M000116656

Leading a Surgical Revolution

Jean-Pierre Jeannet

Leading a Surgical Revolution

The AO Foundation –
Social Entrepreneurs in the Treatment
of Bone Trauma

 Springer

Jean-Pierre Jeannet
Professor Emeritus Babson College
Wellesley, MA, USA

Professor Emeritus IMD Institute
Lausanne, Switzerland

ISBN 978-3-030-01979-2   ISBN 978-3-030-01980-8   (eBook)
https://doi.org/10.1007/978-3-030-01980-8

Library of Congress Control Number: 2018959613

© Springer Nature Switzerland AG 2019
This work is subject to copyright. All rights are reserved by the Publisher, whether the whole or part of the material is concerned, specifically the rights of translation, reprinting, reuse of illustrations, recitation, broadcasting, reproduction on microfilms or in any other physical way, and transmission or information storage and retrieval, electronic adaptation, computer software, or by similar or dissimilar methodology now known or hereafter developed.
The use of general descriptive names, registered names, trademarks, service marks, etc. in this publication does not imply, even in the absence of a specific statement, that such names are exempt from the relevant protective laws and regulations and therefore free for general use.
The publisher, the authors and the editors are safe to assume that the advice and information in this book are believed to be true and accurate at the date of publication. Neither the publisher nor the authors or the editors give a warranty, express or implied, with respect to the material contained herein or for any errors or omissions that may have been made. The publisher remains neutral with regard to jurisdictional claims in published maps and institutional affiliations.

This Springer imprint is published by the registered company Springer Nature Switzerland AG
The registered company address is: Gewerbestrasse 11, 6330 Cham, Switzerland

Foreword

The title of this book reflects, in a few lines, the essence of the AO Foundation and what it stands for. With the invention of a disruptive surgical procedure it revolutionized the world of trauma, reducing pain and disabilities of patients with broken bones and bringing them back into normal social and working life within days, instead of months. In the process, it saved the world's health system billions of dollars—a dream of today's health experts confronting escalating health costs. Practically unnoticed, a worldwide medical device industry developed around this surgical procedure and its surgical instruments and implants—also developed by the pioneer AO surgeons together with a small-scale industry. The social entrepreneurship of a nonprofit organization with changing industrial partners leveraged the dissemination globally on an unprecedented scale.

The idea to present this extraordinary story came out of a research project of Professor Jeannet who identified exceptional success stories of small and medium-sized Swiss enterprises, among them Synthes and Mathys, only to realize the interconnection and further develop the story into a separate book detailing the role of the AO Foundation in this success story.

In today's world, with healthcare costs exploding, a similar approach combining disruptive inventions and innovations with a cost-effective organization might offer ideas for other successful partnerships or private initiatives to remedy illnesses.

The AO Foundation continues to extend its successful work into low-income countries where the burden from injuries and disabilities has assumed epidemic proportions and where treatment methods and care are largely comparable to what the pioneering AO surgeons were confronted with 60 years ago in Switzerland.

The 60th anniversary of the AO Foundation is an appropriate moment to present its history. This book by Professor Jeannet describes the AO history in a comprehensive way, with special attention to the business aspects, making it of interest also for a broader, nonmedical, public.

Nikolaus Renner
Rolf Jeker

AO Foundation, Biel, Switzerland
AO Foundation, Biel, Switzerland

Preface

This book project came my way when I was looking for support for a different, but related, project on Swiss small and medium-sized exporting companies (SMEs) with global success in specific niches. I planned to include Mathys, Straumann, and Medartis, all companies with strong connections to the AO Foundation. However, the AO indicated that they would rather welcome a book on the AO itself with a particular emphasis on its industrial impact. Would I be interested? The AO assured that I would have complete independence as to the approach I would choose. Initially, I hesitated to entertain the idea, since I possess neither a medical nor an engineering background.

My background as a business school faculty member, however, was of interest to the AO leaders since previous books had been written largely by surgeons or medical historians. And so it came that I, with only a cursory acquaintance of the AO, accepted to tackle the challenge of writing a book that would give special emphasis to the AO industrial achievements and impact. My contacts at the AO Foundation board convinced me that my lack of medical training did not disqualify me from writing about the AO and its 60-year history. The readers of this book will have to be the final judges of this decision.

I approached the project in line with my business case research experience gained from writing scores of cases at IMD (Lausanne) and Babson College (Wellesley, MA, USA). This meant that I did not immerse myself only into the archives of the AO, but instead focused on a large number of in-depth interviews with many individuals who had been associated with this enterprise since its inception. While delving into memories about past events, it was to be expected that there would be conflicting perceptions of the what and why of events. Naturally, I made full use of the publications written previously, some of which were crucial to creating the story line I wanted to build, and some helped deal with conflicting memories from interview partners.

As I got ever deeper involved in the AO history, I came to realize that I should not only write a book covering the period since 2002, the year the last book was published. Instead, I needed to tell the entire history of the AO from its inception using the particular lenses that came from my business school faculty background. At first, this meant creating a timeline of the 60 years of the AO and identifying the critical points in its development, be it medical, engineering, or business-related.

Delving deeper, I saw that there was both a social entrepreneurship story centered around the medical aspects of the AO's achievements, as well as a business entrepreneurship story that focused on the industrial achievements triggered by the AO and its purpose. Identifying the two types of entrepreneurial endeavors, social and business, allowed me to approach the AO history from two different angles while using the conceptual lenses from my business school experience for labeling the key events. These business lenses were at the origin of many of the chapter titles and subtitles. Many of these concepts, part of the modern business vocabulary, did not exist when the AO was started. Throughout the text, I have taken the liberty to point out the organizational and business achievements from earlier periods without the access to a technical infrastructure we take for granted in today's business environment.

The intent is to reach an audience beyond the AO community. Reflecting on the potential readers of this book, I was cognizant of the fact that obviously this text is not intended or suited as a manual for surgeons interested in the AO approach to trauma care. And yet, the medical information presented had to find approval of the surgeons involved in trauma care, a constant challenge that was confronting me throughout the two years of working on this project. I hope this text will be read by a general audience, including the large number of patients who have benefited from the result of these efforts, as well as interested readers from the business and research community who might find inspiration in the AO approach.

While this book was written based upon extensive research, it was not intended as an academic exercise. Instead, the aim was to tell the story of the AO Foundation and of the individuals who were instrumental in creating this enterprise and to do so in a captivating, interesting, and also personal way. The AO's tenacity to push ahead with Osteosynthesis for trauma care when confronted with strong opposition from the medical establishment, and to do so with limited resources, could serve as an inspiration for other such projects.

Through the research on the AO, I became aware of the enormous impact of the organization. Millions of people walk the streets having benefited from the breakthroughs achieved by the AO, and yet few members of the general public have any idea who was or is behind these achievements. In that sense, I am happy to have accepted the challenge to write this story and to render it, I hope, in a way to bring it to the attention of a wider audience.

Belmont, Switzerland
August 2018

Jean-Pierre Jeannet

Acknowledgements

This book would not have been written without the generous and active support of the AO Foundation and its Governance. The AO Foundation Board, particularly its President Klaus Renner and its CEO Rolf Jeker, actively worked to open doors and obtain access to countless documentation and offered help with securing interviews. A small steering committee dealing with 60th anniversary issues was always ready to provide guidance. Important financial support for this project was provided through the BLI Institute at the University of Lucerne, assuring that the book project could also find a reputable publisher. Most important, however, was the hands-off approach of the AO leadership allowing the author to express his own opinion while giving ample support that all the relevant facts could be rendered correctly.

The development of this book benefited from very capable authors of earlier works on the AO Foundation, especially for the periods up to about the year 2000. In particular, the publications written by Robert Schneider and Urs Heim on the early part of the AO history, Eugen Kuner on the development of the Osteosynthesis approach, Thomas Schlich on the medical history of the AO and its treatments, Joseph Schatzker's biography of Maurice Müller, as well as the history of AOVET edited by Jörg Auer and his colleagues were a constant guide during the research and writing of this manuscript. All of these authors are extensively cited throughout the book.

Enormous gratitude is owed to about 60 individuals who were willing to sit down for interviews, typically lasting one to two hours. They shared freely of their experience, history with the AO, events they witnessed, and stories they remembered, and offered their reflection on the AO organization, in the past, today, or the future. The summary of these interviews allowed me to gain a much deeper understanding of the importance and impact of the AO, both in medical and business terms. Where appropriate, I have referenced these conversations in footnotes. A complete listing of all persons interviewed is provided in the List of Interviewees.

I am thankful to the surgeons who took the time to explain the intricacies of Osteosynthesis to this not medically trained author, in particular Peter Matter, Reinhold Ganz, and Teddy Slongo who spent extra time with me and reviewed part of the manuscript. The technical issues surrounding the AO *Instrumentarium* and implants were patiently explained to me by Robert Mathys, Jr., and Robert Frigg who also reviewed part of the manuscript as well as Ortrun Pohler, who worked with me on the material science issues. And finally, Rolf Jeker spent many meetings and phone calls with me explaining the intricacies of the AO governance. Without their help I would not have been able to cover, absorb, and organize the entire AO history in one single book.

I would like to express my appreciation to the many institutions, individuals, and copyright holders who allowed us to illustrate important aspects of the AO history. The AO Publication team contributed their skills to converting the many exhibits into publishable visuals for the book. Finally, a special thank you goes to Anita Hussey who edited a rough manuscript into a publishable story.

Last but not least, I would like to thank my wife, Christine Jeannet, who has patiently listened over the past two years to the countless stories I unearthed about the AO Foundation, has debated many aspects of the manuscript and its organization with me, and thus contributed immensely to the story presented in this book.

Contents

About the Author

Jean-Pierre Jeannet served on the faculty of Babson College, USA (1974–2013), where he last held the FW Olin Distinguished Professorship, while simultaneously serving on a joint appointment at the IMD Institute, Switzerland (1981–2010). His teaching and research focused on marketing, strategy, and globalization. He holds the title of Professor Emeritus from both Babson College and the IMD Institute.

He was a frequent consultant in management development and strategic development with companies in Europe, North and South America, and Asia. His consulting practice spanned many industry sectors and included multiple assignments in the healthcare and life science industries.

Professor Jeannet is the author or coauthor of a number of books, including *Managing with a Global Mindset*, *Global Marketing Strategies*, *Global Account Management*, and *From Coal to Biotech: The Transformation of DSM with Business School Support*.

List of Interviewees

The Surgeons
Max Aebi, Switzerland
Janine and Ueli Aebi-Müller, Switzerland (Maurice E. Müller family)
Suthorn Bavonratanavech, Thailand (President 2014–2016)
Michael Blauth, Austria
Chris Colton, UK (President 1996–1998)
Reinhold Ganz, Switzerland
Christian Gerber, Switzerland
Norbert Haas, Germany (President 2010–2012)
David Helfet, US
James Kellam, US (President 2004–2006)
Paul Manson, US (President 2008–2010)
Peter Matter, Switzerland (President 2000–2002)
Robert McGuire, US (President 2018–2020)
Joachim Prein, Switzerland
Jaime Quintero, Columbia (President 2012–2014)
Nikolaus Renner, Switzerland (President 2016–2018)
Thomas Ruedi, Switzerland
Joseph Schatzker, Canada (President 1998–2000)
Theddy Slongo, Switzerland
Marvin Tile, Canada (President 1992–1994)
Chris van der Werken, Netherlands (President 2006–2008)

The Veterinarians
Jörg Auer, Switzerland
Jean-Pierre Cabassu, France
Gerhilde Kása, Germany
Brigitte von Rechenberg, Switzerland

The Scientists & Developers
Robert Frigg, Switzerland
Stephan Perren, Switzerland
Ortrun Pohler, Switzerland

Entrepreneurs and Managers
Fritz Fahrni, Switzerland, ex. Sulzer/Balgrist
Amos Gazit, Distributor, Israel
Jim Gerry, US, retired, Synthes
Jürg Oehy, Switzerland, ZimmerBiomet,
Robert Mathys, Jr., Switzerland, RMS Foundation
Ciro Römer, DPS, USA
Felix Scherrer, Switzerland, ex. Sulzer
Thomas Straumann, Switzerland, Straumann Dental
Hansjörg Wyss, Switzerland, retired, Synthes
Sven Zybell, DPS, Switzerland

AO Executive and Administrative Staff
Claas Albers
Andreas Fäh
Claudio Gubser (retired)
Beate Hanson (ex AO)
Tobias Hüttl
Urs Jann (retired)
Margrit Jaques (retired)
Rolf Jeker
Alexander Joeris
Urban Langer
Christoph Nötzli
Markus Rauh (retired)
Geoffrey Richards
Urs Rüetschi
Stephan Zeiter

The Legal & Financial Experts
Georg Messmer (Curia, retired)
Andrea von Rechenberg (Curia)
Urs Weber (Wenger & Vieli)
Jean-Claude Wenger (retired, Wenger & Vieli)

Prologue: Orchestrating A Cast of Thousands

Davos, Early on a December Morning

A curious sight can be observed early on a December morning in the mountain resort town of Davos, Switzerland. There, on a typical workday before the sun rises above the peak of Pischahorn, and with the street noise muffled by fresh snow, one can see a stream of people walking the streets, all in the same direction. The crowd is much larger than one would expect at this hour, especially in a resort town. These people are not dressed to go skiing or hiking; instead they are wearing comfortable sports clothes, dressed warmly enough for the typical cool mountain air of the season. This stream of humanity, coming out of the various hotels, appear wholly unconnected to all the snow that covers the ground. Instead of skis, they are equipped with computer shoulder bags, books, and folders. These men and women give the impression of young professionals and are, apparently, from all over the world. What are all of these hundreds of people doing in the middle of the Swiss Alps, in winter, if not to go skiing? (Exhibit 1.1)

Following the crowd, along where the stream swells, the people start to head toward the Davos Congress Center, flags draped all over its entrance and giving way to the purpose of this early congregation. This is an annual meeting of the AO Foundation's Davos Courses (AO stands for *Association pour l'Ostéosynthèse* in French; Arbeitsgemeinschaft für Osteosynthesefragen in German; Association of Osteosynthesis in English), which is held each December to expose yet another generation of early and mid-career surgeons to the principles of bone trauma care and related injuries, known the world over as *Osteosynthesis*. Before the sun rises (which happens in the winter sometime after 08:00), the nearly 1000 participants and instructors split into groups, review bone fractures, discuss surgical approaches, learn from experienced colleagues, and become experts at treating bone trauma for patients anywhere in the world applying Osteosynthesis techniques. Bending over artificial models of limbs, skilled and experienced surgeons will teach their younger colleagues how to place sophisticated implants to join broken bones, how to apply

© Springer Nature Switzerland AG 2019
J.-P. Jeannet, *Leading a Surgical Revolution*,
https://doi.org/10.1007/978-3-030-01980-8_1

Exhibit 1.1 Davos, Winter. *Copyright by AO Foundation, Switzerland*

screws to keep them in place, and how to use specially-designed surgical instruments to achieve the best results for patients. The participants will stay inside the conference center, huddled over their simulated operations and bone injuries, until late in the afternoon. By the time they leave the Conference Center, the sun has disappeared and the Davos sky begins to sparkle, the stars becoming clearly visible. This routine will be repeated for the next four days (Exhibit 1.2).

This sight has repeated itself every year since 1960, and over these almost 60 years about 65,000 surgeons and several thousand operating personnel have graduated from the Davos program, becoming skilled at applying the medical technology of Osteosynthesis to bone trauma (not including the approximately 600,000 surgeons outside of Switzerland who have participated in similar courses) (Exhibit 1.3).

Davos Hospital, on a December Morning

Shortly after 07:00, a team of about a dozen surgical staff assembles in the Davos Hospital to man the three operating theaters, each equipped with state-of-the-art instrumentation. They ready the various stations for patient intake, take inventory of medical supplies, and check sterilization stations, as well as the X-ray and anesthesia equipment needed for the operations. Promptly, at the pre-scheduled time, patients are wheeled into the operating area: they are received, transferred to an operating bed, checked, infused, provided with the necessary anesthesia, and moved over into the operating theater where a team of five professionals are ready to perform a demanding procedure—requiring either the application of a fracture fixation, or

Exhibit 1.2 Davos Conference Center with AO Banner. *Copyright by AO Foundation, Switzerland*

Exhibit 1.3 A Davos course. *Copyright by AO Foundation, Switzerland*

sometimes the removal of a metal implant that had been put in about a year earlier—following a complicated fracture, such as of a lower leg or tibia.

The surgeon in charge, helped by an assistant, an operating nurse, and the support staff for anesthesia, X-ray, and supplies, goes over the procedure using medical terminology not always easily understood by laymen. Dr. med. Nikolaus Renner explains:

> The patient, having suffered a trauma to the proximal lateral tibia (fracture to the lower leg), had been originally treated with small cortical screws for inter-fractional compression, bridged using a LISS PLT Less Invasive Stabilization Plate with Self Tapping Locking Screws (5.0), and appeared ready for the removal of these implants as the fracture has sufficiently healed.[1]

The procedure for removing the plate and screws takes a good hour. The approach of applying these implants at the time of fracture, and their subsequent removal, are the same as those exercised each year by the surgeons in the Davos Conference Center. Today's procedure called for a removal of an implant. At another time, the operation might be implantations needed as a result of a fresh bone trauma (Exhibit 1.4).

Elsewhere, on this same December day, hundreds, if not thousands of patients with bone fractures or trauma will be wheeled into operating arenas all over the world. On any given day, thousands of interventions are carried out in line with the procedures taught and practiced in the courses offered in Davos. They may include bone trauma, or trauma to the spine, skull, or face. In a typical year at New York–Presbyterian Hospital, some 37,000 Orthopedic and trauma operations are conducted, with about 8000 being in the area of trauma alone—more than 20 per day.[2]

Some of these procedures may be optional, or elective, and yet still contribute significantly to the improvement of patients' lives. Other procedures may be the result of accidents and are actually life-saving. In all cases, however, patients are treated by highly-skilled teams, specializing in different areas of medicine, ranging from surgery and anesthesia to X-ray technology; each of these professionals is focused on contributing to an optimal outcome for their patients.

Whatever the procedure, surgeons and their skilled operating room staffs will rely on implants, plates, screws, and surgical instruments produced specifically for a given purpose and situation. Supporting these surgical teams, and invisible to patients, is a large support staff ensuring that the correct implant is delivered at the right time, to the right place, and for the right patient. Every day, thousands of specialists travel to hospitals in order to engage with surgical teams and assure optimal patient outcomes.

---

[1] Dr. med. Nikolaus Renner, President of the AO Foundation Board, 2016–2018, and Head of Trauma Surgery at Aarau Cantonal Hospital, Switzerland, reviewing the X-rays.

[2] Source: Dr. David Helfet, Chief Emeritus, Orthopedic Trauma Service, New York–Presbyterian Hospital, 4 December 2017.

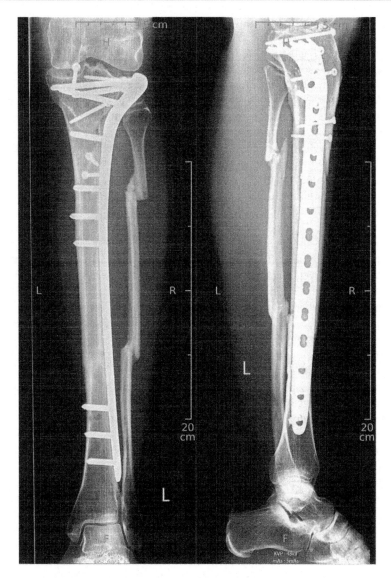

Exhibit 1.4 X-ray of patient for implant removal, Davos Hospital. *By Permission Davos Regional Hospital, Switzerland*

Solothurn, Switzerland, on the Same December Morning

At the same time that the scores of surgeons congregate in Davos to learn how to apply sophisticated medical implants on trauma patients to perform Osteosynthesis, a related and not dissimilar movement is taking place in Western Switzerland.

Looking down from the hills above Solothurn—the capital city of the Swiss Canton bearing the same name—one can see the busy movements of cars, trains, and other transport vehicles going toward a number of factories dotted along the Jura mountain range. Again, it is early morning and the lights of the moving cars and buses are clearly visible, creating, a long line, hemmed in between the Jura mountain chain to the West and the River Aare to the East. In this line of vehicles sit thousands of highly-skilled workers, machinists, engineers, and medical technology experts going to the many factories that, in this region, have created a competence center for the production of medical implants needed for Osteosynthesis—an industry, which supports the surgeries that the teams are performing in Davos, and that the young surgeons are learning about.

In the factories located around the city of Solothurn, as well as in smaller towns beyond the MedTech community, with little-known names such as Zuchwil, Bellach, Bettlach, Grenchen, and Lengnau, a workforce of several thousand are machining metal and titanium parts to exacting specifications, using highly-sophisticated machinery. These enterprises reach up and down along the Jura mountain range, even reaching into the neighboring Canton of Basel-Landschaft, or Basel-Land. The factories have names such as DPS Synthes, Mathys, and Stryker, among others. They manufacture surgical implants and instruments that are so demanding to produce only the most skilled workers will succeed. Their workforces produce these items with sophisticated machinery, titanium steel, LISS PLT plates and the required screws, such as the one implanted in the patient at the Davos Hospital. While the majority of these efforts is concentrated in the Solothurn region, these same companies maintain operations in other parts of the world where, again, thousands of employees machine implants to the most precise of specifications.

The workers, factories, and companies in charge of this industrial effort have been involved in this effort since the early 1960s. When arriving at their workplace for the first morning shift on this early December day, it is still dark outside. When the second shift returns home at the end of their workday, it's dark again. Without the daily contributions of this dedicated workforce, none of the operational procedures supporting Osteosynthesis, the method being taught in Davos, would be possible.

Who Orchestrates This Cast of Thousands?

The thousands of surgeons training in Davos, the thousands of workers streaming towards the factories in the Solothurn area, and the thousands of patients seeking treatment for their bone trauma in hospitals around the world are not random or unrelated. The genius behind these activities is not a governmental, or any other, official body. Instead, this cast of thousands is being orchestrated through the effort of a private, non-governmental organization, known today by the abbreviation of AO (which has since taken the legal form of a foundation). It was originally inspired by a small team of surgeons who came together in Switzerland as colleagues in 1958 and took on the mission to revolutionize the treatment of bone fractures and improve the life of patients around the world. Through the creation of a fraternity of like-minded surgeons, they built an organization largely without government subsidies and created a social entrepreneurial start-up of unprecedented proportion. This was all bootstrapped by their own resources and self-funded through an ingenious business model involving a group of implant producers.

This book tells the story behind this enormous effort, largely performed on a volunteer basis, speaks about the personalities and talents of the founders, as well as the others who joined them, and shows how this small group grew into an ever-larger association, creating a global network of surgeons that would eventually bring their superior surgical methods to every corner of the globe.

The intention is to shed some light on the early challenges that the founders faced, the hurdles they had to overcome, the internal debates they carried out, the structures they built, and the efforts they undertook to enlist the participation of far-sighted industrialists and entrepreneurs needed to supply them with the tools required for their sophisticated surgical procedures—not to mention to help fund the effort. Featured will be how this founding team, and the organization they created, overcame stiff resistance to their innovative surgical techniques from established medical practitioners, how they engaged in research in support of their ideas, and how they built a global organization that has sustained itself to this day, resulting in, among other things, the training courses that still bring thousands of surgeons together every year, and the research program that supports new surgical concepts and practices.

Part I

Launching a Surgical Revolution

Osteosynthesis Explained

2

Osteosynthesis is derived from combining the Greek word for bone (osteon) with synthesis, standing for the combination of various elements into a new and unified entity. The Belgian surgeon Albin Lambotte (1880–1955) is credited with first using the term Osteosynthesis in one of his publications, in 1919.[1] The terminology Osteosynthesis is generally applied to:

> A surgical procedure to restore the continuity, stability and function of a bone, which is indicated if a bone is broken in a certain way in which a conservative treatment, i.e. a treatment without an operation, is not sufficient. Examples for types of bone fractures, where a surgical treatment is indicated are fractures where an articular surface is involved or there is a high-risk of loss of reduction of the fracture when treating it conservatively.[2]

The principles of Osteosynthesis involve a reduction (open or closed) of the fracture, that is bringing the fractured bone fragments in the correct axes again and stabilizing the fracture by attaching a plate to the bone; or, by inserting a nail into the bone, particularly in long bones where you have a medullary canal; or, by using any other implant. In order to apply these implants, open surgery of the injured bone is necessary. Using the implants, the bone fragments might be compressed, or not, depending on the nature of the fracture. Also depending on the type of surgical procedure selected, patients may be allowed to put full to partial weight on the fractured limb. Mobilization, or movement, of adjacent joints is advised to preserve full range, or motion.

Surgeons applying Osteosynthesis to a fractured bone or limb obtain access through open surgery to the bone, thus using an open reduction for the fracture

---

[1]Lambotte (1919), p. 48.

[2]Translation supplied by Alexander Joeri, AO Foundation, Pschyrembel Online (https://www.pschyrembel.de/Osteosynthese/K0G01) Deutsch—Englisch (Definition Osteosynthese), accessed 8 December 2017.

© Springer Nature Switzerland AG 2019
J.-P. Jeannet, *Leading a Surgical Revolution*,
https://doi.org/10.1007/978-3-030-01980-8_2

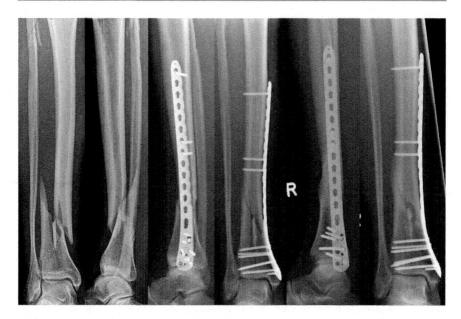

Exhibit 2.1 A ski accident showing broken bone. Application of Osteosynthesis implants, and post-operative control. (**a**, **b**) Accident. (**c**, **d**) Post operation. (**e**, **f**) Post operation control (16 months). *Source: Dr.med. Christoph Sommer, Chief Surgeon Trauma, Cantonal Hospital Grisons, reprinted with permission*

and then internally stabilizing the fracture with specially designed implants, such as plates held in place by purposely designed screws, or sometimes by inserting an intramedullary bone nail. The resulting rigid fixation prevents motion across the fracture lines. This procedure is called Open Reduction Internal Fixation (ORIF), in contrast with Closed Reduction Internal Fixation (CRIF) where no open surgery takes place (Exhibit 2.1a–f).

The traditional method of dealing with bone fractures consisted of resetting the broken bone externally, putting the patient into skeletal traction, and stabilizing the fractured limb with the use of a splint or cast. Until the early 1960s, the vast majority of bone trauma were treated by conservative methods. While the fixation of the fractured bone in a plaster cast helps with its healing, there were considerable negative side effects, such as wasted muscles or stiff joints (Exhibit 2.2).

Osteosynthesis offered several advantages over the earlier dominant methods of treating fractured bones, or external fixation, where after the splint a plaster cast was applied and followed by a longer period of immobilization of the broken limb, usually lasting several weeks. By applying Osteosynthesis it was possible to exactly align the fractured bones in the reduction phase and, thus, restore the correct axes of the bone. This reduction was then stabilized through fixation of an implant onto the bone. As a result, patients could be mobilized; for example, move in a matter of days compared to the more conservative method. This assured preservation of a range of motion, as well as an avoidance of side effects, such as thrombosis. The

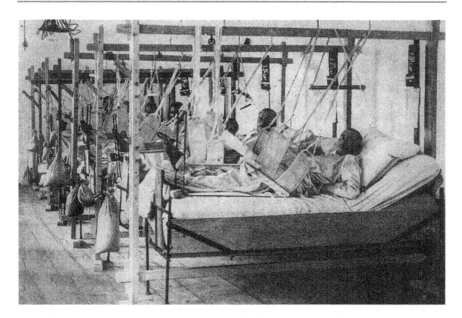

Exhibit 2.2 Conservative treatment of bone trauma in Lorenz Böhler's Austrian Military Hospital during World War I. *(First published in Lorenz Böhler, "Technik der Knochenbruchbehandlung", Maudrich, Wien, 1929, pp. 1–52.) Copyright by AO Foundation, Switzerland*

immobilization of soft tissue around the fractured bone also had the benefit of reducing the risk of infection.

As was the case with any surgical procedure, there existed constant risk of bone infections when applying Osteosynthesis. At some later point in time, an implant removal might be required, usually causing a second surgical procedure. More recently, surgeons have developed the procedure of a minimally invasive Osteosynthesis with the advantage of offering reduced damage to soft tissues and producing smaller, less visible, scars.

Successful Osteosynthesis requires the availability of specially designed, and shaped, implants in the form of plates and fitted screws, as well as surgical tools that have been created to support this type of operation. This will be addressed further in Chap. 4—how the procedure was developed and how the surgeons involved in its development convinced the world that the practice of Osteosynthesis—or internal fixation—merited the replacement of the previously dominant conservative method of external fixation, to treat the world's broken bones.

Reference

Lambotte, A. (1919). *Chirurgie opératoire des Fractures* (p. 48). Paris: Masson.

A Brief Overview of the AO Organization

3

What Does AO Stand For?

Although the AO has undergone several changes, and experienced considerable growth over the years, the term AO has remained constant, whether it took form as an organization, or a foundation. Initially formed in 1958, the moniker of AO began with Maurice Müller, one of the organization's co-founders, who first suggested the French term *Association pour l'Ostéosynthèse* and then used the German equivalent *Arbeitsgemeinschaft für Osteosynthesefragen*; both meaning the same in English— The Association for Osteosynthesis, or AO.

The AO first took on the legal form of a *Verein,* or association, under Swiss law. Its sole purpose was the dissemination and improvement of the practice of Osteosynthesis as the preferred procedure when dealing with fracture care. Since the German name would have been a mouthful for people in many other regions, and the abbreviation AO was owned by another company in the US, the organization used Association for the Study of Internal Fixation, or ASIF, in the English-speaking world. Sometimes both abbreviations were used in combination, forming AO/ASIF as its brand name.

A Humble Beginning

When a group of 13 Swiss surgeons gathered on 6 November 1958, in the Elite Hotel in Biel, Switzerland, few of those present could have imagined that their small gathering would someday evolve into an international force with thousands of member surgeons, cause a worldwide revolution in trauma care, and spurn a global industry for the manufacturing of the necessary implants and related surgical tools. A plaque placed in the hotel, bearing the names of the 13 surgeons attending that meeting, was visible to hotel guests for many years until it was removed during a recent renovation.

© Springer Nature Switzerland AG 2019
J.-P. Jeannet, *Leading a Surgical Revolution*,
https://doi.org/10.1007/978-3-030-01980-8_3

Under the leadership of Orthopedic surgeon Maurice E. Müller (1918–2009), they assembled with the purpose of furthering trauma induced fracture care. Müller had developed a system that successfully applied the principles of Osteosynthesis, up to that time little known in surgical circles and in contrast to the accepted treatment of the era, which dealt with fracture care using the 'conservative method' of splints and casts.

In the original statutes formally adopted by the AO in 1960, the AO referred to itself as an:

> Association for the study of matters pertaining to the treatment of fractures and for the purpose of experimental research in this area. Furthermore, the association has as its aim the practical and scientific exchange of information in the area of fracture treatment, in particular Osteosynthesis.

Today, the AO declares as its mission, and vision, to:

> Foster and expand our network of health care professionals in education, research, development, and clinical investigation to achieve more effective care worldwide (AR 2015).

> Our Vision is excellence in the surgical management of trauma and disorders of the musculoskeletal system (AR 2015.)

After changing its legal status from of an association into in a full-fledged not-for-profit foundation in 1984, the AO moved in 1992 to its current administrative center in Davos. With an annual budget of about CHF 102 million and a permanent staff of approximately 250 (both figures are from 2016), the AO has developed into a formidable force, recognized and appreciated by the global medical community.

With just 13 members in 1958, AO grew into a global organization with more than 20,000 members (2017) spread across the world and organized around several clinical divisions, all based upon the original idea of Osteosynthesis (Exhibit 3.1).

Exhibit 3.1 Views of the AO Center in Davos, Switzerland. *Copyright by AO Foundation, Switzerland*

As the AO organization evolved over the last 60 years, so have its governance bodies and executive units. Today, the ultimate authority at the AO is the AO Assembly of Trustees, a form of parliament, who meet annually; the group elects the AO President, new members to the Board of Trustees, and the members of the AO Foundation Board (AOFB). The AOFB, as the highest supervisory and executive body, is responsible for the execution of the organization's strategy and appoints the AO Executive Management (AOEM), headed by a CEO who is also Vice-Chair of the AOFB (Exhibit 3.2).

Currently, educational programs represent about 45% of AO's annual operating budget. Annually, the AO supports more than 800 educational events globally, involving some 51,000 participating surgeons over 110,000 participant days.

After education, research is AO's second main activity, accounting for about 25% of its budget. Support for AO's many technical commissions (TKs) seeking approval of new implants and surgical procedures, demands about 5% of the operating budget. The remainder of the budget is used for general administrative costs and additional ventures into new areas.

Primarily, the AO is funded by industry contributions, in the form of licensing fees or unrestricted grants, from its main industrial partner Synthes. At the AO's inception, there were three industrial partners (Mathys, Straumann, and Synthes USA), but after a string of producer mergers only Synthes USA remained, which was acquired by Johnson and Johnson (J&J) in 2012 and added to its DePuy Synthes (DPS) division. J&J DPS contributed about 75% of the AO revenue in 2016, intended to support AO educational programs and TK processes for approvals of implant and surgical methods. In return, J&J DPS obtained exclusive rights to all AO developments. AO's remaining income of 25% is accounted for by the return on AO's endowment, currently listed at CHF 1.23 billion (2016).

Organizationally, AO is grouped around its major clinical divisions, of which AOTrauma is by far the largest, accounting for the greatest share of membership and budget. Other clinical units, added over time, include AOSpine, AOCMF, and AOVET. Each clinical division is governed by its own board, under the supervision of the AOFB, and supported by a number of AO administrative support units and institutes, such as for research, clinical investigation, and education. As a separate unit, the AO's TK system guides approval of new surgical techniques and implants. For a complete depiction of AO's organization, see the exhibits below concerning Governance and Executive Levels (Exhibit 3.3).

AO governance level

A clear separation between governing and executive bodies guarantees optimum organizational governance.

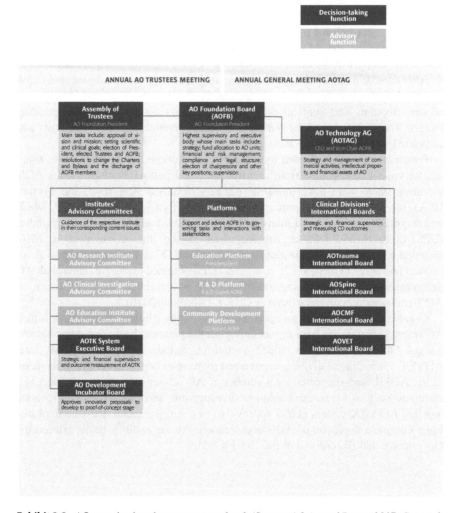

Exhibit 3.2 AO organization chart governance level. *(Source: AO Annual Report 2017) Copyright by AO Foundation, Switzerland*

AO executive level

The executive functions of the AO Foundation are directed by the CEO and Vice-Chair of the
AO Foundation Board and are divided into three layers (institutes, clinical divisions, and support units)
that work closely with each other.

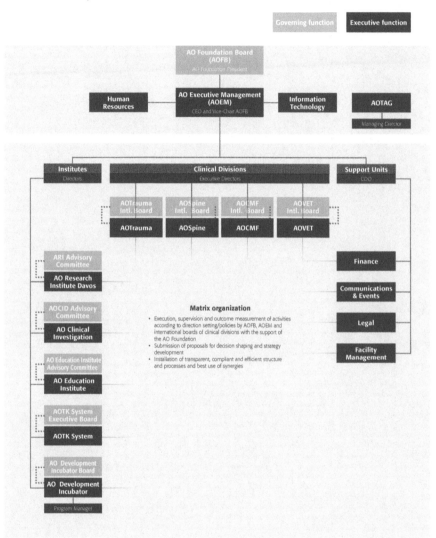

Exhibit 3.3 AO organization chart executive level. *(Source: AO Annual Report 2017) Copyright
by AO Foundation, Switzerland*

Treatment of Bone Fractures Prior to 1960

4

Davos, Another Winter Day, in the 1950s

From today's perspective, it is hard to imagine how fractures were treated well into the 1950s and even into the 1960s. Upon arrival at the Davos Hospital, a patient with a lower leg fracture from a skiing accident was typically treated by first stabilizing the broken limb, then by placing the limb into a plaster cast, and finally by having the patient rest for many weeks in traction, in a hospital bed, until the bone healed. The traction was a complicated looking system, often with a nail put through the patient's heel and weights attached with ropes to the extended limb. The plaster cast would have to be kept on for eight to twelve weeks, during which time the patient was subject to reduced mobility. After the plaster cast was removed, patients would then have to learn how to walk again.

Some older readers might still remember making hospital visits to relatives and seeing legs in casts and suspended. This treatment, referred to as the conservative treatment, employed only external fixation and was considered the gold standard in medical practice for a wide range of fractures well into the decade of the 1960s.

How Conservative Treatment Conquered the World

By 1950, the conservative method of reducing fractures and stabilizing them through splints and plaster, combined with traction, had gained general acceptance in most hospitals throughout Europe and the United States. The leading proponent of this methodology was Lorenz Böhler (1885–1973) who practiced in Vienna and had, over time, developed a complete system for the treatment of fractures.[1]

---

[1] For a detailed approach of Lorenz Böhler, see Schlich (2002), p. 17–19.

© Springer Nature Switzerland AG 2019
J.-P. Jeannet, *Leading a Surgical Revolution*,
https://doi.org/10.1007/978-3-030-01980-8_4

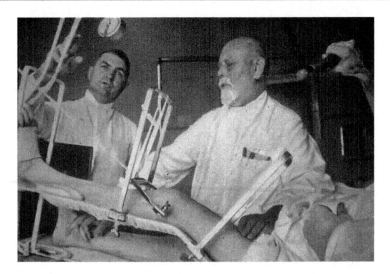

Exhibit 4.1 Böhler with patient in his hospital. *Copyright by AO Foundation, Switzerland*

Böhler, who had started developing his methodology during World War I, while serving in the army. He placed enormous emphasis on the standardization of his approach which he boiled down to a *Schema-F Philosophie*.[2] The control and enforcement of each step of treatment was originally developed in the military hospitals under his control. After World War I, Böhler transferred this methodology to a hospital built for him in Vienna. He convinced the Austrian insurance establishment to do this based on statistics from the pre-war period, which showed very high disability payments. Better treatment could finance a dedicated hospital from the savings gained on these payments. Böhler's Unfallkrankenhaus (Accident Hospital) opened in Vienna in 1925.

One of the central elements of Böhler's conservative system was the employment of traction using weights intended to prevent the fractured limb from shortening during the very long hospitalization period of eight to twelve weeks. Standardized devices, many of those modularized for use under different circumstances, were employed and patients were grouped by different fractures, with patients treated in the same manner. Böhler's approach was inspired by the rationalization processes utilized in industry, which he thought would also bring greater efficiency in the treatment of patients. He published his first standard treatment manual for fracture care in 1929 (Exhibit 4.1).[3]

Although the rigorous application of the conservative method offered many advantages, there were still considerable risks associated with it. The risks had to

---

[2] *Schema-F* is an expression used in the German language to refer to a standardized and routinized process that could be applied without much thought or concentration, such as filling in routine forms and reports.
[3] Böhler (1929).

do with clinical results measured by patient mobility and ability to return to work. The complete restoration of the correct axes of the broken bone was difficult to achieve, and plaster cast and splints did not allow for a completely stable fixation.[4] The long periods until patients could be mobilized resulted in considerable risk through side effects, such as stiffness of joints, loss of range of motion, and in some cases thrombosis.

Even where the conservative method led to a correct healing of the fracture, the long hospital stays and difficult re-entries into active work life remained a major issue, and one of particular interest to both patients and employers. Despite these drawbacks, Böhler's conservative treatment method became the gold standard for fracture care under most circumstances. The spread of Böhler's method was assured by regular visits from abroad to his hospital in the 1920s and 1930s; some reports indicate that international visitors arrived almost on a weekly basis to tour the hospital. Böhler was sometimes using operative treatments, but only when absolutely necessary. He remained, however, very skeptical about the general use of Osteosynthesis.

Negative Experiences with Conservative Method

Complicated fractures of the upper or lower leg near the joints had a high chance of leading to partial or permanent disability. This was particularly true for fractures of the upper (femur) and lower (tibia) extremities, as well as to the spine. Reporting by both the Swiss (SUVA) and the Austrian (AUVA) accident insurers indicate divergent results. While the Swiss SUVA reported in 1945 that the company paid disability pensions for 40% of tibia fractures, and 70% of fractures of the femur, the Austrian AUVA reported required disability pensions in only about 5% of all cases (1955).[5] Swiss surgeon Martin Allgöwer, one of AO's co-founders, would later describe that some form of disability resulted in at least one-third of the cases.[6] Clearly, despite the improvements in fracture care, the results were highly unsatisfactory for patients.

Far more difficult was the employment of the conservative method to the fracture of the femoral neck. These fractures, often incurred by elderly persons, were far more challenging to treat and posed greater risks for patients. For healing, patients suffering from such fractures were usually hospitalized for at least eight to ten, and sometimes up to 16 weeks. Such long hospitalization periods invariably led to complications, resulting in mortality rates of 30–50%.[7] As a result of these

---

[4]It should be pointed out that X-ray technology was not as fully developed, limiting the surgeons' view of the bone fragments around the trauma area.

[5]Bauer (1959), cited by Heim. Heim (2001), p. 26.

[6]Film Interview for Swiss Television SDR, 1980.

[7]Kuner (2015), p. 4.

difficulties, the medical community began to experiment with various surgical procedures.

There were two indications where operative treatment of fractures was often considered and where the conservative method rendered particularly poor results: the first indication were open fractures and the second indication involved femoral neck fractures, a trauma that was particularly difficult for geriatric patients.[8] It would take quite some time for this surgical approach to take hold.

Early Surgical Approaches to Bone Fractures

The developments summarized below took place in different locations, and the pockets of innovative surgeons did not necessarily communicate with each other. New ideas during the time leading up to and through World War II traveled much slower than they do today, in the age of Internet. Among the innovations, those coming from the US, Germany, and Belgium stand out (Exhibit 4.2).

A Nailing Innovation from Boston, Picked up in Europe

Since femoral neck fractures were difficult to stabilize without some type of internal fixation, surgeons tried to find different solutions to this problem. Even as far back as the nineteenth century, attempts were recorded with various forms of 'nailing.' The first generally acceptable technique for nailing was developed by surgeon in the US, Marius Nygaard Smith-Petersen, who was working in Boston and finding favorable results, which he published in 1931.[9] In 1938 already, the Austrian surgeon Böhler documented the use of nails to the hip. This development made its way quickly around Europe and by 1940 it appeared that nailing femoral neck fractures had already become a generally accepted method. This treatment had not been extended to other fractures.

Nailing Rod from Germany Made It Around the World

A second method of surgical treatment of fractures included *intramedullary nailing*, applied to fixing fractures of long bones through the insertion of a nail through the central canal that contained the bone marrow. This method, first developed by the German surgeon Gerhard Küntscher (1900–1972) during the 1930s, was used extensively by German Army surgeons during World War II.

---

[8]A very detailed rendition of the development of surgical procedures can be found in Schlich (2002), pp. 19–27.

[9]Smith-Peterson et al. (1931), pp. 715–759.

Exhibit 4.2 Four pioneers of modern Bone Trauma (Lambotte, Danis, Böhler, Küntscher). *Copyright by AO Foundation, Switzerland*

When Küntscher first presented his innovation at a surgical congress in Berlin in 1940, he was confronted with widespread rejection. Only Böhler, the champion of conservative treatment, supported his idea and adopted it in his hospital. He attended the same congress where two surgeons from Winterthur, Switzerland had managed to smuggle an example of Küntscher's nail back to Switzerland. Sulzer, the Swiss engineering company, produced copies of this rod, which were used successfully in animals and humans at the Winterthur clinic. In 1944, Maurice Müller, one of AO's co-founders, was able to examine an early patient of Küntscher's in order to see for himself.

Küntscher's innovation consisted of a special design for his rod, described as:

A triflanged nail that could provide rotational stability through pressure against the wall of the bone. Because of its triflanged shape the nail did not fill out the whole canal and the pressure on the inner lining of the medullary canal was restricted to three long but very narrow strips. Thus, blood supply was much better preserved then with the usual rods and nails. Moreover, there was no need to open the fracture site itself since the nail was insert through a separate approach at the far end of the bone shaft.[10]

Due to the restrictions of information flow during war times, dissemination of this approach remained limited and was restricted to Germany and Scandinavia. When some Allied prisoners of war returned from Europe with such rod implantations they were giving surgeons in the US and elsewhere in Europe a first exposure to the method. By the early 1950s, the intramedullary nailing of the femur had become common treatment in both Europe and the English-speaking world. However, its application to other fractures remained controversial in both Europe and North America.

Experiments with Compression Plates in Belgium Remained a Local Affair

It was in Belgium where some of the most important experiments and innovations in surgical techniques for bone fractures took place. Visitors to the AO Center in Davos who descend the staircase to the lower level will pass several large portraits celebrating the forerunners of the AO approach to bone fractures; two of these portraits are devoted to the Belgium surgeons Albin Lambotte (1866–1955) and Robert Danis (1880–1962). A detailed description of the two surgeons' contributions can be found in Urs Heim's book *Das Phänomen AO*.[11]

The Surgeon Who Coined the Term Osteosynthesis

Albin Lambotte (1866–1955), the elder of the two Belgian surgeons, began his medical career in Brussels with his brother Élie, who had been considered a highly talented surgeon but passed away in 1912 at age 55. While at the hospital in Brussels, the Lambotte brothers began to conduct surgical fixations for closed fractures. In 1890, Albin Lambotte moved to a hospital in Antwerp where he remained for the duration of his career. He was named Head of Surgery and as a surgeon proved himself to be unusually multitalented. Many publications prove his extensive range of surgical procedures. From about 1900 onwards, Lambotte began concentrating on surgical treatment of fractures. He documented procedures in his two important books, the first one published in 1907, documenting 187 procedures,[12] and the second one in 1913, containing details of 550 Osteosynthesis procedures.[13]

---

[10]Schlich (2002), p. 23.
[11]Heim (2001), pp. 18–21.
[12]Lambotte (1907).
[13]Lambotte (1913).

Exhibit 4.3 Lambotte Atelier. *Copyright by AO Foundation, Switzerland*

In the history of the AO Organization, Lambotte's first book was of particular interest because it contained the first mention of the procedure of Osteosynthesis in any medical publication. His surgical philosophy was highly developed and insisted on absolute stability, not using external bandages. To avoid muscular atrophy, or the development of stiff joints, he allowed for the immediate mobilization of his patients. He developed his own external fixation (*fixateur externe*) and practiced it strictly for asepsis treatments. Influenced by his own friend William Arbuthnot Lane (1856–1943) from the UK, he practiced the 'no touch' operational technique.[14] Reportedly, he aimed at keeping his white gloves pristine throughout an operation (Exhibit 4.3).

Heim found no references in Lambotte's writing to callus and compression.[15] For Lambotte, healing without callus was a natural process, which was furthered through skillful Osteosynthesis. He described this as a condition of a *fracture sous-périostée*.[16]

Lambotte developed a full set of implants and tools: cerclage, screws, nails, and plates, as well as surgical tools and hand drills. Lambotte was both an accomplished artist and artisan. At the beginning, he constructed his own tools and implants, and only later did he rely on external suppliers. Lambotte was also a very talented musician who played in a string quartet and was known to have built a large number

---

[14]Lane (1950).
[15]Heim (2001), p. 132.
[16]Lambotte (1907), p. 11.

of musical instruments, primarily violins, in addition to ultra-light fishing gear, the result of being a passionate fisherman.

Although Lambotte was considered a gifted surgeon and was admired and visited by many other surgeons, beyond a few exceptions, he never developed a school of followers. Among the early founders of the AO, it is believed that only Hans Willenegger was familiar with his work, which he included in a section of a book published in 1963.[17]

The Belgian Surgeon Who Brought Osteosynthesis to the Attention of a Wider Audience

Robert Danis (1880–1962) began his medical career in 1913, in Brussels, focusing on thoracic surgery. Appointed as a professor to the university hospital of the *Université Libre Bruxelles*, he did not begin to work on operative treatments of fractures until about 1930.[18] Danis published his first book on Osteosynthesis in 1932, some 25 years after Lambotte's. It is not known if the two knew each other (Lambotte retired from active surgery in 1946), but the use of the term Osteosynthesis in Danis' first book, and the fact that they had the same publisher, suggests that he must have been familiar with Lambotte's work.

When Danis began to use implants, he was initially disappointed by the quality of his external suppliers. Similar to Lambotte, he began to create his own implants. By doing so, he was able to perfect his screws. In 1938, he first developed a plate capable of exerting axial compression, which he named *coapteur*. His steel plate had a built-in mechanism and with an additional screw, he was able to provide both coaxial compression and immobilization of the fracture.

In a second book published in 1949,[19] Danis reported on some 1500 cases and offered a further refinement of his technique. In many ways, his principles of the treatment of fractures sounded like an early version of what would later become the AO Principles. Danis was against the plaster fixation of fractures because they too often lead to permanent complications and atrophies. He coined the term *Frakturkrankheit*[20] to address the risk of the conservative treatment. In most cases, he suggested surgical treatment and within as early a timeframe as possible. For a successful Osteosynthesis he required optimal repositioning of the fragments. Danis also showed that with continuous compression, bone consolidation could be achieved without visible callus.

Danis was described as a talented teacher, capable of drawing with both hands simultaneously on his blackboard. He was also a skilled engineer, allowing him to make his own surgical instruments and machine tools. He became President of the

[17]Müller et al. (1963), pp. 3–5.
[18]Danis (1932).
[19]Danis (1949).
[20]German, 'Fracture Disease.'

International Society of Surgeons in 1951 and was the recipient of many honorary degrees. Similar to Lambotte, he enjoyed hobbies such as music, painting, and cooking.

Despite his achievements in the field of Osteosynthesis, Danis achieved greater international fame for his breast-cancer operation, which he presented to much acclaim at a 1938 international congress in Brussels. World War II intervened and probably prevented Danis from gaining more notoriety for his Osteosynthesis operations. By the time the war had ended, he had reached retirement age and others stepped into the limelight. Among the AO founders, it was believed that only Maurice Müller was really familiar with Danis' work and had visited him personally in 1950.

Why Osteosynthesis Initially Lost Out to Conservative Treatment in the Race for Global Domination of Fracture Care

Due to the early reputation gained by Böhler with his hospital in Vienna, the conservative method spread internationally and established itself before operative fracture treatment could gain any traction. While Böhler received a steady stream of visitors, Lambotte, in Antwerp, never achieved the same impact and was not able to rely on a large group of followers. By the time Danis published his first findings and his improved instrumentation, Böhler had already achieved an international reputation, although the war certainly imposed limits on the dissemination and diffusion of the new method.

At first, Gerhard Küntscher, with his nail, also struggled to gain acceptance. Eventually, the surgeons in the German army adopted his practice, giving it significant exposure and a rapid adoption during the war (although it was confined to Germany itself). What brought him to the attention of the medical community was the fact that returning soldiers, including Allied soldiers who had been German prisoners of war, returned with fractures that were treated with the Küntscher nail, serving as significant proof of the concept for surgeons on both sides of the Atlantic. Neither Lambotte nor Danis could claim a similar dissemination of their practices.

The Medical World Reacts Negatively to the Practice of Osteosynthesis

A close read of the discussions at surgical congresses concerning fracture treatment provides a clear impression that the majority of surgeons, including some of the most reputable ones, voiced consistently negative views of Osteosynthesis. Schlich[21] cites several examples of the writing of leading surgeons that give us some idea about the hostility Osteosynthesis, as practiced by Lambotte and Danis, faced:

---

[21]Schlich (2002), pp. 25–26.

It was questionable if open bone surgery should ever be done except by highly trained men, with highly trained assistants in highly trained hospitals, otherwise disaster is likely to result (Gray, in a report for an American insurance company, 1982).[22]

The German surgeon Fritz Steinmann was reported to have commented that he did not believe internal fixation would ever become a method of choice, due to the sheer difficulty of the technique and the high-risk for infections.[23]

Böhler, the leading proponent of the conservative method, wrote in his 1929 textbook:

> Internal fixation (is) the most disastrous treatment and responsible for the death of thousands of patients or resulting in permanent disability.

According to Böhler, only very few surgeons would ever be able to employ this method successfully.[24] In later writings (1943 and 1953), Böhler continued to express negative sentiments about internal treatment of fractures. In a comment about super-modern hospitals with highly-sophisticated equipment, Böhler argued that no one was capable of acquiring the knowledge and skill required to use all the modern equipment, including Lambotte's and Danis' Osteosynthesis methods. He feared that once these instruments were available to surgeons, they would be used, even if the users lacked the skill of a Lambotte or Danis.[25]

In the 1950s, several American authors who were also highly critical of Osteosynthesis, advising against its use unless highly qualified operators or equipment and implants were available. In another study, it was concluded:

> If you have a poor surgeon, you can give him the best apparatus in the world and he will still get a high percentage of failures.[26]

As late as the annual conference of the German Association for Surgery in 1960, Böhler continued to criticize Osteosynthesis as one of the most dangerous procedures often applied without proper indication and not mastered technically.[27]

Given these strongly worded comments about the practice of Osteosynthesis, it should not come as a surprise that the technique remained isolated to selective pockets and that most surgeons refrained from using it. This was the situation faced in the early 1950s when a young surgeon from Switzerland, Maurice Müller, entered the scene.

---

[22]Gary (1928), pp. 27–39.
[23]Reference from Schlich (2002), p. 25.
[24]Schlich attributed this comment to Lorenz Böhler (1929).
[25]Thomas Schlich excerpted these comments from Lorenz Böhler (1943, 1953).
[26]Thomas Schlich cites Venable and Stuck (1947) and Reynolds and Key (1954) for these studies.
[27]Kuner (2015), p. 154.

References

Bauer, E. (1959). *Zur Therapie der geschlossenen Unterschenkelfrakturen* (Vol. 39). Suva: Mitteilungen.

Böhler, L. (1929). *Technik der Knochenbruchbehandlung*. Wien: Maudrich.

Böhler, L. (1943). *Technik der Knochenbruchbehandlung im Frieden und im Krieg*. Wien: Maudrich.

Böhler, L. (1953). Unterschenkelschaftbrüche. *LAC, 276*, 192–217.

Danis, R. (1932). *Technique de l'ostéosynthèse*. Paris: Masson.

Danis, R. (1949). *Théorie et pratique de l'ostéosynthèse*. Paris: Masson.

Gary, R. N. (1928). Disability and costs of industrial fractures. *JBJS, 10*, 27–39.

Heim, U. F. A. (2001). *Das Phänomen AO* (p. 26). Mannheim: Huber.

Kuner, E. H. (2015). *Vom Ende einer qualvollen Therapie im Streckverband* (p. 4). Berlin: Kaden.

Lambotte, A. (1907). *L'intervention opératoire dans les Fractures*. Paris: Masson.

Lambotte, A. (1913). *Chirurgie opératoire des Fractures*. Paris: Masson.

Lane, W. A. (1950). *The operative treatment of fractures*. London: Medical Publishing Company.

Müller, M., Allgöwer, M., & Willenegger, H. (1963). *Technik der Operativen Frakturbehandlung* (pp. 3–5). Berlin: Springer.

Schlich, T. (2002). *Surgery, science and industry* (pp. 17–19). Basingstoke: Palgrave Macmillan.

Smith-Peterson, M. N., Cave, E. F., & Vangorder, G. W. (1931). Intracapsular fractures of the neck of the femur, treatment by internal fixation. *Archives of Surgery, 23*, 715–759.

Enter Maurice Müller (1918–2009)

5

When Maurice Müller visited with Robert Danis on 1 March, 1950, he spent just one day with him at the suggestion of a physician he had previously visited in the Netherlands. Müller recounted:

> I realized that I was witnessing a method of Osteosynthesis which allowed one to operate without having to resort to plaster as supplemental fixation. I had never seen this before and had never understood that this was possible. I was always convinced, that many of the complications of fractures, like terrible stiffness, were the result of immobilization.[1]

At the age of 32, Müller had only been practicing medicine and surgery for six years. It was during these years, and the previous six of his medical study, that he became interested in Orthopedics and treating bone fractures and was appalled by the miserable results of the existing practice. The steps Müller took during his medical education, and his early years as a young surgeon, are worth revisiting; they provide some important insights into how he gravitated towards the events leading up to his visit with Robert Danis in Brussels.

How Maurice Müller Decided to Pursue a Medical Career

Müller was born in 1918 in Biel (Bienne), Switzerland, into a French-speaking, entrepreneurial family. His father, who had first emigrated to the US and studied medicine there, returned home during World War I to serve in the Swiss military, as was required. After the war, he ended up taking over the family business. He gave up his dream of becoming a medical doctor because practicing in Switzerland would

---

[1]This and other details on Maurice Müller's early medical experience were taken from Joseph Schatzker's biography about Maurice Müller: *Maurice E. Müller: In his own Words*, AO Foundation (2018), p. 47.

© Springer Nature Switzerland AG 2019
J.-P. Jeannet, *Leading a Surgical Revolution*,
https://doi.org/10.1007/978-3-030-01980-8_5

have required that he redo the entire course of medical studies that he had already completed in the US.

At age 12, Maurice saw that his father had become bitter; he witnessed him burning all his medical books in the garden, the result of losing any chance he had of becoming a medical doctor. Müller credits this scene as the moment he decided to become a medical doctor himself. Later, his father supported that decision and financed his studies. Müller's first year of medical school (1936) in Neuchâtel was spent on foundation courses. In 1937, he transferred to the University of Lausanne for the latter part of his studies. Although his father did not suggest that his son make a career of medicine, it was clear that Maurice was influenced by his father's aborted dreams.

During his medical studies in Lausanne, Müller was offered a chance to participate in a special program conducted by experts from a psycho-technical institute based in Paris. He was one of a few students selected for testing the aptitudes and skills required for different professions. These experts informed Müller that he had talent to become either, in order of priority: an architect, a city planner, or a surgeon. Additional testing showed that he had a great gift for three-dimensional thinking, a skill important for bone surgery; they recommended that he become an Orthopedic surgeon. At the time, Müller had already decided to study medicine, so with Orthopedic surgery, he reasoned he would be headed in the suggested direction. It is amazing that these psychologists were able to identify Müller's exceptional skills so early; he was just 20 years old. How right they turned out to be.[2]

Chance Meetings with First Patients Left a Strong Impression

In April 1944, while the war was still raging, Maurice Müller finished his medical studies at the University of Lausanne. He was just 26 and had, by his own admission, never treated or examined a patient before. As he took turns substituting for physicians on three-week temporary absences, due to their military service, he described his experience of meeting his first patients as the most important in his life.[3]

One of the patients, who had intended to see a specialist in foot problems and vein disorders, walked in perfectly healthy but complained about a nail in his thighbone. The patient told Müller that this nail had started to protrude and yet nobody had been able to help him. Upon further questioning, Müller learned that his patient had been in the war with the French Foreign Legion, prohibited under Swiss law. Because he faced prosecution if he returned to Switzerland, the patient had decided instead to go Finland to join the Finnish army. During forestry work, a tree fell on his leg and fractured his thighbone. He was treated by a German military doctor who inserted a

---

[2]Schatzker (2018), p. 33.

[3]This and other details on Maurice Müller's early medical experience were taken from Joseph Schatzker's biography of Maurice Müller: "Maurice E. Müller: In his own Words", AO (2018), pp. 32–34.

nail. The doctor turned out to be the German Orthopedic surgeon Küntscher (see Chap. 4). Müller had read about this procedure. And here, while the war was still going on, this patient was walking into his office.

> I was totally amazed. Here was a man who had fractured a femur, and after I examined him, I could see he recovered completely and had perfect function of his lower extremity. All other patients with fractured femurs whom I had seen during my studies had severe functional handicaps and were walking with considerable difficulty, frequently with a shorted extremity, an almost completely stiff kneed, and a crooked leg. The treatment in Switzerland at that time was traction for three months or longer and then immobilization of the leg in a body spica cast until the bone hand consolidated sufficiently to allow a gradual resumption of function. Every patient who had a fractured femur ended up as an invalid.[4]

In another few days, a patient visited him who had undergone hip surgery in Paris, where an arthroplasty was performed.[5] The patient could only walk with two canes, and yet appeared happy with the surgical result. In the patient's view, he was without pain, had regained movement of his leg, and could sit still for some extended time. All he was looking for was a shoe lift because his leg was short.

These two experiences were important to point Müller in the direction of finding better treatments for bone fractures or *arthroplasties*, and he committed to become an expert in this field. In Joseph Schatzker's biography of him, *Maurice E. Müller: In his own Words* (2018), Müller explains:

> I wanted to improve arthroplasty so that patients would be free of pain and have mobility, be able to put weight on the extremity which would be of normal length.

Looking for Hospital Position as a Junior Resident

As a result of these experiences, Müller decided to pursue a position as a junior resident in an Orthopedic hospital. With only two Orthopedic clinics in Switzerland at that time, Müller set his eyes on the Balgrist Clinic in Zurich, the larger and more important of the two.[6] Initially rejected for lack of surgical training, it looked as if he would have to settle for the rheumatology clinic; not his first choice. But as it turned out, all the candidates on the short list declined to accept their residency in Orthopedics at Balgrist and Müller was able to start his residency at the Orthopedic clinic at the Balgrist University Hospital in early 1945, the institution of his choice.

---

[4]Schatzker (2018), pp. 32–33.

[5]Arthroplasty was described as a re-forming of a joint's articular surface to relieve pain and or restore function after a joint may have been affected by arthritis or trauma. Wikipedia, accessed 1 May, 2018.

[6]Balgrist Clinic, located in Zurich, was established as a charitable foundation in 1912 to care for disabled children, many of them suffering from polio. In 1945 the Clinic became affiliated with the University of Zurich. Balgrist continued to care for the disabled; surgery was not its main mission.

Pursuing a Gap Year in Africa

Müller, however, quickly became disenchanted with the situation at Balgrist where he found that procedures were traditional and conservative in approach, with no one pushing the envelope. Also, given the personnel situation, there was little chance for advancement. On a whim, Müller put his name in the hat for one of several positions advertised for a Swiss surgical team to be dispatched for service in Ethiopia. Although many surgeons applied, and positions had already been allocated to more senior residents, again by sheer luck, an internal conflict about seniority resulted in the sudden withdrawal of one of the selected candidates. This opened the path for Müller who joined up in 1946. As an interesting aside, the interview process and selection of the team was largely in the hands of Hans Willenegger, then deputy head surgeon at the hospital in Winterthur, later to become one of the AO founders. Prior to applying to the Ethiopia assignment, Müller had pushed through his Doctor of Medicine thesis in just three months, something he had originally thought would take two years while working at Balgrist. He was awarded his degree in April 1946, which he needed to get the assignment for Ethiopia and one month later left for Africa with his fiancée Marty (Exhibit 5.1).

By the end of his 18 months stay, Müller had become a very skilled surgeon, having developed his own efficient and deliberate technique. In doing so, he claimed that he could cut operating time to well below 50% the norm, due to his manual dexterity.

Exhibit 5.1 Maurice Müller and his wife Marty in Ethiopia. *Copyright by AO Foundation, Switzerland*

First Residency in Liestal 1947-1949

Returning from Ethiopia in 1947, Müller changed his plans, realizing that he first had to become a general surgeon before he could tackle Orthopedics. He did this by becoming a resident in the Cantonal Hospital of Liestal, near Basel. It was in Liestal that Müller first came in contact with a significant amount of patient fractures. Müller's recollections from his experience in Liestal was reported in Schatzker's biography and is quoted in full below:[7]

> All over Europe, almost all fractures were treated by general surgeons. All fracture treatment was conservative. For instance, a major joint fracture of the lower extremity, such as a fracture involving the knee, would first be manipulated under an anaesthetic and then treated in traction. One tried to achieve the best possible position of the fragments. Closed reduction and plaster fixation was the method used for most fractures.
>
> Operative treatment of a fracture was rare. One might do a simple cerclage to achieve a better position of a long bone. Some clinics also used Kirschner[8] wire fixation for joint fractures. If closed reduction failed, one might also consider a simple cerclage for long bones and Kirschner wire fixation for some joint fractures. These were the main techniques available.
>
> At Liestal we used cerclage and K-wire fixation. Kirschner wire fixation was particularly useful for ankle fractures and for some fractures in children. For transverse fractures of the tibia or femur, we occasionally used intra-medullary nails, but that was rare and would be used only if a satisfactory position of the fragments was not achieved with closed methods.
>
> All fractures of the femoral neck were treated with the Smith-Peterson triflange nail or the Böhler nail, since conservative treatment of these was usually fatal and if the patient survived, resulted in non-union. On the other hand, because pertrochanteric fractures, unlike the neck, would unite in traction, they were treated in traction in bed for about four months and then in a hip spica cast. Once healed they needed months and months of rehabilitation. Few patients ever returned to an independent level of function. In the elderly, the mortality rate was quite high, but that was the best we could do. The screw and plate combination, like the dynamic hip screw, did not become available until 1956. Once this fixation device became available for these common pertrochanteric fractures, there was a significant drop in the mortality rate.
>
> Femoral shaft fractures were treated most of the time with bed rest and traction for at least three to four months and then in a hip spica for at least another three to four months. A rare exception was the transverse fracture, which was occasionally treated with an intramedullary nail. Once the bone was healed, at least a year of intense physiotherapy was needed to overcome the terrible joint stiffness, muscle atrophy, and weakness. You must understand that in those days a clinic generally knew little else than what they practiced. If they believed in Osteosynthesis, then they either plated everything with the Danis plate or they used intra-medullary nails whenever possible. These clinics were the exception, but if they treated fractures operatively then they used only one method.

As a result of this treatment regime and given that the head surgeon in Liestal was a strong believer in Böhler's conservative method, Müller did not gain any experience with the operative treatment of fractures. Instead, he became familiar with

---

[7]Schatzker (2018), pp. 41–42.

[8]Martin Kirschner (1879–1942), who introduced the Kirschner wire in 1909, became professor of surgery in Königsberg, Germany in 1916 and in Tübingen in 1927.

Böhler's systematic approach to conservative fracture treatment, which proved to be of great value in Müller's further professional development. With one more year of surgical experience, he could obtain his certification in general surgery and was ready to pursue his second certification in Orthopedic surgery, supported by a Swiss government scholarship.

A Second Gap Year: Touring European Orthopedic Centers

After completing two years in Liestal, Müller had fulfilled his promise there. His main professional target remained becoming the chief resident at Balgrist, but that promised position was not to become free until the following year. As a result, he decided to spend the intervening time visiting Europe's major centers of Orthopedic surgery and expose himself to the leading techniques practiced at the time.

Müller began his travels by visiting the leading German centers, among them Bad Tölz where he connected with Professor Lange (1899–1975) and in Munich where he met with Professor Hohmann (1880–1970). He also traveled to Cologne and Aachen. Via Paris, he went to Leiden, the Netherlands, where Professor van Nes was the head surgeon.[9] Here, Müller found the most innovative operative techniques in Orthopedic surgery; he decided to stay several months. In his opinion, van Nes was the most skillful surgeon he had met on this European tour. At Leiden, Müller experienced operations on the hip and spine, and took the chance to publish two articles. Van Nes espoused the view that successful surgeons needed to develop and design their own instruments and tools, something that Müller remembered. It was van Nes who suggested that one day Müller should visit Danis in Brussels, as he had developed modern techniques in fracture care. Müller wrote to Danis and was invited to come visit and review some cases.

The Pivotal Visit to Danis (1950)

When Müller, age 32, arrived in Brussels on 1 March, 1950, he met a surgeon who was already 70 years old. By his own admission, Müller had not heard much about Danis and was only vaguely familiar with his writings, the most recent one having been published the previous year. Some of Danis' techniques were used only occasionally. Danis used compression plates and screws to obtain absolute stability of the broken bone, which he considered essential to achieving a successful Osteosynthesis through primary bone healing. Danis explained that he followed Lambotte's ideas and had been using this, and similar techniques, for the past 25 years. Danis was a 'lone wolf' and worked completely by himself (Exhibit 5.2).

For Müller, seeing Danis' patients and his experience with Osteosynthesis must have been like a revelation. He was particularly impressed with Danis' approach to

---

[9] Cornelis Pieter Van Nes, (1897–1972).

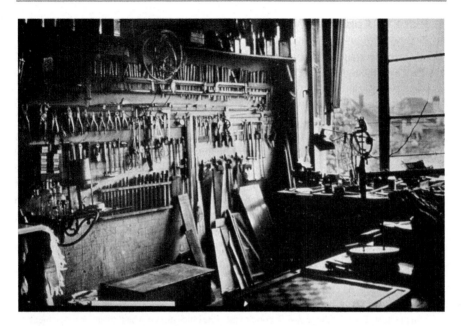

Exhibit 5.2 Danis workshop in Brussels. *Copyright by AO Foundation, Switzerland*

Osteosynthesis, one that did not resort to plaster as a supplemental fixation. At that time, Müller was already convinced that the joint stiffness patients often experienced was the result of long periods of immobilization while their limbs were in plaster. Danis also designed his own instruments—screwdriver, screws, and plates—and had them manufactured by a large Belgian instrument producer. Impressed, Müller took one of the plates and screws along, as well as the address of the manufacturer. Müller admitted that he immediately saw that some things could be done better, and he began the process of thinking about how to improve upon Danis' techniques. From the time of that visit, stable Osteosynthesis, as practiced by Danis, was to become Müller's guiding principle.

Müller was with Danis for just one day, returning to Holland the next. However, it is clear that the visit was, unquestionably, a turning point in his professional development. He later admitted that Danis' 1949 publication was one of the most important works he had ever read. For the future development of the AO organization, this visit can clearly be considered a watershed moment. Much of Müller's development in fracture treatments can be traced back to that single day in March 1950.

A Place to Apply the New Techniques: Fribourg (1950–1952)

Back in Switzerland, Müller again found his path to the coveted position as chief resident at the Balgrist Clinic blocked; the retiring head had promised the position to another person and the new head, while a friend of Müllers, was not willing to reverse the decision. Although certainly disappointing to Müller, something very positive came out of it.

Through some fortuitous circumstances, Müller was accepted to the post of chief resident in general surgery at the general hospital of the Canton of Fribourg, where he promised to stay only for one year. The hospital practiced the conservative fracture treatment method, subjecting all fractures to treatment with traction and plaster. Fortunately for Müller, the chief surgeon was not personally interested in fracture care, giving Müller a free hand to treat fractures in line with the new ideas he had learned from Danis in Belgium. Müller began to treat fractures by applying stable Osteosynthesis without use of plaster immobilization and with immediate mobilization of the extremity.[10] Müller explained:

> From the start, I decided to treat all closed fractures of the tibia either with lag screws or lag screws and plates. I had the necessary equipment to put my new system of fracture treatment into practice. The hospital was very good to me; (the chief surgeon) had given me a free hand and I was able to order a full complement of Danis' screws and plates (coapteurs) from the factory that made all the Danis' implants.
>   My treatment consisted of absolutely stable fixation and immediate mobilization. Once the patients regained a full range of motion and once all the swelling was gone from the leg, only then would we put them in an above-knee cast. They were not allowed to bear weight and were instructed to use crutches. After four weeks, they were re-admitted to hospital overnight. The long leg-cast and stitches were removed. The leg was X-rayed and if all was well and the leg moved freely, it was put into a below-knee walking cast and sent home.

During his time at the hospital in Fribourg, Müller treated and documented 75 tibia fractures. Of that number, there were only three that he considered failures and those, he thought, were due to his own mistakes. As word of his successful treatments spread, something interesting evolved:

> Once I started in my job, I made some interesting observations within a short period of time. Fribourg had five hospitals, which took their turn in fracture treatment. After about five or six months after I started, something very interesting began to happen. The police usually directed where trauma was to be taken, since they kept track of which hospital's turn it was to receive trauma cases. But suddenly, all the trauma cases started to come to us. Almost overnight the other hospitals had no trauma. All patients wanted to come to us. Fribourg was not that big, and word had spread very quickly.

What at first looked like a 'placeholder job' was, in fact, a crucial opportunity to put all the learning from his European tour into practice, and apply, in particular, the ideas he had gained from visiting Danis.

---

[10]These quotes are taken from Schatzker (2018), pp. 49–51.

Finally, at the Balgrist Orthopedic Clinic

In the Fall 1951, a position of assistant opened up at the Balgrist Clinic and Müller left Fribourg to finally assume the role he had always coveted. When Müller assumed his job as resident that year and was then promoted to Chief Resident in early 1952, he must have been elated. He had finally obtained the position he had so long fought for. Additional stays at Liestal, a European Tour, and the time in Fribourg had allowed him to mature his ideas regarding fracture care. Now that he was back in an Orthopedic hospital, he first had to put fractures aside. At Balgrist, most surgeries were elective and trauma cases were few and far between. With the arrival of the polio vaccine in the early 1950s, the large number of polio cases began to diminish, shifting attention from pediatric patients to adults with degenerative arthritis.

Müller very soon embarked on a new mission, namely to show the application of stable Osteosynthesis to the field of Orthopedics and the disease of the proximal femur (hip joints). Once he was named chief resident at Balgrist, he began to develop new surgical procedures. Under his leadership, the Balgrist Clinic transformed itself into a modern Orthopedic hospital, addressing a much wider range of patient needs. From the outset, Müller continued to design new instrumentation, first for hip surgery but also occasionally for Osteosynthesis.

In parallel, Müller worked on research that he wanted to submit for the degree of *Privatdozent* (PD) to the medical faculty of the University of Zurich.[11] It was during this time that Müller began cultivating a circle of surgical friends outside of Balgrist. Over time, he documented a large number of hip cases with an eye towards using them as the basis for his PD degree thesis, both at Balgrist and from operating experiences elsewhere. He published his "Osteotomies of the Proximal Femur" in 1957[12] and earned the Heine Prize from the German Orthopedic Association. The Zurich medical faculty indicated that they would accept this work for his PD degree and after some discussion, following Müller's resignation from Balgrist, the degree was finally awarded in 1958.

Moving to Private Practice at Hirslanden Clinic

Müller's financial remuneration at the Balgrist did not keep up with his professional reputation and it was agreed that he would get one day off each week. He used this flexibility to visit his many friends in regional hospitals around the Berne region. His family, however, which now included three children, was strapped financially. To resolve this, he applied to be allowed a private bed at Balgrist so that he could

---

[11]*Privatdozent* is a form of professorship common at Swiss universities, allowing the bearer to use the academic title of Professor but without necessarily assuming a faculty role, and signaling the qualification to teach at a university in the person's chosen field.

[12]Müller (1957).

supplement his income by seeing a few private patients. The hospital leadership refused this request, and though he even threatened to resign, the hospital wouldn't budge. On top of that, Orthopedic surgeons employed in other hospitals opposed Müllers itinerant habits. These events threatened to derail his medical career but Müller, age 41, stayed the course. On 15 October, 1957, he left Balgrist Clinic to move to the nearby private Hirslanden Clinic, where he began performing surgeries on patients the following Monday. Thus began a period of relative professional freedom and the broadening of his contacts to many other surgeons within Switzerland.

Müller's Closing and Opening Doors Experience: The Power of Persistence

Reflecting on Müllers meandering career development path as a surgeon, it is important to note how many times doors seemed to have shut for him, just to be opened elsewhere, leading to new professional opportunities. A childhood experience influenced his decisions to pursue medicine. Early in his medical training, he was 'diagnosed' with a gift for three-dimensional thinking and it was recommended that he pursue Orthopedics, which he did. After completing his medical training in Lausanne in 1944, the following year he managed to get a residency appointment at the Balgrist Clinic, Switzerland's leading Orthopedic hospital. In just a year he realized that this was not the professional training he had anticipated and so he applied for the Ethiopia tour where he was first rejected, but then could fill in for someone who withdrew at the last minute. His time there, from 1946 to 1947, offered him important experience in the field of general surgery, although it was cut short when his wife was expecting their first child. Back in Switzerland, he completed his general surgical training in Liestal from 1947 to 1949. There, he was confronted with many fracture cases that he was forced to treat in the conservative method. Without planning it that way, Müller became experienced in Böhler's approach to fracture care and was always able to borrow the positive aspects of that method.

When the door shut once more for him at Balgrist, he embarked on a European study tour from 1949 to 1950, which brought him to the steps of Danis' practice in Brussels where he experienced successful Osteosynthesis for the first time. Returning to Switzerland and finding the door into Balgrist still blocked, he joined the Fribourg Hospital. This appointment was made by the head of Fribourg, after all the previously confirmed applicants had withdrawn. There, in the role of a general surgeon, and granted significant freedom by the chief surgeon to operate, he grabbed the chance to practice what he had observed from watching Danis in Brussels. If Müller had joined Balgrist Orthopedic Clinic at that time, his intensive experience with Osteosynthesis in Fribourg would not have been possible. Finally, Müller arrived to find an open door at Balgrist in 1952, just at the time when the patient load changed from mostly younger polio patients to elderly patients suffering from degenerative arthritis. In turn, this led Müller to develop his technique for hip replacement surgery, a surgical procedure he perfected in later years.

Clearly, chance played a role, but once confronted with changed situations, Müller was quick to grasp the opportunity and innovate new surgical techniques. That he also managed to complete his MD, and later a PD thesis, during these years is all the more astonishing. When he later became a core founder of the AO group that innovated Osteosynthesis, it is important to reflect that this was not the result of a direct, linear, planned career path. Many other surgeons would have veered from the meandering path and gone for the known and comfortable, rather than the adventure of constantly plunging oneself into something entirely new.

The move to Hirslanden Clinic, covered in the next chapter, was an important development; Müller became free to perform surgeries at other hospitals and to adopt the model of the itinerant surgeon. These new arrangements in a private clinic also enabled him to improve his financial situation. It is during this time that the key steps towards the creation of the AO organization were taken.

References

Müller, M. (1957). *Die hüftnahen Femurosteotomien*. Stuttgart: Thieme.
Schatzker, J. (2018). *Maurice E. Müller: In his own words*. Davos: AO Foundation.

Recruiting a Circle of Friends

6

When Lecturing Failed to Convince

Upon arriving at Balgrist, and assuming his role as chief resident, Müller was eager to share the Osteosynthesis experience he had gained in Fribourg over the prior two years. His first lecture there was held in Winterthur for the hospital surgeons and residents. A second lecture was given at the Balgrist Clinic, with Müller inviting a number of chief residents from regional hospitals, including the chief resident for general surgery at the Zurich University Hospital. Müller shared his experience about visiting Danis, passed around his book, and talked about his surgical experiences prior to joining Balgrist. In his words, he showed them "fantastic cases" to demonstrate the then new concept of absolute stability with compression, combined with early mobility of the affected limbs. Müller was astounded to find his audience unimpressed. Worse, even those who he could motivate to visit Danis in person came away with a kind of "we found nothing to learn" reaction.

This must have convinced Müller that simply lecturing in his new position at Balgrist would not be enough to share his experiences, and that he would probably need an academic degree for some added credibility. By observing Danis he learned that if one practices alone, without a team or research funding, it is difficult to have impact beyond one's own practice. He saw general surgeons who were practicing trauma as being his main target. At that time, traumas were not treated at any of the Orthopedic departments in Switzerland; most of the surgeons who dealt with trauma cases practiced outside of university hospitals in the country's many regional hospitals.

In addition, Müller must have realized that practical application was the only way to change the minds of other surgeons. He was also not clear to what extent the lack of French language capability prevented his colleagues from truly immersing themselves in the publications by Danis, which were all written in French (Müller's mother tongue, although he was bilingual, having spent several years practicing in German-speaking regional hospitals).

© Springer Nature Switzerland AG 2019
J.-P. Jeannet, *Leading a Surgical Revolution*,
https://doi.org/10.1007/978-3-030-01980-8_6

Making His First Adherent

During his time at the Balgrist Clinic, Müller began what would later become known as his routine of itinerant surgeon—on free days or weekends, he would pack his bag of surgical tools and implants and operate on difficult cases at the invitation of professional friends. These friendships were later instrumental in forming the organization that would become the AO organization.

In 1952, Müller's first year as a chief resident at Balgrist, he reconnected with Robert Schneider,[1] a high school friend from Biel, over the time of his annual military service. As kids (Schneider was four years his senior), they had rowed in the same club, and on the same boat, on Lake Biel. Müller was small in stature and was always the coxswain steering the boat, while Schneider rowed at the head of the bow. When Müller was promoted to be a unit leader in the medical corps of the Swiss Army, Schneider, by then a surgeon, was assigned to his unit.

As Müller and Schneider regularly met in the military service, they were naturally 'talking shop.' As Müller explained his experience and ideas surrounding fracture care based on Osteosynthesis, it turned out that Schneider had also known of Danis and attended a lecture of his in France. Schneider, who had become the chief surgeon at the region hospital in Grosshöchstetten (the Berne region), was skeptical and was not easily convinced of Müller's ideas (Exhibit 6.1).

One day Schneider approached Müller about a very difficult medical case:

> You know I am a close friend of the head of our medical fraternity. His sister had a bad accident and broke her shoulder. She had a four-part fracture of the proximal humerus. The surgeon who treated her excised the fractured head since he did not know what else to do. She now has a very painful pseudo arthrosis. A shoulder arthrodesis would be the best way to treat her, but unfortunately, she is a short, obese woman who weights 120 kg. She would not survive a week in a shoulder spica cast, never mind a few months. If everything you have been telling me is true, then you should be able to help her. If you can secure an arthrodesis without putting her in a shoulder spica, then I will believe all your tales about the new form of Osteosynthesis that you have been talking about.

In those days, the only way to obtain some form of *Arthrodesis* of the shoulder required an immobilization of the fragments for a minimum of four months in a shoulder spica cast. Müller, who at the time had already had some Orthopedic experience at Balgrist, first constructed a temporary cast anchored around the patient's waist, and then a buttress for her arm made of plaster. Only after the patient confirmed that she would be able to support this did Müller schedule an operation for which he used his newly designed external compression clamps and additional wire tension bands. Within two months the patient experienced a solid Arthrodesis, was painless, and regained the function of her extremity.

---

[1]Robert Schneider (1912–1990), Chief of Surgery Regional Hospital Grosshöchstetten, near Berne, from 1951 to 1970.

Exhibit 6.1 Maurice Müller (right front) and Robert Schneider (left front) in Military Service in Switzerland. *Copyright by AO Foundation, Switzerland*

Life on the Road as a 'Star Surgeon'

Müller's friend Schneider was both elated and impressed. He, like many of his Swiss colleagues, were general surgeons and believed that Orthopedic surgeons knew little about actual surgery, since normally they did not treat fresh trauma and avoided the treatment of fracture complications. This general belief was also predicated on general reputation of the Balgrist Clinic, which was perceived to handle chronic conditions and avoid trauma cases.

Having convinced Schneider of his exceptional surgical skills, Schneider began to introduce Müller to his friends in the Berne-area hospitals as the new 'surgical star.' Many of Schneider's friends were also the heads of surgery in those regional hospitals. These word of mouth recommendations led to invitations to operate in those hospitals on difficult cases. Although they were usually Orthopedic cases, they did give Müller a chance to demonstrate how the technique of Osteosynthesis applied in Orthopedics. In many of these operations, Müller could show the advantages achieved by stability, teach atraumatic approaches, and the importance of maintaining blood supply to the bone. In the process, Müller could also teach his fellow surgeons the principle that later became the core of the AO organization's teaching on Osteosynthesis.

In his early days at Balgrist, Müller was not able to perform many surgeries in other hospitals but as time went on, he went more often on weekends, always at the invitation of the hospital's chief surgeon. However, when Müller switched to private practice, based at the Hirslanden Clinic, he had more time. His visits consisted not only of performing surgery, but also of discussion about, and teaching of, the procedures. According to Schatzker's biography about Müller, he was able to continuously develop his thinking about stable Osteosynthesis and his particular surgical techniques.

His appearances as guest surgeon in Schneider's Grosshöchstetten Hospital became more frequent. Schneider's daughter is cited in a letter by Urs Heim as[2]:

> I remember well how Marty Müller (Maurice Müller's wife) played with their three children and us in our home, sometimes well into the Saturday evening, as our fathers operated in the hospital.

The early experience with Danis in Brussels continued to influence Müller's thinking. He remembered that despite being a sophisticated user of the Osteosynthesis technique, Danis was not able to have a wider impact because he worked as a single practitioner. Early on, Müller realized that in order to achieve a wider adoption of these practices, he needed to create something like a school for operative fractures, in order to, as he called it, "form a circle" of devoted and enthusiastic followers who would come together to push ahead in the development of Osteosynthesis.

Müller made more surgical visits to the regional hospitals of Langnau (Head Surgeon Walter Schär) and Interlaken (Chief Surgeon Walter Bandi), where many of the skiing-originated fractures from ski resorts in Grindelwald, Wengen, and Mürren were sent. He added to those in 1955 a visit to Courtelary (Chief Surgeon Walter Stähli) in 1955. Robert Schneider reconnected Müller with Hans Willenegger who by then had become chief surgeon in Liestal, where Müller had spent the previous two years as a resident in general surgery. However, that was prior to the time that Willenegger was appointed (it was Willenegger who selected Müller for the Ethiopia team in 1946, see Chap. 5).

By 1956, Müller's core group of like-minded surgeons had grown to five—Schneider, Bandi, Schär, Stähli, and Willenegger (who, in this group, was the most experienced general surgeon). This was the group that Müller decided to invite to his Balgrist Clinic for a three-day practical course.

Just prior to organizing this first course, Müller travelled to visit Böhler in Vienna. He saw Böhler's approach, spoke with his residents, and came away impressed, even though this all involved the conservative treatment. Despite the fact that the Böhler team had little experience with operative fracture treatment, Müller judged the systematics developed by Böhler to be the best fracture treatment system of any kind. The system, not the treatment, became a model for him.

In the mini-course Müller arranged for his close surgical friends, he showed them his cases, gave some demonstrations, and let them see how he used stable Osteosynthesis for Orthopedic patients. The group spent three days together, and

---

[2]Heim (2001), letter written by Regula Matthison-Schneider, translated by author.

Müller pitched them his ideas on fracture treatments, some of which were developed during his Fribourg time. Müller's circle of friends had now expanded to include five heads of surgery at regional Swiss hospitals.

Already, Müller saw the opportunity to develop a large-scale treatment regime that would become international in application. Based on his Fribourg experience he had, at the end, articulated the principles for treatment, which were to become the guiding principles for the AO organization, yet to be founded.

In December 1957, on the occasion of receiving his degree as PD, Müller was offered a chance to deliver an important lecture on Orthopedic surgery and fraction treatment to a larger audience at the University of Zurich. The principles he cited read like a forecast of what was to come when the AO was founded one year later[3]:

- Bone is a living tissue
- Blood supply to the bone must be preserved
- Dead bone cannot heal
- Only normal form guarantees normal function
- Restoration of normal form requires open reduction
- For the maintenance of open reduction, internal fixation was required
- To guarantee healing of bone after open reduction, absolute stability was mandatory
- Absolute stability was achieved through compression
- Absolute stability abolished post-operative pain and made immediate rehabilitation of soft tissue and joins possible

These principles, combined with Müller's thoughts, were eventually published in his book *Proximal Femoral Osteotomies.*[4]

Following the lecture, Müller had invited guests for a drink. Some in his circle stayed on to have a longer discussion and they ended up accepting the proposal to create a school for surgical techniques; one like Müller had observed in Vienna while visiting Böhler. It was Müller who suggested the French term 'Association pour l'Ostéosynthèse' as a name for the school, abbreviated to AO.

Can Anyone Help with a Difficult Orthopedic Hip Case?

Willenegger, a member of the core group, and present at the Balgrist mini-course, was approached by Martin Allgöwer, Chief Surgeon of the Cantonal Hospital in Chur.

---

[3]Schatzker (2018), p. 64.
[4]Müller (1957).

Allgöwer[5] was looking for help in treating a patient with a difficult hip problem. Willenegger immediately suggested that he contact Müller, who would be able to help, and that he read Müller's recent book.

Since Müller had just left Balgrist to move into private practice at Hirslanden, he had time to respond to Allgöwer's request, agreeing to visit Chur. The two had never met but Allgöwer had heard very positive reports about Müller from Swiss Army friends, despite never having served in the same medical unit. During several visits to Chur, Müller performed surgical procedures and demonstrated his instrumentation and implants, which he transported in the trunk of his car. Allgöwer, a general surgeon, warmed up to Müller and eventually became one of the most important advocates of operative fracture treatment through Osteosynthesis. As a result of Müller's monthly visits, within the period of a few months, Allgöwer absorbed Müller's operative fracture care ideas and had transformed fracture care in Chur, eliminating casts, and adopting the ideas of early mobilization—that in a hospital known to manage an important flow of bone fractures from nearby winter resorts attracting an ever-growing number of skiing enthusiasts. Müller's circle of friends now counted six chief surgeons at regional hospitals.

Reviewing Müller's careful documentation of his previous cases, Allgöwer helped him publish the results in a leading Swiss medical journal.[6] He suggested another training course, similar to the one held the previous year, in Chur. Allgöwer suggested expanding the group beyond the five attending the Balgrist meeting to include other surgeons, some of whom Müller had previously worked with.

This course for the expanded group took place in 15–17 March, 1958. A total of 13 surgeons were invited, with ten actually attending. Beyond those that had been present in Balgrist, the additions included Allgöwer, as well as three other surgeons. The circle had grown to ten surgeons, six of whom came from the Berne region and shared a similar background with Müller because he was looking for experienced surgeons already familiar with his approach and willing to take it a step further (Exhibit 6.2).

During this course in Chur, the group examined existing practices of Osteosynthesis and the currently available instruments—surgical tools, as well as implants—resulting in a joint decision that an effort was needed to standardize the full range of instruments. Their time together ended with an agreement to create a new association for Osteosynthesis. It was to be named, at Allgöwer's suggestion, a group for the 'study' of Osteosynthesis, to signal intent to go beyond existing practice. In addition, the group tasked Müller with suggesting ways to develop a more uniform *Instrumentarium*, since he was the most experienced in the development of instruments and implants.

---

[5]Allgöwer, Martin (1917–2007), Chief Surgeon of the Chur Cantonal Hospital (Canton of Graubünden) in 1956, and in 1967 Professor and Chair of Department of Surgery of the University of Basel.

[6]Müller and Allgöwer (1958), p. 253.

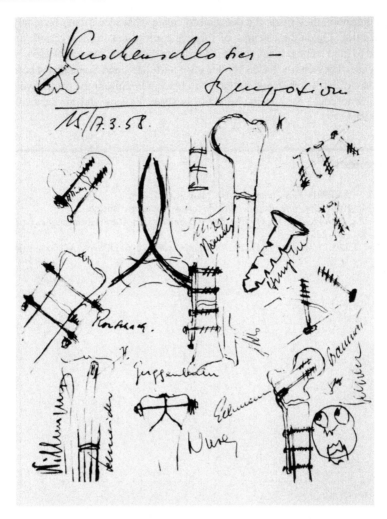

Exhibit 6.2 Card Signed by Participants in Chur Course 1958. *Source: Janine Aebi-Müller, published with permission*

From Müller's handwritten notes, four major goals are laid out in the approach to Osteosynthesis:

1. Best possible anatomical reconstruction in form and function of the injured extremity
2. Immediate mobility
3. Hospitalization period as short as possible and rapid transfer back into the working life (rehabilitation)
4. Protection of soft tissue, (added in handwriting, possibly by Allgöwer)

Furthermore, they made the decision to create what would later become the AO Organization. Given the calendar of surgical conferences in Switzerland, the group decided to hold its next meeting the day prior to the Swiss Surgical Society's annual conference. They chose Biel as the location—Müller's and Schneider's home town and close to Berne, the venue of that conference. Organizational details were left to Müller, who could rely on the help of his sister Violette and his surgical friend, Schneider.

References

Heim, U. F. A. (2001). *Das Phänomen AO*. Mannheim: Huber.
Müller, M. (1957). *Die Hüftnahen Femurosteotomien*. Stuttgart: Thieme.
Müller, M., & Allgöwer, M. (1958). Zur Behandlung der Pseudoarthrose. *Acta Chirurgica Helvetica, 25*, 253.
Schatzker, J. (2018). *Maurice E. Müller: In his own words* (p. 64). Davos: AO Foundation.

The AO Kick-Off Meeting

7

The Kick-Off Meeting

With Müller and Schneider as organizers, the group of 13 surgeons gathered for their first meeting on 6 November, 1958, at the Hotel Elite in Bienne. This was convenient for the invitees who all had to attend the next morning's meeting of the Swiss Surgical Society in Berne (Exhibit 7.1).

What's in a Name?

As early as December 1957, Müller proposed forming such a group that would be called the *Association pour l'Ostéosynthèse* (AO). At the kick-off meeting, it was decided that the association's official name, in German, would be *Schweizerische Arbeitsgemeinschaft für Osteosynthesefragen* (Swiss Association for the Study of Osteosynthesis). Although the translation of association is widely understood in both French and in English (Association of Osteosynthesis), it cannot fully capture the original meaning of *Arbeitsgemeinschaft*, consisting of two terms, *Arbeit* and *Gemeinschaft*: *Arbeit* is meant to signal that this group wishes to undertake a project, or accomplish something; *Gemeinschaft* is best translated as fraternity, brotherhood, or community of surgeons. With this wording the group wanted to signal that it was to be understood as a group of independent surgeons, coming together for the purpose of studying Osteosynthesis, and doing so as a group of equals without an established hierarchy. The addition of the term *Fragen* (in this the English translation would be 'issues') to the name of the group came at the insistence of other members, Willenegger in particular, that the group was to investigate issues surrounding the practice of Osteosynthesis.

All but one of the surgeons present were Swiss and certainly aware of the many types of associations that exist in every town for almost every purpose, including sports. A *Verein*, or association, would have provided context for their undertaking

© Springer Nature Switzerland AG 2019
J.-P. Jeannet, *Leading a Surgical Revolution*,
https://doi.org/10.1007/978-3-030-01980-8_7

Exhibit 7.1 Hotel Elite in Bienne, site of the first AO meeting. *Copyright by AO Foundation, Switzerland*

as the most common legal form in Switzerland in terms of forming groups. Although forming a *Verein* to promote a specific medical treatment was not common, the legal form came with specific benefits: as long as the association had formal statutes that ruled its governance, its membership, and controlled its finances, it could obtain a tax-exempt status; this was critically important since the AO intended to engage in a number of fund-raising activities to finance research.

G13: The Group of 13[1]

The 13 surgeons and founding members of the AO included ten surgeons who had participated in the courses held at Balgrist (1956) and in Chur (March 1958), plus three who had been invited to previous events but had not been able to attend.

- Maurice, Müller (Hirslanden, Zurich), initiator
- Schneider, Robert (Grosshöchstetten)
- Bandi, Walter (Interlaken)
- Schär, Walter (Langnau i.E.)
- Stähli, Walter (St. Imier)
- Willenegger, Hans (Liestal)

---

[1]Heim (2001), pp. 41–57.

- Guggenbühl, August (Grenchen)
- Allgöwer, Martin (Chur)
- Hunziker, Willy (Belp)
- Ott, Walter (Rorschach)
- Baumann, Ernst (Langenthal)
- Brussatis, Fritz (Balgrist)
- Patry, René (Geneva)

G5: The Founding Fathers of the AO

The surgeons assembled at the Hotel Elite were, by and large head surgeons at regional hospitals, and who, in one way or another, had developed a friendship with someone else in the group. The core members of the AO, also seen as 'the founding fathers'—Müller, Schneider, Bandi, Willenegger, and Allgöwer—were the most active in developing the organization. Müller's professional progress has been detailed (see Chap. 5), as has the nature of the connections others had with him, but for the record, here is a review of the professional pedigrees of the other core members, so as to better understand the surgical experience of the assembled group.[2]

Robert Schneider (1912–1990)

Raised in Biel and Delémont—the German and the French parts of the Canton of Berne, respectively,—Schneider, like Müller, was bilingual and would later help him with formulations of articles in German. Four years his senior, and taller than Müller, he was active in the Biel rowing club, where they had met. In his youth, Schneider had already excelled in the use of mechanical building sets (*Meccano*). He undertook his medical studies at the University of Berne. During his early medical career, he was very close to Walter Bandi, also a 'founding father' and the same age. Because he saw that his progress at the university hospital was blocked, he switched in 1945 to private practice in nearby Grosshöchstetten, eventually being appointed head surgeon there in 1951. The following year, he reconnected with Müller when Schneider was assigned to Müller's Swiss Army medical corps unit. From then on, Schneider and Müller shared a very close friendship and Müller frequently operated in Schneider's hospital on weekends. In terms of personality, he was described as domineering in appearance but conciliatory in behavior. As time progressed, Schneider became particularly active in spreading AO's thinking to many German clinics through frequent visits and as a guest surgeon.

---

[2]The descriptions of the background of the founders of the AO were taken from Heim (2001), pp. 48–56.

Walter Bandi (1912–1997)

Bandi showed talent for science and mathematics as a young student. When it came to decide on further studies, he chose medicine and met Schneider at the University of Berne. The two hit it off well, quickly becoming good friends, and even sharing a semester experience in Paris. First, Bandi joined various Berne University clinics and hospitals and then left for appointments at regional hospitals in the area. In 1951, he was appointed head surgeon of Interlaken's regional hospital, which was quickly becoming a center for sports and skiing related fractures, due to its proximity to the nearby winter resorts of Grindelwald, Wengen, and Mürren. He met Müller, through Schneider, for the first time in 1952. He remained active in the expanding the AO organization, working as a talented speaker, developing some of the screws needed for Osteosynthesis, and after his retirement, taking on some of the duties to spreading the thinking abroad.

Hans Willenegger (1910–1998)

When the AO was founded, Willenegger was chief surgeon at the hospital in Liestal and previously chief resident at the University Hospital Basel. He knew Bandi and Schneider (both two years his junior) from his medical studies in Berne, who reconnected him with Müller who had operated occasionally in Liestal and was thus familiar with Willenegger. As has been pointed out, Willenegger met Müller in 1946 as part of the selection team headed for Ethiopia. At that time, in Winterthur, Willenegger also used the Küntscher nailing technique.

Prior to his nomination as head surgeon, Willenegger was active in research. His publications about blood transfusions were widely circulated.[3] He was also an animal lover who occasionally operated on animals with dislocated fractures in his operating rooms. This brought him in contact with veterinarians, which later led to a close cooperation with an AO subgroup, namely the AOVET. By temperament, he was the born educator, a skill that was to turn out very important in the later development of the AO organization.

Martin Allgöwer (1917–2007)

Raised in St. Gallen, Allgöwer spent some time studying in Geneva where he became fluent in French. He earned his medical degree in 1942 from the University of Basel and was exposed to research early on while working in laboratories of a local pharmaceutical company. He joined the University Hospital Basel as an assistant in surgery where he learned to perfect his surgical technique on animals in his own laboratory. With the appointment of a new chief of surgery—who was

---

[3]Willenegger (1947).

coming from Winterthur and brought along his own team, including Willenegger as chief resident—Allgöwer managed to finance a stay in Texas through some local foundations. This move was supported by Willenegger, his new head resident.

In 1952, during his Swiss military service, Allgöwer suffered a complicated fracture of his lower leg during a skiing exercise. It was Willenegger who performed the operation through *cerclage*. After the removal of his cast, he had a dangerous clot in his lungs, one of the complications typical when treating fractures through the conservative method. Once Willenegger became chief of surgery in Liestal a year later, he promoted Allgöwer as his chief assistant. Just three years later, Allgöwer was named head of surgery at the cantonal hospital in Chur. During his initial years heading surgery at that hospital, he became increasingly interested in trauma triggered by the ever-increasing fracture cases from the region's ski resorts. This is when he came in contact with Müller, at his friend Willenegger's suggestion.

Allgöwer's time in Texas, fluency in English, and understanding of the US culture, came in handy later when the AO's development reached the US. Equally important for the AO, was his early research experience with animals, which laid the basis for the AO's initial research effort.

The G5, or core founding group, brought different talents and skills to the table, which were effectively leveraged in later years as the AO grew. There was a gifted surgeon (Müller), a solid organizer and diplomat (Schneider), an excellent speaker and presenter (Bandi), an experienced researcher (Allgöwer), and a talented educator (Willenegger). At the first meeting there was no talk of a core group, or that they would assume these various roles. Those differentiations would emerge over time (Exhibit 7.2).

Other Founding Members of the AO (G13)

Beyond the five members described above, there were eight additional surgeons present at that first meeting. Four of these surgeons were to play an active role in the further development of the organization. Walter Schär (1906–1982) head of the regional hospital in Langnau, Walter Stähli (1911–2009) head of the regional hospital of St. Imier, and Ernst Baumann (1890–1978) head of the regional hospital of Langenthal. These doctors were all part of the 'Bernese connection' and friends of both Schneider and Bandi, who connected them to Müller, and who had attended the earlier courses at the Balgrist and in Chur. They were all active participants, either with regard to the use of AO implants and instruments, or the contribution of various technical improvements and/or tools.

August Guggenbühl (1918–2009), head surgeon of Grenchen's regional hospital, came to the AO through Willenegger, his former boss in Liestal. He played an important role in the development of some of the surgical tools, as well as being a well-known animal lover who had a habit of driving around in his convertible car with several of his big dogs in the back, and was also instrumental in making connections to veterinarians and the creation of AOVET.

Exhibit 7.2 Core founders G5 with Müller (center) and clockwise Allgöwer (top right), Willenegger, Schneider, and Bandi. *Copyright by AO Foundation, Switzerland*

The remaining surgeons present: Fritz Brussatis (1919–1989), René Patry (1890–1983), Walter Ott (b. 1915), and Willy Hunziker (1915–1987) were all friends with either Allgöwer or Willenegger, although none stayed very long in the orbit of the AO. Brussatis, the only non-Swiss of the group, returned to Germany shortly afterward where he did stay connected with the AO. Patry, from Geneva, admired Müller as surgeon but never used his instrumentation in his surgery practice. Ott, head surgeon in the Rorschach regional hospital, left the AO in 1962 as a result of a disagreement on how to treat some indications. Hunziker remained in the AO but was not very active.

Of all of the AO founders, Müller was the only Orthopedic surgeon. All the others were general surgeons who had to handle an increasing number of trauma patients. They all had a significant amount of surgical experience and were mostly heads of regional public hospitals, directing a team of residents and assistants. Of the founders, only Müller, Willenegger, Baumann, and Patry were university-affiliated, or had achieved university faculty status, a fact that will play out later and affected the roll-out of the group's ideas among other Swiss hospitals.

Müller and Guggenbühl were the youngest of the founding members; Müller was the only one who worked in a private clinic treating private patients. Half of the G13 could be counted as belonging to the 'Berne faction', whereas the others were either recruited by Willenegger (Liestal) or Allgöwer (Chur). With Müller driving the group's instrumentation, it is interesting to note that an Orthopedic surgeon was instructing a group of general surgeons about trauma, something generally treated only by general surgeons.[4]

The First Meeting Agenda

In addition to the formal decision to create the AO organization, there were several important items on the the kick-off agenda. That evening, the Osteosynthesis implants, screws, and tools, referred to as the *Instrumentarium*, were presented, for use in the coming winter 'season,' presumably by Müller. He had been working since the Chur meeting with Robert Mathys, a mechanical engineer. Additional agenda items concerned deciding on the producer of the AO implants and instruments, a short discussion about surgical techniques and experiences from the previous winter, dialogue about how best to record the surgical results, and plans for research and the creation of a research laboratory in Davos. Different members were tasked with different responsibilities. Müller drove the development of the *Instrumentarium*, while other members were tasked with taking them to their hospitals and evaluating their usefulness.

The group also elected Schneider as chairman, Müller as secretary, and Allgöwer as treasurer. The formal adoption of legal statutes and by-laws had to await subsequent meetings.

References

Heim, U. F. A. (2001). *Das Phänomen AO*. Mannheim: Huber.
Willenegger, H. (1947). *Der Blutspender*. Basel: Schwabe.

---

[4]For the 50th Anniversary meeting held in Biel in 2008, three of the four surviving founding members attended the celebration (Müller, Stähli, and Guggenbühl).

AO Formulates Its Credo

8

Drafting By-Laws

In order to be formally recognized as an association under Swiss law, the group needed to adopt written by-laws in line with legal requirements—only then could they obtain tax-free status. It was not until the second membership meeting that a draft was submitted to members for their consideration and adoption.[1]

The fact that it took some 18 months from the Biel kick-off meeting in 1958 to arrive at formally adopted by-laws did not keep the AO group from making major progress in the development of surgical techniques and instruments. Willenegger had presented a first draft, but this was not submitted to the entire group until Fall 1959. The by-laws document was formally approved and published, dated 19 March, 1960.

The first by-laws, issued in German, incorporated several important elements that, over time, were to remain central to the AO. Some changes and refinements were reported between initial and final drafts.[2] The by-laws contained 16 articles of which the most important ones are cited here.

The Purpose of the AO

Article 1 emphasized the creation of an association for the study of issues involving bone fracture treatment, the undertaking of experimental research, and the exchange of practical and scientific experience, particularly as it related to Osteosynthesis. From the outset, the organization was intended to be a grouping of surgeons who not only exchange surgical experiences, but also actively engage in research.

---

[1]For a full text rendition in German of the AO statutes, see Heim (2001), pp. 228–230.
[2]Heim (2001), pp. 65–67.

© Springer Nature Switzerland AG 2019
J.-P. Jeannet, *Leading a Surgical Revolution*,
https://doi.org/10.1007/978-3-030-01980-8_8

The Role of the AO General Assembly

The AO General Assembly was intended to be the top decision-making unit, and its role is detailed in several articles (Articles 4–8) of the by-laws. At each annual meeting, activities of the previous year were to be reviewed and the elected leaders were to report on the organization's financial status. The AO intended to hold two to four scientific meetings annually, and members could be asked to contribute additional financial resources. Very early in the life of the Foundation, member surgeons were encouraged to willingly engage in detailed discussions and share their respective experiences.

Defining the AO Leadership Positions

The AO leadership was to be elected from among its membership for two-year terms, including the position of *Obmann*, or chairman, secretary and treasurer. These three roles were to be executed on a voluntary basis and without compensation.

The choice of the term *Obmann*, which is similar to the US jury trial court system's use of Foreman, is important. AO members decided not to have a 'president' for their association, but instead *primus inter pares*, a person with limited decision-making powers. An important role, however, was the role of the 'convener' of the membership to its meetings. Robert Schneider, one of the AO 'founding fathers', and close friend of Müller, was elected, and subsequently re-elected to fill this role, remaining in it until 1978. Müller was elected to be the group's first secretary, and Allgöwer its first treasurer.

Membership Rules

Membership was open to surgeons from all nationalities provided they supported the goals of the AO and had an independent professional standing, per Article 3 of the statutes. All existing members had to agree on any new members, thus effectively providing a veto right to each existing member. Clearly, the intention was to limit membership to practicing surgeons only; an included provision was that, upon retirement, or at the time when a surgeon could no longer perform Osteosynthesis, the member would be moved to the status of senior member. An entry fee of CHF 500 was also established as a requirement to membership. In fact, this was already the amount being contributed by the founding members for their first meeting.

Up to 1965, 18 new members were admitted to the AO. By 1983, on the Foundation's 25th anniversary, some 120 members had been admitted, seven of which had passed away, two had quit, eight were in the scientific members category, and another 13 were listed as corresponding members.[3] During this time, nine

---

[3] Schneider (1983), pp. 249–251.

surgeons had reached the status of senior member. The roles and activities of both the scientific and corresponding members of the AO will be discussed in coming chapters.

Members' Privileges and Duties

Each member of the AO enjoyed same privileges and was asked, at the same time, to accept some duties, as detailed in the lengthy Article 12 of the statutes. All members were expected to attend AO meetings. Of particular importance in this same article was the duty to document all of their treated fractures, according to an agreed upon standard format, while at the same time earning the right to access the documentation of all the other members. With this requirement, the AO threw open the doors to a review system of all cases accessible to all members.

Members were expected to engage with one another in a supportive spirit, adopting collegial interpersonal relationships, similar to a fraternity. Every single member could count on the support of all the other members. By adopting this as part of its by-laws, the founding AO members set the direction about how they intended to engage one another and eventually leading to the AO philosophy further described below.

Finally, and relating to the AO's further development, great importance was placed on the commitment of each member to make any and all scientific developments related to surgical treatment of fractures available to the AO membership-at-large. This would lead to complete sharing of technical developments, making them available license-free to the AO community.

Adhering to the AO Credo

A final, but equally important, duty of membership was the requirement that members follow AO guidelines relating to the treatment of fractures—a principle that went to the heart of the AO's *raison d'être*. Also related to the AO guidelines is the use of the term 'credo,' one that became popular in management circles as a result of a document initially published by Johnson & Johnson(J&J).[4] In retrospect, the application of credo to the founding principles is of interest because J&J ended

---

[4]Source: Johnson & Johnson (J&J) Website, accessed 16 February, 2018. Robert Wood Johnson, J&J chairman from 1932 to 1963 and a member of the Company's founding family, drafted its credo himself in 1943, just before J&J became a publicly traded company. This was long before anyone ever heard the term 'corporate social responsibility.' J&J's credo is more than just a moral compass. The company believes it is a recipe for business success. The fact that J&J is one of only a handful of companies that have flourished through more than a century of change is advanced as proof of that. The values that guide the company's decision-making are spelled out in its credo, and views this as a challenge to put the needs and well-being of the people that the company serves first.

up acquiring all of the medical implant assets initially designed and created by AO surgeons (see Chap. 40).

Bootstrapping the Organization

In summary, the AO's founding members were all practicing surgeons, who came together to form what they called 'a community of surgeons,'—one with equal status for all members, intending to advance the practice of Osteosynthesis. They were prepared to engage in research, share all of their cases (both successful and not), and to support this organization on a volunteer basis based upon their own personal financial resources.

There was no talk about subsidies of any kind, outside capital, or any resources beyond their own. It is this fact that leads us to borrow the term 'bootstrapping' from the world of business ventures. That such a loose organization, with minimal structures, would eventually be able to create a veritable surgical revolution for the treatment of bone fractures was not self-evident at the time. How this happened is explored in subsequent chapters.

Defining AO Treatment Guidelines

AO members were committed to follow the agreed upon AO treatment guidelines for Osteosynthesis. What were these guidelines, and how were they created?

A draft with annotated handwritten comments stemmed from the Chur meeting in March 1958, led by Müller.[5] In this draft, Müller articulated four goals, as well as five principles that would result in a successful Osteosynthesis. The goals and principles later became the foundation of AO teaching, and were more fully developed through publications authored by the core founding group. By 1962, they were articulated as follows[6] (Exhibit 8.1a, b):

Restoration of Anatomy[7]

To return the fractured limb to its proper anatomic shape was the principal goal of fracture treatment. According to the AO, the reconstruction of the anatomy generally offered the best chance for optimal recovery of function and was preferred to "tolerable misalignment."[8] In later publications, this process was described as

---

[5]Heim (2001), p. 216–217.
[6]Müller et al. (1963).
[7]Müller et al. (1991), p. 2.
[8]Müller et al. (1991), p. 8.

Ziele und Grundprinzipien der modernen Osteosynthese beim Erwachsenen

Ziel

Folgende 3 Ziele sollen erstrebt werden :

der Muskeln und

1. Die sofortige Mobil--postoperative aktive Betätigung der frakturnahen Gelenke muss vor allem ermöglicht werden, denn sie stellt den besten Reiz zur Normalisierung dar. Dann braucht nach erfolgter Knochenheilung nicht noch die Folgen der Frakturkrankheit, wie Gelenksteifen und Muskelschwund, behandelt werden.

Der Vorteil dieser Frühmobilisierung kann nicht hoch genug eingeschätzt werden. Nur dann kann eine Osteosynthesemethode befriedigen, wenn sie unmittelbar nach der Operation einsetzen kann.
Dabei soll nicht danach getrachtet werden die Frühbelastung zu erzwingen ! Vor der Belastung sollte die Knochenwunde weitgehend überbrückt sein.

2. Die Wiederherstellung der anatomischen Form des Knochens, denn nur die ideale anatomische Form kann normale Funktion erzeugen. Form und Funktion sind so sehr miteinander verknüpft, dass eine veränderte Form zwangsläufig die Funktion ungünstig beeinflussen wird.

3. Die per primam Heilung der Fraktur ohne sichtbarer Callusbildung. Jeder überschüssiger Callus ist minderwertig, muss um- und abgebaut werden, ist unnötig, wie hunderte Beispiele es zeigen können .

Die Grundprinzipien nach denen eine gute Osteosynthese durchgeführt werden sollte sind schon seit längerer Zeit bekannt :

1. (Lambotte 1890, Lane 1893) : Eine lückenlose Asepsis vom Moment des Unfalles an bis zur Heilung, ist Grundbedingung jeder Osteosynthese, denn die Infektionsgefahr ist der einzige stichhaltige Argument der Gegner der Osteosynthese .

Jede Gewebsinduration (Verhärtung), jede röntgenologischesichtbare Aufhellung auf im Bereich einer Schraube spricht für eine leichte Infektion, für ungenügende Asepsis. Eine Schraube muss nach 6 oder 12 Monaten mindestens so fest wie zu Beginn den Knochen fixieren!

Schonungsvolles, anatomisches Operieren Grundbedingung.
Maske über Nase , Plastikeinlage vor Mund, Op.Schurz hinten verschlossen. Abdecken mit antiseptischem Mastix und Plastik.
Hautmesser sofort wechseln, peinlichste Haemostase(oder Blutleere !) Schonungsvolle Reposition unter Zug . Sorgfältigste Hautnaht !
Zur Ausschaltung der Gefahren des lokalen Haematoms, Draenieren mit Polyaethylendrains und Saugapparat (z.B. Wasserstrahlpumpe!) (besser als alle Antibiotica !) .

2. (Lambotte 1890, Lane 1893) : Die Osteosynthese soll die Frakturstelle in einem absolut stabilen Block verwandeln, deren Festigkeit im Laufe des ganzen Prozesses der Bruchheilung nicht nachlässt.

Nur dann ist eine "per primam" Heilung zu erwarten. Jede überschüssige Callusbildung nach Osteosynthese zeugt von einer Unruhe im Frakturbereich! Die Erzielung einer stabilen Osteosynthese ist oft überaus schwierig. Es handelt sich aber meist um ein mechanisches Problem. Jedenfalls sollen stets alle Fragmente an Ort und Stelle gebracht werden und niemals exci-diert werden !

Exhibit 8.1 (a, b) Notes from Maurice Müller used for Chur Meeting in 1958. *Source: Reproduced with kind permission of the Hofgrede Verlag, Berne*

ziele und Grundprinzipien der O.   -2-

Beispiele einer stabilen Osteosynthese :
- Cerclage + Verschraubung bei langen Spiralbrüchen u. langen Schrägfr.
- Küntschner Marknagel bei Oberschenkelbrüche im mittleren Drittel nach
  Ausbohrung der Markhöhle bis auf 12 bzw. 14 mm und Einsetzung eines
  entsprechend dicken Marknagels.
- Danisplatten bei Vorderarmquerfrakturen
- Nichtsperrende Laschenschrauben nach Pohl (modif.n. Müller) bei
  pertrochanteren und subtrochanteren Frakturen.

3. **Materialfrage** : Das eingesenkte Material soll gewebeverträglich sein
   und das jeweils notwendige Instrumentarium soll zur Verfügung stehen.

   Nur bei ungleichem Material, die Prothesen entfernen, sonst belassen
   genau wie die Zahneinlagen. Das Quantum des Material ist belanglos .

   Nach Orsös 1925 sollen die eingesen versenkten Metallstücke weder
   einen chemischen, noch einen mechanischen, noch einen elektrischen
   Reiz ausüben !

4. Danis prägte den Satz 1931 ein : Zwischen den Fragmenten sollte einen
   axialen Druck ausgeübt werden .

   Die Struktur des Knochens ist funktionell bedingt nach genauen mathema-
   tischen Prinzipien und die Knochen und Knorpelzellen richten sich stets
   nach den Druck- und Zugkräften aus (weest Bauprinzip der maximalen
   Materialersparnis) .

   Ein Abbau der abgestorbenen Knochenenden (Osteolyse) findet nur dann
   statt wenn kein axialer Druck ausgeübt wird (Müller) und die Fragmente
   nicht absolut ruhig gestellt sind (mikroskopische Bewegungen genügen) .

   Bei Pseudarthrosen, die Pseudarthrose nur dann anfrischen , wenn ein
   richtiges Falschgelenk mit Knorpelüberzug und Gelenkkapsel besteht oder
   wenn eine hochgradige Fehlstellung nur durch Sprengung der Pseudarthrose
   möglich ist. Sonst heilt die Pseudarthrose (nicht Endzustand, sondern
   Stillstand) unter einem axialen Druck überaus rasch.

   Nach einer O. darf nie einen Zug (Extension) ausgeübt werden, da sonst
   beide Kräfte sich neutralisieren.

5. Müller 1951 : Es soll möglichst **früh operiert** werden. Ideal ist die
   8 Std-Grenze die bei geschlossenen Schaftbrüche bis 12 Std verlängert
   werden kann.   Nur in bestimmten Fällen Operation nach dem 5.Tag.
   Jedenfalls sollte während des Stadiums 2 der Callusbildung (Organisation
   der Gewebszerstörungen und des Blutergusses durch Granulationsgewebe)
   möglichst nicht operiert werden !

   ──────────

Bemerkung : Bei jeder Pseudarthrose ist vorerst das bestehende mechanisch-
biologische Problem aufzudecken und die schädigende Beanspruchung
zu identifizieren, damit diese vor allem ausgeschaltet werden kann.

Vortrag in Chur gehalten 15. 3. 58

Anwesend : Allgöwer, Bandi, Baumann, Guggenbühl, Hunziker, Ott, Solèr, Schneider, Stähli, Wf, Wittenger + Sanromà

Exhibit 8.1 (continued)

anatomical reduction of the bone fragments, particularly for joint fractures.[9] It has remained the first principle until today.

Stable Fracture Fixation

AO doctrine required that "all methods of operative fixation must provide adequate stability to maintain length, axes, and rotation. Stability in internal fixation is used to describe the degree of immobility of the fracture segments.[10] Lag screw fixation, with or without neutralization plates, depended on 'absolute stability' for optimal bone healing, which occurred by direct bridging of the precisely reduced fracture." The appearance of callus was viewed "as indicative of lost stability for which nature tried to compensate." This would later require a need for reduced weight bearing of the fracture area. Stable internal fixation (plates, screws) had to be designed to fulfill the local biomechanical designs. Maintenance of stability during the healing process could be achieved by applying pressure to the fracture using intramedullary nails, screws, or compression plates, resulting in a functionally stable Osteosynthesis.[11]

Preservation of Blood Supply

The preservation of the blood supply to the bone fragments and the soft tissue required an atraumatic surgical technique. Over time, this principle had risen in importance and it concerns both the treatment of soft tissues as well as any bone fragments and their vascularity.[12]

Early Pain-Free Mobilization of Limb and Patient

The adoption of the principle of postoperative immediate mobilization has significantly decreased risks of permanent impairment after most fractures.[13]

Patients who were free of pain and unhindered by a plaster cast, or any other traction devices as was typically used for a conservative method, were able to actively move muscle and joints much more readily and sooner. Prior to the AO, not using plaster casts as an additional method of immobilization had been used occasionally but complete abandonment of the cast after Osteosynthesis was a radical step at that time.[14]

---

[9]Ibid., p. 2.

[10]Müller et al. (1991), p. 12.

[11]Schlich (2002), p. 35, citing research by Maurice Müller to make this point.

[12]Müller, Ibid, p. 3.

[13]Müller, Ibid, p. 3.

[14]Schlich (2002), p. 35.

In the draft based upon Müller's discourse at the Chur meeting, several handwritten notes and additions have been identified. Müller himself had listed only three principles (anatomical reconstruction, primary bone healing through compression, and functional rehabilitation through early mobilization).[15] The handwritten insertion concerning a fourth point including traumatic surgical processes was believed to be an addition contributed by Allgöwer who, as a gifted surgeon, had published extensively on the treatment of wounds and soft tissues in surgery and was known to be able to close patient's wounds from surgery in exceptional ways, minimizing later scars. The addition is a testament to the collaboration of surgeons from different fields for a better patient outcome, something that can be detected in the further development of AO in a number of later initiatives.

Evolution of AO Credo Over Time

Although the articulation of the AO Principles from 1962 evolved over time, there were no major changes made, and, even after almost 60 years, they have stood the test of time.

As surgical experience and increased understanding of soft-tissue problems evolved, AO principles were slightly adapted, as was the differentiation between the initially pursued absolute fracture stability versus the later introduced, relative fracture stability, leading to a number of innovations in implant design highlighted in later chapters of this text. Although the AO guidelines maintained that absolute stability remained the treatment goals in articular fractures, relative stability was often a preferred option in multi-fragmentary fractures.[16]

In 2018, AO's valid treatment principles are remarkably similar to those published in 1962. There are still four major principles, which the AO lists as follows[17]:

1. Fracture reduction and fixation to restore anatomical relationships.
2. Fracture fixation providing absolute or relative stability as the 'personality' of the fracture, the patient, and the injury requires.
3. Preservation of the blood supply to soft tissues and bone by gentle reduction techniques and careful handling.
4. Early and safe mobilization and rehabilitation of the injured part and the patient as a whole.

The question might be raised about why the principles of the AO did not change, despite the advent of new technologies, such as minimal access surgery, computer-aided navigation, and newly-designed internal fixators offering many more new

---

[15]Schlich (2002), p. 35.
[16]AO website, philosophy, accessed 15 January, 2018.
[17]Ibid., AO Website.

treatment options. During all of this time, although technology evolved, the under-lying biology itself did not change and thus, the AO's Published Principles did not have to be altered.[18]

Development of AO Surgical Principles

As can be gleaned from the Chur draft, Müller not only articulated the four principles and goals of Osteosynthesis, as described above, but also lectured about the surgical principles necessary, or best practices, to achieve a successful Osteosynthesis. He noted five principles that he had already mentioned and had been known for for some time. In describing these five best practice elements, he referred to Lambotte and Lane, as well as to Danis, when articulating best practices:

1. Thorough asepsis throughout the surgical procedures, starting from the arrival of the patient. He pointed out that the danger of infection was the only major criticism that could be raised by those opposed to Osteosynthesis. It is interesting to note the extent to which Müller described the necessary steps to be taken to prevent infections, even including how to put on the surgical masks.
2. For the second operating principle of converting the fracture into a stable block, Müller referred to Lambotte and Lane. He pointed out that Osteosynthesis should take place without callus, and that the emergence of callus pointed towards some instability around the fracture. He admitted that complete stability was difficult to achieve, but that this was largely a technical problem. He then went on to list various techniques that could be employed to arrive at a stable Osteosynthesis. He pointed out that there were several technical ways to proceed.
3. Surgical implants and instruments were detailed in the third point.
4. Here Müller referred to Danis and the need to achieve axial compression between bone fragments. He offered reasons why this should be so and referenced some of his own published research.
5. The last point referred to the timing of an operation. Müller argues for the earliest possible point in time, even specifying the time window in hours.

The extent to which the principles of successful surgery were outlined foreshadowed the focus on surgical skills needed to perform successful Osteosynthesis. It also demonstrated how the AO founders, through meetings and attending as guest surgeons in each other's hospitals, were focused on their surgical craft, sharing it amongst themselves. This would later find its way into the many AO courses that were launched two years later.

Frequent references to Lambotte and Danis attested to the fact that Müller saw himself as adopting their principles, even though, admittedly, he viewed himself as having significantly improved and gone beyond their techniques.

---

[18]Ibid., AO Website, accessed 15 January, 2018.

Over the next three years, AO members were to systematize these good surgical principles in a series of instruction sheets (*Merkblätter*).[19] Under the leadership of Müller, ten instruction sheets, numbered one through ten, plus drawings, were collated into a set of about 90 pages. These sheets, shared among the AO community, were intended to standardize the practice of Osteosynthesis and to make the ideas available to a larger group of surgeons. The instruction sheets were to become the basis of the first book published by the AO founders in 1963.[20] Some chapters authored by Müller in that book were almost identical, word for word, to the earlier published instruction sheets.[21]

AO Built on Four Pillars

The founders of the AO had early on included a number of statements in their by-laws as to how they intended to achieve their collaboration. Some of these were aimed at certain activities and others were more focused on how they intended to govern and interact amongst themselves.

In *The Origins of the AO Foundation* (2001), his history about the early years, Urs Heim included a drawing that has been republished many times.[22] This drawing did not exist in the early days of the AO, but was created later for the book. However, the Foundations' four pillars were evident in the very first documents published by the AO. In the drawing, the four pillars hold up a structure, or roof, labeled 'Cooperation,' referring to the spirit of AO members who wanted to share openly, and support each other (Exhibit 8.2).

The four main activities envisioned for the Foundation were: Instrumentation, Teaching, Documentation, Research. All were depicted as pillars. Each grew over time and at different rates of speed (and not necessarily in a coordinated fashion) but they did prove to be connected in a symbiotic relationship. Each of the pillars is critical to the Foundation and its work, and each will be addressed in greater detail (see following chapters).

Instrumentation, or as Müller preferred, the *Instrumentarium*, included all surgical instruments, screws needed for fixation, plates implanted, as well as the medullary nail. Later, this led the AO to be involved in an industrial collaboration that was necessary for the ultimate realization of this pillar.

Teaching was a key activity from the beginning for members of the AO. It had its origin in Müller having been an itinerant surgeon for a time. During that period, he visited many surgeon friends in regional hospitals, and it was in these settings that they all gained surgical technique experience—learning-by-doing. Later, teaching took the form of more formal presentations and speeches at congresses. This form

---

[19]Müller (1961).

[20]Müller et al. (1963).

[21]Heim (2001), p. 134.

[22]Heim (2001), p. 101; drawing by Klaus Oberli.

Exhibit 8.2 AO: The four pillars. *Copyright by AO Foundation, Switzerland*

was then eclipsed by formal training courses, which eventually became one of, if not the most important, pillars of the Foundation.

Documentation was seen early on as an important element. All member surgeons were expected to document their cases, before and after surgery. The benefit of complete documentation was not invented by AO surgeons but was observed by Müller, and others who found out that all of their forerunners in fracture treatment—namely Lambotte, Danis, and Böhler—had engaged in detailed documentation. From the very beginning, AO surgeons were convinced that this was an important and necessary activity and contributed to the further development of the AO's human capital.

Research was the fourth and final pillar. In Article 1 of the by-laws, it is made clear that the AO was intended to study issues surrounding bone fractures. Studying, understanding, and eventually researching were central to the AO's understanding of its own mission. At the Foundation, research covered clinical research (predominant in the earlier years), experimental research (which assumed greater importance over time), and metallurgical research (the nature of materials used for the implants, which gave rise to several problems over time and needed to be addressed).

Labeling the roof of the AO structure 'Cooperation' signals that any of the four activities, or pillars, to be undertaken were to be tackled in this spirit. The AO founders did not intend to create a top-down administration grouping, but a bottom-up community of organized surgeons, coming together voluntarily in the spirit of cooperation. For them, cooperation means the concept of achieving a goal together instead of as lone individuals; to contribute something to a common goal, as opposed to simply being a consumer or bystander, and an active collaboration rather than just waiting for something to be done by others. To use a metaphor from the US, it means to help draw the cart instead of comfortably sitting in the cart.

It is certainly clear that the surgeons assembled on 6 November, 1958 at the Hotel Elite in Biel, Switzerland, were not coming together to simply enjoy good meals, practice camaraderie, or build professional connections for their own benefits. Rather, by joining this group, each and every one of the 'founding fathers' signed up for a major enterprise that would demand much of their time, energy, and resources. They all knew that it would be for the benefit of patients who, after suffering from bone fracture, all too often ended up disabled and unable to continue an active life.

References

Heim, U. F. A. (2001). *Das Phänomen AO*. Mannheim: Huber.
Müller, M. E. (Ed.). (1961, July and December). *Operative Frakturbehandlung*. Instruction Sheets of AO. Unpublished Manuscripts.
Müller, M. E., Allgöwer, M., Schneider, R., & Willenegger, H. (1991). *Manual of internal fixation* (3rd ed.). Heidelberg: Springer.
Müller, M. E., Allgöwer, M., & Willenegger, H. (1963). *Technik der Operativen Frankturenbehandlung*. Berlin: Springer.
Schlich, T. (2002). *Surgery, science and industry*. Basingstoke: Palgrave Macmillan.
Schneider, R. (1983). *25 Jahre AO–Schweiz* (pp. 249–251). Berne: Arbeitsgemeinschaft für Osteosynthesefragen.

Pillar One: Developing the AO *Instrumentarium*

9

Decision to Develop AO-Specific *Instrumentarium*[1]

When the AO founders gathered in Chur, at their first full three-day course in March 1958, the group assigned Maurice Müller the task of creating an *Instrumentarium*. There was extensive discussion among the surgeons present and based on their hands-on experience with human cadaver bones, it became clear to all concerned that, to a considerable extent, successful Osteosynthesis depended on a dedicated and proprietary *Instrumentarium* suited to their surgical needs.

The *Instrumentarium* in use up to the meeting could only be described as a hodge-podge of tools, plates, and screws, often not fitting together in an ideal way, and assembled for each surgery in the hospitals based upon what was available. Various members of the group were familiar with some of the tools, such as Smith-Peterson or Böhler nails, Küntscher nails, cerclage, occasional compression plates, and various drills. Baumann, one of the AO founders, had developed his own lag screw. Schneider, another founder, described this situation as a matter of luck to find the drills, screws, and plates that all fit together.[2]

When the group tested the available *Instrumentarium* in Chur, they quickly accepted Müller's idea for the need of a standardized set. Müller was tasked to develop this Osteosynthesis *Instrumentarium* under the condition that it would be easy to handle, compatible in use with all elements, and made of the same material.[3]

---

[1] *Instrumentarium* is the terminology used by the AO founders for the combination of surgical instruments, implants (plates), and screws. Otherwise specific terms are used for only one of the elements, i.e. surgical instruments, etc. In later years, the producers internally used the term "instrumentation" for all three elements. For ease of understanding, the term *Instrumentarium* is used throughout this book and always refers to all three elements (surgical instruments, implants, and screws).

[2] Schneider (1983), p. 14.

[3] Heim (2001), p. 102.

© Springer Nature Switzerland AG 2019
J.-P. Jeannet, *Leading a Surgical Revolution*,
https://doi.org/10.1007/978-3-030-01980-8_9

This development task was the result of Müller's prior experience in designing instruments for his Orthopedic surgery. He had learned from both Van Nes and Danis during his visits in 1950, that for a surgeon to become successful, he had to design his own *Instrumentarium*. This left a deep impression on Müller. Upon returning to Switzerland, he had begun, step by step, to design instruments and have them produced by a local supplier. In particular, he worked with Zulauf of Langenthal, a company specializing in woodcarving tool making near Berne. While Müller's instruments were suited for his Orthopedic surgery, they were not designed for Osteosynthesis. As the result of his itinerant practice, he had impressed many surgeons with his own tools. However, Müller himself was not completely satisfied with his suppliers and began looking for alternatives.

Müller Locates Robert Mathys

No sooner had he been asked to devote time and energy to this development, he took immediate steps to locate a suitable producer by asking around for a recommendation of a skilled craftsman able to work with material made from specialty steel. His contact, a supplier of specialty steel to machining workshops supplying parts to the watch industry, suggested he go and see Robert Mathis, owner of a small workshop in the town of Bettlach, halfway between Biel and Solothurn.

Mathys (1921–2000) was born into a middle-class family in the region and completed an apprenticeship as a technical draftsman and mechanic at a local engineering firm. He was an eager tinkerer with small engines, constructing little diesel engines for use in model airplanes and, in his town, earned himself the nickname *Motörli Röbu*.[4] At the age of 19, and in his spare time, he earned a pilot's license. During World War II, Mathys spent long stints in the Swiss army, not unlike Müller. He had applied for a professional pilot position in the Swiss Army, receiving his acceptance in 1946 just two months after he had opened his own workshop. He declined the offer and opted to build his business. He was 25 years old.

On 8 April, 1958, only about three weeks after the Chur meeting, Müller showed up in the Mathys workshop. What Müller found turned out to be a pivotal connection for AO's further development and its *Instrumentarium*. Mathys was an expert in constructing, designing, and machining stainless steel screws, a skill Müller was looking for and had not found among his early suppliers. By the time Mathys met Müller, his business had grown to 14 employees. He had never manufactured any parts for the medical industry! (Exhibit 9.1).

When Müller arrived, unannounced,[5] on Mathys' door steps, he came with a design for a screw. In a matter of days, Mathys returned to Müller with a prototype. They continued to collaborate, with Müller visiting every ten days or so. Just how

---

[4] 'Engine Rob' translated into English.
[5] Interview with Robert Mathys, Jr., conducted on 3 February, 2017, in Bettlach.

Exhibit 9.1 Robert Mathys, Sr., in his workshop. *Copyright by AO Foundation, Switzerland*

detailed instructions for Mathys were can be gleaned from Schatzker's biography about Müller[6]:

In the spring of 1958, I designed the 4.5 cortex screw with a special thread. This screw was undoubtedly an important breakthrough in the design of a bone screw. The head of the screw was rounded and had a hexagonal recess to couple with the hex profile of the screwdriver tip. The thread of the screw was designed to withstand pull-out and provide optimal holding power and compression. This determined the ratio between the diameter of the shaft and the diameter of the thread, as well as the angle subtended between the thread and the shaft. The greater the surface area and the closer the angle was to 90 degrees between the thread and the shaft, the greater the holding power of the screw. It was a non-self-cutting screw and required a tap (thread cutter) to minimize the damage to bone by the dullness of the threads of a self-tapping screw. It also made the process much more accurate.

Mathys was a genius. He seemed to understand intuitively what I needed and what would work. We began to develop an unbeatable team. He was an expert at making screws. Since Mathys was an expert with screws, I started with the design of a cortical screw as the first implant, before we moved into other things.[7]

The screws, designed by Müller and manufactured by Mathys, represented a substantial improvement over designs used by Lambotte or Danis. Since the cortex screw required pre-tapping of a matching threaded hole, such a tap was prototyped by Mathys as well (Exhibits 9.2 and 9.3).

---

[6]Schatzker (2018), pp. 71–72.
[7]Schatzker (2018), p. 76.

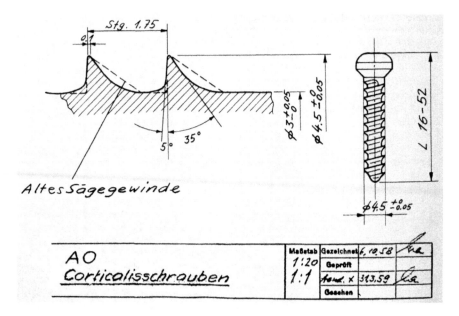

Exhibit 9.2   First AO screw designs. *Source: Mathys, reproduced with the permission of Hogrefe Verlag, Berne*

To provide Mathys with some surgical experience, Müller arranged for him to visit in October 1958 when he was operating as a guest surgeon in Grenchen, a nearby regional hospital whose head surgeon was August Guggenbühl, one of the AO G13. This proved to be a decisive experience for Mathys and resulted in immediate improvements to the screws and instruments. In just a few weeks, Mathys developed some 16 improvements, which were then offered to the AO for consideration. Throughout this design process, Müller demonstrated a penchant for ergonomics in the design of the surgical instruments, and this at a time when the concept of ergonomics itself was not commonly known (Exhibits 9.4 and 9.5).[8]

It was only seven months between their first meeting on 8 April and the AO kick-off meeting on 6 November. In that time Müller had assembled, in close collaboration with Mathys, the basic elements of the *Instrumentarium*. This was presented, discussed, and approved for further testing by the 13 founding surgeons present. Their speed of development was extraordinary given the circumstances of the era—there was only the telephone and regular mail, no Internet, no Google, no electronic files, no transfers, and no computer CADCAM.

---

[8]Interview Robert Mathys, Jr., Op. cit.

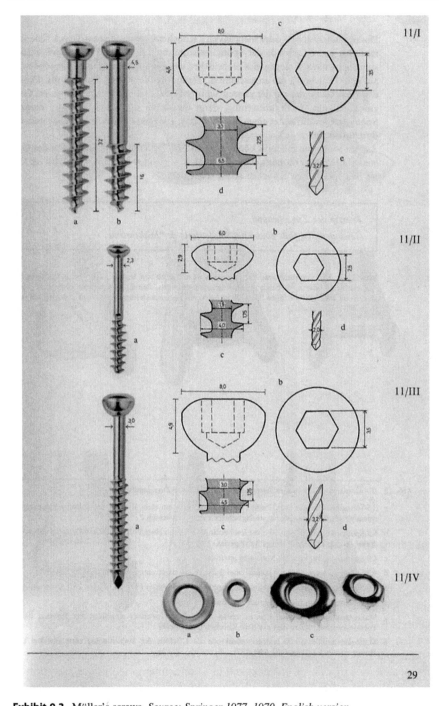

Exhibit 9.3 Müller's screws. *Source: Springer 1977, 1970, English version*

Exhibit 9.4 Robert Mathys, Sr., at drafting table

Exhibit 9.5 Robert Mathys, Sr., with Maurice Müller. *Copyright by AO Foundation, Switzerland*

Agreeing on a Suitable Finance Model

Although Mathys had the right technical skills, there remained the issue about how he would be paid. It is important to remember that Müller and his AO friends did not possess a stock of financial capital. Each AO member paid his own expenses and the AO organization had no separate financial resources beyond the CHF 500 each new member paid for admittance. With only 13 members, the organization's cash resources at that time were less than CHF 10,000. Somehow, Müller needed to convince Mathys to wait for his payment until sometime in the future, but for how long? The AO members had, after all, agreed to test all of the *Instrumentarium* for several years before putting it on sale.

Mathys had to promise that he would not directly sell any elements of the *Instrumentarium* (surgical tools, screws, plates) to the outside until it was permitted by the AO. Everything was to remain Müller's property and such a release would only come after all of the *Instrumentarium* had been tested. Equally, AO members had to promise not to pass any elements on to third parties.

In previous business arrangements, Müller often had problems with suppliers who wanted to put his designs on the market right away. Müller promised Mathys that he would be reaching "sales by the millions" within four years.[9] Of course, this was easier said than done since Mathys ran a small company and did not have extensive financial resources. Nevertheless, Mathys accepted these conditions and the two of them agreed on the deal with a simple handshake: no contracts, no lawyers, no patent attorneys, no purchase orders, no confidentiality agreements, and no non-disclosure forms. This would be unimaginable in today's business world, but at the time it was rather typical for business conducted in Switzerland.

The issue of payments still had to be settled. At first, Müller thought that he and Mathys could set up a company and go to a bank for a loan. But it quickly became clear to him that such an arrangement would not only put him in conflict with his AO colleagues, but also with the entire medical community. He felt that he could not design plates and screws, then recommend their use to surgical colleagues and patients, and finally ask them to pay him.

To circumvent this ethical problem, he had Mathys send all instruments and implants, as well as his invoices covering only direct manufacturing costs, to his younger sister Violette Moraz-Müller, who was residing in Biel. She had been recently widowed and agreed to adapt her small house to the needs of the growing AO organization. She would become the center of logistics and invoicing, staying in that role for about five years.[10]

The growing need for logistics presented a challenge. Mathys, who was fully absorbed in designing prototypes for the AO, would at times come daily in the early evening, delivering new models. The original 13 hospitals soon expanded to 20; they would call in orders and Mrs. Moraz's daughter would bring the packages to the post office the same evening for next day delivery—mail order sales of implants with pretty prompt service for a business at that time.

Any orders from doctors would go through Moraz-Müller, as would any payments from hospitals or surgeons. Violette Moraz-Müller would retain 15% for administrative costs and transfer the rest to Mathys. The problem with this system was that payments to Mathys were only made once the transfers had been received, and that could take up to three months. When Mathys, who spent considerable time on this project at the expense of his core business, developed financial difficulties,

---

[9]Schlich (2002), p. 49.

[10]Violette Moraz-Müller became an active member of the AO organization, participating in research meetings and AO training courses. After she stepped away from the AO, her functions were transferred to Waldenburg where several employees from Straumann Company took over her responsibilities. Later on, she became also involved when her brother, Maurice Müller established Protek to market his hip implant designs.

Müller provided a letter of comfort to the local bank who would then give a loan directly to Mathys. These arrangements were made to finance the development of the AO *Instrumentarium*, essentially moving the financing burden to Mathys as the producer, always with the promise that he would eventually be having a business 'selling millions in about four years time,' the time Müller thought it would take to fully test the AO *Instrumentarium*. Try doing business like this with a bank today!

From Individual Tools to Standardized Toolsets

Müller and AO members had to resolve another issue about the future use of the *Instrumentarium*. It was the intent of Müller and his AO colleagues that only surgeons familiar with the AO principles were allowed to order the *Instrumentarium*. That meant that from the outset, volume was expected to be small and unless more surgeons became familiar with the AO procedures sales would grow slowly.

The first version of the *Instrumentarium* was ready for demonstration to the AO surgeons at their kick-off meeting in November 1958. Over the following months, Mathys and Müller designed more elements, ranging from screws, plates, and a version of the *Intramedullary* nail with a design superior to the widely used Küntscher nail. Also developed were the necessary surgical tools.[11] A tension device to be applied to bone fragments before plates and screws were used was readied for the March 1959 AO meeting.

The AO *Instrumentarium* was intended as a modular and standardized system. No longer would operating nurses, asked by surgeons for a screw driver, bring two sets for the surgeon to try them on in search of the one which would best fit the available screws. All sets were identical, and so were the tools, resulting in interchangeability and similarity in surgical techniques across hospitals. Tools, plates, screws, and other elements came sterilized, and packed in color-coded aluminum cases, six in total, that must have reminded observers of the toolboxes used in car repair shops. It was said that the idea of using boxed sets stemmed from Mathys who, when observing early operations, looked to remedy the "tool chaos" in the operating room.[12] In a final push, Mathys manufactured some 20 sets of six aluminum boxes each, for use in the first AO course planned for Davos in December 1960, previously tested by the AO surgeons in real surgery (Exhibit 9.6a–c).

A letter, preserved from the early 1960s by Müller to Mathys, serves as example of the detailed collaboration between the AO and Mathys. Some three pages long, the letter listed feedback from AO surgeons with their suggestions for improving the toolsets. It covered such specifics as the subdivision of the toolboxes, as well as comments on every type of screw, screwdrivers, and other tools. In particular, the drills had been subject to some criticism. Not even the smallest details were overlooked. The complete surgical experience, driven by a sense for ergonomics,

---

[11]Heim (2001), pp. 106–111.
[12]Schlich (2002), p. 51.

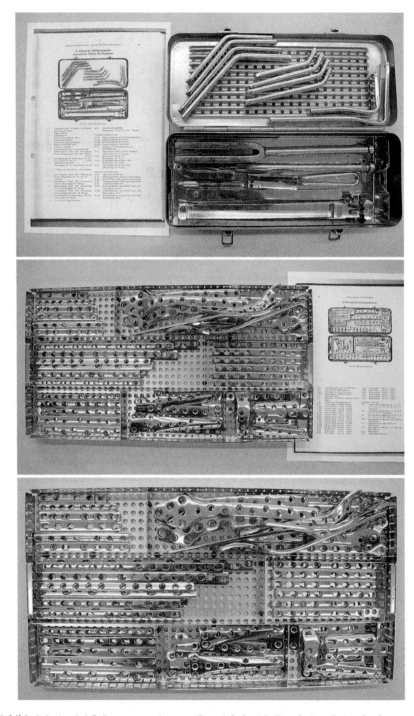

Exhibit 9.6 (a–c) AO *Instrumentarium* set. *Copyright by AO Foundation, Switzerland*

Exhibit 9.7 Maurice Müller
presenting AO
*Instrumentarium. Copyright
by AO Foundation,
Switzerland*

was communicated and, in the end, executed with great precision by Mathys and his workshop crew.[13]

Until late in 1960s, Müller's collaboration with Mathys remained based on the business model described above. At that time, just before the first AO course, held in Davos, a new company, Synthes AG in Chur, was founded. From that time on, Mathys paid license fees to Synthes, owned by AO founders, who used the proceeds to fund AO-related research.

Managing Successfully in "Crossing the Chasm"

The creation of a standardized set of instruments and implants to be created for all AO surgeons was a major difference to the approaches that had been taken by Danis and Lambotte, the forerunners of the AO approach to Osteosynthesis. Those two Belgian pioneers created tools for themselves, either in their own workshops, or in conjunction with an outside supplier. The sharing of tools and implants was not facilitated, and both Danis and Lambotte worked as sole pioneers, unable to create a

---

[13]Schneider (1983), p. 27, citing letter dated 22 February, 1960 from Maurice Müller to Robert Mathys, Sr.

larger following. The AO surgeons, under the leadership of Müller, managed to reach a much larger group, leading to wider dissemination and standardization. Using a phrase coined much later to describe sales of innovations and their successful implantation in the market, the AO surgeons managed successfully in "crossing the chasm" leading to a faster adoption among other surgeons (Exhibit 9.7).[14]

By moving early from designs for specialist-only ones, and satisfying averaged skilled surgeons, the AO allowed non-specialists to participate in this new form of surgery. The AO prepared to reach the larger market of mainstream surgeons by not aiming solely at the innovators and early adopters. When Müller had the *Instrumentarium* tested by the larger G13 group, he was soliciting a wider market test response.

References

Heim, U. F. A. (2001). *Das Phänomen AO*. Mannheim: Huber.
Moore, G. A. (1991). *Crossing the chasm, marketing and selling high-tech products to mainstream customers*. New York: Harper-Collins.
Schatzker, J. (2018). *Maurice E. Müller: In his own words*. Davos: AO Foundation.
Schlich, T. (2002). *Surgery, science and industry*. Basingstoke: Palgrave Macmillan.
Schneider, R. (1983). *25 Jahre AO–Schweiz*. Berne: Arbeitsgemeinschaft für Osteosynthesefragen.

---

[14]Moore (1991).

Pillar Two: Teaching Osteosynthesis 10

Maurice Müller on the start of the first AO course in Davos, 1960[1]:

> I think the first AO course in Davos was the real beginning of the AO.

Teaching at the Core of the AO

The decision to make teaching one of the four pillars of the AO was no accident. The founders chose not to make training or courses, per se, one of the pillars. They wanted to signal that their organization was intent on emphasizing the teaching of Osteosynthesis principles. They also felt that the term 'teaching' conveys a certain way to be actively involved and go beyond simply conveying information or theories. As already seen, much of the first two years were spent designing the *Instrumentarium* (Müller sometimes also referred to it as *Armamentarium*) in an intensive collaboration between Müller, Mathys, and his AO colleagues, who provided valuable feedback on improvements for each element. Many of the elements were also tested in real surgery. But once the AO surgeons agreed on complete surgical sets, they were ready to take it into the classroom.

There is history behind this need to teach the practice of Osteosynthesis. Lambotte, one of the early pioneers of Osteosynthesis, insisted that he could never fully capture in writing all of the steps necessary for a successful surgical procedure. Lambotte likened surgical training to apprenticeship demonstrations, and to practical training, in something akin to an operating room environment, on human cadaver bones. The model would become one of watching the Masters perform—being close to a person who could pass the skills on to younger surgeons. Watching and

---

[1]Schatzker (2018), p. 99.

© Springer Nature Switzerland AG 2019
J.-P. Jeannet, *Leading a Surgical Revolution*,
https://doi.org/10.1007/978-3-030-01980-8_10

practicing would be far better than reading about it. Schlich referred to it as "tacit knowledge."[2]

As AO surgical sets were all standardized, Müller strongly believed the method of instruction, or teaching, needed to become standardized as well. Again, he had had exposure to some ideas from his visit to Böhler in Vienna, where he appreciated the regulated form of instruction. Böhler, however, did this only at his own hospital, and the AO founders had their sights set on surgeons operating at numerous hospitals, even beyond Switzerland. This required that they find a method with standardized tools and in a standardized format, for surgeons to use so that they could replicate results and compare among different cases.

Commentary from AO founders gives us insights into how they thought and where they knew the pitfalls were in Osteosynthesis. In their first published text-book, as well as in later editions, they consistently warned fellow surgeons against over-confidence:

> We cannot advise too strongly against internal fixation when it is carried out by an inadequately trained surgeon and in the absence of full equipment and sterile operating room conditions. Using our methods, enthusiasts who lack self-criticism are much more dangerous than skeptics or outright opponents.[3]

What the AO founders conveyed here was their deeply felt conviction that access to the *Instrumentarium* alone would not be sufficient. Without adequate training and instructions, surgical success could not be guaranteed. This belief led them to prevent an open sale of their *Instrumentarium*, and to make sure that it would only get into the hands of trained surgeons who fully understood the AO techniques.

In the years leading up to the beginning of the AO, Müller had experienced different types of teaching environments. When he first joined Balgrist, he had tried to share the experience with Osteosynthesis that he'd gained with surgeons from the Zurich area, at the Fribourg hospital. By his own account, simply showing slides with charts, X-rays, and giving a lecture didn't convince anybody, certainly not those who, by disposition, were opposed to Osteosynthesis.

Towards the end of his Balgrist years, and as he was transitioning to private practice at Hirslanden, Müller held the two workshops for his circle of friends. In both Balgrist and Chur, surgeons practiced principles on human cadaver bones. Additionally, when attending a course on hand surgery in Paris in early 1960, Müller again experienced the power of learning when practicing surgery on human cadaver hands. What was new in Paris was the simultaneous transmission via television monitors, an idea that Müller was later to integrate into the AO's courses designed for Davos.

---

[2]Schlich (2002), p. 65.
[3]Translated by Schlich (2002), p. 66 from Müller et al. (1963).

Techne Versus Episteme

The importance of practical skill versus book knowledge, or theory, was recently described by another author when commenting on the professional training prevalent in Switzerland. Nassim Taleb, best known for his book *The Black Swan*,[4] referred to this idea using the Greek terms *Techne* versus *Episteme*, or know-how versus know-what.[5] At the time, the notion that the skill of a surgeon and the use of the *Instrumentarium* needed to be taught through hands-on exercises was a novelty. It was to become ever more apparent as the AO developed into an organization where surgical skills were highly prized, and perhaps considered even more important than the AO *Instrumentarium*.

Preparing for the First AO Course in Davos, 1960

Towards the end of 1960, the AO surgeons decided to launch a new instructional course, with the intention of broadening the base by inviting both the AO membership, as well as their residents and surgical assistants. If every member were to invite two assistants, there would be a group of about 25, plus the AO members. By the time the responses poured in, there were more than 60 applications. Most of these came from regional hospitals in Switzerland, thus attracting general surgeons. A few non-Swiss participants applied, most notably Dr. Howard Rosen from New York, Professor Krauss and Dr. Weller from Freiburg, and Dr. O. Russe from Vienna, all individuals who were later to play important roles in the development of the AO in their countries. In addition to the AO members, the assembled group exceeded 92 persons.[6]

Preparation for the course content had started earlier that year and had been piloted at the AO meeting in Interlaken. In a letter sent by Müller, on behalf of AO leadership, he reminded members that it was important to join the meeting with documentation of their own cases.[7] The Interlaken meeting was also intended to prepare AO speakers for the Congress of the Swiss Surgical Association in Geneva (May 1960) and their extraordinary meeting in Berne in November of that year. That material became the foundation of the course in Davos. However, that was just the 'theory,' the practical exercises still needed to be shaped.

The venue selection for the first course was AO's recently acquired laboratory building in Davos. Space was at a premium. In later years, the courses made use of a cinema for presentations and speeches, as well as empty rooms in nearby hotels for the practical exercises.

---

[4]Taleb (2007).

[5]Taleb (2012), p. 90.

[6]Heim (2001), p. 117.

[7]Schneider (1983), p. 26. The letter by Maurice Müller is very detailed in terms of instructions to the AO membership and illustrates that members were to be active and well-prepared for the meetings.

Exhibit 10.1   AO course faculty Davos 1960. *Copyright by AO Foundation, Switzerland*

Müller acted as the main course designer for this four-day seminar. The principal design idea, which turned into the guiding philosophy of all the AO courses to come was that a small group of participating surgeons gather around a table and, under the guidance of a more experienced AO surgeon—a table instructor—practice the application of plates and screws on human cadaver bones. Participants used real instruments for this exercise. The course took them through the AO techniques, step by step, starting with the concept of a trauma surgery (Exhibit 10.1). Müller would later explain:

> The participants had to be reminded that since only living bone can heal, exposing the fracture must be atraumatic to preserve the viability of bone. Next, one must restore form in order to restore function. This means anatomic reduction of the fracture. Once form is restored, it must be preserved. This means internal fixation. To ensure healing and freedom from pain the fixation must be absolutely stable. Then, early mobilization of the extremity is undertaken so that a full range of motion can be regained. By following these fundamental steps, post-traumatic complications can be avoided.[8]

Müller shared the speaker duties with his core AO founders. He reserved for himself the lecture on principles of Osteosynthesis, and how to avoid complications such as "plaster disease." Allgöwer addressed lag screw fixation. Willenegger spoke on articular fractures, such as ankles. And finally, Schneider presented issues around intramedullary nailing of the tibia. These lectures had been initially prepared for the

---

[8]Schatzker (2018), p. 99.

Exhibit 10.2 Maurice Müller instructing in Davos course. *Copyright by AO Foundation, Switzerland*

Swiss Surgical Society meeting held earlier in the year. Each of the lecturers was followed by practical exercises on human cadaver bones for which all AO members were present to serve in the role of table instructors. Müller took active part in the practical instructions. At the age of 42, most participating surgeons were considerably older than he, a fact that most certainly did not make it easy in terms of the course dynamics (Exhibit 10.2).

From the beginning of the Davos course, a special feature was the early afternoon break the entire seminar group would take—they'd all put on their skis and join the tourists on the slopes of Davos. The AO members Müller and Allgöwer, in particular, were avid skiers. This tradition was preserved for many years until they had to yield to the demands of compliance officers and regulators, who would no longer approve seminars for anything other than those that contained scientific content, exclusively.

In a 2018 interview, Peter Matter, who had attended the first AO course in 1960, recalled[9]:

> I was not attending as a regular course participant. Due to my position as a young resident at the Chur hospital headed by Allgöwer, I was put in charge of course logistics. One of my duties was to keep up the supply of beer and frankfurters. The course took place at the

---

[9]Interview with Peter Matter, former Chief Surgeon Davos Hospital, (1971–1997), former Head of Swiss AO 1982–1992, and President of AO Foundation (2000–2002), conducted on 21 February, 2018, in Davos.

Research Institute just a short walk from the Hotel Schweizerhof where all participants and faculty stayed. Already then, there was a number of international participants: eight from Germany, three from the US, two from Austria, and one from France. After the morning session, everyone went skiing and lunch was on the slopes. Work recommenced at around 16:00 hours and often went on until 19:00 or 20:00 hours.

What was striking was the openness of discussing real cases from the past. Presented for discussion were mostly failures, often from among the surgeons present in the course. All course participants would contribute comments. It was not unusual for someone who owned up publicly to mistakes and identify himself or herself as the surgeon who committed the failed surgery. This openness was to become part of the AO culture.

The first seminar in Davos was by all accounts a complete success. The AO had managed to be inspired by a number of earlier bone trauma pioneers, such as Böhler and Danis, to take from their teaching experience the most suitable points for its purpose, and to create a unique experience different from anything attending surgeons had ever experienced. The multiple requests to purchase the *Instrumentarium* sets on the spot were declined because the AO founders did not want to confuse teaching principles with selling instruments.

When organizing their first course, the founders thought that they might run one additional course; after all of this teaching, trained surgeons would all be able to go on and teach others by themselves. A follow-up course for the attendees of the first course was held, as promised, shortly before the second Davos course, at a Zurich hospital. The AO founders harbored the idea that they would be able to offer more of these courses, but little did they know that this would turn out completely different. For the next course in 1961, 102 participants registered. This created quite a stir and the AO organizers began to doubt whether their unique model, with its hands-on practice could survive. Offering follow-up courses for an ever-growing number of past participants was an idea that had to be discarded. Instead, past participants frequently came back to attend another course to keep up with latest developments.

When the AO founders became absorbed with drafting their first major textbook on Osteosynthesis in 1962, they decided not to hold a course that year.[10] Instead, they offered two courses in 1963, after which time they intended to stop. In their minds, publishing their textbook, and making more openly available their *Instrumentarium*, the need for institutionalized instructions would become obsolete. Little did they know! Continued demand for the poplar courses, and additional support from the *Instrumentarium* producers, lifted the courses to a new level, eventually developing into an ever-growing activity. How this growth occurred, and how the AO managed it, will be discussed later in the book.

Since all of the AO members were practicing surgeons, they were well aware how much successful surgical procedures depended on skillful assistance by operating room personnel. For the second AO course in Davos, the AO developed a parallel program just for operating room (OR) nurses. Müller's sister, Violette Moraz, who, as the logistics hub of the group, had accumulated considerable knowledge about the

---

[10]Müller et al. (1963).

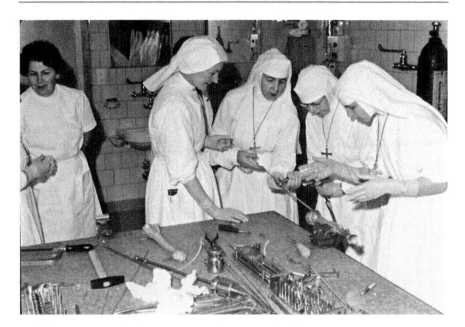

Exhibit 10.3   AO course for OR nurses and assistants. *Copyright by AO Foundation, Switzerland*

AO tools and implants, played an active part in those courses. Just like all of the other AO courses, this one was continued for some time (Exhibit 10.3).

Inviting VIPs to Davos

As the Davos courses became more established, the AO started to invite leading Orthopedic and trauma surgeons from outside of Switzerland, opening up a dialogue and contributing to the spread of the AO methodology. Among these VIP visitors, and sometimes even as course participants, were Professor Krauss from the University of Freiburg (Germany), who was the first university professor to openly and actively support the AO principles, as well as the UK's John Charnley and Lorenz Böhler from Vienna.

Reflecting on the Davos courses that were, at first, meant to be temporary activities until the AO practices became better established, one can only conclude: What was meant to be temporary turned into a venerable institution.

References

Heim, U. F. A. (2001). *Das Phänomen AO* (p. 117). Mannheim: Huber.
Müller, M., Allgöwer, M., & Willenegger, H. (1963). *Technik der Operativen Frakturbehandlung.* Berlin: Springer.
Schatzker, J. (2018). *Maurice E. Müller: In his own words* (p. 99). Davos: AO Foundation.

Schlich, T. (2002). *Surgery, science and industry*. Basingstoke: Palgrave Macmillan.

Schneider, R. (1983). *25 Jahre AO–Schweiz* (p. 26). Berne: Arbeitsgemeinschaft für Osteosynthesefragen.

Taleb, N. N. (2007). *The black swan*. New York: Random House.

Taleb, N. N. (2012). *Antifragile (How to live in a world we don't understand)* (p. 90). London: Allen Lane/Penguin Books.

Pillar Three: Maintaining Complete Documentation

11

From the outset, AO members were committed to documenting all of their cases and, thus, enshrined this commitment in the AO by-laws. Members were required to make a copy of each case available to other members. The by-laws further stated that members must document their own Osteosynthesis, according to common guidelines; record the cases in such a way that they could be analyzed statistically; grant all other members access to their documentation, while at the same time be granted access to all of their fellow AO colleagues' documentation. At that time, when surgeons were eager to talk about their successes while also keeping a lid on their failures, this represented a far-reaching commitment among members.

The Early Models of Documentation

Müller realized early on the importance of a full and detailed documentation. During his initial visits to the clinics of van Nes (Netherlands) and Danis (Belgium), he experienced the absence or incompleteness of reports first hand. He found that van Nes maintained no documentation at all. Danis, who could record only those patients who volunteered to return sometime after the operation for a control, documented his cases using X-rays. Lambotte, who had retired before Müller's time, created drawings and X-rays focusing on the type of fracture and operating procedures, but was lacking full histories for comparison purposes.

Upon Müller's appointment as resident of the hospital in Fribourg (from 1951 to 1952), he carefully documented his experience with his 75 Osteosynthesis procedures that were carried out during his stay. He quickly learned that the availability of this documentation became an important aspect in recruiting like-minded surgeons from the regional hospitals in Switzerland.

When Müller visited Böhler's hospital in Vienna, in 1956, he came away with a sense that Böhler's careful documentation of each and every case was an important contributor to his success. The full documentation of these cases, including results

© Springer Nature Switzerland AG 2019
J.-P. Jeannet, *Leading a Surgical Revolution*,
https://doi.org/10.1007/978-3-030-01980-8_11

after treatment, were due to the fact that Böhler's patients were all insured and could be made to return for follow-up checks. Böhler maintained his documentation by diagnosis types, which also contained accident type next to the treatment, and included drawings of any fracture. In Vienna, Müller saw the first use of punch cards (originally introduced in the US at the end of the nineteenth century), which could be sorted mechanically.[1]

Müller's documentation approach was triggered by the need to archive his habilitation at Zurich University, submitted in 1957. Using a Leica camera, he took photographs of his X-rays. This eventually led to the idea of using small-frame photos of X-rays and sticking them on the back of the reporting cards, thus making it possible to do away with the unwieldy X-rays themselves. This was, of course, very much in the middle of the analogue age; the digital age, as it's known today, was still some 50 years in the future.

Creating a Standardized Documentation System

When the AO founders committed to share their documentation with one another, they realized that only a standardized format, or reporting, would be useful. Whatever documentation was assembled by Lambotte, Danis, or Böhler, it applied only to a single clinic. But AO, with its 13 founding members, representing 13 hospitals, with more being added over time, faced a multi-point reporting system with the idea of creating a single hub. Unless order was established, this initiative carried the risk of quickly descending into chaos.

As with fracture diagnostics, X-ray images were seen as the most objective means of therapy control. In this respect, the AO used Böhler as their example. Over the years, the Viennese surgeon compiled series of X-rays tracking patients' progress. In 1938, he published a study containing three X-rays for each of 78 femoral neck nailings performed in his clinic. In 1943, Böhler's collection was comprised of some 4000 cases, and included about 20,000 individual pictures (conventional photographs were also part of this collection). By 1954, he had the meticulously recorded case histories of all 78,349 in-patients and 507,772 out-patients, as well as the X-rays of 241,000 injuries treated in his Vienna hospital since 1925.

Like Böhler, the AO used standardized forms for its documentation project. In 1959, Müller introduced colored code sheets for documenting operations and the check-ups, conducted after four and twelve months. He also designed punch cards to which miniature copies of the X-rays could be attached. After discharging an Osteosynthesis patient, surgeons were expected to first send the yellow code sheets to the Davos Documentation Center (Exhibit 11.1).[2]

---

[1]Heim (2001), p. 112.
[2]Schlich (2002), p. 125.

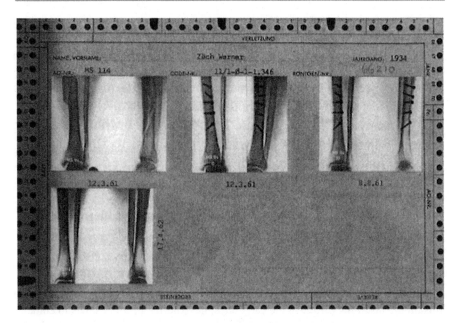

Exhibit 11.1 Punch card. *Copyright by AO Foundation, Switzerland*

Traditionally, each surgeon had to fill in three forms on each patient. The A-Form collected information on the type of fracture, or injury, as well as the type of surgery adopted, and the type of implant used; an indication of the post-operative results was also requested. The B-Form, a control after four months was recorded, and X-rays attached. The C-Form, filled in after a control that was to take place one year after the initial injury, requested details about the anatomical results, the function of the injured limb or extremity, and information about an 'economic result,' or how long it took to reinsert the patient back into regular or work life. The questions covered included:

- Total lengths of all hospitalizations (in days)
- Time lapse until first part-time work
- Time lapse until full employment
- Type of work compared to earlier employment
- Amount of earnings compared to earlier income
- Ability to undertake sporting activities
- Ability to serve in the military

All of these answers were also supported by X rays taken one year after the operation.

The question about returning to work was always important to Müller, who had included this question in his very first documentation when he began surgery using Osteosynthesis in 1951. This was an initial attempt to come to grips with the issues of health economics, a notion which was to become more important much later.

At each turn, these forms went to the Documentation Center in Davos. The information was then used to make two new punch cards, one of which remained in Davos while the other was sent back to the respective surgeon. The AO surgeons also needed to send along a set of pre- and post-operative X-ray pictures. These were copied and miniaturized, pasted onto the punch cards, and returned to the operating surgeon for safe-keeping.

The year after the Documentation Center was opened, 1000 cases were registered, and 10,000 X-ray copies were made available for analysis. The workload quickly overwhelmed the staff, and delays in reporting occurred. In the AO tradition of paying their own expenses, each case had a recording fee to be paid for by the surgeon.

Müller himself admitted that it was hard to convince his colleagues to undertake this time-consuming effort. In the early days, he exhorted his colleagues to come to the meetings with full documentations.[3] Early on, when AO surgeons ran into heavy opposition, it proved invaluable to have this material ready and for presentation. Realizing how valuable this was to their cause, AO members changed their minds about the documentation effort. In hindsight, Müller thought that they were clearly at the forefront of evidence-based medicine.[4]

Based on their documentation, the AO team consisting of Müller, Allgöwer, and Willenegger were able to make an important presentation to the German Association of Surgeons in 1963, presenting several hundred completely documented cases, adding to the AO's standing in that country.

Although AO surgeons were praised for their documentation efforts, it turned out that much of the credibility built by the AO was caused by their superior clinical outcomes. The documentation was actually running behind the clinical results, but nevertheless contributed to the reputation of the AO as a serious endeavor. Müller remained the one responsible for the Foundations' Documentation Center, eventually moving it with him to Berne when he took up the position there. He invested a considerable amount of energy and resources in a computerized version of the databank. The term 'Big Data' had not yet been created but was, implicitly, the ideal that Müller and his colleagues pursued so they might extract insights into the best treatment algorithms for their patients.

---

[3]Schneider (1983), p. 26, letter by Maurice Müller to his AO colleagues on the need to document their cases.

[4]Schatzker (2018), p. 79.

The challenge of the AO documentation had to do with the complexity of coding all the relevant facts, and the often not completely returned information. Critics also pointed out that, although a wealth of information was collected, the nature of the different fractures treated by different surgeons, representing a wide variety of fractures, would not allow for any kind of statistically relevant studies on the basis of randomness. That proved to be the major weakness of the project.

By 1983, 25 years after the creation of the Documentation Center, a total of 130,000 fractures had been documented. Of those, some 80,000 were completed with code sheets and X-rays. During the same time period, 550,000 X-rays were copied photographically. The data set had helped in the answering many complex clinical questions and was the basis for many publications and dissertations.[5]

This wealth of information was eventually used by Müller, and several teams from Berne University, to go through the documentation which by 1986 had grown to more than one million X-rays, covering more than 150,000 operatively treated fractures and was eventually used to draw up a classification.[6] This classification was important because now surgeons anywhere could communicate across the cases and have a basis to compare treatment results.

Since Müller stepped down from the leadership of the AO organization, the strategy surrounding documentation has been changed. What the changes were, and why it was changed, will be discussed with regard to research in more recent years.

AO on the Forefront of Creating a Learning Organization

With limited resources, and possibly acting ahead of its time, the AO was on the way to pool all its participating surgeon's experience in a single, combined learning curve. Prior to that, Lambotte, Danis, and Böhler were assembling data for only one single clinic. If the AO were able to manage pooling the data of all of its members, and place that data on a single learning curve, the members could, if done properly, move through that learning curve much faster than if each member just kept the data to themselves. Naturally, the data had to be standardized, and Müller pursued that, at time driving his colleagues up a wall (Exhibit 11.2).

---

[5]Schlich(2002), p. 130.

[6]Müller et al. (1990), Preface, p. V. The original classification appeared in French under the title "AO-Classifications des Fractures."

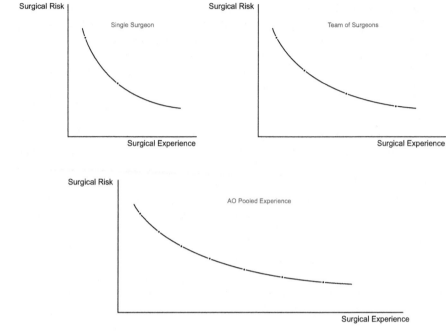

Exhibit 11.2   Institutional Learning at AO. *Source: Drawing by Jean-Pierre Jeannet*

References

Heim, U. F. A. (2001). *Das Phänomen AO* (p. 112). Mannheim: Huber.
Müller, M. E., Nazarian, S., Koch, P., & Schatzker, J. (1990). *Classifications of fractures*. Berlin: Springer.
Schatzker, J. (2018). *Maurice E. Müller: In his own words* (p. 79). Davos: AO Foundation.
Schlich, T. (2002). *Surgery, science and industry*. Basingstoke: Palgrave Macmillan.
Schneider, R. (1983). *25 Jahre AO–Schweiz* (p. 26). Berne: Arbeitsgemeinschaft für Osteosynthesefragen.

12

Research as Part of the AO Mission

In the AO by-laws, the founders listed the study of fracture care as one of its main purposes, specifically citing 'experimental research' as part of its goals. The determination of AO membership was demonstrated by actions taken prior to their constituting a kick-off meeting in Biel in November 1958. The previous instructional course in Chur had already triggered some important steps that preceded the formal adoption of those activities.

Finding a Research Location

Allgöwer, practicing in the hospital in Chur, had been active with his own research stream dealing with wound healing. Searching for a place to undertake experimental research, he came across an unused building in Davos, formerly used to house a now shuttered Swiss institute researching tuberculosis patients. Before World War II, several sanatoriums and health centers dedicated to tuberculosis patients existed in Davos that were later converted into hotels.

The building in question contained rooms suitable for laboratories and came equipped with a marble table previously used for dissecting human cadavers. Allgöwer was able to adapt the entire unit for his medical research, using animals. He created the Laboratory for Experimental Surgery, Research Institute Davos, and formed a foundation with an injection of CHF 10,000 as start-up capital, convincing his two AO friends, Müller and Willenegger, to contribute similar amounts. Further contributions from industry and local government allowed for the venture to commence on 18 June, 1959, just seven months after the AO was started. Financial support for the laboratory was not put on a steady footing for a couple of years when the financial structure of the AO was changed. With this singular initiative,

© Springer Nature Switzerland AG 2019
J.-P. Jeannet, *Leading a Surgical Revolution*,
https://doi.org/10.1007/978-3-030-01980-8_12

Exhibit 12.1 First location of AO research center in Davos. *Copyright by AO Foundation, Switzerland*

supported by AO colleagues, the AO Organization was physically implanted in Davos, and had a location it could call home (Exhibit 12.1).[1]

Aside from housing the research laboratory, the AO Documentation Center was moved into the same building. The Center grew from the initial five employees to a staff of 25 by 1967. Allgöwer led the Center as director, spending two days a week there to direct research of wound healing, shock, and burn injuries. The research program related to Osteosynthesis commenced in 1962.

When Reliance on Clinical Results Would Not Suffice

The growth of the AO Documentation Center in Davos contributed to the creation and publication of clinical research. AO members were eager to show the world that their particular approach to Osteosynthesis was successful and led to superior results over the conservative, plaster cast, method practice advocated by Böhler. Despite the accumulation of a wealth of clinical data, many non-AO surgeons still had substantial doubts about whether or not the AO approach really worked, and how the claimed results were achieved. This was the period of time when the AO was clearly

---

[1]Heim (2001), p. 36.

eminence-driven; for example, the argument was, 'We, or Müller, can prove it, just look at our clinical results.' The problem was that this type of argument only went so far.

From the start, AO surgeons operated on the same assumptions as Danis—one of the Osteosynthesis pioneers—in believing in anatomical reduction after a trauma, then subjecting the fracture to a rigid fixation with compression Osteosynthesis, thus allowing for post-operative mobilization, as well as believing in primary bone healing.

These tenets, however, were not universally accepted. Danis had to admit that he had relied only on his clinical results as proof, had no funding to conduct experimental research, such as with animals, and owned only a workshop, not a true laboratory. However, he also pointed out that all of his experience with Osteosynthesis and compression was empirical only, and that an experimental investigation would eventually be required to prove the point.[2] Given that the underlying tenets of the AO philosophy were not generally accepted by the Swiss medical community, and at universities in particular, it was now necessary to use experimental research to demonstrate that these assumptions could be substantiated. AO members had accepted meeting this challenge from the outset.

Confronting Opposition at Surgical Conferences in Switzerland

The debate, both within the AO and the medical community as a whole, was centered around two major issues. First, there was no clear indication why compression should work, why it would not lead to bone resorption, and why it should be a major contributor to healing. Second, there was no confirmation regarding the issues surrounding primary bone healing. Unless these two central issues could be answered and confirmed definitively, the debates were likely to continue, and detractors could claim that the AO lacked sufficient scientific confirmation for its treatment regime. In a meeting of the Swiss Society of Surgeons in Geneva in the summer of 1960, AO founders were granted a total of 40 minutes speaking time. Four short talks were given on the principles of Osthesynthesis (Müller), on fixation of fractures to the lower leg (Allgöwer), on fracture dislocations of the ankle joint (Willenegger), and on medullary nailing (Schneider). There was no time allocated for a formal discussion. Because the four talks created such a stir, the Association decided to have a second meeting in November. At that second meeting, held in Berne, the same AO presentations were confronted with massive criticism from major university hospital centers, particularly those in Berne and Zurich. As AO *Obmann* Schneider pointed out, "nobody was prepared to believe that bone healing could take place without traditional callus formation."[3]

---

[2]Heim (2001), p. 119, quoting Danis (1949).
[3]Schneider (1983), p. 19.

The Argument Against and for Rigid Fixation[4]

When the AO was formed, the medical community generally held the view that any form of rigid fixation, with or without compression, would impede fracture healing. Traditionally, surgeons believed that a fracture resulted in dead bone cells (necrosis) at the ends of a fracture. These dead bone cells would, over time, be replaced by newly created living cells. If one were to apply a rigid fixation to the fracture, the natural approximation of the bone cells and the corresponding absorption process would be prevented. A gap resulting from this in the fractured bone could lead to a delay in the healing process, or worse, a non-union. Proposed by those surgeons were fixation plates without screws, held in place by muscles, and the use of the Küntscher nail, as discussed earlier. Some leading surgeons even argued that any form of compression would result in instability and non-union. Because most surgeons accepted this view, they rejected the use of bone plates and continued to adhere to nailing and conservative treatment.[5]

The AO retorted that these risks, or non-unions, came as a result of incomplete stabilization, and that even the smallest of movements around the fracture could lead to loss of bone tissue in the affected area.

Biomechanics to the Rescue[6]

Experimental research undertaken by the AO depended on the invention of new measurement techniques involving the collaboration between a surgeon (AO member Willenegger), an engineer (Fritz Straumann), and an anatomist (Robert Schenk). Later, researchers Stephan Perren (bio-mechanic) and Max Russenberger (engineer) joined the effort and improved the device to register even the smallest loss of pressure to bone fragments. As a result, the team was eventually able to report that no resorption caused by necrosis had occurred.[7] In addition, the AO researchers could demonstrate that so-called pressure necrosis was nothing other than the result of insufficient stability of fixation (Exhibit 12.2).

These results were then used by AO surgeon Müller to confront their most consistent opponents at the University of Zurich and challenge them to refute the AO experiments with their own research, and to stop opposing the AO ideas *ex cathedra*. This was a turning point for the AO as the positive effect of compression and stability could be supported. Complete vindication of the AO's point-of-view

---

[4]This section relies heavily on Schlich (2002), Chap. 5, offering an excellent description of the scientific arguments and the AO research program to overcome resistance in the medical community.

[5]The leading proponents of this view were Böhler and Watson-Jones.

[6]A detailed review article of this research effort can be found under Perren 2002, see reference.

[7]Hutzschenreuter et al. (1969), pp. 77–81.

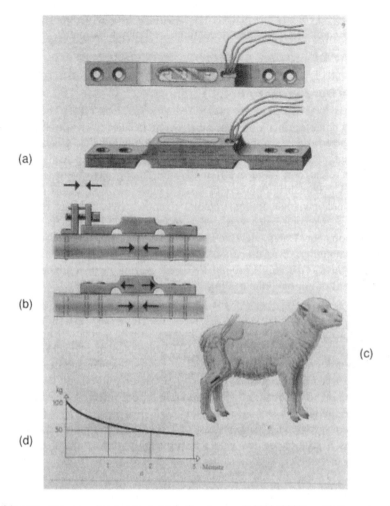

(a)

(b)

(c)

(d)

Exhibit 12.2 Perren tension measurement device. *Source: Schlich (2002), p. 92. Reproduced with permission*

came in 1971 when the conclusion of its research was integrated into leading text books on Orthopedics used on both sides of the Atlantic.[8]

With regard to its research program, it is interesting to note how the AO was able to involve scientists from other disciplines, but not necessarily from the medical field. Included in the effort were bio-engineers (Perren), matallurgists (Steinemann and Straumann), and anatomists (Schenk), who combined with AO surgeons (Willenegger) to build the compelling argument for other AO surgeons (Müller)

---

[8]Campbell and Canale (1971).

attending medical conferences. This cross-disciplinary collaboration was a hallmark of the AO research effort and was to continue well into the future.[9]

The Battle Over Primary Bone Healing

The phenomenon of 'primary bone healing' was to occupy AO researchers for some time. Until the emergence of the AO, the surgical community had given the creation of bone callus a central role in the process of fracture healing. Only a few lone surgeons, or researchers, argued differently and among them were Lambotte and Danis, the two Belgian forerunners of Osteosynthesis. It was Danis, in particular, who had maintained that optimal internal fixation would actually reduce callus formation, and its appearance was a sign of imperfect treatment methods, not a natural phenomenon. Danis' view stood in direct contrast to the majority view of the medical community. By the time AO surgeons first presented their full *Instrumentarium* to the public around 1963, the general view continued to be that callus was part of normal bone healing.

Max Geiser from Berne University's Clinic for Orthopedics, and a vocal opponent of the AO philosophy, conducted research to prove the AO view wrong. He based his research on rabbits; by artificially fracturing their bones, he examined the different stages of the bone healing process. He concluded, that bone healing always started with the formation of callus protecting the fracture site and dead bone ends gradually replaced by living bone tissue.[10] For Geiser, and others, the absence of callus was sign of an overzealous surgeon. It is only natural that this type of argumentation required a response from the AO.

AO surgeons, reviewing Geiser's research, were of the opinion that his use of cerclage[11] as a fixation device was not sufficiently stable, and that the callus observed on the rabbits was due to instability caused by the fixation device used. So far, only AO surgeons were skilled enough to achieve absolute stability through their own fixation devices.

Anatomist to the Rescue

AO member Willengger had previously taught at the University of Basel, reached out to Robert Schenk, an anatomist at the university, with the assignment to study the nature of bone healing using histology. This scientific tool, well known to anatomists and other life scientists, involves the use of microscopes to look at tissue and offer a

---

[9]Stephan Perren joined the AO Research Center in 1964 as director; he had previously worked for Allgöwer in Chur and was to play a major role until he stepped down in 1996.
[10]Geiser, M., 1961 and 1963, in Schlich (2002), citations on p. 315.
[11]Cerclage was a form of wiring wrapped around the injured bone.

glimpse of what happens in the callus area not revealed by regular X-rays. Up to this point, no one had been able to decipher actual healing inside the bone.

Schenk and Willenegger obtained access to test animals (dogs) through a regional pharmaceutical company. The animals, subjected to *Osteotomies*, were implanted with fixation devices and histology; recently developed tracing materials were then used to investigate the effect. Schenk aimed to show that bone healing did occur through bone vessels inside the Haversian system, eventually leading to bone formation along the fracture ends reconnecting them. Normal and healthy bones are in a constant restructuring process by *Osteoclasts* and *Osteoblasts* forever producing new *Osteons*. In addition, the research showed that necrosis was not caused by the implants, or by pressure, but instead by the fracture itself. During the entire healing process described, no additional callus was formed. This description of the primary bone healing process, using the more sophisticated histologic fact base, proved to be enough to turn the tide in the medical community to come around to the AO view. The AO could now claim that, while callus was not a negative per se, the condition of callus-free healing was, however, an indication that the Osteosynthesis fixation had been performed properly (Exhibit 12.3).

The cycle was not completed until 1969 when AO scientist Berton Rahn applied the same methods used on dogs again on rabbits. Using the latest AO dynamic compression plate (DCP) he could prove the AO position and that Geiser's erroneous findings on rabbits was due to poor fixation methods.

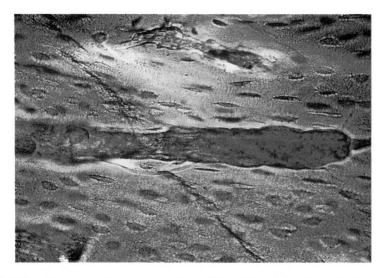

Exhibit 12.3 Histology and bone healing. *Copyright by AO Foundation, Switzerland*

References

Campbell, W. C., & Canale, S. T. (1971). *Campbell's operative orthopedics* (12th ed.). St. Louis: C. V. Mosby Co.

Heim, U. F. A. (2001). *Das Phänomen AO*. Mannheim: Huber.

Hutzschenreuter, P., Perren, S. M., Steinemann, S., Geret, V., & Klebl, M. (1969). Effects of rigidity of internal fixation on the healing pattern of osteotomies. *Injury, 1*, 77–81.

Schlich, T. (2002). *Surgery, science and industry*. Basingstoke: Palgrave Macmillan.

Schneider, R. (1983). *25 Jahre AO–Schweiz* (p. 19). Berne: Arbeitsgemeinschaft für Osteosynthesefragen.

Pitching the AO Philosophy to Hostile Audiences

13

Pitching the AO Philosophy

As indicated in the last chapter, there had been several instances where the AO leadership was challenged to lay out its philosophy to an audience of hostile Swiss surgeons. Initially, the arguments could be made only on the basis of the founding members' clinical experience; it took more time to assemble the supporting evidence to win their arguments.

First Disputation in Geneva (1960)

Founding the AO and developing its *Instrumentarium*, AO surgeons thought it time to take their project to a larger audience. Until then, AO membership had met largely among themselves, developing the guiding instructions, reacting to surgical experiences of members, and giving feedback about the use of the *Instrumentarium*. The opportunity for a first debate arose on the occasion of the Congress of the Swiss Surgical Society to be held in Geneva in May 1960.[1]

Apparently, there had been quite some buzz generated in the Swiss surgical community about the AO and its philosophy; as a result, a time slot of 40 minutes was created at the end of the agenda for the AO speakers to present their ideas. Having met previously to coordinate their messages, the AO members decided to divide the time into four slots of ten minutes each. Representing the AO were four core members: Müller, Allgöwer, Willenegger, and Schneider. The idea was to provide some informational content about the activities of the AO.

Müller took the first speaking slot, addressing the principles of Osteosynthesis and internal fixation. Allgöwer discussed lag screw fixation of fractures of the tibia,

---

[1]Schatzker (2018), p. 92.

© Springer Nature Switzerland AG 2019
J.-P. Jeannet, *Leading a Surgical Revolution*,
https://doi.org/10.1007/978-3-030-01980-8_13

citing 400 cases he had treated in his hospital in Chur. Willenegger spoke about 118 fracture ankle dislocations, which he treated with stable lag screw fixation and plating when necessary. And in closing, Schneider explained intramedullary nailing of fractures of the tibia, citing 246 documented cases. All four of these presentations were later published.

As mentioned, the presentations of the four AO surgeons created significant reaction. Because they had been added to the end of the agenda, there hadn't been any time allocated for discussion. Because this became a hot topic among the Swiss surgical community, the society decided to schedule a second, extraordinary, meeting in Berne later the same year and offer more time for debating this issue.

Second Disputation in Berne[2] (1960)

The Swiss Surgical Society held a second meeting in Berne on 24 November in a large auditorium at the University of Berne, with some 400 members present. During this day-long meeting, the morning was reserved for general issues of treatment of fractures and Osteosynthesis, while the afternoon was devoted exclusively to the treatment of fractures of the tiba.

In the morning meeting, Müller was allocated 30 minutes to make his case about internal fixation and Osteosynthesis. He discussed bone healing without visible callus and cited some animal experiments that were available at that time. Müller presented his clinical experience, as well as nailing long bones and the best nails suited for this procedure. He also addressed the risks and failures of Osteosynthesis experience by AO members.

The leadership of the Swiss Surgical Society arranged for three speakers from its own membership to follow Müller, to give their side of the story, as a rebuttal, and point out the dangers of using Osteosynthesis. The purpose of the meeting was clearly to discredit the AO and put a halt to its efforts. Three formal lectures were readied by the Surgical Society. Leading the charge was Hans-Ulrich Buff (1913–2004), chief surgeon at Solothurn who was about to become the director of one of the University of Zurich's surgical clinics. The second opponent was Karl Lenggenhager, head of general surgery at Berne's Insel Hospital, who was followed by Max Geiser,[3] an Orthopedic surgeon, also from Berne. All three, board members of the Society, led the frontal attack against the AO group.

Due to the meeting's importance, we have to rely on Müller's memory, in addition to some other sources. First, this is what Müller recalled, years after the meeting:

---

[2]The Berne meeting on 24 November, 1960 has been recounted in several publications. Schatzker (2018), p. 97, but also Heim (2001), p. 70; Schneider (1983), p. 18 and pp. 37–38.

[3]Max Geiser (b. 1926) had been the chief resident of Professor Dubois, becoming a senior surgeon of the Orthopedic Department at the University of Berne.

In his talk, Dr. Buff described lag screw-fixation as an old method no longer in use. He believed that if tibia fractures required surgery, intramedullary nailing was the only suitable technique. He really had no idea what he was talking about. He showed cases of distal tibia fractures he had nailed, which had to be immobilized in plaster because they were all unstable and were shortening. Drs. Lenggenhager and Geiser (both of the University of Berne) treated all tibia fractures first with traction and then with cast immobilization. They maintained that this was a technique supported all over the world and that the AO surgeons were about to commit serious malpractice. Dr. Geiser had visited England where he was persuaded that closed fractures must remain closed.

At the time, general surgeons were familiar with only two indications for surgery. First, the cerclage technique could be used for torsional fractures of the tibia, but it had to be combined with cast immobilization. Second, mid-shaft transverse fractures could be treated with intramedullary nails. The AO claim that tibia fractures should have open reduction and stable internal fixation, achieved with compression and mobilization after one week was revolutionary. They simply could not accept it.

Some of what we were presenting had been used in the past. The lag screw principle, for instance, had been published by Danis in 1941, but no one knew anything about it. The AO method was based on the principles of stable internal fixation that I had written down after my experience in Fribourg. Over time, I made only minor modifications, but everything had been presented publicly, particularly in my lecture on form and function, which I gave in Zurich in 1957. Since 1957, Allgöwer's clinic had become very good at treating torsional fractures of the tibia with lag screw fixation. Three years later these early AO cases, which we had prospectively documented, were described in a book published in German in 1963. In 1965, it was published in English as Technique of Internal Fixation of Fractures.[4]

My AO colleagues and I felt that we had won a minor victory, because the society could have taken measures to shut us down. Somehow reason prevailed, and they held back from official censure. But it was apparent that the AO faced a hostile world, which was far from ready to accept anything we had to offer. Things were heating up with the first AO course in Davos only a couple of weeks away.

The afternoon was dedicated to fractures of the tibia. There were again three AO presentations by AO surgeons as in Geneva: Bandi replaced Allgöwer, who was ill, and presented the AO treatment of internal fixation with plates and screws, Schneider covered nailing techniques of the tibia, and Willenegger commented on overall results. When the discussion was opened, Müller's recollection is again highly instructive:

> The atmosphere at the end of the meeting reminded me of hostile armies facing off in battle. The anxiety of the surgeons present was palpable. My appointment to the St. Gallen clinic had further fuelled their apprehension. There was also talk of my recent trip to New York in September 1960 to attend the SICOT meeting, news of which had filtered back to Switzerland. What raised the general anxiety even further was the fact that just prior to this extraordinary meeting, we had announced the first AO instructional course to be held in Davos on 10 December 1960. The surgeons learned that the course would include lectures on our new surgical principles and that participants would be able to practice the new techniques on actual bones using our instruments and implants. We stressed that only the new AO instruments and implants would be used at the course but that they would not be for sale. There was great alarm at this announcement. The general surgeons not only saw the dwindling number of patients but now they realized that they would not be able to get their

---

[4]Müller et al. (1965).

hands on the new AO implants and instruments. As soon as they heard this, they accused us of acting unprofessionally by withholding information necessary for patient care. To make things worse, they were upset that we were opening the door of our AO clinics to many new, visiting surgeons who would come to learn about the new techniques.

They had cause to be concerned and angry. What really surprised me was that the Orthopedic surgeons opposed us. Up to this time, their professional lives had been virtually free of emergencies; now they suddenly faced the idea that Orthopedic surgeons would do trauma surgery and fracture treatment. To make matters even worse, we were preaching immediate surgery for all lower extremity fractures, which meant frequent emergency operations at night.

AO Surgeons in the Role of Disruptors

The Harvard Business School professor Clayton Christensen published a book on the introduction of new technologies and coined the phrase 'disruptive technology' to explain the impact of major innovations. Although this term was coined about 40 years after the creation of the AO *Instrumentarium*, the issues faced by the AO founders preceded the formulation put forward in Christensen's book.[5] The reactions of the assembled community of surgeons in Berne were typical of the reactions usually received by innovators; in this case, they were heaped upon AO surgeons.

Müller's recollection of those meetings showed that the AO surgeons were perceived as a major disruption to the then dominant practice of the surgical community. In general, Orthopedic surgeons were confronted with a totally different surgical technique, which, if accepted, would change the way they worked. In addition, the AO surgeons were not Orthopedic surgeons, with the exception of Müller. They were perceived as general surgeons from regional hospitals (again, except for Müller), none had achieved the status of professor, and not even Müller had a university appointment yet. The AO innovations of treating bone fractures through internal fixation was a triple threat: disrupting existing treatment regimes, disrupting an entire professional group of Orthopedic surgeons, and disrupting the roles that surgeons themselves were inhabiting. The fact that the source of disruption was a group of young, not-yet-established surgeons without university affiliation, did not make it any easier.[6]

The opposing camp was also against AO's approach on philosophical grounds; this charge was led by two professors from the University Hospital of Berne (Lenggenhager and Geiser), as well as the about to be appointed head of one of the university surgical departments from Zurich (Buff). It was Buff, in particular, who favored the conservative method of treatment of fractures and viewed the AO approach as mechanistic and scientific. Buff saw the role of the surgeon as being one of an artist, not a scientist. In his view, the role of the surgeon was to resist the internal fixation techniques, to guide and accompany the patient through the much

---

[5]Christensen (1997).
[6]Christensen (2003).

longer conservative method by using external fixation devices and plaster casts, using only surgical approaches later on should a non-union occur. Of course, this was in total opposition to the AO philosophy.

The fact that Müller had just been appointed head surgeon to the new hospital wing of the Cantonal Hospital in St. Gallen was a factor in the strong resistance emanating from the established medical community. The main driver of the AO had finally secured a major hospital appointment and was likely to have a much stronger base from where to pitch the AO's ideas.

Following the Berne meeting, the AO surgeons considered themselves lucky that they could hold off a formal censure from the Swiss Surgical Association, something that would have frustrated their progress in view of the upcoming AO course in Davos.

Pitching the AO Philosophy Abroad

Initially, the reception experienced overseas was also very hostile. A few presentations were made early on by AO surgeons at some international conferences. One of the first presentations was made by Müller at the International Society of Orthopedic Surgery and Traumatology (SICOT) conference in New York in 1960, where Müller gave several presentations about different aspects of Osteosynthesis. Although not much is known about the reception he received in New York, the presentation by an AO-friendly surgeon at a La Société Française de Chirurgie Orthopédique et Traumatologique (SOFCOT) meeting in France was interrupted with the call, "don't follow the Swiss farmers."[7]

Likewise, the reception in Germany was for a long time rather cool, if not hostile, to the AO thinking. In 1962, a leading German Orthopedic surgeon wrote in his textbook that "it would be utopia to believe that a simple bone screw could hold for long."[8] Schneider, one of the AO founders, also recalled situations in Germany when presentations showing AO implants were accompanied by whistling from the audience.

Inviting Guests of Honor to Davos to Overcome Resistance

As has been reported, in looking for support for their treatment philosophy, AO surgeons invited a number of leading trauma surgeons to Davos for their annual courses. These guests of honor came from many different countries and included some of the best-known trauma and Orthopedic surgeons of the era.

One of the first university professors to support the AO philosophy was the German surgeon H. Krauss and his team from Freiburg. Following visits in 1960

---

[7]Heim (2001), p. 85.
[8]Heim (2001), p. 85.

made by Müller and Willenegger to explain the AO thinking, he also sent some of his residents to attend one of the first Davos courses. Freiburg became the first German hospital to fully adopt the AO technique and Siegfried Weller, one of their surgeons, later became president of the AO. In the early phase of rollout, it was Weller who transported scarce implants and surgical instruments across the border into Germany.[9]

The renowned surgeon J.G. Charnley was invited to be a guest of honor at the Davos course in 1961 (Müller's extensive contacts and interaction with Charnley will be covered in Chap. 25). Lorenz Böhler from Vienna also attended the Davos course as an honored guest in 1964 (previously, his son Jörg had attended the first course and had taken the AO philosophy back to Austria). This practice of bringing leading surgeons to Davos certainly helped spread AO's internal fixation philosophy, although it would still take several years before a breakthrough was recorded in Germany, Austria, and beyond (Exhibits 13.1 and 13.2).

Exhibit 13.1 Visit of John Charnley to Davos course 1961. Martin Allgöwer (second from the left) and John Charnley (second from the right). *Copyright by AO Foundation, Switzerland*

---

[9]Schlich (2002), p. 154.

Exhibit 13.2 Professor Lorenz Böhler (at the right) visiting the Davos course. *Copyright by AO Foundation, Switzerland*

Taking on the Entire Medical Establishment

The AO founders were mostly young surgeons without the accolades of university professor positions. They took on the leaders of their profession in a battle for Osteosynthesis that had been described by surgical leaders outside of Switzerland as a 'dangerous procedure,' fit only for the most skilled surgeons, and one to be avoided in favor of the established, conservative, treatment of bone fractures. Some might have considered this a suicidal mission, but the early AO surgeons believed fervently in the superiority of their techniques, as well as the patient benefits. Eventually, their dedication, combined with their surgical skills, won the day.

References

Christensen, C. M. (1997). *The innovator's dilemma: When new technologies cause great firms to fail*. Cambridge, MA: Harvard Business School Press.

Christensen, C. L. (2003). *The innovative solution*. Brighton, MA: Harvard Business Press.

Heim, U. F. A. (2001). *Das Phänomen AO*. Mannheim: Huber.

Müller, M. E., Allgöwer, M., & Willenegger, H. (1965). *Technique of internal fixation of fractures*. Heidelberg: Springer.

Schatzker, J. (2018). *Maurice E. Müller: In his own words*. Davos: AO Foundation.

Schlich, T. (2002). *Surgery, science and industry* (p. 154). Basingstoke: Palgrave Macmillan.

Schneider, R. (1983). *25 Jahre AO–Schweiz*. Berne: Arbeitsgemeinschaft für Osteosynthesefragen.

In Search of a Business Model

14

Trying to Find a Business Arrangement

Even since Robert Mathys shook Maurice Müller's hands to seal an agreement, in the Spring of 1958, he collaborated in the design of many prototypes; these were showcased to the AO membership on the organization's kick-off day the in November 1958. Mathys, a skilled craftsman, understood that he would not be able to commercialize any of the implants and instruments until positive surgical experiences had been confirmed and that this could take up to three to four years.

In the process of developing prototypes and making demonstration sets, Mathys had to get new machinery and equipment, some of which were acquired after securing loans. By the end of 1959, his total debt accumulation was about CHF 300,000, a significant amount for the owner of a small tool machining workshop. He had not yet been paid for anything other than direct material and labor costs, but that was far less than the accumulated investments of his time and machinery. The arrangements for delivering his products to hospitals was executed by Müller's sister, Violette Moraz-Müller, but this also meant that he would not receive payments until the hospital paid the sales coordination office. Delays in invoices paid contributed to Mathys' problems.

At this moment, Müller contacted Mathys' bankers to assure them that eventually there would be a substantial amount of revenue to be made, due to scaled-up production and implants and instrumentation being offered for commercial sale. The banker accepted Müller's assurance on face value due to his growing reputation as a surgeon, and because he was from a reputable commercial family in Biel. It became clear to Müller, however, that the arrangements had to be firmed up and made more formal, so as to give some comfort to Mathys who had invested so much of his time. From Mathys' point of view, he had up to that time dealt only with Müller and his sister, never having met any of the other AO surgeons. In order to reduce his perceived uncertainty, he also aspired to receive a formal exclusivity contract from the AO. Up to this time, no contracts had been signed.

© Springer Nature Switzerland AG 2019
J.-P. Jeannet, *Leading a Surgical Revolution*,
https://doi.org/10.1007/978-3-030-01980-8_14

As an aside, for those familiar with the creation of today's high technology start-ups, these arrangements might appear rather exceptional and extraordinary. Today, in the same circumstances, inventors, investors, and entrepreneurs would sign countless non-disclosure forms, engage in lengthy negotiations, deal with numerous lawyers, and go through any number of business plan versions and financial pro forma statements. Shipping surgical instruments and implants without any purchase orders is surely unimaginable from a modern business perspective.

In early 1960, a contract was finally drafted for a meeting in Chur held on 6 January between Mathys and the AO surgeons Müller, Allgöwer, Willenegger, and Schneider. In this document, the signatories agreed to create a new company with Mathys having a 50% ownership. This company, anticipating growing sales, was eventually turned into a shareholding firm, whereby the AO could own as much as 50% of the share capital. This clearly would take care of Mathys' business interest and formally treat him as the sole and exclusive supplier.

A Trusted Advisor Joins the AO Team

As a result of these discussions and negotiations, a new personality joined the AO founders who was to have considerable influence on the development of the Foundation from an organizational and financial point of view. Because the founders themselves, with the exception of Müller, had little commercial and financial experience, Allgöwer sought the advice of his accountant in Chur, Peter von Rechenberg (1920–1992). As a partner in a local accounting firm, Curia AG, he had earned a reputation as a tax specialist and was often consulted by not-for-profit organizations on fiscal matters.[1] For the first 30 years of the AO, von Rechenberg would become an important advisor on all major re-organizations, get involved in all commercial agreements with producers such as Mathys, and with his temperament often intercede to quell conflicts and disagreements in the surgical community. From what is known, von Rechenberg, and his firm Curia, already had their hands on the first contract draft that had never been formally approved. He was to play a much bigger role in the next stage of creating formal structures between the AO and producers.[2]

This first proposed agreement was never consummated. The surgeons, upon some reflection, soon adopted the viewpoint that it was impossible that they, as a non-profit organization devoted to the study of Osteosynthesis, could at the same time participate financially in a commercial, for-profit company, producing and marketing implants and instruments. It would take another year to find a solution

---

[1]Heim (2001), p. 75.
[2]Curia AG, located in Chur, has been the accounting firm for the AO organization ever since Peter von Rechenberg became involved. His son, Andrea von Rechenberg, is active at Curia and is still involved with AO matters to this date. His daughter, Brigitte von Rechenberg, became a veterinarian surgeon and had been involved with AO for many years.

and to propose a different organizational structure, leading to the establishment of a new company in December 1960 named Synthes AG and domiciled in Chur.

Creating Synthes AG Chur to Monetize AO Innovations

Throughout the year of 1960, discussions were ongoing about establishing a company that would be compatible with the not-for-profit status of the AO, and yet allow for the commercialization of the AO-approved *Instrumentarium*. Wherever the AO surgeons displayed their surgical sets at conferences, interest was considerable. Up to now, only AO members, and a few selected course participants, were allowed to purchase implants. It was planned that sales would be open to the general medical community two years hence, in September 1962. Because the volume of ordered implants was expected to rise rapidly, the AO wanted to make sure that the necessary arrangements were made and that the commercial agreement with Mathys was signed.

Contrary to the version at the beginning of the year, the creation of Synthes AG Chur now was planned as an organization with AO shareholders only. The AO was a non-profit organization, and the group wanted to prevent that only the producers realized financial gain. After all, the surgeons considered the ideas behind the AO *Instrumentarium* to be their own, and the organization still had large funding needs in terms of research and education, as well as establishing the AO philosophy in the medical community against considerable resistance. But the surgeons considered it unethical to personally profit from their innovation.

Business Model Innovation to Secure Revenue Stream

As the surgeons looked for possible solutions to their quandary, it was Müller who came up with an idea that became the foundation of the new, to be established, company named Synthes AG Chur. Created as a limited company and incorporated according to Swiss law, Synthes was to coordinate production, represent the *Instrumentarium* to the public and medical community, and be involved in the distribution of its profits.

The main revenue source of Synthes Chur AG was to be the licensing fees that producers would pay on sales of implants and instruments. These licensing fees would be used to fund AO activities, such as the research and the Documentation Center, as well as its educational efforts. It was pointed out, that for licensing fees to be charged to producers, the company needed to possess its own intellectual property. The envisioned Synthes AG Chur, however, did not own any intellectual property. All patent rights and design rights on the *Instrumentarium*, developed with Mathys, was the sole property of Müller. Under these circumstances, the idea of a pass-through licensing fee, not subject to taxation, would not be possible. To resolve this dilemma, Müller took one of those defining decisions that still impacts the AO to this day.

Making a Magnanimous Donation

Müller donated, without any compensation, all of his patent rights, including those going back to his pre-AO days in Fribourg and while at the Balgrist Clinic, to the newly created Synthes AG Chur. This included what was later called the 'Müller Set'—the cassettes for screws and cassettes for plates, plus a cassette for hip plates. In the same vein, all future developments by Müller, or any of the AO members, were likewise to be donated free of charge to Synthes AG Chur. With this unprecedented act of generosity, the very important aspect of volunteerism without compensation for contributions to the AO organization was strengthened, and the spirit of this can still be felt, even though, as will be seen later, some changes in these arrangements emerge over time.[3] Years later, Müller commented on this selfless act[4]:

> I had given this issue a great deal of thought. My gift of intellectual property would ensure the necessary funding for AO Switzerland for the future. This act of giving intellectual property subsequently became a standard of practice for those who belonged to AO. AO surgeons voluntarily transferred new intellectual property that they developed to Synthes AG Chur in order to ensure the growth and welfare of the group and its common goals.

A Single Exception

When Müller signed all of his patents over to Synthes AG Chur, he made one exception. He withheld any patents and developments related to hip surgery or replacement and kept those in his name. Included were activities such as the manufacture, distribution, and sale of Müller's hip products. Later, this decision allowed him to move in a different direction when it came to hip replacement, and to start a separate commercial operation in the form of Protek AG, which he did in 1967, selling it later in 1989[5] (this development is covered in more detail in Chap. 25).

---

[3]The Synthes AG Chur founders were well aware of the practice in other countries of surgeons licensing their designs to manufacturers, having their names put on those, and receiving up to 20% of the business profits in return. The AO surgeons wanted to prevent such practice, and Müller's donation of his designs and patents allowed them to do so.

[4]Schatzker (2018), p. 103.

[5]Schatzker (2018), p. 113.

Arranging for Control of Synthes AG Chur

Synthes AG Chur was created in the legal form of a limited, or incorporated company, with a nominal share capital of CHF 50,000, divided into 50 shares of 1000 each. Some 40% of the capital was paid up. The shareholders were the four AO founders—Müller, Allgöwer, Willenegger, and Schneider. Despite the urgings by his friends, Müller was satisfied to take just 14 shares, leaving the three others to share the rest. Schneider and Willenegger each received 12 shares, and Allgöwer kept 11 and ceded one of his 12 shares to their fiscal advisor, von Rechenberg, as owner of one single share (Exhibit 14.1).

Müller later argued that he did not need any more than 14 shares; with that number he could exert control of the firm as long as he could get one of the other three to agree with him. Because Schneider was his closest friend, this arrangement worked well for about 20 years until Schneider's retirement in 1978. As a result, Müller could concentrate on the business arrangements, and Allgöwer and Willenegger were satisfied getting their research projects funded. According to Müller, he spoke with Allgöwer almost daily on the phone on matters related to Synthes AG Chur and during the first 20 years there were no disagreements between them.

Shares could be sold only at their nominal value, and the surgeons adhered to this agreement until a more formal agreement was signed. The shareholders took into

Exhibit 14.1   AO founders (from left to right) Willenegger, Schneider, Müller, von Rechenberg, Allgöwer, and Bandi (latter not a Synthes AG Chur shareholder). *Copyright by AO Foundation, Switzerland*

consideration the case of retirement from the company, or the case of death.[6] How this important stipulation influenced the long-term development of Synthes AG Chur will be explored later.

In both the by-laws and the shareholding agreement, Synthes AG Chur was designed as a non-profit company, stipulating that the shareholders not assume any financial benefit from their shares. All funds were targeted toward the undertakings of the AO, such as research and education.

Explains Müller:

> Synthes AG Chur was designed in such a way that we, as surgeons on the board, would retain guidance and full control of our funds and their distribution, never for personal use, but only for research, teaching, and development.

This agreement was completed and signed just prior to AO's first course in Davos in December 1960. Although it did not yet clarify the business arrangements between Mathys and the AO, the formation of Synthes AG Chur nevertheless made it possible to proceed with formalizing the business relationship. At the very beginning, the creation of Synthes AG Chur was meant to monetize the AO innovations and establish a recurrent revenue stream that would guarantee the long-term survival of the AO and its projects.

References

Heim, U. F. A. (2001). *Das Phänomen AO*. Mannheim: Huber.
Schatzker, J. (2018). *Maurice E. Müller: In his own words*. Davos: AO Foundation.

---

[6]Heim (2001), "Synthes Shareholders Agreement," dated 17 January 1968, p. 232.

A Metallurgist Joins the AO Team

Some developments created tension in the collaboration between AO surgeons and Mathys. Quality issues arose as Mathys ramped up production to move from prototyping to mass production. Implant failures occurred and began increasing. What worried the AO surgeons even more was the appearance of signs of corrosion, which caused local inflammations in patients and were difficult to distinguish from more serious and acute infections. Mathys himself became aware of this and on his own contacted a local physicist but was unable to find the underlying cause of the problems.

As these issues were discussed among the surgeons, Willenegger was also actively participating in the search for answers to the implant imperfections. Through his Rotary Club contacts in Liestal, he reached out to local businessman Reinhard Straumann (1892–1967),[1] who since 1938 had been the owner of Tschudin + Heid AG, Waldenburg, a company producing watch components, and an expert in metallurgy. He was a successful entrepreneur and owned several other businesses. While previously having managed a watch component company, he developed two global patents for balance springs (Nivarox) and on special alloys (Nivaflex). Nivarox SA, founded in 1934 in Le Locle (Neuchâtel), was acquired by The Swatch Group in 1984. Nivaflex, founded in 1951 in Saint-Imier, and Nivarox both produced special steel alloys used for key components in the watch industry.

In 1954, Straumann turned his research laboratory into the Research Institute Dr. Ing. Reinhard Straumann, equipped with laboratory facilities for metallurgical research and investigations, in order to capitalize on his previous experience in the watch and medical industries. In recognition of these accomplishments, Straumann

---

[1] Professor Dr. Ing. Reinhard Straumann, Professor at Technical University in Stuttgart.

© Springer Nature Switzerland AG 2019
J.-P. Jeannet, *Leading a Surgical Revolution*,
https://doi.org/10.1007/978-3-030-01980-8_15

had been granted an honorary doctorate and nominated Professor at the Technical University Stuttgart.

It is worth noting Straumann's wide range of interests; he was described as a lateral thinker with interests in many different fields[2]—Swiss Air Force officer, passionate ski jumper, pioneer in sports medicine, as well as a student of ski jumps and aerodynamics of ski jumpers. He came to study bone structures after spending time in a hospital due to a ski jumping accident. Not surprisingly, Straumann was immediately interested in the metallurgical issues surrounding AO implants. His son Fritz Straumann, who was in charge of the research department at the Institute, was appointed as the conduit for all AO-related issues. He also signed up for the first AO course in Davos as an observer. Straumann's organization not only brought metallurgical know-how to the AO organization, but also an industrial acumen, as a result of operating several manufacturing businesses.

His son, Fritz Straumann (1921–1988), was also a trained engineer. He was schooled at *Ingenieurschule HTL* (*Höhere Technische Lehranstalt*) or, Engineering School, Higher Technical Studies, in Le Locle, an institution with close ties to the watch industry. Later, he headed the Straumann Institute's metallurgical testing department and interest in science led him to become a contributor of the first book, the *Manual of Internal Fixation*, published by AO in 1963.

Important for the AO was the technical team that the Straumanns had assembled at the Waldenburg location. This team worked on the corrosion issues and was able to identify the underlying causes for a series of metal defects. Important members of that team were: Ortrun Pohler, who had joined in 1957 and worked on the AO's metallurgical studies, Samuel Steinemann (1923–2016), ETH-Z physicist, Fridolin Sequin (1921–1989) responsible for the documentation of the AO *Instrumentarium*, and Paul Gisin (1925–1995) who as technical designer and developer, later worked on drills, which were incorporated into the AO *Instrumentarium*.

As far back as Danis, the issue of stainless steel had been raised. Danis favored the V2A steel containing chromium, nickel iron, and traces of carbon. As it turned out, stainless steel was not stainless steel, and it mattered how it was produced. Research conducted at the Straumann Institute determined that the stainless steel sourced for the implants were at fault. Under the leadership of Ortrun Pohler, the impact of different surface treatments and destructions to corrosion resistance in the human body were explored.[3]

Reflecting on that time, Ortrun Pohler remembers the day when Fritz Straumann walked into her office placing the corroded and broken implants he had just received from Willenegger on her desk. With this gesture, he asked her to investigate the problems. An analysis of the defective implants resulted in detecting the underlying

---

[2]Interview with Ortrun Pohler, metallurgist and employee at Straumann Institute during that time, conducted 24 May, 2018, in Lörrach. Ortrun Pohler also reviewed later drafts of this chapter and contributed additional details on the resolution of the metallurgical issues related to the AO *Instrumentarium*.

[3]Mathys (2014), p. 423.

causes for the failures. The fracture surfaces of the broken plates showed typical signs of slowly progressing metal fatigue cracking. The plates had undergone cyclic loading in the fracture zone under weight bearing, indicating unstable conditions of the Osteosynthesis.

The corrosion signs on the implants were of different intensity and arose from different reasons. There were distinct corrosion pits which went as channels into the material and were caused by longitudinal "slag" inclusions which had been dissolved by the corrosion process. These impurities were caused by undesired "elements", such as oxygen, silicone, and manganese sulfides. Furthermore, the implant steel had a chemical composition not optimal for resisting general corrosion, even though it was a type of V4A steel containing also molybdenum for improved corrosion resistance. These findings meant that AO implants required a stainless steel of improved quality: a steel of higher cleanliness and optimal composition, microstructure, and mechanical properties.

It proved difficult to source stainless steel of this quality, and at a high level of reproducibility, on the market. Eventually, the Straumann team located a steel producer in France with a rare slag-remelting process unit to eliminate slag components and who accepted the strict material specifications. Pohler and her colleagues began a cooperation with the French producer who met initial tests for all requirements. However, quality of the supplied material began soon to decline, and Straumann Institute had to take up a new collaboration with a producer duo in Germany. The German suppliers were able to meet the exceeding standards on a consistent basis.

Pohler investigated AO implant steel regarding various properties to demonstrate optimal quality. It could be shown that even cold worked steel for plates was not sensitive to stress corrosion cracking, and that the material did not develop general nor pitting corrosion in critical testing solutions.

Throughout this time, Pohler managed any quality issues directly with the producers and became engaged in the relevant international standard organizations, often in the role of chair person of working groups, representing both Swiss and AO interests.

Eventually, the steel alloys specified for AO implants became a global standard, with some exceptions. US suppliers never arrived at the absolute same specs as the Europeans had, and so, in a compromise, the ISO standard was patterned after what US suppliers could manage. The AO standard, however, remained the tighter one. What complicated matters even more was the fact that certain implant applications required different mechanical properties, such as soft, hard, extra hard, which had to be specified for the different types of raw material for specific implants. Reported Ortrun Pohler[4]:

> It took up the better part of two years to get this resolved, holding countless meetings in Waldenburg and Davos.

---

[4]Interview Pohler, O., Op. cit.

Furthermore, test on biocompatibility of metals and alloys were carried out with the AO research center in Davos. To assure consistent material quality, Straumann Institute became the sourcing point for ordering all stainless steel for both Mathys and Straumann, conducted material and quality checks, and then shipped the material to Mathys in an arrangement that was to last many years and was later even extended to the US production plants Synthes USA.

Crafting an Agreement Between Synthes AG Chur and Producers

The AO surgeons, just having put the finishing touches on their own financial arrangements in the creation of Synthes AG Chur, which they completed without the participation of any producer by not involving them directly in the organization, could finally think about the nature of the arrangement they, as surgeons through the AO, wanted to have with Mathys and any other producer.

There was still one hitch before a final agreement between AO's Synthes AG Chur and producers could be reached. Fritz Straumann, quickly grasping the market potential of the AO implants, was keenly interested in also becoming a producer and could, through his collaboration, help Mathys in his financial squeeze. However, Mathys was apparently concerned that he might lose the AO business entirely if he did not get a resolution regarding the metallurgical issues—the AO, through Synthes, might turn to another producer. This situation needed to be addressed.

The negotiations, involving the essential business interests of both Mathys' and Straumann's companies, became very complicated. Their resolution was taking more time than anticipated and lasted for more than a year, well into 1961. In March of that year, Mathys suddenly stopped delivering prototypes. He refused to hand over mechanical drawings to Straumann, insisting that a new agreement was needed, and that he wanted to be compensated for set-up expenses, documentation, and other direct costs related to help get Straumann under way—a total of about CHF 225,000. Confronted with the choice of either terminating Mathys or paying the considerable compensation, the AO surgeons got both producers around a table to try and get them to accept a deal that would name them both as producers and ask them to deliver identical products.[5]

The negotiations took about two years, and it was not until 21 November, 1963, that the final version of the agreement on the co-operation between Synthes AG Chur on one side and the two producers, Mathys and Straumann, on the other side, was finalized. A sense of urgency was introduced as the official commercialization of the AO *Instrumentarium* was fixed for September 1962; everyone was aware that this required a resolution of the various commercial conflicts between the two producers. Synthes AG Chur's fiscal advisor, von Rechenberg, played an important diplomatic role keeping the two producers engaged and moving towards an agreement everyone could sign.

---

[5]Heim (2001), p. 58.

The first public exposition of the entire *Instrumentarium* was held at a surgical conference in Schaffhausen, Switzerland, in September 1962, right after the decision to bring it to the market. This decision was much anticipated, and the AO group found it increasingly difficult to hold off making the *Instrumentarium* more widely available due to the pressure they felt from the surgical community. Originally, market entry had been planned for 1963 to give the AO enough time with clinical experience, but everyone was clamoring for access. As it turned out, use of the *Instrumentarium* without sufficient instruction and training was likely to result in surgical failures. Those failures were later often used by the opponents of the AO method as proof that Osteosynthesis was inferior to the conservative treatment.

Two instrument sets were initially offered in a catalogue: the basic set for simple use of screws went on the market for CHF 1110. The more complete set, with cancellous screws, was available at CHF 1778. Additional elements were available on special order. Special orders could be delivered within eight to ten days, at a 20% premium over standard units. All of these sets and elements were produced by Mathys in Bettlach.

Dividing the World in Olten

Before a final agreement could be signed, the parties concerned realized that havoc would rule if both Mathys and Straumann were to be let loose on the world markets. To prevent confusion, Mathys suggested that the allocation of major markets be done by drawing lots. Straumann's staff had organized all the markets into bundles of similar potential, according to the views of the time. The meeting took place in a 'neutral' spot, which meant neither at the company sites of Mathys (Bettlach) or Straumann (Waldenburg). The location choice fell to the restaurant in the Olten railway station, roughly equidistant to both companies (Exhibit 15.1).

For the lot drawing, Straumann's staff had put the names of these agreed upon bundles of commercial values on small pieces of paper. There was one market exception, which was Germany, considered to have by far the largest potential. To solve this problem, Robert Mathys simply bought a map of Germany in the newspaper kiosk at the station, on which the two parties drew a line across Germany, dividing the country into a northern section, including the then GDR or East Germany, and a southern section. By drawing lots, Mathys got the northern part and Straumann the southern. For the rest of the world, more lots were drawn and because Mathys was senior to Fritz Straumann, Robert Mathys drew first.

Mathys drew the entire continent of Africa. Straumann drew Switzerland. The two continued to take turns. Mathys ended up with Asia, Germany North, Austria, the Middle East, France, Italy, Yugoslavia, and Greece. Straumann drew Germany South, Great Britain, Spain, Scandinavia, Latin America, and North America. Both companies were now free to develop these markets by building their own sales channels.

Two years later, in a further refinement of the market allocation between the two producers, they opted to share equally all sales to the (West) German Army. Mathys,

Exhibit 15.1   Fritz Straumann and Robert Mathys, Sr., during a dinner at an AO Course in Davos, 1962. *Copyright by AO Foundation, Switzerland*

in addition to East Germany, had also gotten Romania and Bulgaria. Straumann, in return, obtained sales rights for Czechoslovakia, Poland, and Hungary.

You might think at this point, 'Hold it, this is illegal!' Well, it would be illegal today, according to the international regulations of competition statutes. At the time, in 1963, the laws were different; it was not illegal, per se, to divide markets outside of Switzerland. The competition laws governing monopoly situations in Switzerland were ruled by the assessment of whether there was actual market restraint with negative impact on the part of the actors. The creation of a monopoly situation was not ruled out by or in itself, which differed considerably from the prevalent competition and monopoly laws in place in the US, for example. Rarely had ever such a large global market potential been divided and allocated among players in such a small, unassuming railway station restaurant.

In any case, the participants of this exercise did not believe they had done anything wrong. However, as we shall see in the later developments of the AO and Synthes, this decision would come back to haunt them some 25 years later.

The commercial agreement, signed on 21 November, 1963, was the first of many such contracts, involving the AO through Synthes AG Chur, and with the producers Mathys and Straumann. The parties treated each other as having the same rights under this agreement and stated as its purpose "cooperation in the manufacturing and distribution of instruments and implants for bone surgery." It is interesting to note, it did not list Osteosynthesis.

The signatories confirmed Synthes AG Chur as the sole owner of all rights related to the *Instrumentarium* designed according to the principles of the AO, and Synthes conferred on the two producers the exclusive rights to produce and market such surgical tools and implants. They would use the same product listings and maintain identical product specifications but would be allowed to charge different market prices. The producers committed to mutually cooperate and support each other in order to guarantee an equal supply of implants across all markets. In return for this agreement, Mathys and Straumann would pay Synthes AG Chur a contribution of 15%—computed on official list prices—to be used for further research, as well as a contribution towards documentation. For the computation of licensing fees, the manufacturers and AO maintained a shadow-pricing list with identical costs and prices for each item, which was used for the purpose of determining licensing fees only.

Both producers signed their exclusive licensing agreement with Synthes AG Chur, not with the AO organization at large. At Synthes, the decision makers were the four shareholder surgeons (Müller, Allgöwer, Schneider, and Willenegger). At this point, other surgeon members of the AO were effectively excluded from the decision-making process, including the details of the financial arrangements and the directions given to the surgeons on the commercialization of the *Instrumentarium*.

In parallel, discussions continued within the AO and among its surgeons on the release of the *Instrumentarium*. Demand and market pressures continued to grow, and in order not to be accused of 'monopolizing the system,' the surgeons accepted beginning market entry towards the end of 1962. Because Straumann had not yet been able to ramp up its own production capacity, they were initially forced to source implants from Mathys, which in turn helped Mathys with his own financial situation as volume grew quickly.

Looking back at this first cooperation agreement, it can be concluded that the AO managed, through the creation of Synthes AG Chur, to 'have its cake and eat it too'. The surgeons could distance themselves from the commercial aspects of marketing their *Instrumentarium*, while at the same time manage to create a financing vehicle that would contribute to the further development of the AO's goals.

Financial records preserved going back to 1961, when all sales where through the Biel coordinating office managed by Violette Moraz-Müller, show sales of about CHF 770,000. Of that, about 415,000 were paid for purchases, presumably to Mathys for supplying implants and instruments. The coordinating office transferred CHF 73,000 to the Laboratory in Davos, and after paying all expenses, had a small net profit of CHF 22,000. Laboratory expenses had reached CHF 250,000 and were partially funded through industry donations. From 1961, the AO, and later through Synthes AG Chur, began to absorb an ever-larger part of the operating budget.

From 1962 onwards, through the creation of Synthes AG Chur, the financial records tell a story of growing licensing fees, starting at CHF 164,000 in 1962 to 224,000 in 1963, and 279,000 in 1964. This licensing income, stemming from both the Mathys and Straumann companies, and remitted to Synthes, allowed for growing contributions to the AO's Research Institute Davos' laboratory, started at CHF 70,000 in 1962 and increasing to 180,000 in 1964. Figures indicate that about 60% of the Synthes income was used to support the AO research effort, with ever-larger sums in later years.

References

Heim, U. F. A. (2001). *Das Phänomen AO*. Mannheim: Huber.
Mathys, R., Jr. (2014). Schlossern für die Gesundheit. In F. Betschon, et al. (Eds.), *Ingenieure bauen die Schweiz* (Chap. 12.4, Band 2, p. 423). Zurich: NZZ Libro.

A Commission to Steer the Enterprise 16

Surgeons Looking for Ways to Control Producers

As Maurice Müller tells the story, the origin of AO's *Technische Kommission* (TK), or Technical Commission, goes back to a need to ensure quality control: once producers received exclusive rights to produce the AO *Instrumentarium* from Synthes AG Chur, a process needed to be instituted to assure that all such implants and instruments produced and sold by the producers, Mathys and Straumann, were properly approved by the AO and its surgeons.

The creation of the AOTK became necessary since all rights to the AO *Instrumentarium* rested with Synthes AG Chur, and within Synthes, only four of the AO founding members were shareholders. In some way, these four shareholders (Müller, Allgöwer, Willenegger, and Schneider) possessed a monopoly in terms of giving instructions to Mathys and Straumann, the two designated AO producers. Producers had to accept Synthes instructions and, thus, accept that their freedom was restricted.

When the TK first met in November 1961, it was an informal group consisting of the four AO founders and Synthes AG Chur shareholders, together with producers Mathys and Straumann. The group met several times each year and its decisions, made by majority vote, were binding for all TK members, surgeons, and producers alike. The nature of the TK composition ensured that surgeons were always in the majority. The TK decisions were also binding for AO surgeons who could not have their own instruments produced by Mathys or Straumann. Any proposals for additions to the AO *Instrumentarium* had to be made through the TK whose decisions were final. However, AO surgeons were free to adopt other instruments or, on occasion, implants from other sources—a requirement to use only Synthes supplied implants did not exist.

The first TK meeting was attended by the four AO founders, and included: Robert Mathys, Sr., Fritz Straumann, two Straumann staff members, Vogt and Karpf, Violette Moraz-Müller, who until that point had handled all shipments from her

© Springer Nature Switzerland AG 2019
J.-P. Jeannet, *Leading a Surgical Revolution*,
https://doi.org/10.1007/978-3-030-01980-8_16

home in Biel. Meetings were chaired by Müller, and the administration of the meetings was in the hands of von Rechenberg, fiscal and legal advisor to the AO and Synthes AG Chur.

Discussed were all elements of the AO *Instrumentarium*, the surgeons' experience with new implants and new developments. Although the producers had an exclusive contract with Synthes AG Chur, the AOTK became the forum where decisions were made on any part of the AO *Instrumentarium*. Effectively, neither Straumann nor Mathys could produce and market implants or instruments related to AO procedures without express TK approval.

Müller served as chair of the TK from its inception until 1987, when he retired from the Commission. By all accounts, he was the dominant person, and although decisions were to be taken by majority vote, most of the time there was simply an emerging consensus driven by Müller without any formal votes taken. The effect of this group was to assure safety and efficacy of any Synthes/AO-branded product. Once a product had been accepted by the TK, it was listed by its functional name, thus de-personalizing all innovations. The item was now an AO item, not one made by surgeon X.

AOTK as Powerful Focus Group

Today's business world is replete with references about the use of focus groups, where customers tell manufacturers what they think about their products. Companies maintain extensive consumer panels to get firsthand information about the requirements for successful products. The AOTK system can be viewed as an early version of such instruments, one that no modern-day marketer would want to do without. The role of the AOTK preceded the term 'focus group,' as it is known today, but was certainly an important part of the modern marketing approach to the *Instrumetarium*.

Although initially installed as a way to distill surgeon experience into standardized surgical products and implants, the TK system utilized by the AO also benefitted the producers Mathys and Straumann. Mandating the two companies to produce and market only what was approved by the TK eliminated market uncertainties in terms of medical acceptance. The development of the entire AO *Instrumentarium* was the result of AO surgeons' initiative, and neither Mathys nor Straumann would have ever launched any of these products without the urging of Müller and his AO colleagues. Every AO product added to the Synthes product catalogue had been previously tested in surgery, discussed, approved by experienced surgeons, and once added to the catalogue, assured of some level of demand.

AOTK Practicing Open Innovation

The presence of the TK acted like a highly specialized marketing research department, constantly coming up with new ideas, improving what was on the market, and putting the producers into a supply chain role. Any member of the AO could propose innovations to the TK for investigation, testing, and eventual approval. This also applied, essentially, to non-AO members, although initially most of the proposed innovations came from the core team of founders.

Since producer representatives were always present, AOTK sessions turned into a feedback loop for both surgeons and producers. Producers could propose product alternatives as well, but if turned down by the TK, the producers were obligated to desist and could not add them to any product catalogue.

AOTK as a Conservative Influence

From the outset, Müller was the dominant force in the TK during the first three years and all the new design ideas came from him. Then, other surgeons slowly began to contribute design ideas as well. Müller's grip on the AOTK during his chairmanship was seriously challenged in 1978 when he favored the introduction of locked intramedullary nailing as part of the AO concept. Despite a passionate plea on the part of Müller, and the favorable report by Perren as Director of Research, he could not convince his other surgeon colleagues on the TK to add this innovation to the AO *Instrumentarium*. Years later, Müller would remember this situation as a painful turning point in his role and the beginning of his waning influence at the AO and its TK.[1]

The discussion surrounding the introduction of the interlocking medullary nail also showed the limitations of the TK system. At first it was refused, but later accepted and quickly became a major sales success. The refusal of the introduction had its origin in the AO philosophy of insisting on absolute stability and the belief among most AOTK members that an intramedullary nail was not suited to provide this. Within some 20 years of starting their mission to bring internal fixation to the treatment of bone trauma, the once revolutionary disrupters were at risk of becoming fixed to their own ideas and were having difficulty absorbing new developments from outside AO circles. The disruptors were about to become disrupted themselves.

AO Activities Serving as Indirect Promotion

There were a number of other activities undertaken by AO surgeons, or the AO organizations, that had a beneficial impact on the business volume of the producers. Neither Mathys nor Straumann were medical equipment companies, and neither had

---

[1]Schatzker (2018), p. 132.

any established sales or marketing channels to the medical community, or to hospitals.

Any research papers published in medical journals about the AO experience and, indirectly, the AO trauma experience, had an impact on the Foundation's reputation, as well as a powerful and positive effect on the sale of AO-approved implants. The same can be said for the courses offered by the AO. It has been reported that as much as one-half of the *Instrumentarium*'s annual business stemmed from orders the producers could link directly with course participants.

These activities by AO surgeons created free publicity beyond what a single producer might be able to put up. If the publicity was not free, as was the case for typical companies in the medical space, spokespeople or consultants would have had to be hired and their fees paid. When this collaboration started, Mathys and Straumann were still small companies with very limited resources. They could concentrate on investing in production equipment and, later on, into sales operations abroad. At the beginning, to ramp up AO sales, they were largely playing a logistical function: produce and ship. Over time, this would change, in particular as the producers accumulated an increasing amount of medical experience themselves.

The AOTK as Arbiter for Delicate Business Situations

Early on in the development of the producer relationships, AO and the TK were faced with an event that became known internally as the 'Voka Affair.'[2] Two Straumann executives, Vogt and Karpf, had, for three years, attended all of the TK meetings and, as a result, obtained deep insights into the AO *Instrumentarium*. When they left Straumann and founded their own company, named Voka, they did so in a nearby village to Mathys' operations. They established a manufacturing operation and marketed copies of AO-approved products. Having only manufacturing and no research or development expenses, Voka was underselling Mathys and Straumann by about 25%. In the ensuing discussions at TK meetings, AO surgeons were reluctant to be pulled into what they considered a 'commercial issue,' and the TK recommended to the producers that they abstain from price competition.[3] Instead, the AO, Synthes and the TK, pursued a strategy of competing against knock-off competition by emphasizing the research, education, and a quality-controlled *Instrumentarium* to win over surgeons.

---

[2]Schlich (2002), p. 64.

[3]Voka, domiciled in Selzach, a neighboring town of Bettlach, eventually became Osteo and was later acquired by Stryker, who today still operates the plant at that location producing Osteosynthesis implants.

AOTK as a Marketing Forum

Aside from technical developments, the AOTK also controlled market development and the marketing communications activities of the producers. The TK members were particularly concerned about assuring that the information provided by the marketing arms of the producers was in line with the AO books and educational materials.

There were also situations when the TK intervened as both Mathys and Straumann started to expand their overseas sales and agent networks. The AOTK prevented the Spanish AO group from having implants designed or shipped circumventing the AOTK or suggested when some producer needed to establish better shipping and stocking service if complaints were made.

AOTK as a Permanent Fixture at the AO

The institution of the AOTK has remained a very important part of the AO organization until the present day. It reigned supreme until 1984, when the AO Foundation was created and some of its role, particularly with respect to marketing and budget allocations, was then assigned to the Foundation leadership. After 1984, the AOTK has been much more focused on approving implants and instruments, as well as surgical procedures. How it evolved from there will be featured later, when the role of today's AOTK is discussed (see Chap. 44).

References

Schatzker, J. (2018). *Maurice E. Müller: In his own words* (p. 132). Davos: AO Foundation.
Schlich, T. (2002). *Surgery, science and industry* (p. 64). Basingstoke: Palgrave Macmillan.

AO Vision, Mission, Values, and Strategy   17

Accomplishments of First Three Years

By 1961, just three years after founding the organization, the initial group of 13 AO founders had reached a number of very important milestones. They had not only managed to create a formal organization but had also developed a full set of surgical implants and instruments, called *Instrumentarium*, and tested its use in actual surgery; enlisted a group of producers ready to ramp-up the production of implants; and, crafted a unique business model allowing them to bootstrap and finance their efforts. Finally, and perhaps most importantly, they were beginning to win debates with the established medical community on the validity of their internal fixation and surgical techniques. All of this was undertaken on a volunteer basis while the AO members were fully occupied with their own surgical careers. By any measure, this was an astounding accomplishment that would lay the groundwork for more to come.

Vision, Mission, Values, Strategy

Certainly, the medical accomplishments of the AO have been detailed here. However, there must be a recognition that many of the actions undertaken during the organization's first years were not only medical in nature. There was an astounding amount of organization building undertaken in the venture, reminiscent of what it takes to create a business enterprise. AO surgeons created a venture that resembles the work of entrepreneurs, even though they did not see themselves as such. They viewed themselves as creating a social enterprise in the non-profit realm.

Leaders of larger business organizations often see their directional strategies as addressing an enterprise's vision through its mission, its values, and, of course, setting its strategic direction. It is of value to look at the AO's early existence through the lens of a business leader gaining a fuller perspective of an organization's

© Springer Nature Switzerland AG 2019
J.-P. Jeannet, *Leading a Surgical Revolution*,
https://doi.org/10.1007/978-3-030-01980-8_17

achievement, instead of narrowing it to the perspective of surgeons building a non-profit foundation.

From the outside, the AO's 'vision' was one of revolutionizing the treatment of fracture care, from what the founders believed to be the failure of existing treatments, resulting in decreased mobility and increased disability. AO members aspired to have a broad impact and envisioned a different, and better, form of fracture care. They were not inventors of the basic techniques or technologies, but they were surely the prime movers in terms of making their preferred approach the new global standard.

The AO had its own, clearly articulated, 'mission,' which was to impart the basic capability of Osteosynthesis surgery to all surgeons, taking it out of the hands of a few gifted geniuses. The AO efforts to establish courses, train surgeons, and equip them with the best possible tools and implants, were all designed to maximize treatment results for their patients. AO surgeons did not approach their work as something that would make them, and them alone, superior surgeons. They intended to share their skills, and to collectively help one another to become better still.

Looking through the AO by-laws and reading between the lines bring out the 'values' underlying the AO. There was no specific 'values section,' as would be the case for a modern company, or organization. Instead, the AO had some clear language on member responsibilities. The values of the AO encouraged open discourse among members, not hampered by considerations of seniority, which was not always the practice in hospitals at that time.

In addition to the values, there was also a clear statement about how to interact with one another, and this was all to be done on a voluntary basis. The AO was not founded for personal gain. There were no paid positions in the organization and the member surgeons volunteered their time. Maybe the biggest gesture of generosity was exhibited by Maurice Müller, certainly the driver of the early years, to gift the AO with his patents related to the *Instrumentarium*. This set the standard of passing on any and all developments, or intellectual property, to the AO, free of charge.

And, last but not least, the AO defined a 'strategy' about how it intended to further its development. Compared to other inventors of surgical techniques, the AO surgeon innovators successfully navigated the Innovators' Dilemma by moving very quickly to reach out to early adopters of their surgical techniques. The creation of the business model of having producers pay license fees to the AO-affiliated company Synthes AG Chur, and to use this licensing-based revenue stream for the benefit and growth of the AO vision, mission and values, meant that these items were not just words but were, instead, turned into tangible concepts that could be acted upon. With funding thus assured, the AO became master of its own destiny and largely independent of contributions from governmental or other institutions. Organizationally, through such units as their AOTK, they created vehicles that would ensure continued innovation.

During a review of AO's development, one is struck by how easy it is to apply modern-day business concepts to something undertaken by surgeons 60 years ago. Without formal business training, the AO actions in many areas precede what is now commonly referred to as 'modern strategic concepts.' Describing AO innovation quickly brings to light concepts such as Open Innovation. The AO approach to opening up markets brings up terms such as Crossing the Chasm, Test Marketing, and Focus Groups. The AO's financial arrangements bring to the fore concepts of 'Revenue Stream,' 'Business Model,' and 'Bootstrap Financing.' The arrangements the organization had with the production of its implants renders talk about 'Supply Chain Management.' All of this terminology is familiar to today's student of business, but at the time the AO was created, none of these terms were part of daily parlance.

Thus, testing the first three years of the AO as an organization against today's standard corporate strategy processes, as taught in business schools all over the world, the founders of the AO followed principles that were not generally known at the time. They did this almost intuitively, and in some ways were ahead of their time. None of the founders had any formal business training or experience other than running hospitals. They instinctively found a way to come together in a surprisingly effective way. And on top of that, they did so very rapidly, without any of the modern communications aids that are taken for granted today.

What started as an association of like-minded surgeons evolved into a veritable 'Social Enterprise' with complex structures. Neither the term 'Entrepreneurship,' nor the concept of 'Social Entrepreneurship' was known to the AO founders. Sixty years later, they are part of the common business vocabulary.

How these principles and strategies served the AO, and how they influenced the future, will be addressed in the coming chapters. At this point in time, a new phase for the AO had begun.

Part II

Growing the Organization

Growing the Enterprise

18

Moving from Start-up into Growth Phase

The AO Foundation's start-up phase extended from the mid-1960s until 1984, ending with the most important agreements in place: the adoption of the by-laws, the conclusion of the agreements with the producers, and the market introduction of the *Instrumentarium*. This era also included the struggle for acceptance in the traditional medical community and the launch of the first AO courses in Davos.

What started as a group of surgeons coming together, committed to revolutionizing the treatment of bone trauma and taking tangible action, had grown into an enterprise espousing a profound social commitment. The organization had now taken on a more concrete form, resulting in a number of institutions with clear mandates, ready to confront a medical world that was not receptive to its basic ideas.

The history of the growth phase of the AO Foundation no longer followed a distinct chronological order as the early years had. Instead, one sees that events splinter a bit, sometimes happening simultaneously and at other times not. The illustration below helps to make this point and shows how AO's growth phase becomes more complicated. To avoid having to jump between different, individual, time lines, a single strand will be maintained through to the end of AO's growth phase in the mid-1980s. The chapters in this section about growth should be viewed as having taken place simultaneously and in parallel, where each string is eventually combined to form a stronger fabric, which represents the entire AO organization. (Exhibit 18.1)

© Springer Nature Switzerland AG 2019
J.-P. Jeannet, *Leading a Surgical Revolution*,
https://doi.org/10.1007/978-3-030-01980-8_18

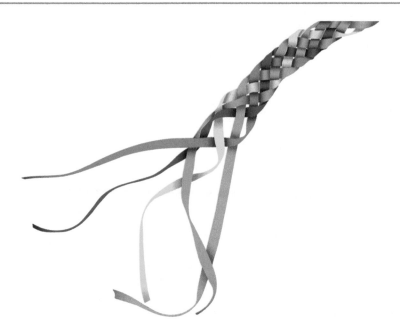

Exhibit 18.1 Individual strands forming a strong fabric. *Copyright by AO Foundation, Switzerland*

The Moment of Lift-off

In the life of a dynamic enterprise such as AO, it's very difficult to ascertain the flashpoint of change, when the pioneering phase changes to the growth phase. But, if there is one single point of time that can serve as the tipping point it would be from 1961 to 1963. Over that period, a number of important elements came together: The conclusion of the producer arrangements with the Mathys and Straumann companies, while the AO moves into mass production for implants and surgical tools. The Davos courses for surgeons, and their repeats, had been launched. A research laboratory had been created, also in Davos, and important projects were already under way. There was progress being made to convince the Swiss surgical community of the benefits of AO's approach to bone fracture care. And, finally, the AO had created for itself some important institutional units, such as the Technical Commission (TK) and Synthes AG Chur, that put structure into its financing and innovation processes, as well as the settlement of some governance issues. With the creation of these multiple organizational units, the launch of several initiatives, and the increased activity regarding the fight for acceptance, the single association had evolved into a complex enterprise, still dependent on the voluntary participation of its members.

The Growth Phase of the AO Enterprise

This growth period, ranging from about 1963 to 1984, can be said to have ended with the creation of the AO Foundation in 1984, an important organizational step in the history of the AO. It also coincides roughly with the 25th anniversary, in 1983, of the AO's creation.

Describing the events, actions, challenges, and talent recruitment necessary to move this enterprise forward can pose a great challenge, particularly when all of these initiatives roughly cover a 20-year time period. In order to manage an overview, it is important to isolate the various development strands into something more homogeneous; describing one at a time until the end of the growth period, before tackling another. While this might create the impression of a series of discrete activities, versus taking a longer and wider view at first, it is nevertheless necessary to absorb the complexity of the AO enterprise, whose strength will be exemplified towards the end of this section.

Mathys Company Ramping up from Humble Beginnings

With the creation of Synthes AG Chur in late 1960, which was to act as the vehicle to grant exclusive licenses to instrument producers Mathys and Straumann, in addition to the conclusion of agreements with the two companies to produce AO-licensed implants and surgical tools at the end of 1961, the path was clear for ramping up a more professional and large-scale production. Until 1962, Mathys and Straumann produced the *Instrumentarium* exclusively but the two companies, and their owners, needed to agree on how to move forward. As described in Chap. 15, the final hurdles were cleared when global markets were allocated between the two firms.

There were two issues which still remained to be resolved in this arrangement. Most immediate was the problem that arose from reported corrosion and the occasional breakage of early implants. Since incoming stainless steel needed to be of a very specific grade and composition, it was the Straumann organization that had equipment and skills to test all of the material. As a result, the sourcing of raw material for both producers was initially handled by Straumann in Waldenburg, about an hour's drive north of Bettlach.

The second issue concerned the scaling up of production. Since both licensee firms sold from a single catalogue, both producers had to assure that whoever produced a given implant element that it would be compatible, and identical, to the one produced in the other plant. This could only be achieved through standardized production of both equipment and processes.

Initially, it was not easy for Robert Mathys, Sr., to accept that he needed to share the impending production ramp-up and the accumulated production know-how with a second supplier. After all, he had invested an enormous amount of time over the years working with Maurice Müller producing prototypes and working on developments of the entire AO *Instrumentarium*, and with no compensation for his time. The tension and conflict of adding Straumann as the second producer was diffused by the AO legal and fiscal counsel, von Rechenberg, who played a critical

© Springer Nature Switzerland AG 2019
J.-P. Jeannet, *Leading a Surgical Revolution*,
https://doi.org/10.1007/978-3-030-01980-8_19

role as moderating diplomat between the two companies, resolving the issues that could have led to extensive legal fights.

Mathys had an advantage over Straumann due to having set up production earlier; as a result, he was in a position to produce for Straumann until the latter set up a new factory in Waldenburg, home of the Straumann family business. Producing the first volume for Straumann on a supplier contract basis was critical in resolving Mathys' financial squeeze; it became an important bargaining chip to get everyone back on track. Since production of the AO *Instrumentarium* turned out to be a very profitable affair from the beginning, the Mathys financial issues were quickly resolved.

Capacity Expansion of the Mathys Company[1]

Robert Mathys, Sr., established his small workshop in Bettlach in 1946 as a single proprietorship. His workshop was located in a small building serving both as workshop and family home, across from the Bettlach railway station. In 1955, the workshop employed ten people. In 1958, when he first met with Maurice Müller, there were about 15 employees and Mathys ran a profitable business. Four years later, just before the official market launch of the AO *Instrumentarium*, employment had reached 40 people and sales were in the low single millions (Exhibit 19.1).

The company maintained the legal form of a sole proprietorship until 1976 when the firm was transformed into the Robert Mathys Co., a form of partnership, only to be transferred a second time into Robert Mathys AG Bettlach, a limited company, in 1990.

In order to meet growing demand, Mathys expanded its manufacturing capacity several times; initially in 1963, a second time in 1966, and then a third time in from 1968 to 1969. Both employment and sales figures showed a dramatic rise. The workshop grew continuously and rose to about 400 by the mid-1980, with most of this growth coming during the first 20 years of its role as AO producer. Over the same time, Mathys sales rose from a recorded CHF 2 million in 1966 to CHF 98 million in 1985.[2] How the Mathys group of companies grew again five-fold in the following 20 years, will be addressed (see Chap. 34).

Dealing with Manufacturing Complexity

From his early experience of supplying Bosshard, a wholesaler of industrial screws, Mathys was familiar with screw production of high precision and quality. The machining processes for screws required the intake of steel rods. Production involved several steps, ranging from turning to whirling, for which special machine

---

[1]Details based upon two long interviews with Robert Mathys, Jr., in Bettlach, on 3 February, 2017 and on 28 February, 2018.
[2]Information provided by Mr. Robert Mathys, Jr.

Exhibit 19.1 The Mathys company early beginnings. *Source: Robert Mathys, Jr., reprinted with permission*

tools needed to be acquired. One local machine tool supplier, Monnier + Zahner, was to become a world leader in screw manufacturing equipment for many other producers, simply as a result of collaborating with Mathys on production of medical-grade screws.[3]

As far as plate manufacturing was concerned, the plates were sourced in rectangular form as raw stock. The processes of milling, as well as hole drilling and punching, were applied. Contours on plates were forged. When the AO shifted towards newer models of dynamic compression plates (DCP) plates, more powerful computer numerical control (CNC) machines needed to be installed.

The medullary nail, part of the AO *Instrumentarium* from the beginning, was substantially redesigned by Schneider, the AO Swiss Chair, and Gysin, a Straumann employee, and first produced by Mathys. This nail, designed along the folding nail principle, required a different manufacturing process than other implants.

The Mathys Company expanded factory space continuously over the next few years. The first expansion took place in 1958 and was attached to the existing family workshop. Several additional expansions were undertaken in Bettlach, where visitors to the small town can still observe the various development stages on the

---

[3]Monnier + Zahner was founded in 1964. See company history on website https://www.monnier-zahner.ch/en/portrait.html, accessed 8 March, 2018.

Mathys company campus. Additional manufacturing space was acquired in other nearby towns, preferably through buying existing factories, namely in Grenchen and Selzach, and later in Balsthal. Purchasing and converting existing manufacturing space was a faster and less expensive process than building greenfield factories, although new factory construction was undertaken on the Bettlach campus.

The production of surgical instruments posed a special challenge—the required volume increased in parallel with the AO courses. Mathys, who had primary responsibility for the production of instruments, soon ran into the problem of hiring enough skilled workers. Because Switzerland did not recognize the production of medical instrumentation as a separate craft with its own apprenticeship program, Mathys acquired a company in Salzburg, Austria, where the craft of surgical instrument maker was a recognized profession with an ample supply of skilled craftsmen.

Ramping up the AO Implant manufacturing capacity, given its wide assortment of initially 200 elements growing to some 1200 elements over the next 20 years, required several different manufacturing processes, which was best handled in different plants, or sites. Mathys, coming from the production experience of a small workshop, mastered this complexity in an admirable way. He grew his business from a sales volume to CHF 30 million with 170 staff in 1975, to a quadruple of its size over the following ten years.

Staffing the factories was also aided by a deep recession in the Swiss watch industry in the mid-1970s, affecting many production sites in the vicinity of the Mathys plants. The skills required for watch component manufacturing were related to what it took to make medical implants. To some extent, the Mathys and AO production cushioned the blow suffered by the Swiss watch makers when the first Asian digital watches arrived on the world market in the early 1970s (Exhibit 19.2).

International Expansion at Mathys

In the markets allocated to Mathys, the company established its first sales subsidiary in Bochum, the Northern German territory and a center of trauma surgery. France, Belgium, and Italy followed in 1964. Australia was also one of the first sales subsidiaries. Other markets served with their own sales subsidiaries were South Africa (1978), Singapore (1979), and India (1977).

Robert Mathys, Jr., says:

> The market for AO implants was clearly driven by the courses offered by the AO. We as producers just supplied according to the demand created and very little selling was needed. We created sales subsidiaries when demand in a certain region surged and that had mostly to do with the launching of AO courses away from Davos.

Exhibit 19.2 Mathys factory in Bettlach, 1974. *Source: Robert Mathys, Jr., reprinted with permission*

How Robert Mathys, Sr., Bootstrapped His Company

How could a single proprietorship, that as early as 1960 had suffered a financial squeeze, finance this considerable growth? Robert Mathys could not depend on any personal or family wealth. He built his company entirely on his own resources, without any outside capital injection, in what today would be referred to as a classical form of bootstrapping the enterprise. As a classical entrepreneur, his wealth consisted of the value of the company.

Robert Mathys, Jr., continues:

> Robert Mathys, Sr., financed this entire growth from his own resources. Although technically illiquid, you might even say almost bankrupt, when the real production of AO implants took off, the healthy profitability soon generated sufficient cash flow that further growth could be entirely financed from internal financial resources of the business. We paid no dividends, all profits were reinvested in the business, avoided external debt financing, such as through banks, and supported our sales subsidiaries usually for one year before they were expected to pay their own way.

Pre-funding sales subsidiaries, purchasing equipment to expand production, acquiring new plants and sites for capacity expansions, and continuously retooling the factory to follow the developments and improvements of the AO Implants, were all financed by the Mathys business. The underlying profitability of the implant business was instrumental to generating sound profits and cash flow. Mathys achieved rapid expansion despite not accessing help from investment bankers, not receiving assistance from private equity companies, or any other institutions in the business community, or taking advantage of government subsidies—all tools so often utilized in today's business world.

Mathys Having a Lasting Industrial Impact

The industrial impact of the Mathys Company's growth was not based on the AO implant production alone. The company became involved with the development and production of Maurice Müller's early hip prosthesis, triggering the growth of the Monnier + Zahner machine tool company, as well as eventually leading to the creation of Thommen Medical—a dental implant company that owed its foundation to the Mathys business and technology leveraged from the manufacturing of AO implants.

Through its payments of licensing fees to Synthes AG Chur over the course of time, and almost as an add-on, Mathys became the largest single contributor to the financial flow that supported the AO organization. By the mid-1980s, the annual contribution by Mathys to Synthes AG Chur, and indirectly to the AO, had reached about CHF 6 million.

Straumann Assumes Role of Manufacturer 20

The Rotary Club Connection

The Straumann Institute, as the company was officially referred to, joined the AO as co-producer following the implant corrosion resolution (this process is described in Chap. 15). When Reinhard Straumann (1892–1967), who met AO co-founder Hans Willenegger through their Rotary Club connection, accepted the challenge to help with the metallurgical investigation, he also made a deal with Willenegger to become an AO implant producer.

Straumann Leveraging Industrial Experience

Straumann was already a successful entrepreneur who owned several businesses other than the Straumann Institute.[1] While managing a watch component company until 1938, he developed two global patents for watch balance springs (Nivarox) and special alloys (Nivaflex). Both companies produced watch components using special steel alloys. In addition, Straumann was the owner and CEO of Tschudin + Heid, a machinery component manufacturer located in Waldenburg where the Straumann family lived[2] (Exhibit 20.1).

When the Straumann organization became a full-fledged producing partner of the AO, as co-signer of the Synthes AG Chur producer agreement, the company did not have an operating factory or capacity for implants. Within a short period of time, a manufacturing capacity needed to be created from scratch and also located in

---

[1]The full name was 'Institut Dr. Ing. Reinhard Straumann,' afterwards referred to as Institute in our text.

[2]Tschudin + Heid goes back to an initial operation in 1892; it continues to operate until today producing components for various industries.

© Springer Nature Switzerland AG 2019
J.-P. Jeannet, *Leading a Surgical Revolution*,
https://doi.org/10.1007/978-3-030-01980-8_20

Exhibit 20.1   Tschudin + Heid in Waldenburg. *Source: Thomas Straumann. Reprinted with permission*

Waldenburg, home of the Straumann Institute. For the initial market introduction period, Mathys supplied Straumann with the needed implants for the Straumann markets but it did not take a long time until Straumann was ready to commence production.

The Straumann organization was more than just a metallurgical research institute. Founder Reinhart Straumann was heading the operations of Tschudin + Heid, in Waldenburg, and the original business of Reinhard Straumann's in-laws. Tschudin + Heid produced watch industry components.[3] In connection with the two technical developments Nivaflex and Nivarox, both targeted at the watch industry and partially owned by Reinhard Straumann, a considerable amount of manufacturing experience for demanding components had been accumulated at the company. The Straumann organization in Waldenburg was, at that time, still small, with 40–60 employees involved with the research institute. The manufacturing of parts to exacting standards in specialty steel was Reinhard Straumann's expertise, a fact that helped him to quickly get on top of the manufacturing challenges for the AO *Instrumentarium* (Exhibit 20.2).

---

[3]Tschudin + Heid goes back to an initial operation in 1892 and continues to operate to this day producing components for various industries. The privately-held company is based in Waldenburg.

Exhibit 20.2 Reinhard
Straumann. *Copyright by AO
Foundation, Switzerland*

Fritz Straumann Steps In

When Reinhard Straumann met Willenegger in 1960 to discuss the AO corrosion issues, he quickly appointed his son Fritz to head the investigation into its cause. Throughout the entire collaboration between Straumann and the AO, Fritz Straumann assumed the lead. As a result, he was a participant in the first AO course in Davos and represented the Straumann interests on the AOTK, its technical committee, created to steer the collaboration (Exhibit 20.3).

Both AO producers Mathys and Straumann were of additional help to quickly get on top of the manufacturing challenges. Since the *Instrumentarium* needed to be identical, Straumann had to take the same equipment on board as Mathys had, and thus did not have to create an entire manufacturing process from scratch. Rather, it was a matter of correctly duplicating the production methods pioneered by Mathys.

The Straumann organization had two specific roles to play in the context of the sharing with Mathys. First, due to its depth of knowledge in the area of metallurgy, Straumann served for many years as the purchasing office for metallic materials, stainless steel, and later titanium for both companies. Second, Straumann assumed the Mathys sales office when it was transferred from Biel, at the time Violette Müller, Maurice Müller's sister and long-time office and logistics manager,

Exhibit 20.3 Fritz
Straumann at AO Davos
course, 1969. *Copyright by
AO Foundation, Switzerland*

remarried. It was from Waldenburg that shipments were made to the Swiss hospitals because the Swiss market had been allocated to Straumann in the Olten deal.

As the Straumann organization continued to grow, Straumann reorganized its operation in Waldenburg and transferred the Synthes/AO Implant Unit into a separate business unit, referred to as Straumann Medical, still part of the Straumann Research Institute. The metallurgical research operations were also part of the Institute, as well as the watch component companies in Waldenburg and in the Jura.

Even before the Straumann organization joined up with the AO, the Straumann Institute had moved into new quarters in Waldenburg in 1957. In 1973–1974, Straumann occupied a new building there, the *Unteres Gebäude*, which became dedicated to the AO implant production. Financing of the expansion was accomplished through internal resources aided by the steady stream of licensing incomes from the Nivaflex and Nivarox metal alloy patents. The difference with the Mathys organization is apparent: the Straumanns had a going and profitable business to fund their institute research and the implant production, while Mathys needed to rely on internal funds directly generated from the implant production. Straumann was already a successful entrepreneur and industrialist when he teamed up with the AO, whereas Mathys was still on his way to becoming one.

In the early phase of the Straumann/AO production, the organization was perceived by those who worked there as being a mix of different talents, with a variety of specialist craftsman, skilled in producing prototypes for all kinds of applications. They were not organized along the lines of modern manufacturing enterprises. Physicists and metallurgists worked next to mechanics and machinists. This kind of work environment suited the free-flowing minds of both Reinhard Straumann and Fritz Straumann, who took over the entire Waldenburg operation after Reinhard's death. Accounting and record-keeping of the divergent operations where not separated in clear cost accounting modes. It was in this environment that the resolution of the AO implant corrosion issue could happen because it was supportive of both collaboration across multiple disciplines and lateral thinking.[4]

Expanding Straumann Internationally

International sales were developed and supported with foreign sales subsidiaries, or distributors similar to the Mathys operation. Offices were created throughout the assigned Straumann 'territories,' covering most of Latin America and including Argentina, Bolivia, Brazil, Chile, Columbia, Ecuador, Mexico, Paraguay, Peru, and Venezuela. In Europe, Straumann built operations in Germany South with its offices in Freiburg, as well as in the Czech Republic, Hungary, Greece, Great Britain, Ireland, Norway, Poland, Portugal, Spain, and Sweden.[5]

The US market, also allocated to Straumann in the previously reported Olten agreement, took some time to develop. Initially, Straumann assigned Smith Kline French (SK), a large US-based pharma company, as its US distributor, with all supplies shipped from Switzerland. After a slow start and disappointing results, the Straumann organization relinquished the sales rights to the US territory to the AO but kept the right to act as the implant supplier. The experience behind the US market development will be reported in the following chapter.

By the mid-1980s, Synthes AG Chur received research contributions from Straumann, in a range of about 80% of the contributions earned from Mathys. By 1984, Straumann contributions reached about CHF 4 million annually, smaller than the CHF 5.6 million reported by Mathys. This difference was partly attributed to the fact that once Synthes USA became independent of Straumann in 1977, the US revenue was no longer included in the figures Straumann reported.

Straumann Industrial and Technological Impact

Parallel to the build-up of Straumann's AO business, Fritz Straumann had undertaken the early developments of dental implants through Straumann Institute. This culminated in 1974 with the first successful clinical testing at the University of Berne, and the creation of the International Team of Implantology (ITI) in 1980, with the aid of Professor André Schroeder. This collaboration, which benefited from the Straumann experience with AO implants, was later to become the basis of the Straumann Institute's dental implant business and a successful international spin-off, which we shall review later on in more detail (see Chap. 49).

Given the diverse technical nature of the skills housed under the Institute's umbrella, the Straumann contribution to AO's development went beyond production

---

[4]Based upon interviews with Ortun Pohler and Margrit Jaques, two long-serving Straumann employees who worked in Waldenburg at that time.

[5]Schlich (2002), p. 165.

and sales. The Straumann technical staff played important roles in the development of various AO projects and were also, as will be seen later, at the forefront of the AO expansion into the veterinary sector (see Chap. 24).

Reference

Schlich, T. (2002). *Surgery, science, and industry* (p. 165). Basingstoke: Palgrave Macmillan.

The Experience in Europe

With the advent of selling the AO *Instrumentarium* publicly, and the resolution of dividing world markets between the instrument producers Mathys and Straumann, an earnest effort was undertaken to market the products outside Switzerland. The first efforts to find adopters abroad was concentrated in Germany and Austria, two countries where the AO surgeons maintained extensive professional contacts. Characteristically, both countries had extensive hospital networks dealing with accidents and trauma. However, *Unfallchirurgin* (trauma surgeons) in the leading trauma centers in both countries had to be convinced. This did not happen overnight.

Building a Beachhead in Germany

The Küntscher nailing technique had already been adopted in Germany. Typically, this combined the conservative fracture treatment involving plaster with a stretch bed. The AO method of internal fixation met with an extensive, and at times emotional, rejection on the part of the leading German trauma surgeons. If sales of AO implants and tools were to increase, this resistance had to be overcome.

Similar to what had taken place earlier in Switzerland, there was intense debate about the pros and cons of conservative versus operative trauma treatment. The leading German trauma surgeon and head of the world's oldest trauma hospital, Heinrich Bürkle de la Camp (1895–1974) gave the keynote speech at the annual German Surgical Conference in Munich in April 1960. He reiterated his support for the medullary nailing technique but warned his colleagues of dangerous methods of introducing "foreign objects" into the human body in order to deal with trauma. This

© Springer Nature Switzerland AG 2019
J.-P. Jeannet, *Leading a Surgical Revolution*,
https://doi.org/10.1007/978-3-030-01980-8_21

address was followed up by Lorenz Böhler (from Vienna) who labeled Osteosynthesis as one of the most dangerous methods to treat bone trauma.[1]

Against this backdrop of hostility, AO surgeons were able to use their own personal contacts to avoid a confrontational meeting as the ones held in Switzerland. AO co-founder Willenegger, who headed the Liestal hospital not far from the German border, was in close contact with Professor Ludwig Heilmeyer from the University of Freiburg. They collaborated on issues of blood transfusion. Through this contact, Heilmeyer probably connected Willenegger with the Chair for Surgery, Professor Hermann Krauss. An invitation was issued for Willenegger and Müller to attend the Southwestern German Trauma Association, held just prior to the above-cited, larger meeting held in Munich and they were able to address the meeting on the principles of operative fracture treatments. From Willenegger's hospital, seven recently operated patients were brought in so they could demonstrate their mobility to all those present. Krauss was impressed and dispatched his senior intern Leo Koslowski to the next AO meeting in Interlaken to learn more about the AO philosophy, with other guests from that Freiburg meeting also attending. Just months later, Krauss and one of his interns, Siegfried Weller, joined in the first AO course in Davos.

Given the AO rules on the supply of *Instrumentarium*, it was difficult to provide sufficient supplies directly to the Freiburg Hospital. AO rules stipulated that only surgeons who were trained by the AO, for example those who attended their courses in Davos, could order implants. Because Weller had attended the first course in Davos, he became the go-between for implants by personally shuttling back and forth between Waldenburg, the base of the Straumann operation, and Freiburg, transporting sets, implants, screws, and X-rays in his car across the German–Swiss border. This shuttling of supplies came to an end when Straumann, who was responsible for the Southern German market according to the country allocation, opened a sales office in Freiburg in 1963.

These intensive contacts led to Freiburg becoming AO's first beachhead in Germany, and to the University Hospital there becoming the first German 'AO Hospital.' During the 1959–1960 period, there were 177 Osteosynthesis operations performed in the Freiburg Surgical Clinic. By 1967–1968, this had risen to 1261. Weller went on to become President of the AO Foundation from 1994 to 1996.[2] Freiburg was also the location for the first AO course conducted outside of Switzerland in 1965.[3]

From this first beachhead in Freiburg, the AO philosophy was carried through personal contacts and movements of surgeons to other German hospitals. The first important move was Jörg Rehn who went from Freiburg to Bochum where he assumed the position previously held by Bürkle de le Camp, a vocal opponent of the AO philosophy. Given the importance of Bochum, Mathys selected the city as

---

[1]Kuner (2015), pp. 153–154.
[2]Heim (2001), pp. 68–69.
[3]Schlich (2002), p. 70.

the location for its Northern German offices, within the region allocated to his company.

More important were the moves of several AO supporters to Mainz where two surgeons from Freiburg—Fritz Kümmerle and Carl Heinz Schweikert—assumed positions in 1963, followed by Fritz Brussatis in 1969 who returned to Germany, the only non-Swiss member of AO's founding group.

The diffusion of the AO philosophy in Germany followed different patterns when compared to Switzerland. In Switzerland the surgical skills to apply the AO techniques were disseminated and taught through an independent network of autonomous surgeons practicing in mostly regional hospitals. However, in Germany the diffusion took place through junior surgeons from key hospitals, such as in Freiburg. It is interesting to note that Krauss, an early supporter of the AO in Freiburg and head of that clinic, fully supported the AO method but never applied it personally in surgery. Osteosynthesis was carried out by junior surgeons that had initially been trained in Switzerland.

Building a Second Beachhead in Austria

To establish the AO philosophy in Austria was no small task. Lorenz Böhler, often referred to as the 'Pope of Traumatology,' was the country's dominant figure, well entrenched throughout Austria's network of specialized accident units. Müller had made earlier visits in 1958 to introduce the Austrian medical community to his idea of Osteosynthesis. At that time, most surgeons were highly skeptical. By chance, Jörg Böhler, Lorenz Böhler's son, was exposed to an AO presentation in Freiburg. He, together with other young Austrian surgeons, was among the first to attend the Davos courses and carry the message back to Austria.

Even more important was the visit by a young Austrian surgeon, Harald Tscherne from Graz, who met up with the AO philosophy while visiting Bochum in 1963. He obtained the support of Franz Spath, his head of surgery in Graz, who dispatched his son to check out Müller, then Chief Surgeon in St. Gallen, to see if he was good enough to operate on his daughter. Coming back with glowing reports, the entire Graz Hospital converted to the AO philosophy and within less than four years had carried out almost 1000 Osteosynthesis procedures.

Similar to the trend in Germany, the encouragement for adopting the AO philosophy came from a head surgeon who was not normally involved in fracture care and left this type of intervention to younger physicians. Through such active support, it was Graz, not Vienna, that became the AO's Austrian beachhead. By 1982, more than 200 Austrian surgeons had attended Davos courses. Eventually, all of the more than 50 independent accident hospitals in Austria were adherents of the AO philosophy. Austria was part of the Mathys sales territory; the company established a subsidiary there in 1963 and a production plant in Salzburg for the production of surgical tools.

By 1984, the market share for Synthes AG Chur and AO-branded implants was estimated at 80% in Germany, 90% in Austria, 70% in Belgium, 50% in France, and

10% in Italy.[4] No figures were reported for Switzerland, but one can safely assume that the share was also about the same level as Austria or Germany.

Forming a Beachhead in Canada

The expansion of the AO philosophy into Canada followed a pattern resembling some of the core European countries: a cluster of interested surgeons became converts to the AO method and the message emanated from there. Toronto was the center of this Canadian concentration, and some of the early adopters of the AO philosophy played an important role in the future development of the Foundation, not only in Canada but worldwide. Two of them stand out: Marvin Tile and Joseph Schatzker, both assuming the presidency of the AO Foundation from 1992 to 1994 and 1998 to 2000, respectively. Tile came into contact with the AO during a fellowship in London in 1965 when it was recommended that he see "a man named Maurice Müller in St. Gallen." He did just that. Tile attended the AO course in Davos in 1968 and returned to help with the first AO course in North America, held in 1969 for residents in the Toronto area.[5]

While still a young resident in Toronto in 1965, Schatzker came in touch with the AO surgeons; he remembers a lecture held by Müller in front of a large audience explaining the AO philosophy of fracture treatment. At the time, Müller did not speak English fluently and Schatzker was sitting in front with a large stick, translating slides; he recalls a comment at the end of the session from one of the most senior trauma surgeons in Canada, a group generally attached to the UK school of conservative fracture treatment, who got up and said, "Professor Müller, you may be famous, but you are the biggest liar!"[6] This was the kind of reception AO surgeons received early on in Canada, something that changed very quickly and which was in no small part due to the work of Schatzker and Tile.

Schatzker also attended the Davos course in 1967 and soon became involved in the translation of the leading AO textbook into English, followed by a second book that he wrote with Tile, "because the initial book did not have any explanations."[7] To establish the validity of the AO philosophy, Schatzker asked other trauma surgeons to send them their failures. In two years, Schatzker had dealt successfully with about 40 difficult cases, which he presented, in an open meeting to other trauma and Orthopedic surgeons. This event very much helped convert the more traditional Toronto surgical community to the AO philosophy, culminating in the first AO course held there.

The successful work of the Canadian AO adherents not only paved the way for the AO in Canada but those surgeons also attended many conferences in the United

---

[4]Schlich (2002), p. 165.
[5]Interview with Marvin Tile conducted on 9 December, 2016, in Davos.
[6]Interview with Joseph Schatzker conducted on 9 December, 2016, in Davos.
[7]Schatzker and Tile (1967).

States, helping to turn the tide there. James Kellam, from Toronto where much of the activity was centered, had trained with Tile and Schatzker and became the third Canadian president of the AO from 2004 to 2006. The massive size of the US market with its many centers of excellence in Orthopedic surgery made the market entry much more difficult (see Chap. 22).

References

Heim, U. F. A. (2001). *Das Phänomen AO*. Mannheim: Huber.
Kuner, E. H. (2015). *Vom Ende einer qualvollen Therapie im Streckverband* (pp. 153–154). Köln: Kaden.
Schatzker, J., & Tile, M. (1967). *The rationale of operative fracture care*. Berlin: Springer.
Schlich, T. (2002). *Surgery, science and industry*. Basingstoke: Palgrave Macmillan.

Cracking the US Market

22

Establishing a Foothold in North America[1]

Progress in the North American markets, particularly in the US, moved much slower for AO than it did in Europe. The adoption of the AO philosophy had usually occurred through contacts in the medical community, in addition to the recruiting of eager surgeons committed to the new technique. The entire US market and Canada had been allocated to Straumann, as part of the Olten agreement, but if the AO methodology were not adopted by a sufficient number of surgeons, sales of implants would be very slow.

On the surgical front in the US, there was also widespread skepticism towards Osteosynthesis. In 1960 the president of the American Orthopaedic Association went on record warning against it; the prevailing attitude at the time was 'keep the fractures closed.'

Müller made his first trip to the US in the summer of 1959, just a few months after the establishment of the AO. He travelled by boat, at the invitation of an American surgeon he had met in Europe. Upon arriving in New York, and without a prior appointment, Müller visited the head of Columbia University's Orthopedic department, who was so impressed by Müller's slide documentation that he spontaneously called many of his surgical friends across the US to arrange for visits on the spot. Thus, Müller was introduced to many of the leading Orthopedic hospitals; he gave 27 lectures in all and by the time he left to return to Switzerland, he had also been invited to the well-known International Society of Orthopaedic Surgery and Traumatology (SICOT) conference to be held in New York in 1960.[2]

Returning to SICOT in September of 1960, Müller was confronted with the skeptical attitudes of leading Orthopedic surgeons from both the US and the UK. At

---

[1]Schlich (2002), pp. 180–195.
[2]Schatzker (2018), pp. 93–94.

© Springer Nature Switzerland AG 2019
J.-P. Jeannet, *Leading a Surgical Revolution*,
https://doi.org/10.1007/978-3-030-01980-8_22

this time, however, another critical contact was made that was to influence the development of the AO in the States. Howard Rosen (1925–2000), practiced at a New York hospital and had a friend who was also an Orthopedic surgeon. The latter's elderly uncle, a tennis enthusiast, had experienced a non-union of his humerus (upper arm). After four failed surgeries, no one in the US seemed to be able to help. After looking at the X-rays, Müller told them to "bring him to Switzerland and his arm will be healed in no time, and within three months he will be playing tennis again." Shortly thereafter, the elderly patient went to Switzerland and Müller performed the operation. Upon returning to the US with a plate in his arm, Müller made Rosen responsible for the local follow-up; he was so impressed with the operation results that he and his friend Herbert Sandick signed up for the first Davos course in December 1960. They returned home with full sets of the AO *Instrumentarium* in their suitcases.

What happened after this illustrates the uphill fight the AO experienced in the US. The head surgeon at Rosen's hospital would not allow him to use the *Instrumentarium* and also prohibited him from doing so for several years. Rosen turned to his veterinary friends and found a good use of the AO *Instrumentarium* in veterinary surgery, gaining experience with their use in that way. This also made Rosen a founding member of what was to become later AOVET—AO's global network of surgeons, scientists and other specialists in the field of veterinary surgery of the musculoskeletal system.

Surgeons as Marketers in the US

During the SICOT Conference in New York, Müller got acquainted with representatives of Howmedica, a US company active in the implant business. Following further discussions, Müller agreed to leave one set of the AO *Instrumentarium* and, with a handshake, granted them the right to make six copies. If no sales occurred, the company promised to destroy the sets. When Müller returned two years later, he got in touch with the company to ask about progress in marketing the AO *Instrumentarium*. As far as he could determine, they made excellent copies, some were successfully used by US surgeons, but the company had decided to stop distribution out of fear that they could be subject to lawsuits in case of failures. As promised, Howmedica company had destroyed all of their copies.

An editorial published in the US *Journal of Trauma* a few years later illustrated the issues the AO was confronted with when introducing US surgeons to the AO philosophy.

According to Thomas Schlich:

The AO created a serious problem in the development of their technique, due primarily to the excellency of their surgery and the precision of their instruments. They are master surgeons who have spent years in developing their technique. They have perfected a beautiful set of instruments and use them with great skill. As a result, every young surgeon interested in fracture treatment becomes intrigued with the instruments and wishes to try them out immediately in his own hospital. This, then, is the problem. The beginner can no more hope quickly to emulate the work of these surgeons than a week-end skier can successfully duplicate the efforts of a champion Olympic skier.[3]

This shows how senior surgeons were intimidated by the AO procedures but that younger ones were still eager to try. However, the network and support and training that had been built in Switzerland was missing in the US, heightening the risk of failures.

Creating Synthes USA

This period was the end of Müller's direct engagement with the US market as he became totally immersed with hospital duties in St. Gallen and was already planning a move to the University Hospital Inselspital Berne. He was more than happy to leave further development of the US market to Martin Allgöwer, an AO co-founder who had had experience in the US during his early training. He worked with Straumann on developing this important market. Straumann appointed Smith, Kline & French (SKF), a pharmaceutical company based in Philadelphia, to be its distributor in the US.

At the same time, the AO was faced with issues surrounding its abbreviation and brand name. As it turned out, a US company, American Optical, had already registered AO for its company name abbreviation. In order to avoid unnecessary litigation, the AO decided to use the term ASIF (Association for the Study of Internal Fixation) for the US.[4]

Development of the US market continued at a very slow pace. SKF successfully organized a charter flight for US surgeons to attend the Davos course.[5] The pharma company also complained to the AO about delivery and supply issues from Switzerland, despite very low sales, averaging around USD 400,000 annually. Even the creation of a beginner set to reduce initial entry costs for hospitals did not sufficiently turn demand around. Capacity constraints of both producers in Switzerland continued and when the newly developed DCP plate generation was introduced in 1972, Straumann could not keep up with the US market demand.

In 1974, the core Swiss AO group, led by Allgöwer, and the other shareholders of Synthes AG Chur, decided to join with Straumann and form their own company, Synthes USA, by discontinuing the distribution arrangement with SKF. Synthes USA, however, did not have any distribution or sales activity of its own in the country, and given the size of the market, the already low sales had declined and losses began to pile up. The local Synthes USA management was arguing with the Swiss surgeon shareholders about the need for a sales force, as well as being

[3]From Schlich (2002), p. 183, citing a 1970 editorial in the *Journal of Trauma* by Watts.
[4]Schlich (2002), p. 186.
[5]Telephone Interview with Jim Gerry conducted on 18 April, 2017.

equipped with cars, neither of which had been necessary in building the European market.

Ownership of Synthes USA, as well as the operations in Canada and in Mexico, was held with ASIF Holding, a Zurich-incorporated company allowing the names of AO surgeon shareholders to be kept confidential. Originally capitalized with CHF 700,000, the capital investment had to be successively increased to make up for the accumulating losses. The shareholders were the AO founders and TK members Müller, Allgöwer, Willenegger, and Schneider, as well as Fritz Straumann (it was his market after all). Mathys, without any rights to the North American markets, was not a shareholder. Over time, a few others joined but it remained a closed affair.[6]

Straumann continued with the exclusive arrangement to supply the venture from its Swiss plant, and Synthes USA became the exclusive distributor for the US. This was the third time that AO surgeons had had to inject capital into one of their companies. The first was to capitalize the AO Research Institute; the second time when creating Synthes AG Chur, and now Synthes USA required start-up capital, as well as a subsequent infusion of cash.

It was not until August 1975 that the negotiations with SKF came to an end and the payments for existing inventory were negotiated. For a total of USD 196,000 newly-formed Synthes Ltd. USA acquired all remaining inventory from SKF. The trademark DCP was transferred from SKF to Synthes AG Chur.[7]

To run the US operation, the AO surgeons hired a manager from Protek Canada, the Müller-owned distributor of his hip implants which went through the DePuy Company for Canada and the US. Jim Gerry, who had been part of the earlier SKF effort, came back as marketing manager. When sales were slow to develop and losses continued to pile up, Müller loaned the company funds from his Protek hip implant business to tide it over. The real breakthrough, however, came through a chance meeting between Allgöwer and a passenger on a transatlantic flight.

Enter Hansjörg Wyss

Martin Allgöwer and Hansjörg Wyss connected through their passion for flying private planes. In 1975, working for Monsanto, the US Company, and based in Brussels, Wyss had developed a side business selling US private planes to European individuals. One of those people was Allgöwer who had acquired a pilot's license. Through this contact, Allgöwer approached Wyss with some questions about Synthes USA because Wyss seemed to have considerable management experience. Wyss, however, was cautious and did not want to jump into this right away. He became a part-time consultant to the venture, working on the Synthes USA

[6]Interview Margrit Jaques, Honorary AO Foundation Board Member and author of TK Minutes from 1971 to 1991, conducted on 27 May, 2018, in Lausanne.
[7]Letter to shareholders of Synthes USA dated 26 August, 1975, issued by Margrit Jaques, secretary to the Synthes Board.

Exhibit 22.1 Hansjörg
Wyss, 2004. *Copyright by AO*
Foundation, Switzerland

management and budgeting systems, and meeting regularly with local managers. It took some two years before Wyss committed to take over as the full-time manager. At that time, Synthes USA had a staff of about 25 people and annual sales of USD 3 million (Exhibit 22.1).

Initially, Wyss acquainted himself with all the intricacies of trauma and Orthopedic surgery. Prior to accepting the responsibility for Synthes USA, he also posed some conditions that he thought were necessary to ramp up the company in order to be successful in the US market. Specifically, Wyss first wanted to become co-investor, and second, he asked for a commitment from the AO to offer at least two basic courses in the US, annually, over the next ten years.[8]

Wyss anticipated that it would take about five years to reach a profitable sales level. With supplies from Switzerland at high prices compared to local alternatives, Wyss insisted that a production plant be built in the US to serve the North American market. This could not happen without changing the existing contractual and exclusive arrangements struck between Synthes AG Chur in Switzerland and Straumann as exclusive producer for the US market, in addition to Synthes USA with exclusive sales rights in the US. At a contested board meeting for Synthes USA, held in Europe, Wyss got his way and received the go-ahead to open a factory which he located in the state of Colorado. Production commenced in 1979.

Although Robert Mathys, Sr., was not involved with the US market, he had repeatedly made it known that, if he were Straumann, he would build a factory there himself. As events unfolded, Straumann yielded the entire North American market to the newcomer Wyss, with only a minimal financial participation through co-ownership in Synthes USA. This turned out to be a pivotal moment in the development of the US market.

---

[8]Hansjörg Wyss invested CHF 400,000 into Synthes USA when joining (Source: Interview with Hansjörg Wyss, conducted on 2 December, 2017).

Through courses and the granting of many young surgeon fellowships, sales increased. By 1980, the US operation was still not out of the woods yet. At a board meeting, Wyss proposed a number of changes in the marketing operation that went counter to what was done by AO producers in Europe. One of those suggestions was to create a direct sales force, paid partially on commission, which led to a heated board meeting. Wyss eventually got his way with the support of some of the other AO shareholders and Müller, who had argued against these practices, ultimately lost the argument. This was an important moment for the future development of the relationship between Wyss and Müller: Müller later complained about his loss of influence, as, in his view, one of his closest friends and partner, Allgöwer, seemingly succumbed to Wyss' influence.[9] With the entrance of Wyss into the AO organization, and the resulting shifts of alliances among its founders, a process began that eventually led to Müller's disengagement and finally, his resignation from the AO board. Business arguments held more weight than personal ones.

The results of the new US market strategy were encouraging. From a low of only USD 2.2 million in 1975, growth finally picked up and sales reached USD 13 million in 1980, increasing by 15–20% every year and reaching USD 30 million in 1984. Similar trends could be observed in the payments of licensing fees, which were now also paid by Synthes USA on its US production volume. By 1984, the US operation paid about CHF 2 million in licensing fees to Synthes AG Chur, the holder of all AO-related IP, compared to Straumann with CHF 4 million and Mathys with CHF 5.6 million. In 1982, employment at Synthes USA reached 183. It was not until the early 1990s, however, that the US operation surpassed both Mathys and Straumann in sales and licensing revenue generation and thus becoming the most important revenue source for the AO.

Jim Gerry, who witnessed the growth of Synthes USA close up from his position as marketing manager, observed that the astounding growth was largely due to the change in sales models. The Synthes sales force was highly trained in trauma and Orthopedic surgery; they were also more technically proficient than competing sales forces, spent considerable time supporting surgeons in the operating rooms, and were on call all the time. By doing this, they did not serve merely as a traditional sales force but became friends and associates of the surgeons. Gerry explained, "We revolutionized trauma surgery in the US."[10]

Cracking the US market was the most difficult part of AO's building a global sales network. While producers Mathys and Straumann had established either fully-owned sales companies or distributors in all of their assigned countries, the size of the US market posed special problems. It was not sufficient to establish the AO ideas only through courses held in Davos. And in the end, it did require a dedicated operation that visited surgeons and hospitals on a regular basis. Wyss was the first to

---

[9]Schatzker (2018), pp. 128–129.
[10]Telephone interview with Jim Gerry, Synthes executive (retired in 2008), conducted on 18 April, 2017.

realize this and with Synthes USA eventually accomplished the company's strategic objectives.

Now, there were three producers for the AO to contend with.

References

Schatzker, J. (2018). *Maurice E. Müller: In his own words*. Davos: AO Foundation.
Schlich, T. (2002). *Surgery, science and industry*. Basingstoke: Palgrave Macmillan.

Expanding the *Instrumentarium*

23

Continuous Improvement Process of the *Instrumentarium*

The AO *Instrumentarium* was subjected to a continuous improvement cycle over the first 20 years of its use. The driving force of this continuous development was the AOTK, its Technical Commission, where all important decisions concerning the *Instrumentarium* and surgical methods were made. However, in parallel, there was important work taking place at the AO Research Center in Davos that, at times, was supporting the practice, while at other times also generated improvements in implants as a result of new scientific insights.

The two producing companies represented by Robert Mathys, Sr., (the Mathys company) and Fritz Straumann (the Straumann company) also contributed as they gained more and more experience with implants and materials. Likewise, at the Institute Straumann in Waldenburg, important work in material science generated new insights to the material composition of the AO implants.

When the AO went public with its first set of the *Instrumentarium*, there were about 200 items combined into different surgical tool boxes. Twenty years later, there were more than 1400 different items.

As always, the AO did not operate as a single, closed, organizational entity. It functioned as a collection of different players, all located in various communities and working for different organizations or companies without co-location, independent of each other but working in unison for a single purpose and toward a common goal of achieving better clinical results for patients. Using terms of modern management, the AO worked as a self-managed team and was held together by their common purpose, without the presence of a chief executive officer (CEO).

© Springer Nature Switzerland AG 2019
J.-P. Jeannet, *Leading a Surgical Revolution*,
https://doi.org/10.1007/978-3-030-01980-8_23

First Generation of *Instrumentarium* Centered on Round Hole Plates

The first generation *Instrumentarium* was created under the aegis of the AO philosophy—achieve absolute stability and combine that with pressure on the bone to maximize healing. The implant designs reflected this understanding. The central plate of this period was the compression plate (CP) with round holes and screws. These pressure plates came in narrow, broad, long, and short versions, as well as in the form of a tubular semi-pipe plate issued in 1963 (Exhibit 23.1).[1]

Initially, the *Instrumentarium* came in five color coded 'cassettes,' or aluminum boxes, that contained all the necessary shapes and forms of implants, screws, and surgical instruments for the main procedures listed below:

1. Cassette for screws (corticalis [red] and spongia [red/yellow]), developed by Müller
2. Cassette for plates (yellow), developed by Müller
3. Cassette for hip plates (blue), developed by Müller
4. Cassette for medullary drilling (green), developed by Müller
5. Cassette for medullary nailing, developed by Müller, Allgöwer, and Weber (introduced in 1963)

This initial standard *Instrumentarium* was used in the first Davos courses in 1960 and 1961, predating the creation of the TK. The use was primarily intended for long bone fractures to the upper and lower leg. Over time, additional cassettes for other types of fractures were added (Exhibit 23.2).

Compression and tension devices, developed by Müller, were used to apply temporary pressure on bone fragments prior to applying a plate and screws. In annual or semi-annual steps, the AOTK approved additional elements of plates for specific purposes and situations and made them available for distribution.

Exhibit 23.1   Round hole plate, 1958–1959. *Copyright by AO Foundation, Switzerland*

---

[1]Müller et al. (1963), p. 54.

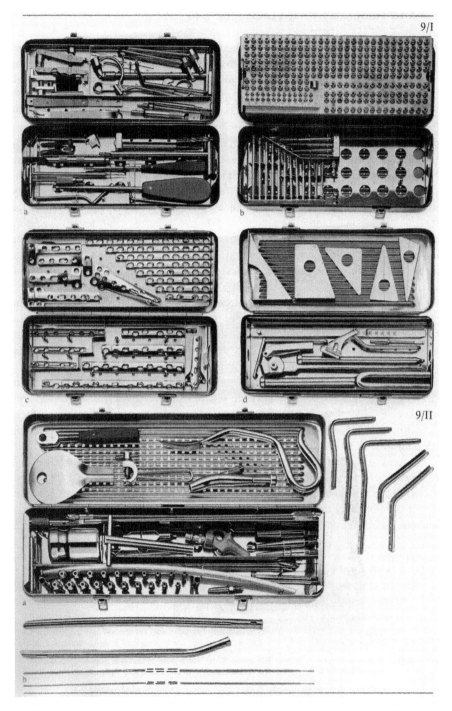

Exhibit 23.2 AO *Instrumentarium* layout. *Source: AO Technik der Operativen Frakturenbehandlung, Springer, 1977, p. 21*

Second Generation with DCP Plates (1966)

The development of the dynamic compression plate (DCP) was a major improvement in the AO *Instrumentarium* and had its roots in the observations made by Stephan Perren, a bioengineer, who had joined the AO research group in Davos from his previous assignment in the Chur hospital.[2]

Ever since the creation of the AO Research Institute (ARI) in Davos, scientists had been investigating the impact of pressure on bone healing. This research stream, which allowed the AO to demonstrate that pressure had a positive influence on bone healing, was based upon the development of a special device built into a standard round hole plate. The AO research method of applying the plate and screws to the fracture relied on a removable tension device. With the small measuring device inserted, the research team realized that even during the initial application of the tension device, substantial variations in pressure occurred. Further investigation showed that even experienced surgeons could not always achieve the required compression with the tension device and round hole plates. Perren concluded that an elongated form of the plate hole would be able to avoid compression loss (Exhibit 23.3).

Further development work determined that with such a different plate, the standard use of a removable compression device prior to plating would no longer be necessary. Each additional screw in the DCP plate contributed to the tension along the fracture line. Tested by AO co-founder Martin Allgöwer in clinical trials, and patented in 1966,[3] the DCP was initially made available only to AO surgeons and those attending the AO courses; standard sets were later added in 1971, after sufficient experience with them had been accumulated. Eventually, the DCP became a highly versatile plate that could be produced in various sizes, offering the AO an opportunity to develop instruments for surgeons specializing in other anatomic specialties, such as the maxillofacial and veterinary disciplines.

In hindsight, this important development and major addition to the AO *Instrumentarium*, came about as a result of a confluence of events. At first, there was a need to substantiate clinical experience of AO surgeons with compression. The device developed for this test also brought to light that it was difficult for surgeons to achieve sufficient compression regularly. This then led to the creation of the DCP

Exhibit 23.3 Dynamic
compression plates (DCP)

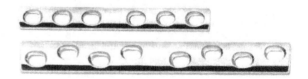

---

[2]Hutzschenreuter et al. (1969), pp. 77–81.
[3]Hutzschenreuter et al. (1969), pp. 77–81.

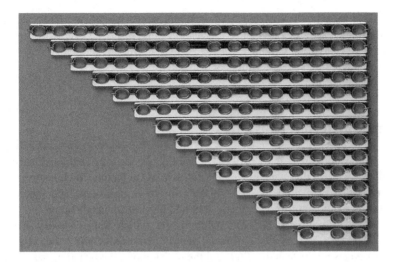

Exhibit 23.4 DCP sets. *Copyright by AO Foundation, Switzerland*

with elongated wholes. This process involved a number of scientists and surgeons with different backgrounds, ranging from biomechanics, engineering, and, of course, surgery. Needless to say, it also required an industry that was able to convert its equipment to the production of this new plate (Exhibit 23.4).

Introduction of Dynamic Hip Screw (DHS) in 1978

The dynamic hip screw was a device that became part of the AO *Instrumentarium* only after extensive debate.[4] Devised initially by Küntscher's instrument designer, it gained considerable traction in the US and was also in use among AO-trained US surgeons. The AO way was to use its angled plates in fractures of the upper end of the femur—the same application as for the DHS. Such angled plates had been part of the AO surgical sets since 1959. AO surgeons considered the easier use of the DHS a sign of 'inferior surgical skills' related to hip surgery. However, when clinical experience indicated that the easier use of DHS resulted in shorter surgery times and fewer complications, combined with the fact that competitors were making inroads, the AO felt compelled to act. Eventually, Straumann collaborated with surgeons in Basel and in the US to develop a device; this development added pressure on the TK to approve it for AO use. The device became both a clinical and a commercial success. The full cassette for DHS was introduced in 1980.

The eventual introduction of the AO-designed DHS demonstrated the flexibility of the AOTK system. New developments from outside the AO could find their way into the system, although usually only after competitive producers had made the first

---

[4]Schlich (2002), p. 204.

move. This early practice of a form of open innovation was always tempered by the need to subject each idea to intensive clinical testing. Many AO surgeons supported this approach and often reminded colleagues that serving the market quickly was not to be considered equal to serving patients safely.

Expanding Surgical Cassettes

Under the leadership of the TK, the AO went about the introduction of successive sets of cassettes, or complete instrument sets, by AO surgeons. Such instrument sets were re-issued in regular intervals to keep the tools up-to-date and incorporated singular innovations or improvements that had been introduced earlier.

The AO differentiated between standard sets, which were re-issued at regular intervals, and specialized sets. Following their initial introduction in the early 1960s, standard sets were reissued in 1969, and the revision of all outstanding sets occurred in 1975. Successive generations of standard sets included any improved implants and surgical instruments.

As the utilization of the AO *Instrumentarium* began to expand to many different fracture types, so did the need to supply different sets. Increasingly, they became very specialized. The following is a list of sets introduced to the market over the first 20 years with their corresponding lead surgeon (where this information is available):

1962 set for nailing (Schneider)
1964 set for small fragments (Heim)
1970 set for vets (small animals)
1971 set for DCP plating
1972 set for instruments for small fragments
1973 set for broken screws (Mathys)
1975 set for external fixator
1976 sets (3) for general instrumentation
1976 set for maxillofacial surgery
1979 set for chisel and pestle
1980 set for small fixator (hand wrists)
1980 set for DHS system
1980 set for *Gewindespanner* (turnbuckle)
1981 set for spongia screws (fully-threaded)
1981 set for screws for US market
1982 set (revised) for small bone fragments
1982 set for screws
1982 set for sterilization
1983 set for cerclage

Multiplying Plate Shapes and Sizes

As the *Instrumentarium* became more specialized, AO surgeons continued to contribute their clinical experience to add an ever-growing number of types of shapes. These shapes, re-issued with the corresponding plate generation, added significantly to the increase of items over time. They included:

Neutralization plates
Angled plates
Tubular plates
Contoured plates
Buttress plates (in many different forms)
Spoon plates
Cloverleaf plates
T-plates
Bridging plates

These plates were also made available in numerous sizes, with different numbers of holes, adding to the number of variations available. As a result, the complexity of the entire *Instrumentarium* continued to grow.

Screws of All Types

Part of the AO *Instrumentarium*, screws performed two major functions: they were designed to either fasten plates onto the bone, or to hold fragments of bone together when they were called lag screws.[5] Screws could be further differentiated by the manner in which they were inserted into the bone and their size, and the type of bone they were intended for. In addition, screws differed by the manner of connecting with a screw driver. Then there were self-tapping screws, which required pre-drilling of a pilot whole before insertion. The non-self-tapping screw required an exact pre-drilling, corresponding to the thread of the screw.

This large number of screw types required the inclusion of up to 150 different screws into a boxed *Instrumentarium* set, constituting more than 50 screw varieties, or models. Needless to say, such a large number of different screws invariably added significantly to manufacturing complexity and the challenge of distribution logistics.

In a research effort that stretched over several years (from 1960 to 1963), scientist Heinz Wagner (University Münster, Germany) tested the various AO screw designs on animal models and confirmed the superiority of the AO screws in both corticalis screws and spongia screws versions.[6] Both of these screw types were part of the

---

[5]Müller et al. (1991), p. 179.
[6]Heim (2001), p. 119. Wagner was nominated a Scientific Member of the AO.

original Maurice Müller designs and considered one of the essential elements of the AO *Instrumentarium*.

Overcoming the Material Challenge

Initially, all implants were made of stainless steel and, as already mentioned, it was the corrosion issue that eventually led to the involvement of the Straumann Institute to develop a special steel treatment to assure consistency in grades.

Early on, research was undertaken at the Straumann Institute and at the AO Research Laboratory in Davos with regard to different materials. Titanium was extensively tested and proven to be well tolerated as an implant material. Commercially available, pure titanium was devoid of any toxic components. With improvements in the titanium alloy composition, it became possible to reach about 90% of the strength of a stainless steel implant, making it a material of choice if the issue was tissue tolerance or immunological complications.

The titanium debate was to go on for some time and also exemplified the differences between the European and US markets. In Europe, initially, concerns with steel implants led to experiments with titanium as a material of choice. Although it had about twice the manufacturing costs when compared to steel, European surgeons observed fewer complications and allergies with titanium. In the US, the view was different. Tests had shown that steel allergies were surface, or skin driven, and did not occur once it had been implanted in the bone. As a result, the US remained largely a 'steel' market, whereas Europe and Asia moved much more forcefully to titanium. Given that the US market for implants eventually outgrew the European markets, stainless steel remained the material most often used in plates and screws.[7]

Expansion into Different Types of Trauma Surgery

The AO *Instrumentarium* experienced further expansion when the AO group added two major groups of surgeons. Expansion into veterinary medicine required the addition of new surgical tools, plates and screws. Even more so, when the AO formed expert groups for maxillofacial (MFC) and spine surgery, entire new sets of implants were added. These were typically smaller in size than the initial standard sets, with smaller plates and screws, and additional surgical tools.

The resulting rapid expansion of individual items came at a time when AO methodology of bone fracture surgery expanded into many different geographies, forcing the AO manufacturing partners to expand output while adding to the variety

---

[7]Source: Robert Frigg, former Head of Synthes Global Development. The latest generations of medullary nails, craniomaxillofacial implants, and spine implants are manufactured from titanium alloys.

of parts. It should not come as a surprise that in some geographies occasional supply problems existed.

Of particular importance were the supply issues to the North American market, originally allocated to the Straumann organization. With the foundation of Synthes USA as the exclusive distributor of Straumann-originated AO implants, supply challenges remained. This was certainly one of the reasons why under the new leadership of Hansjörg Wyss, Synthes USA insisted on being granted permission to produce in the US for their local market. What resulted was a considerable realignment of decision-making power within the American operation, ranging from AO governance to a new constellation among producers of AO implants, as well as changes in the roles of surgeons versus producers as it related to further development of the AO *Instrumentarium*. As the AO approached the mid-1980s, this realignment among surgeons and producers generated conflicts that took years to resolve.

References

Heim, U. F. A. (2001). *Das Phänomen AO*. Mannheim: Huber.
Hutzschenreuter, P., Perren, S. M., Steinemann, S., Geret, V., & Klebl, M. (1969). Effects of rigidity of internal fixation on the healing pattern of osteotomies. *Injury, 1*, 77–81.
Müller, M. E., Allgöwer, M., Schneider, R., & Willenegger, H. (1991). *Manual of internal fixation* (3rd ed.p. 179). Heidelberg: Springer.
Müller, M. E., Allgöwer, M., & Willenegger, H. (1963). *Technik der Operativen Frakturenbehandlung* (p. 54). Berlin: Springer.
Schlich, T. (2002). *Surgery, science and industry* (p. 204). Basingstoke: Palgrave Macmillan.

AOVET: Humans Helping Animals

24

The Animal Lovers Affiliated with the AO[1]

Some of the early AO-affiliated surgeons and entrepreneurs were animal lovers and owned both small and large animals, particularly horses. Among those, two stand out. First, there was August 'Urs' Guggenbühl (1918–2009), a member of the G13 and chief surgeon of the regional hospital in Grenchen from 1957 to 1983. The Hospital Grenchen was also the place where Maurice Müller first took Robert Mathys, Sr., to observe surgeries. 'Guggi,' as his friends called him, had previously trained under Willenegger in Liestal, was a recognized dog lover and known to drive around with his many large dogs in the backseat of his Jaguar convertible. Disappointed with his local veterinarian's surgical skills for dogs, he had set out on his own to teach AO surgical techniques to this veterinarian, at times even carrying out the surgeries himself.

Occasionally, Guggenbühl showed his AO colleagues X-rays of the Osteosynthesis he had performed with his veterinarian. Willenegger, knowing about Fritz Straumann's support of veterinary surgeons, arranged that they meet. Straumann, the second animal lover involved with the AO, was to have a major impact on the AO's connection to veterinary medicine. Straumann owned a number of horses, which he kept on the grounds of the Straumann Villa in Waldenburg and the nearby Bechburg, where the family trained their horses. Dogs were also part of their household.

The meeting with Guggenbühl initiated a fruitful cooperation, eventually leading to the creation of AOVET and the spread of systematic AO Osteosynthesis techniques in the veterinary medical discipline on an international scale.

---

[1]This chapter relies heavily on the AO Publication by Auer and Pohler (2013), as well as extensive chapter reviews and text inserts by Ortrun Pohler and Gerhilde Kása.

© Springer Nature Switzerland AG 2019
J.-P. Jeannet, *Leading a Surgical Revolution*,
https://doi.org/10.1007/978-3-030-01980-8_24

Background to Orthopedic Surgery in Animals

As in human medicine, bone surgery in the veterinary field appeared for several reasons much later than in general surgery on soft tissues and organs. Operative bone repair had been carried out here and there on individual cases in an improvised way, ending very often with complications due to great gaps in understanding the prerequisites for successful Osteosynthesis, analogous to human medicine. With the creation of the AO in 1958, all these issues were investigated systematically resulting in a rapid adoption of the AO principles and techniques, eventually also in animal surgery.

Orthopedic or trauma surgery on animals dates back to the 1940s when knowledge about Küntscher's intramedullary nailing techniques began to be occasionally transferred to animals. Adjustments needed to be made to the size of the nails, but it was largely a transfer of human surgical techniques to animal surgery. One such early surgery in the 1940s involved AO founder Hans Willenegger, who assisted a Swiss veterinarian, Jacques Jenny, with the implantation of a Küntscher nail into the medullary cavity of Kai, Mrs. Willenegger's dog. This story is of significance because it involved one of the founders of the AO, Willenegger, before he even became involved with AO-type Osteosynthesis, and a veterinarian, Jenny, who was to play a significant role in the further development of large animal veterinary surgery in the US. It was Willenegger who supervised and performed with Schenk the early animal experiments in Liestal, which supported the AO with important research findings about bone healing mechanisms as reported earlier (Exhibit 24.1).

Exhibit 24.1 Kai, the dog.
Copyright by AO Foundation,
Switzerland

The Concerned Veterinarian from Berne

There were several chance meetings and events before veterinarians and AO members came together formally. At the Equine Clinic Berne, part of the University of Berne, a practiced and dedicated veterinary surgeon, Björn von Salis, had been concerned about the treatment of injured horses for quite a long time. He had decided to become a veterinarian when, as a boy, he attended a horse jumping event and witnessed one of the horses break a leg; the horse was put down on the spot. He later learned how to anesthetize horses but was never satisfied with the outcome of treatments applied to bone trauma in horses. As part of his desire to earn his doctorate, he moved to the Basel area in the mid-1960s, while continuing to work in a small animal practice nearby. There he met the two veterinarians, Dr. Ferenc Kása ('Feri,' 1935–2017) and Dr. Gerhilde ('Geri') Kása, who continues to practice to this date in their small animal clinic together with their son.

In 1967, Fritz Straumann took his dog to the veterinary practice in Basel where he met von Salis, and through this connection the two became acquainted. Von Salis treated Straumann's dog and often visited the Straumann family, owner of several horses, at their home in Waldenburg, looking after his horses too. When von Salis noticed how extensively Straumann was involved with the AO organization, its Osteosynthesis techniques and implant development, he told Straumann about the lack of adequate fracture treatment for large and small animals and asked him if he could imagine using AO implants and methods for application in large and small animal surgery, and if he would be willing to help explore this. Straumann, who had asked himself the same question before, found this a worthwhile investigation and was willing to support this effort with implants and instruments and to have the needed development work to be carried out in the laboratories and workshops of his Institute.

On the occasion of von Salis' next visit to Waldenburg he brought along a collection of frozen horse bones with fractures that had occurred in natural accidents. Straumann involved Ortrun Pohler, who was working at that time on AO research projects at his Institute and had been occupied since 1960 with resolving issues around broken and corroded implants. Pohler was asked to support the veterinarians to explore the usefulness of AO implants and to develop, where necessary, required equipment, and already on the same day she examined with von Salis the bones brought he had in.

Pohler, von Salis, and Straumann agreed that a systematic weekly working program should commence. Using AO standard *instrumentarium* the collected fractures were stabilized and then tested for load resistance to obtain first indications about their usefulness in Osteosynthesis. X-rays taken with a new mobile ambulance recently developed by von Salis confirmed that available AO *instrumentarium* could work on horse bones for relatively simple fractures, under the condition that the biomechanical principles established by AO for human trauma cases would be obeyed. Complicated fractures would be not treatable with available AO *instrumentarium*. However, for adequate treatment, some elements of the AO *instrumentarium* required modification, and in some instances totally new implants and instruments needed to be developed. Little was known about the bone healing process in large animals at this time, but early clinical cases pointed to a much longer healing time for horses compared to humans.

The Kásas were invited by von Salis who suggested that the AO methodology might also apply to small animals, such as cats and dogs. Being keenly aware of the lack of satisfactory fracture treatments for small animals through their veterinary practice, the Kásas were more than happy to join the effort undertaken at the Straumann Institute in Waldenburg, and they quickly found out that the AO *instrumentarium* could indeed be useful in the treatment of small animals. Their further engagement contributed immensely to the spread of the AO stable internal fixation techniques in small animal bone surgery.

Creating the Waldenburg Circle

There was, however, still one piece of the puzzle missing. Veterinarians, as well as implant designers, had little surgical experience and certainly not with Osteosynthesis. Nevertheless, Pohler and Straumann were both regularly involved with the AO surgeons through their development work and participation in the AOTK, and reached out to Guggenbühl, whom they knew personally through Willenegger.

The veterinarians, the Kásas and von Salis, together with Pohler, Straumann and Guggenbühl, set up a small working group in 1968 that began to meet regularly in Waldenburg on Wednesday afternoons and evenings.[2] Later, some local veterinarians joined the meetings bringing in their problem cases. In these meetings, Guggenbühl assumed the role of instructor teaching the veterinarians how to conduct an effective Osteosynthesis on animals—a surgeon for humans was teaching veterinary surgeons. Every single parameter used in the instruction of the Davos courses applied to Osteosynthesis on animals. Even methods of X-ray techniques and surgical planning were applicable. It was then up to the veterinarians to select the best methods for whichever fracture or type of animal they were treating. Often on weekends and evenings, Guggenbühl attended surgery on patient animals giving instructions.

The Story of a Horse Named Maxlie

In order to test the healing process of Osteosynthesis with implants on a horse, Fritz Straumann saved a horse, Maxlie, from slaughter. Perren, head of ARI, the AO Research Institute in Davos, performed an Osteotomy on the horse, along with two human surgeons—Guggenbühl and Peter Daetwyler—and the veterinarian von

---

[2]Interview with Dr. Gerhilde Kása, AOVET, and Professor Ortrun Pohler, conducted on 24 May, 2018, in Lörrach.

Exhibit 24.2 Surgery on
Maxlie, the horse. *Copyright
by AO Foundation,
Switzerland*

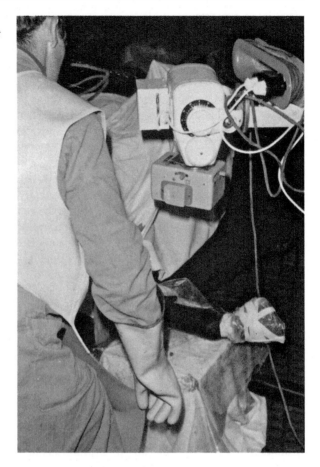

Salis; they were assisted by Fritz Straumann and two of his employees. This
opportunity was used by Perren to test the AO's new titanium plate developed for
humans. And so, it happened that in November 1968, the first two 4.5 mm DCPs in
titanium were applied to a McIII Osteotomy on a horse near von Salis' practice in
Frauenfeld. Again, the transfer of developments between human and animal
implants was a success (Exhibit 24.2).

The fixation remained stable during the full healing time. After healing, the plates
were removed and investigations showed that neither the plates, nor the plate/screw
connections or tissue had any signs of metal loss or degradation. Maxlie enjoyed the
rest of his life without complications and in good care.

Creating AOVET

The group of vets who met informally, beginning in 1967, became generally known as the Waldenburg Circle. The positive and promising results of the experimental work, and the quick healing in the first series of clinical Osteosynthesis cases on dogs and cats created the desire to form an AO-type organization for veterinarians. The AO Board and the AO surgeons acceded to the request for help to create an AO for veterinarians and to assist in the transfer of know-how from human to veterinary surgery.

AOVET was formally created on 31 August, 1969 by Willenegger in Waldenburg, with von Salis as its first president, a position he held until 1980. Pohler was asked to accept the function of secretary. The by-laws were closely patterned after those of the AO with, of course, the necessary changes for membership. Financial and technical support for the development of new implants and organizational needs came first from Straumann. Through Pohler, indirectly and later also directly, AOVET became member of the AOTK, the central coordinating body where all implants and surgical tools were discussed and approved. But for some time, AOVET remained a separate entity legally until later when it became a division of the AO and was supported by the entire organization.

Leveraging Veterinarian Implants for Human AO Implants

The story of the exchange between veterinary and human implants would not be complete without including the necessary development work with regard to the size and shape of implants, particularly, the screws. Because animal bones differ in sizes and structure from human bones, it was soon clear to the Waldenburg team members that the standard AO instrumentation used for human trauma was not entirely suited for animal use. A special DCP was designed. The small cortex screws of 3.5 mm created for veterinary surgery by Pohler also eventually became the standard 3.5 mm cortex screw for human Osteosynthesis as well. Further developments concerned small plates and the use of 2 mm screws.[3] At this point, work on the *Instrumentarium*, the formation of a group of concerned veterinarians, and their relationship with the AO, came full circle.[4]

The process involving this group of scientists and surgeons coming together from different fields at Waldenburg began rather informally. Over time, the processes became ever more scientific and resembled the AO processes in its own implant designs. Fritz Straumann made his own team available, particularly Ortrun Pohler,

---

[3] AOVET Dr. Gerhilde Kása remembered a presentation to AO trauma surgeons in Freiburg on their new mini plates and screws, and the interest expressed by Professor Schilli, resulting in a transfer of this small instrumentation to CMF surgery.

[4] Some of this context was based on interviews with Jörg Auer, AOVET member (conducted in Lenzburg, Switzerland on 25 July, 2017) and Brigitte von Rechenberg, Head of SWISSVET, (conducted by telephone on 4 January, 2018).

Exhibit 24.3 From Great
Danes to small dogs.
Copyright by AO Foundation,
Switzerland

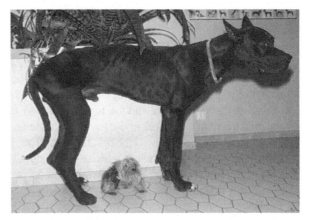

who worked on the design and prototyping of implants. But the time put in by all the participants was essentially voluntary and not compensated, again patterned after the earlier AO experience. The drive was to help animals, and this bound the group together.[5]

The exchange between veterinary and human implants was only possible because of a strict adherence to AO principles. The implants were of the same quality as the human implants, subject to the same stringent controls and manufacturing procedures as implants for humans, and the same materials were being used. Other collaborations between veterinary and human trauma groups included the experience with 2.0 mm screws for small animal surgery. Here, the experience of the Kásas was important because their practice centered around small animals. These implants and screws were later successfully used in craniomaxillofacial (CMF) surgery, as is covered in the next chapter (see Chap. 25). Along the same lines as the adoption of Osteosynthesis in the medical community, the Kásas, with their small animal practice in Lörrach, were ahead of the veterinary practices of animal surgery in German universities, which adopted Osteosynthesis for animals much later. This was not for a lack of interest, but simply because it took time to adapt their internal operating procedures to the demanding AO methodology. Over time, very positive exchanges developed with German universities.

Leveraging AO know-how to animals had its challenges. Most of the AO implants had been tested on sheep. However, the bone structure of sheep is different from that of humans so that compatibility with implant materials could be successfully modeled, but not the proper shape of the implants themselves. The vast range of animal sizes was a significant challenge because implants had to fit large animals, such as large dogs, all the way down to very small animals and even birds (Exhibit 24.3).

---

[5]Interviews with Ortrun Pohler and Gerhilde Kása conducted on 24 May, 2018, in Lörrach.

How a St. Bernard Dog Helps the AOVET Expand into North America

It is safe to assume that many developments of the AO-related expansions were a result of a chance event, or meeting. This was not much different for AOVET. The reason for the group's jump over the Atlantic was owed to the fracture of a femur of a St. Bernard, the most typical and folkloric dog in Switzerland. A veterinarian, Bruce Hohn, practicing in New York and attending to the dog, had heard of Howard Rosen, a US surgeon and participant in the first Davos course. When Hohn contacted Rosen to borrow his *Instrumentarium* to operate on the dog, Rosen suggested that they do the surgery together rather than having Hohn learn the procedures by himself. Through this contact, which resulted in a lifelong friendship, Rosen became close to the US veterinary community. Hohn, together with some other veterinarians from the US, joined the Davos course in 1969, shortly after AOVET was founded.

When Hohn moved to Ohio State University in Columbus, Ohio, he created one of two beachheads for AOVET in the US. The first was hosting an AO course for veterinarians in 1970, with 99 participants. The second was a course created at the University of Pennsylvania where a Swiss veterinarian, Jacques Jenny, was a faculty member who had also assisted Willenegger in 1943 with the very first dog intramedullary nailing. In a way, it developed that AOVET beat the human AO surgeons to the US, with courses and the adoption of the AO philosophy. It would take some time until the AO course about human patients offered in Davos made it across the pond to the US.

Creating Infrastructure for AOVET

Beginning in 1970, regular annual courses were offered, first in Switzerland (Bettlach) and then in the US (Ohio). Courses began to be offered in different languages and publications followed; the organization continued to grow internationally. In 1986, Ferenc Kása established a first AOVET "chapter" in Germany and acted as its president, and the first course in Germany took place in Giessen in 1982.

In order to better coordinate activities, an AOVET Center was established in 1976 in Waldenburg under the direction of Dieter Prieur, a German small-animal specialist, who held the position until his retirement in 1991. For many years, the Straumann Institute organization generously supported the group's need for an office. After Fritz Straumann's death, the office was moved to Zurich in 1992 and was attached to Zurich University when Jörg Auer assumed the role of general secretary. AOVET's further development, beyond the mid-1980s, will be covered later in the book (see Chap. 43).

Reference

Auer, J., & Pohler, O. (2013). *History of AOVET: The first 40 years*. Davos: AO Publication.

The AO Enters Additional Trauma Segments

Until the mid-1970s, much of the activity at the AO was focused on long bone fractures. These were the fractures around which the AO built its initial *Instrumentarium*. Over time, there was an increase of activity that took the AO away from 'long bones only' into other parts of the human skeleton (adult human bodies have 206 bones), namely the craniomaxillofacial (CMF) and spine disciplines, and later also hand and foot.

Entry into CMF Surgery[1]

The use of AO implants in CMF surgery started to develop when a leading CMF surgeon, Professor Bernd Spiessl (1921–2002), moved from Hamburg to Basel in 1966 to be the head of CMF surgery there. Word from Orthopedic and trauma colleagues had spread, increasing interest in the AO methodology among CMF surgeons.

Spiessl brought with him a young surgeon, Joachim Prein, to Basel who was to become a major driver in having AO implants and *Instrumentarium* made accessible for CMF surgery. Prein became involved in research early on through the AO Research Center in Davos where he collaborated with Perren, its head, as well as Berton Rahn and Reinhold Ganz, who was later to play a major role in furthering development of the AO trauma implants.

At about the same time, the AOVET team led by Feri and Geri Kása gave a presentation to a general meeting of AO in Freiburg, Germany, to let them know how

---

[1]This section relies heavily on an interview with Professor Joachim Prein, conducted on 20 March, 2017, in Zurich.

© Springer Nature Switzerland AG 2019
J.-P. Jeannet, *Leading a Surgical Revolution*,
https://doi.org/10.1007/978-3-030-01980-8_25

veterinarians were approaching trauma. As part of that presentation, some of the newly piloted small implants were shown, which piqued the interest of the CMF surgeons—they would finally have access to the type of implants they needed for CMF trauma indications.[2]

At the AO, research was initially conducted on sheep only and the available AO *Instrumentarium* was poorly suited to CMF research on those animals, the plates were too thick. A breakthrough was achieved when Robert Mathys, Sr., came up with a three-dimensional, foldable plate, an accomplishment that Prein later described as simply "ingenious."

By 1974, after the first CMF course in Davos, the AO surgeons began to recognize CMF as a specialty area within trauma, and two years later, the AOTK approved the first CMF *Instrumentarium* set for general distribution. Although Mathys had solved the foldable plate issue, there was more support forthcoming from the Straumann Institute regarding further developments in the area of CMF (Exhibit 25.1).

At the Straumann Institute, Fritz Straumann had begun as early as 1970 with developing and applying AO implants to dental surgery. This interest probably led to a greater affinity to CMF issues. As noted previously (see Chap. 20), 1974 marked a milestone for Straumann; it was the year that he took the dental implants to the

Exhibit 25.1 CMF course practical exercises. *Copyright by AO Foundation, Switzerland*

---

[2]Interview held with Dr. Gerhilde Kása, conducted on 24 May, 2018, in Lörrach.

University of Berne for further development. Eventually, this action would lead Straumann to take a bigger interest in dental implants, resulting in the creation of a separate dental business, in the form of a freestanding company.[3]

In the US market, Synthes USA supported the development of dedicated implants for CMF as Paul Manson, who later to become President of the AO (2008–2010) and was a CMF/neurosurgeon himself, became actively involved in the implant development process. The first CMF course in the US took place on Amelia Island (Florida) in 1985.

Since CMF was not a singular subject but more of a 'field,' there was always conflict and competition between different surgical specialties, all having something to do with CMF. The interested medical specialties included oral and maxillofacial surgery, plastic surgery, Otorhinolaryngology (ear, nose and throat, or ENT) and dental surgery. It was Prein's contribution to create courses under the AO umbrella that brought all of those specialties to the same table, and not just the narrower CMF specialties, per se. This was fully implemented for the first time in 1984 in the US; it later became the standard for further AOCMF courses.

The evolution of CMF within AOTrauma started the process of addressing additional areas of the human anatomy, starting with the lower and upper extremities, and eventually dealing with areas that required ever smaller implants and adapted instruments.

The Evolution of the Spine Specialty Within AO[4]

Spine fractures had been discussed at AO meetings as early as 1977, when an extensive part of the scientific meeting was devoted to spine surgery.[5] It took several years until the first sub-program on the spine was included in the 1981 Davos course. AO surgeons and producers alike were questioning the commercial potential of dedicating resources to spine surgery, implants, instruments, and special courses. Many within the AO did not think the volume generated from this discipline was sufficient; the number of spine specialists was also viewed as being quite small.[6]

New energy was injected into the debate with the arrival of Max Aebi on the scene, a young surgeon who had started his surgical career in Basel. There he came in contact with Allgöwer who encouraged Aebi by saying that spine surgery would become "the future." In the late 1970s, Aebi visited a number of international spine surgery centers on a Swiss National Science Foundation grant, including going to several spine centers in the US. Upon his return to Switzerland, Aebi connected with

---

[3]The Straumann dental business was separated from its AO medical implant business after the spin-off in 1999.

[4]This section is based in part on interview with Prof. Dr. med. h.c. Max Aebi, conducted on 20 March, 2017, in Zurich.

[5]Schneider (1983), p. 85.

[6]Schlich (2002), p. 206.

the AO and its TK Spine that had previously been formed under the leadership of Erwin Morscher (Basel), the doctor who had pioneered the internal fixator.

Aebi, however, was not satisfied with the existing approaches to spine surgery. He had seen different methods used in France and became the first surgeon to utilize them in Switzerland. Eager to improve on the existing technology, Aebi reconnected with Allgöwer. Aebi was pushing the need to create a separate AO chapter for surgery on the spine. By teaming up with John Webb (Nottingham, UK), the two quickly moved on a parallel TK for the spine. Formalized in January 1987, and enlisting the help of Robert Frigg, a gifted mechanic and developer at the AO, the group found support from the Straumann Institute. Their work culminated in the design of a 'universal spine system' dealing with fractures, deformities, and degenerative disease, simultaneously.

The universal spine system was to supplant the older generation of internal fixator propagated by Morscher, creating tensions between the two factions. Unofficially described as a 'palace revolution' by some 'young rebels,' a new spine TK was formed, receiving financial support from the AO organization and now named AOTK Spine. Educational programs were launched, and research programs undertaken when Aebi moved to McGill University in Montreal for several years. When the AOSpine group was formally established in 1999, John Webb and Max Aebi became its first Chairs (Exhibit 25.2).

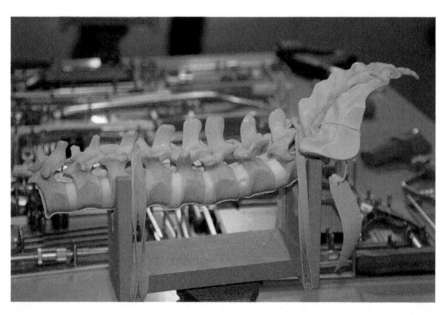

Exhibit 25.2   Spine course. *Copyright by AO Foundation, Switzerland*

Differences Between the Creation of AOCMF and AOSpine

The development of the two specialties, CMF and Spine, did follow different pathways. CMF had started earlier and had a formal organization, preceding Spine with courses and programs. The development of CMF was less contentious and evolved more harmoniously within the mainstream of the AO organization. The same applied to the development of a CMF-specific *Instrumentarium*. The CMF specialty did not comprise a single group of surgeons but always involved a combination of several surgical specialties, coming together to create a common approach.

By contrast, the development of the spine specialty was characterized by a clash of an older, more traditional approach with a group of 'young Turks.' There was obviously a controversy within the group of spine surgeons, and this disagreement had to be addressed first before progress could be made. Getting access to a significant set of resources from the available funding for the entire AO was another issue of continuing disagreement; when spine licensing revenue from the three producers began to grow, issues of appropriate allocation of funding became part of the debate.

What About Total Hip Replacements?

Hip surgery had always been an area dominated by Orthopedic surgeons, although there was a considerable trauma aspect to it. The entire development of hip surgery and total hip replacement, however, was to develop separately, but in parallel, with the core AO trauma surgery.

The connection between trauma, hip replacement, and the AO was a personal story, at times overlapping and involving some of the AO's main players in different ways, primarily Maurice Müller. In fact, many AO surgeons were also involved in hip surgery. It's important to emphasize that from the beginning, the AO *Instrumentarium* did not include hip replacement surgery. There was a reason for this.

On 9 February, 1961, Maurice Müller implanted the first total hip replacement on the European Continent, while serving as head surgeon in the Cantonal Hospital in St. Gallen.[7] This did not come out of the blue as Müller, when still chief resident at Balgrist Hospital in Zurich (1952–1957), had concentrated on hip surgery, not bone trauma. His interest in hip surgery went as far back to his stay in the Netherlands, when he visited the Dutch surgeon van Nes in 1950.

When taking on the surgical assignment at the Hospital of Fribourg (1950–1951), Müller had performed a few hip surgeries among the mostly long bone trauma cases. While serving at Balgrist, as well as during his itinerant surgeon time in Switzerland (1958–1960), he had performed numerous hip surgeries using implants and technologies from the US or the UK. He also taught his AO colleagues his hip surgery procedures.

---

[7]Müller worked there from 1960 to 1967.

Throughout the period that the AO *Instrumentarium* was being developed with Robert Mathys, Sr., the two also collaborated on hip prosthesis for total hip replacements using a stainless steel pilot model; these were made by Mathys and included the part for Müller's first implant in early 1961. For later models, which were made from cobalt steel alloys, Müller switched implant production to Sulzer, a large technology and engineering company located in Winterthur, outside Zurich. Mathys, however, continued to produce the surgical instruments for hip replacements.

When Müller donated his designs and patents to Synthes AG Chur for the creation of the AO contract between the instrument producers and Synthes AG Chur, he expressly excluded any patents or models related to his hip surgery project from both the early producer draft agreement in 1960 and the final one concluded in 1963. Müller's AO colleagues involved in the creation of Synthes AG Chur approved and accepted this, signaling from the outset that the paths of AOTrauma and the total hip replacement prosthesis were meant to be separate.

Other AO surgeons maintained intensive exchanges with J. G. Charnley, the leading surgeon in the UK for total hip replacement who was the AO guest of honor at the December 1961 Davos course. Several AO surgeons, including senior surgeons from hospitals in Chur and St. Gallen had visited Charnley on their own, and Müller's chief resident in St. Gallen, Hardy Weber, spent some extra time with Charnley in the UK. Some AO surgeons designed their own models for total hip replacement, leading to some friction among them. As long as Müller was chief surgeon in St. Gallen, Weber was not allowed to implant his own design at the hospital. He did so only after Müller moved to assume his role as professor in Berne; Weber then became head of St. Gallen, eventually creating his own company (Allopro) with some co-investors, sourcing his implants at the same company, Sulzer.

In terms of managing the business arrangements for his hip prosthesis business, Müller largely duplicated the structure he had advocated for the AO. He created the Protek Foundation in 1965, followed by Protek AG, a company incorporated and dedicated to the marketing of his hip implants. This was similar to the Synthes AG Chur and Mathys/Straumann production arrangements. Consistent with his beliefs that surgeons should not profit personally from implant sales used in their own surgery, Müller had all the accumulated profits transferred from Protek to his Protek Foundation, using the money to fund his research at the University of Berne. Müller appointed the AO's legal counsel, Peter von Rechenberg, to serve as chairman of Protek for a time. For the benefit of transparency, he physically separated the hip implant operation from any AO-related activities by moving Protek AG out of the University of Berne and into another regional location.

As a company, Protek AG was fully-owned by Müller. Initially Protek, distributed through DePuy, didn't fare very well in the US market. In a second iteration, Müller created Protek Inc. as a subsidiary in the US; that, too, struggled. On his third try, when Müller hired an executive from Synthes US, who had been trained by Wyss, sales finally started to track expectations. This was also the time that Wyss became interested in Protek, but at a point when he was immersed in building the AOTrauma business with Synthes US. The parallels between the Synthes/AO struggle to move business to the US and Müller's experience with Protek are striking. [8]

Years later, in 1989, Müller divested the Protek business to Sulzer, its implant producer, who had previously acquired Hardy Weber's Allopro business. At the time of the sale, there was tension between Protek and the AO due to the fact that in international markets, some 25 agencies combined AO Implant (mostly Mathys) with Protek sales. AO surgeons were unhappy with the sale of Protek to Sulzer because it placed them too close to a commercial business with both AO implants and Protek hips being sold through the same units.[9] When Protek was still in Müller's hands, it served the benefit of medical research. With Sulzer as the owner, it was now in the for-profit sector.

Eventually, the Sulzer implant business was acquired by Zimmer, another large US multinational company who was an AO implant competitor. The hip implant business, with the large number of operations being performed worldwide and reaching the position of 'surgical procedure of the century,' went on to surpass the trauma-related business by a large margin. In hindsight, AO members who played a role in the early creation of the organization realized that the AO should have entered this business, especially as they continued to perform total hip replacement surgery as part of their surgical practice.

At first, Hansjörg Wyss, CEO of Synthes USA and a growing force in the AO group, was interested in handling the hip replacement business. Müller had already appointed a different US firm, DePuy, to be its distributor in the US and Canada before Wyss had joined Synthes USA. Later, Wyss came to realize that if the hip replacement business had been added earlier to the Synthes USA trauma business, his sales force would have pursued the low-hanging fruit of selling hip prostheses rather than ploughing the more demanding field of creating business for bone trauma implants.

When it comes to the industrial logic behind a possible combination of medical implants, such as hip prosthesis, with trauma implants, producers who started with hip prosthesis grew quickly, and then used their resources to buy into the trauma implant business. Did the AO miss a major opportunity? Business strategists could probably debate this forever. In either case, this is not the last to be said about Müller's Protek—a company that was to play a role in other developments related to the AO.

References

Schlich, T. (2002). *Surgery, science and industry*. Basingstoke: Palgrave Macmillan.
Schneider, R. (1983). *25 Jahre AO–Schweiz*. Berne: Arbeitsgemeinschaft für Osteosynthesefragen.

---

[8]Interview with Prof. Ueli Aebi-Müller, conducted on 18 April, 2018, in Berne. Ueli Aebi, son-in-law of Maurice Müller, had considerable exposure to Müller's ventures.

[9]Interview with Urs Jann held in Davos on December 7, 2016.

Carrying the Message: Apostles, Missionaries, Translators, and Baggage Carriers

26

Bringing the AO Message to Every Corner of the World

A picture of a growing organization has been painted in the previous chapters—new members and resources were added every year, the AO's *Instrumentarium* expanded, and an entire industrial base was built in collaboration with entrepreneurs. The energy and efforts that went into this expansion rested with the people that made up the AO community. Therefore, it is necessary to show both the means by which they carried the message elsewhere, as well as provide some additional background about the various talents that were responsible for much of this effort.

Apostles as Principal Disseminators of a Revolutionary Message

Gonzague de Reynold, a Swiss historian (1880–1970) and a keen observer of European history, once commented that all political revolutions were bound to become expansionary at some point. Since the AO philosophy could be viewed as a surgical revolution, it should not be surprising to see that this movement assumed an expansionary mode. It was not about conquering countries here but, instead, the minds of surgeons anywhere in the world and establishing the AO philosophy in all corners of the globe.

At the outset, it was the core AO founding members, or the G5, who became actively involved in traveling abroad in support of the AO ideas. Müller was probably the first to travel to the United States for the AO, in 1959, only a few months after establishing the organization,[1] to spread its new philosophy. Müller made this trip by boat and, just as many other passengers, suffered from sea sickness. He used this two-month journey to see as many Orthopedic centers in the US as he

---

[1]Schatzker (2018), p. 87.

© Springer Nature Switzerland AG 2019
J.-P. Jeannet, *Leading a Surgical Revolution*,
https://doi.org/10.1007/978-3-030-01980-8_26

could manage. He was to make several other trips to the US and Canada, becoming a regular in terms of delivering lectures.

Among the other founding members, Schneider traveled most frequently to Germany. Walter Bandi did not begin traveling often until his retirement from his post in Interlaken. Martin Allgöwer also made trips to the US, and other countries, once he stepped down from his hospital post. Among all the AO founders, Allgöwer was the most gifted with language—he spoke several—and had built a worldwide reputation as a general surgeon. His trips to the US were also related to his close connections to the Straumann organization, which covered the US sales territory. Hans Willenegger, sometimes referred to as 'Apostle of the AO' may have been the most consummate traveler among the G5. As the first president of AO International (1973–1983), he became the point man in making overseas trips. His efforts to bring the AO philosophy and *Instrumentarium* to the then separate East Germany (GDR) became legendary. He also took trips to many countries in Latin America and Asia. By many accounts, he was a born teacher and tireless in propagating the AO philosophy. Through his travels, he recruited many young surgeons to join the AO community (Exhibit 26.1).

Exhibit 26.1 Willenegger teaching at an early Davos course. *Copyright by AO Foundation, Switzerland*

Willenegger maintained copious notes of his trips and had calculated that by 1990, even beyond the time of his tenure as president of AO International, he had visited 244 cities in 123 countries, accumulating some 1.25 million km by plane. While traveling the world as an AO ambassador, he had become personally acquainted with thousands of surgeons.[2]

Peter Matter, a member of the first Davos course, and later the head surgeon of the hospital in Davos, commented on Willenegger's role as an apostle:

> In his role as the first AO International President, Hans Willenegger was the AO missionary and travelling more than one million miles around the world to introduce the AO philosophy. He started with personal contacts in different countries, gave presentations at medical meetings and introduced more intensive activities with AO courses after he had found some local supporters in the country or region. He even tried hard to communicate in the native language, especially in the Spanish speaking world although, I might add, that his thinking and his language expressions were always in Swiss German. Willenegger was the AO apostle with immense dedication to teach.[3]

Many early members of the AO can still recount how they got connected with the organization through one of these travelling apostles and how, in the process, they themselves became disciples of the AO philosophy. That many of them became later presidents of the AO attests to the strong and inspiring personalities of the AO founders.

From Translators, Drivers, and Suitcase Porters to AO Disciples

The AO founders made many personal contacts when they traveled in the early days of the organization. They often were assigned a young staff surgeon to assist them on trips, including translating, and some amazing friendships developed from these contacts. Due to the large number of experiences, only a few will be related here in order to provide the reader a better idea of how some doctors in other countries became recruits of the AO community.

Joseph Schatzker, a European born (in today's Lliv, Ukraine, originally Poland), Orthopedic surgeon practicing in Canada, found himself assigned to take care of Müller who was visiting in order to attend a conference in 1965. Schatzker was selected by his senior professor due of his fluency in German, and when he picked him up in an old VW Beetle, Müller, who didn't speak English very well at that time, was very pleased to find someone with whom he could converse in German. When Schatzker visited Europe on a scholarship a year later, he wrote to Müller but didn't receive a reply. During a stay in Sweden he accidentally bumped into Müller traveling through the same hospital, who immediately suggested that he needed

---

[2]"AO—The First 50 Years—AO Foundation," in *Transforming Surgery, Changing Lives, AO Foundation Annual Report 2008*, p. 13.

[3]Source private notes from Peter Matter on the early creation of AO's international network. Matter was President of AO International (1993–1999) and President of the AO Foundation (2000–2002).

Schatzker to translate the AO book on internal fixation from German into English. Out of this contact sprang an in-depth collaboration and the publication of the first English language issue of the *The Manual of Internal Fixation* (1980). Schatzker became a strong advocate of the AO philosophy in North America; he was later elected President of the AO Foundation (1998–2000) and authored a biography about Müller, *Maurice E. Müller: In His Own Words* (Davos: AO Foundation: 2018).[4]

In his early training, Jaime Quintero, from Columbia, was exposed to Willenegger when he traveled to Latin America. Quintero, who grew up in Bogota attending a German school there, wanted to experience something new and through his father, also a surgeon, secured an internship in Brazil and had to learn Brazilian Portuguese. In about 1975, Willenegger visited Brazil and the senior surgeon at Quintero's hospital assigned him to act as a translator for Willenegger, since he was, after all, 'a Gringo who speaks German.' At the conclusion of the visit, Willenegger suggested that Quintero accept an internship to Augsburg, a hospital in Germany staffed with many AO-trained surgeons. He eventually did come to Europe on such a fellowship. Quintero became an active member of the AO, rising to become President of the AO Foundation (2012–2014), as well as a founding member of the AO Alliance.[5]

Suthorn Bavonratanavech, a young surgeon from Thailand, experienced Willenegger's charisma in Asia. Suthorn, as he is affectionately called by everyone within AO, was assigned to be a personal driver for Willenegger during one of his first visits there. He described Willenegger's style as being missionary as he preached the gospel of the AO, humble in style but charismatic, someone who could captivate an audience in a matter of minutes. Eventually, this led to Suthorn becoming connected to the AO, and he, like Quintero, rose to the position of President of the AO Foundation (2014–2016) and became a founding member of the AO Alliance; he also assisted Siegfried Weller from Germany in launching courses in Asia.

Siegfried Weller, one of the participants of the first AO course, was a member of the hospital staff in Freiburg, the first in Germany to become a 'AO Hospital.' In 1974, when Weller had already become President of the AO in Germany, a position he occupied from 1970 to 1991, he was contacted by Willenegger who asked for his help with AO courses in Asia. He accepted and frequently traveled to countries, such as India, Thailand, Indonesia, and Japan, during which time he also connected with Suthorn from Thailand. He remembered finishing his regular surgery schedule in his Tübingen hospital on a Friday, jumping into a plane to going to some Asian city, carrying along with him used implants because patients there could not afford new ones, operating on Saturday, and flying back on Sunday evening to arrive in

---

[4]This anecdote was shared by Joseph Schatzker during an interview with the author, conducted on 9 December, 2016, in Davos.

[5]Anecdote shared by Jaime Quintero during interview with the author, conducted on 5 December, 2016, in Davos.

Germany early Monday morning and go directly to surgery where most of the staff had no idea that he had just returned from Asia. Weller also became AO Foundation President from 1994 to 1996.[6]

David Helfet, a South Africa-born surgeon, came to Johns Hopkins, in the US city of Baltimore, for training; he had a strong interest in trauma surgery. Helfet's senior colleague knew Willenegger and one day Müller arrived as a visiting professor. Then a young surgeon in training, Helfet was nominated to act as *Handlanger*, a sort of jack of all trades, to aid Müller, the famous Swiss surgeon. His helper role resulted in an offer for two stints as a fellow in Switzerland, first for a three-month fellowship in Berne, followed by a further three-month stint in Basel with Allgöwer. In 1981, Helfet came to Davos for the first time as part of helping Müller, then teaching an AO course:

> I was carrying Müller's attaché case and helping him in general. I stayed at the Hotel Schweizerhof in the cellar while he resided in the penthouse apartment.

As this relationship blossomed, Helfet was asked to organize the first AO course for trauma in the US. During his life-long association with the AO organization, Helfet is believed to have spent some five years of professional time on AO business, including AO courses and other roles worldwide.[7]

There are many more of these examples circulating in the AO community than can be recounted, but what they all show us is the enormous outreach practiced by the AO founders to enlist younger surgeons to join them and learn about the AO philosophy. Over time, AO fellowships became a more formal process to bring young surgeons to Europe, and later to other countries as well, so that they could all experience AO surgical practice for longer periods of time.

AO Fellowships for Training to Recruit Disciples

The AO founders realized early on that the Davos training courses were not enough, by themselves, to induct young surgeons into the AO way of thinking. Initially, the Davos courses were largely attended by more senior surgeons, often heads of clinics. All those attendees had young surgeons at home whom they wanted to develop and, as a response, the AO Fellowship program was created.

Even though the AO organization had begun to publish textbooks on its surgical techniques, AO members realized that the best form of instruction was to join in real operations with experienced AO surgeons. To help train such budding surgeons, the AO created a separate foundation in 1968 specifically to support young surgeons experience actual surgical procedures; this happened first in Swiss hospitals and then later in other countries as well. Starting with just a few participants in 1969, the AO

---

[6]"AO—The First 50 Years—AO Foundation," Op. cit, p. 73.
[7]David Helfet, interview with author conducted on 3 December, 2017, in Davos.

managed to grant 86 surgeon fellowships over the period from 1971 to 1974. In the following years, the numbers of fellowships granted rose steadily from 50 in 1976 to 142 in 1983, at that time bringing the total of fellowships granted to 949. Fellows hailed from 74 countries and originated from all continents. In later years, annual fellowships granted exceeded 200.[8]

In the beginning, fellowships were granted for young doctors to join Swiss, German, and Austrian hospitals with a strong AO orientation. Problems arose when the Swiss authorities limited their stays to three months. AO members intended for fellows to return to their home hospitals and become advocates of the AO philosophy there. The personal contacts that arose from these fellowships often lasted a lifetime.

Globetrotters Flying on Goodwill Tours

Possibly the most dramatic gesture of bringing the AO philosophy and *Instrumentarium* to all corners of the world was Robert Mathys, Sr.'s goodwill flight around Africa in 1966. Mathys, a passionate aviator since childhood, spent two years planning a trip circumnavigating the African continent together with a medic, Robert Meier, and a cameraman, Roland Koella, to record the trip. The entire cost of this trip was covered personally by Robert Mathys, Sr. He had acquired a new twin-engine plane, an Aero 45, Czechoslovakian-built, and had it equipped with extra instrumentation to make it fit for the flight.

Mathys was motivated by the status of bone trauma surgery in Africa where often even modern hospitals were poorly equipped—not having the latest surgical equipment—and surgeons were insufficiently trained. Mathys, Sr., brought with him a full set of the AO *Instrumentarium*. Demonstrations of surgeries were done through playing instructional films. No sales were made, and all demonstrations were performed free-of-charge to the hospitals visited. The flight took off from Berne on 13 October, 1966, and the team returned on 14 December, 1966, just about two months later, having covered more than 30,000 km and visited some 50 hospitals in 28 different countries (Exhibits 26.2 and 26.3a–c).

Mathys, Sr.'s flight was not to remain the only such endeavor. In 2005 and 2006, Stephan Perren, long-time head of AO Research Institute (1967–1996) decided to make an around the world flight with his son Nicolas Perren. In a single-engine plane, the Perrens flew from Zurich to Sydney, covering the 23,000 km in 23 stages, between 27 September and 4 November, 2005. Their second leg took place the following year between 19 June and 23 July, 2006, covering the remaining 30,000 km, in 48 stages. The purpose of their trip was to draw attention to the dangers of osteoporosis; he held numerous lectures, showing how the achievements

---

[8]Schlich (2002), pp. 79–81.

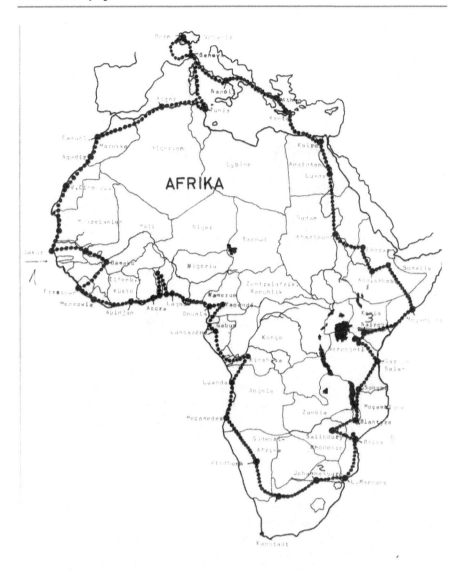

Exhibit 26.2 Mathys flight around Africa. *Source: Robert Mathys, Jr., reprinted with permission*

of the AO Foundation and AO-trained surgeons could successfully deal with fractures occurring from this condition (Exhibit 26.4).[9]

These examples, and collected stories, demonstrate the enormous commitment by the AO leaders to bring their message to as many people as possible. They invested unstintingly of their time, were generous with their own resources, and became an

---

[9]Perren and Perren (2008).

Exhibit 26.3 (a–c) Photos depicting Robert Mathys, Sr., Pilot, and his Crew. *Source: Robert Mathys, Jr., reprinted with permission*

Exhibit 26.4 Perren flight around the world. *Source: Stephan Perren, reprinted by permission*

important element in the constantly growing AO organization. Beyond being missionaries, the AO membership employed other means to get their message across.

References

Perren, S., & Perren, N. (2008). *Great circle: The world eastbound*. Davos: BUDAG Verlag.
Schatzker, J. (2018). *Maurice E. Müller: In his own words*. Davos, AO Foundation.
Schlich, T. (2002). *Surgery, science and industry*. Basingstoke: Palgrave Macmillan.

Laying the Foundation for a 'Trauma University'

27

It Started as a One-Off Event

Teaching had always been one of the four main pillars of the AO organization. Initially, the AO founders thought that they would start by offering a few courses, and then go forward with other aspects of the organization's development. The first Davos course in 1960 was not conceived of as an annual, repeating, event. Instead, the idea was centered on a cadre of trained surgeons who would be able to continue training their young residents in their own hospitals. On that score, the AO founders must have been overwhelmed by the continuous demand for instructional courses in line with the model first developed for Davos. What was at the origin of this constant pressure to keep running courses and to dramatically expand their availability around the world?

The Persistent Demand for Surgical Instruction

When the AO made its *Instrumentarium* available for sale in 1962, it quickly became clear that availability of this *Instrumentarium* itself did not guarantee satisfactory surgical outcomes. Mistakes were committed by insufficiently trained or inexperienced surgeons, prompting AO leadership to intervene in order to prevent acquiring a poor reputation. Even policing the sale of the *Instrumentarium* by restricting it to AO-trained surgeons only could not prevent abuse. As a result, the AO leaders accepted that they would have to continue the courses for 'a while,' not realizing that this would become one of the organization's central activities. An example of the use of the AO *Instrumentarium* and surgical techniques by unskilled or inexperienced surgeons was offered by Norbert Haas, longtime AO member and past President of the AO Foundation (2010–2012). In the hospital in Hannover, where he began his career, there was a 21% infection rate when they started using the AO methodology.

© Springer Nature Switzerland AG 2019
J.-P. Jeannet, *Leading a Surgical Revolution*,
https://doi.org/10.1007/978-3-030-01980-8_27

At the same time, the infection rate in Allgöwer's hospital in Chur was only 1%. Just having the tools was obviously not enough.[1] The largest learning event, by far, for surgeons remained the annual course in Davos. Starting in 1960, it was repeated annually and by 1982 some 13,491 participants had attended the course, which was always held in early December. Increasingly, the event attracted surgeons from all over the world so that, of the total participants who had attended by 1982, only a little more than 10% originated from Switzerland. Germany, the US, and the Netherlands delegated more participants than Switzerland. The vast majority of participants came from European countries.[2]

The Challenge of Managing a Growing Course Portfolio

For the course organizers, the growth of participants from the initial 66 the first year to 1270 in 1982 was a double-edge sword. The design of the first course, already oversubscribed at the time, was built around a smaller group of surgeons who had been taught by the AO's founders and experts. Experiencing a growth rate factor of 20 times required a significant redesign of the logistics while still preserving the hands-on learning style that had been the core element of the courses. This was accomplished by splitting the December course into two offerings of one week each, which still implied growth by a factor of ten for each cohort of surgeons. A larger venue was procured, first with the rental of two adjacent cinemas and later by obtaining access to the Davos Conference Center through the town management. The course offerings were supported by a special staff, and the important institution of having table instructors for the small groups going through practical exercises was maintained.

The logistics of running a large course event in Davos were daunting. For each small table group of six to eight attending surgeons, the course required one or two table instructors, the corresponding *Instrumentarium* for the practical exercises and other course materials, such as videos. All of this had to be transported to the course site, prepared, packed up afterwards and shipped back to where it was all stored.

A sufficient supply of bone material for the practical exercises became a particular issue. Since the AO founders considered it essential that surgeons were put in a situation where they would use the real elements of an *Instrumentarium* and apply the drills, plates, and screws, they needed to source human cadaver bones used in hospitals around Switzerland. As the number of participants scaled, the sourcing of cadaver bones also became more of a problem.

Many stories were related by members of the AO community about these early years when some cadaver bone shipments went astray. One truck bringing such bones to Davos had a road accident on the way, with the driver taking off for fear that he would be arrested by the police for the truck's content. Another time, one of the

---

[1]Interview with Professor Norbert Haas conducted on 7 December, 2016, in Davos.
[2]Schlich (2002), p. 164.

instructors driving to Davos was late and ran into a speed control on his way. Apparently, there was some time spent explaining to the police the content of his trunk, which was filled with human cadaver bones. Other stories were circulated about courses held outside of Switzerland. One AO member, a consummate pilot himself, used his private plane to ferry bone supplies to courses held in Italy. Clearly, this situation was only going to get worse unless the AO organization found a way to deal with the logistics of bones.

In 1975, help came from a Swiss company which had become a supplier of materials to the Swiss army. Experienced in producing components made of polyurethane, the company agreed to start supplying artificial bone models for the AO courses. At that time, the AO used about 750 different bone models. In 1982, the AO was able to acquire a local firm to become a dedicated supplier of bone models. With courses expanding, this company, in 1988, turned into SYNBONE and continued to supply the AO with artificial bones (we will return to SYNBONE again later; see Chap. 45).

Instructional resources came from AO members and residents of AO-dominated hospitals. Producers Mathys and Straumann, and later Synthes US, provided instructional help in the form of a staff familiar with the use of the *Instrumentarium*. The course budget was partially supported through the licensing fees of the producers, which, at first, absorbed about 5% of the AO budget. This appeared to be a low figure for the number of courses offered. However, the faculty members were working largely on a volunteer basis, with only direct expenses paid, and all participants paid a tuition fee for attending, as well as covering their own travel and hotel expenses. During the early phase, very few full-time AO staff was involved with the course program.[3] To a large extent, AO course staff and instructors were a virtual resource, or a virtual teaching staff, not compensated by the AO and yet available on a flexible basis without incurring any substantial fixed costs for the organization. Courses were held in rented premises only for the duration of the courses. Clearly, this was a very lean operation with a maximal impact (Exhibit 27.1).

For an international course, language also had to be considered. When only Swiss participants attended, German was acceptable. In 1963, a first French language section was offered, with the challenge of recruiting French-speaking table instructors. At that time, English was not as widely spoken by surgeons as it is today.

Special tracks were also offered for operating room nurses. Some 670 nurses attended the special courses during the 1960s. In 1974, a first course for CMF surgeons was added; it was repeated many times over as other specialist courses joined what had originally been only a trauma curriculum. This specialization took off in the late 1980s and early 1990s. The AOVET group, as reported earlier, began to offer separate courses away from Davos in 1970, and hosted its first course for

---

[3]Interview with Claudio Gubser, a retired AO course organizer during the early part of the programs, conducted on 8 December, 2016, in Davos.

Exhibit 27.1 Table course instruction. *Copyright by AO Foundation, Switzerland*

veterinarians in English in 1971, in Davos. For those courses, animal cadaver bones were easier to source than human ones.[4]

International Expansion of Courses

It didn't take very long for the AO to start offering courses in other countries. Driven by surgeons who returned home from Davos, and to serve young surgeons who were not able to take the trip to Switzerland, already an expensive locale at that time. A total of 20,242 participants attended AO courses outside of Switzerland in the period up to 1982, making up almost 60% of all AO course participants. Again, Germany accounted for the largest share, followed by North America, and Austria.

The first foreign course was held in Freiburg, Germany, in 1965, followed by Ljubljana (today's Slovenia), Canada (1969), and the US (1970). The list of countries with the first courses offered up to 1982 are listed below:

1965 Germany
1968 Slovenia
1969 Canada
1970 Austria, United States
1972 Australia, Mexico

---

[4]Auer et al. (2013).

1973 UK, Israel
1976 Several Nordic countries
1977 Egypt, Ecuador, Indonesia
1978 India, Kenia, Uruguay
1979 Argentina, Peru, Venezuela, New Zealand, Tunisia
1980 Costa Rica, Netherlands, Nigeria Portugal
1981 Bolivia, Morocco
1982 Columbia, Libya

In some of these countries, such as Germany and the US, courses were held in multiple city locations. In case of the US, it was the AOVET group that led the charge, offering courses in multiple cities and driven, in part, by the expansion of Synthes USA. Some courses became almost annual affairs, others were one-time events. The course offering, and the locations, were often driven by the preference of local surgeons who had attended Davos courses.

The Continued Value of AO Courses

As the annual Davos course became an institution, the venue was never questioned. In the early years, there was sufficient downtime for outdoor sports, primarily skiing in the Davos area, which was a big attraction for surgeons who could combine their medical training, as well as take advantage of being in a top skiing resort. The course program was interrupted in the early afternoon, allowing participants to enjoy lunch on the slopes, and then reconvened in the late afternoon for an additional session, which lasted into the early evening. Changes in the regulatory environment no longer allowed the combination of leisure with medical training; today's courses take place over the entire day. The avid skiers among the participants either came earlier or stayed until after the conclusion of the course. There are still older AO members and course participants who lament the absence of skiing in the mid-day. Surprisingly, the Davos course has so far survived both global warming and the lack of spare time during the day for hitting the slopes (Exhibit 27.2).

The value of the courses should also be appreciated in terms of marketing the AO *Instrumentarium*. From the outset, no sales of the *Instrumentarium* took place at seminars and all orders had to go directly to the respective producers. Although all instructional materials were AO-approved, as was any instrumentation used from the approved AO producers, no attempts were made to sell or to market the AO brand. Clearly, the familiarity of the attending course participants with the AO *Instrumentarium* was critical to later sales, but this came more as a result of the courses and was not pushed during them. Producers saw the courses as the best sales tool and admitted that this allowed them to concentrate on supplying implants, not selling them. The AO did not want its instructors to be viewed as sales personnel, and participants were free to return home and order implants from any supplier.

Over the first 30 years, the AO courses, offered at first as a way to get initial acceptance, became a major activity of the organization. Increased penetration of the

Exhibit 27.2   Table course instruction with drills. *Copyright by AO Foundation, Switzerland*

AO philosophy among trauma surgeons did not diminish the demand for courses because every year a new crop of residents started their careers with a continuous need to be trained in the AO way.

References

Auer, J., et al. (2013). *History of AOVET—The first 40 years*. AO Foundation.
Schlich, T. (2002). *Surgery, science, and industry* (p. 164). Basingstoke: Palgrave Macmillan.

Publishing the AO Philosophy

28

Instructional Notes at the Beginning

Writing about the concept of Osteosynthesis, and its practice, preceded the 1958 creation of the AO. Maurice Müller had set down the first written instructions on Osteosynthesis in 1951, while at the hospital in Fribourg and following his visit to Danis. As the AO group started to take up its work, it was again Müller who created the well-known instruction sheets (*Merkblätter* in German), which were carefully reviewed by all AO members and regularly amended to include their commentary.[1] They carried the title *Operative Frakturbehandlung*, or Internal Fixation, which would become the title of the AO's first full textbook.

The first complete collection of the instruction sheets was issued in 1961 by Müller during his time at the hospital in St. Gallen. A booklet of about 90 pages in regular page format, this work became the basis for the first full text issued by the AO founders in 1963 under the title *Technik der Operativen Frakturbehandlung*, or *Technique of Internal Fixation of Fractures*, published by Springer-Verlag.[2]

The AO founders must have been motivated to put their own practice to paper, similar to books published by their role models Lambotte,[3] Danis,[4] and Böhler.[5] Given the intense debates about the usefulness of internal fixation, the AO group was most likely interested in putting their own ideas first and not letting them be described by authors skeptical of the practice.

The AO surgeons first text book was about 350 pages with many illustrations of the AO practice. The foreword was written by Professor Krauss, head of the surgical

---

[1] Schlich (2002), p. 76.
[2] Müller et al. (1963).
[3] Lambotte (1907).
[4] Danis (1949).
[5] Böhler (1929).

© Springer Nature Switzerland AG 2019
J.-P. Jeannet, *Leading a Surgical Revolution*,
https://doi.org/10.1007/978-3-030-01980-8_28

clinic of the University of Freiburg and the first university professor to come to publicly support the AO ideas. While Müller, Allgöwer, and Willenegger were listed as the book's authors, there were important contributions from other AO surgeons on particular chapters, including the two other core AO members Schneider and Bandi (both members of the G5). Comparisons between this publication and the earlier one show that cited instructional notes regarding the sections authored by Müller were largely identical to his instructional notes from two years previous. This book truly represented best practice as experienced by the AO group of surgeons. It came enhanced with 459 illustrations and 2000 individual exhibits (Exhibit 28.1).

Aside from treating the various indications suitable for internal fixation, the book covered the general practice required for a successful internal fixation and paid attention to the fact that poor operational practice would not lead to a successful surgery. The part about the entire set of implants, and the issue of selected metal, was covered by Fritz Straumann and Professor Samuel Steinemann, one of his main metallurgists, and was maintained in later publications as well. The *Instrumentarium* and its use were described again in detail by Müller himself.

The time required to author this book must have been considerable given the fact that all of the participating surgeons were heading their own surgical practices in regional hospitals. In order to allocate enough time for this collaboration, the AO decided to skip the Davos course in 1962. The book was first published in German, and later translated into English but that was not published until 1965 by Dr. Gottfried Segmüller, a surgeon from the hospital in Chur. Since the English edition was obviously targeted to the UK and the US, the section 'Tibia Fractures' was omitted due to the ongoing controversy about this treatment in the US.

Despite the copious documentation, the many illustrations, and the background materials included about the *Instrumentarium*, the AO surgeons did not believe that simply studying the book would make a successful surgeon. The AO surgeons were still of the view that successful practice and practical experience were essential to guarantee successful internal fixation results.

As the AO surgeons convened to prepare a second edition of their text, their methodological and painstaking approach took much time. By 1967, the *Technik* had sold out, and the second edition seemed a long time off. As a result, the group decided to issue a technical manual for surgeons intended as a temporary solution to the full text.

Manual as 'Placeholder'

This 'temporary' text, *Manual der Osteosynthese*, was composed more as a technical book, and the format resembled the illustrations of the earlier instructional notes. The book came illustrated with a large number of drawings (683 images) and very few X-ray documents compared to the *Technik* book. Published in 1969, it was an

TECHNIK DER OPERATIVEN FRAKTURENBEHANDLUNG

VON

M.E.MÜLLER
M.ALLGÖWER   H.WILLENEGGER

MIT BEITRÄGEN VON

W.BANDI · H.R.BLOCH · A.MUMENTHALER
R.SCHNEIDER · S.STEINEMANN · F.STRAUMANN
B.G.WEBER

MIT EINEM GELEITWORT VON

PROF.DR.H.KRAUSS
DIREKTOR DER CHIRURGISCHEN UNIVERSITÄTSKLINIK, FREIBURG i. BR.

MIT 459 ABBILDUNGEN IN
2000 EINZELDARSTELLUNGEN

SPRINGER-VERLAG BERLIN HEIDELBERG GMBH
1963

Exhibit 28.1   Front page 'Technik 1963'. *Source: Müller et al. (1963). Reprinted by permission*

immediate success, with drawings and illustrations, and more in line with what surgeons required for instruction[6] (Exhibit 28.2).

---

[6]Müller et al. (1969).

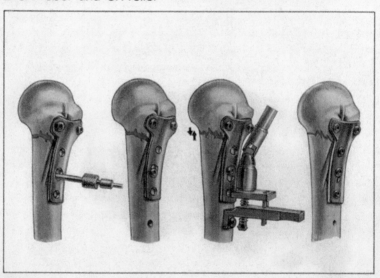

Exhibit 28.2 Cover page first manual (German). *Source: Springer Verlag. Reprinted with permission*

The Manual included Robert Schneider, chair of the Swiss AO group and one of the founding members, as the fourth author. In the foreword, the authors point out that the experience of more than 50,000 documented procedures formed the basis of the Manual.

This became the model for Schatzker's translation into English, *Manual of Internal Fixation*, equipped with some 300 figures and published in 1970, with drawings by Oberli, a frequent illustrator of the AO books.[7] Schatzker spoke fluent German and completed his medical studies in English in Toronto, thus making him an excellent choice to do the translation. He was also one of the early 'disciples' of the AO founders and was personally recruited by Müller for the project[8] (Exhibit 28.3).

The first edition of the Manual was eventually translated into a number of other languages, including French (1974), Italian (1970), Japanese (1971), and Spanish (1971). A second edition of the Manual was published in 1977, which was also translated into Spanish (1979), French (1979), Italian (1981), Chinese (1983), and Japanese (1988). Eventually, a third edition was published in 1990 and by the year 2000, it was estimated that Springer had sold close to 110,000 copies of the Manual; quite an accomplishment for a text that was supposed to be a placeholder until something more complete could be published.[9]

While the Manual described the standard AO practice for internal fixation, there were other books published by AO members that focused either on special situations or, later, on some deviations of standard practice, already signaling an impending evolution that was to be led by a second generation of gifted AO surgeons. Weber published a book on ankle fractures in 1966[10] and, with another AO colleague, a book about his experience with Osteosynthesis at the St. Gallen hospital, bringing some differing views on the standard AO procedures.[11]

A book on small and peripheral fractures was published by Heim and Pfeiffer in 1972.[12] The book was intended to be a companion to the AO Manual and was translated into English in several versions.[13] Many other specialized books were to follow, including some by AOVET, AOSpine, and AOCMF. They helped establish AO's reputation as the originators of a serious surgical procedure, while at the same time assisting in the training of surgeons (Exhibit 28.4).

---

[7] Müller et al. (1970).

[8] J. Schatzker, interview conducted on 9 December, 2016, in Davos.

[9] Schlich (2002), p. 79.

[10] Weber (1966).

[11] Brunner and Weber (1982).

[12] Heim and Pfeiffer (1972).

[13] Heim and Pfeiffer (1988).

M. E. Müller   M. Allgöwer
R. Schneider   H. Willenegger

Manual of Internal Fixation

Techniques Recommended
by the AO-ASIF Group

Third Edition, Expanded and Completely Revised

Springer-Verlag

Exhibit 28.3   Schatzker translation of manual. *Source: Springer Verlag. Reprinted by Permission*

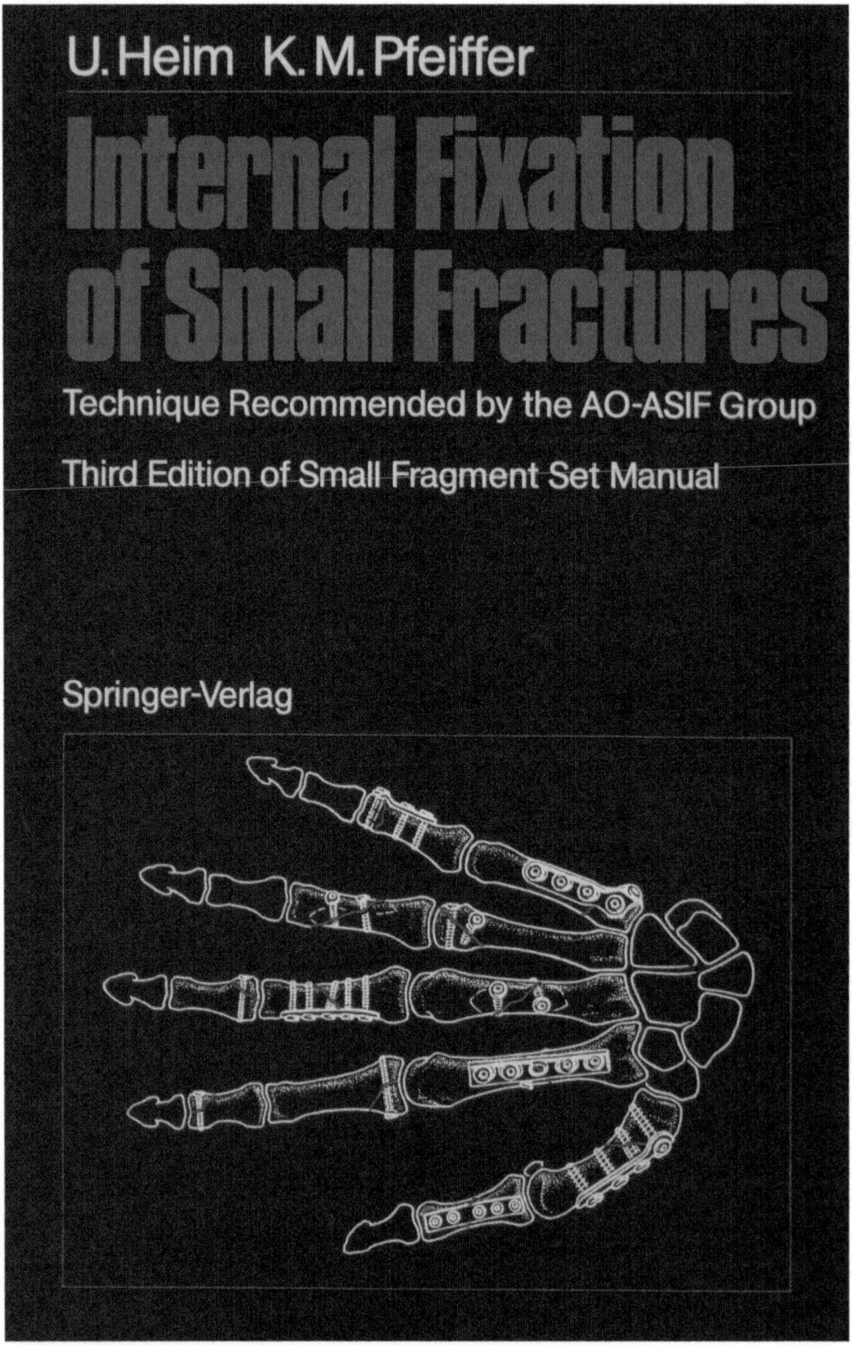

Exhibit 28.4 Book cover of text on small fractures by U. Heim and K. M. Pfeiffer. *Source: Heim and Pfeiffer (1988). Reprinted by permission*

Scientific Publications

In the early years of the AO's growth, a large number of publications appeared in scientific journals dealing with the underlying assumptions of Osteosynthesis. As noted earlier, the findings on bone healing and the impact of pressure on healing— the relevant issues as researched both the AO Research Institute in Davos and other universities—were important elements in moving the AO philosophy from 'speculation' to proven medical concept. The book publishing, however, was very important for the support of the surgical craft, and as such very much in line with the inclination of the early AO surgeons who strongly believed that training surgical skills would achieve better results for patients. Book publishing constituted the Techne (or craftsmanship) side of their interests, whereas scientific journals played to their Episteme (the knowledge) side. How this was to evolve over the next phase of the AO's development will be covered later in the book (see Chap. 45).

References

Böhler, L. (1929). *Technik der Knochenbruchbehandlung*. Wien: Maudrich.
Brunner, C. F., & Weber, B. G. (1982). *Special techniques in internal fixation*. Berlin: Springer.
Danis, R. (1949). *Théorie et pratique de l'ostéosynthèse*. Paris: Masson.
Heim, U., & Pfeiffer, K. M. (1972). *Periphere Osteosynthesen unter Verwendung des Kleinfragment-Instrumentariums der AO*. Berlin: Springer.
Heim, U., & Pfeiffer, K. M. (1988). *Internal fixation of small fractures* (3rd ed.). Berlin: Springer.
Lambotte, A. (1907). *L'Intervention Opératoire dans les Fractures Récentes et Anciennes*. Brussels: Lamertin.
Müller, M. E., Allgöwer, M., Schneider, R., & Willenegger, H. (1969). *Manual der Osteosynthese, AO-Technik*. Berlin: Springer.
Müller, M. E., Allgöwer, M., & Willenegger, H. (1963). *Technik der Operativen Frakturenbehandlung*. Heidelberg: Springer.
Müller, M. E., Allgöwer, M., & Willenegger, H. (1970). *Manual of internal fixation* (trans: Schatzker, J.). Heidelberg: Springer.
Schlich, T. (2002). *Surgery, science, and industry*. Basingstoke: Palgrave Macmillan.
Weber, B. G. (1966). *Die Verletzung des Oberen Sprunggelenkes*. Berne: Huber.

Internationalizing the AO Organization

29

From a Swiss to an International Base

With the success of the AO organization's rollout of its *Instrumentarium*, and the increasing acceptance of its philosophy, requests were fielded from surgeons outside of Switzerland who wanted to have their own, local AO organizations. When the AO was founded in 1958, all but one of the 13 founding surgeons were Swiss. The expectation of active participation in the regular meetings to further develop the AO philosophy must have put a break on the enrollment of more AO members. Surgeons attending the Davos courses hailing from other countries were not willing to leave AO contacts at the course-level alone.

The Italians Take the Initiative

Italian surgeons were the first, in 1966, to form the *Club Italiano degli Amici dell'AO*, without prior approval or support from the AO in Switzerland. They went on to publish an AO manual in Italian, partially illustrating the procedures with their own drawings and documenting them with clinical experience from their own hospitals. Until that time, publications were only available in German and it was understandable why Italian surgeons would move to translations for their own publications. The group issued its own newsletter and some of the Swiss AO surgeons took exception to a few of the surgical instructions included in the publication. This experience started a whole process about how to deal with an emerging global network from the Swiss base.

Alarm bells were set off in Switzerland when it was discovered that the Italian group had concluded a supply agreement directly with Mathys without consulting either Synthes AG Chur, the patent owners, or the Swiss AO organization, and its TK in particular. As a result, the Swiss AO tried to enforce that any such

© Springer Nature Switzerland AG 2019
J.-P. Jeannet, *Leading a Surgical Revolution*,
https://doi.org/10.1007/978-3-030-01980-8_29

arrangements required TK approval.[1] The AO saw it as a risk to let various groups make arrangements in their own countries, thus diluting the AO brand. One of the principles of the AO was a coherent, standardized, and uniform set of instruments, plates, and screws. To avoid confusion, the AO had to ensure that all decisions relating to *Instrumentarium* stayed with Synthes AG Chur, and were overseen by the TK.

Austria and Germany Move Next

Austrian surgeons had also been frequent participants in the AO courses. In 1969, AO surgeons from the Graz cluster created an informal AO group, a fact that Schneider, the AO Chair in Switzerland, found out only after the fact. However, the grouping was informal and did not become a formal entity until 1973; it was named the Austrian Section of the AO.

Germany, the largest market for AO implants and surgical implants, presented a worry for AO leadership because surgeons there had also begun to form their own organization, the German AO. Created in Frankfurt, in 1970, it was an exclusive Club (AO Deutschland) with founders determining who would be part of the group, basing their decisions on member standing and sympathy to the philosophy. Initially, members needed to be of high standing, have two recommendations, and be admitted with a unanimous vote of all other members, thus reducing growth of the chapter; it was by invitation only and admission was intended to be reserved for the best.[2] The more formalized creation of the German AO Section took place in 1971.

Admission criteria were already a subject for debate when the Swiss AO was founded. A new member had to be recommended, or proposed, by at least one existing member, and then confirmed unanimously by all others. In that sense, the restrictive handling of member admissions in Germany was not all that different from Switzerland.

Developing and Charter Local Chapters

When a Spanish section of the AO was formed by local surgeons in early 1972, it became clear to the AO leadership in Switzerland that some action had to take place to prevent the original idea of a single network of surgeons from dissolving into a large number of local initiatives. Admitting all these international surgeons to the Swiss AO chapter was ruled out; it was feared that it would substantially change the character of the Swiss group, which was conceived as a community of surgeons who met regularly in face-to-face meetings.

---

[1] Schlich (2002), p. 221.
[2] Interview with Norbert Haas, past President of AO (2010–2012), conducted on 7 December, 2016, in Davos.

The first proposal advanced by Schneider, the AO Chair in Switzerland, was to suggest that the AO allow the formation of local chapters, or sections, that were based on a similar model as the Swiss one: a relatively small group, which is based on personal contacts and bound to the original Swiss group with a contract that would ensure the respect of the existing AO structure regarding innovation, practice, and the sourcing of implants. Since controlling new groups in several countries might become a larger task, the Swiss AO group moved towards the creation of an entirely new organization, the AO International (AOI). Created in 1972, all the AO sections in different countries were required to become members of AOI, including the Swiss AO. Thus, AOI thus became the umbrella organization of AO organizations and affiliates.

In order to assure that local chapters would become members of the AOI, some benefits and resources had to be shared between the central AO in Switzerland and the local affiliates. Important conflict potential could come from the distribution of producers' royalties, which were collected centrally by Synthes AG Chur and was allocated, through the TK process, to different AO activities. To avoid the risk of the distribution of royalties by source of country sales, as some might have requested, the AOI offered a number of services with respect to clinical research, education, and documentation, although the latter was to be created locally and connected to the central documentation center in Switzerland.

Formal Creation of AO International

The AOI was formally established in 1972 in Berne with Switzerland, Austria, Germany, Italy, and Spain as participants. AOI by-laws contained the same goals as the Swiss by-laws. Any activities under the AO brand had to be coordinated with the AOI office in Switzerland. Each section could delegate three members to the governing assembly. With Hans Willenegger appointed President and Maurice Müller secretary, with several other international members appointed to the board, the AOI still remained largely in Swiss hands. There continued to be considerable concern among Swiss AO members that this move to internationalize would result in a dilution of their original ideals.

Conflict with Spain

Developments in Spain caused conflicts with the umbrella organization. When the first Spanish AO chapter was founded, local surgeons had formed their own instruments company, violating the rules of central sourcing and causing concern in Switzerland. The conflict was resolved by the Swiss group by promising to make additional resources available to the Spanish chapter for development and documentation. Two years later, the Spanish group started to collaborate with another local producer who had promised a greater share of the profits. Since Spain was part of the Straumann sales territory, the AO encouraged Straumann to open a local sales subsidiary that would improve supply and logistics, thus protecting the AO business and its source of licensing fees derived from sales. This was further supported by conducting a big AO congress in Madrid to stake out the ground for the AO organization. Similar problems were reported in other countries and the AO Switzerland, in tandem with the TK and the producers, moved swiftly to protect the source of its revenue.

The AOI envisioned that 'mini Swiss AOs' would be founded in many countries. Aside from the more formal groups in Germany, Austria, and Switzerland, the formal establishments with by-laws and ratification at the AOI office never materialized. New chapters had to have at least six qualified surgeons to start with and were expected to participate in scientific exchange, collaborating with AO institutions in research and documentation. Prohibited was any personal gain from the sales of the *Instrumentarium*, and its many new elements could only be approved by the central TK in Switzerland.

Different Purpose for AO International

Attempts to form AO chapters in some countries, such as Belgium, Norway, or Mexico, had to be abandoned due to a lack of broad support in the respective countries. With few formal member organizations, the planned assembly of delegates did not take place. This meant that in the end the AOI turned into a service organization led by President Willenegger for the first 12 years. During this time, Willenegger traveled extensively, which allowed him to identify the best surgeons in the many countries he visited, as well as share the AO organizational philosophy—that it was not just a business venture and that surgeons should not personally profit financially from the organization.

Even though the AOI did not fulfill its intended role as the umbrella organization to many local chapters, it was very effective in standardizing the AO philosophy around the world. Often referred to within AO as the *unité de doctrine*, or doctrinal unity, the AOI implemented the requirements set by the AOTK to ensure that at every course using AO instrumentation at least one AO member had to be present. This policy was enforced to ensure the quality of various courses at a time of rapid internationalization.

The AOI did serve the strategic need of the organization's development beyond what was envisioned. By enforcing some key rules globally, such as the role of the AOTK for everyone, the need to order through official AO channels and producers, served to strengthen the producer network, which, in turn, grew AO's annual royalty base. Using the budget commitments that were generated, the AOI and AOTK were able to keep everyone in line. This was particularly important as the AO philosophy spread to more and more countries.

Reference

Schlich, T. (2002). *Surgery, science and industry* (p. 221). Basingstoke: Palgrave Macmillan.

The Diverse Talents Shaping the AO

30

A Range of Talents

Throughout the first 25 years of AO's history, many different personalities had an enormous impact on the direction of the organization. In order to appreciate their many contributions, it is necessary to consider their full range of talents, both professionally and personally, that have combined to build this enterprise. Today, diversity is a term that is used extensively in describing organizations but it was just as relevant when the AO was created. It is not possible to mention all of the players involved with making the AO what it is today, but it is important to consider the range of talents, from various cultures, that came together to make their contributions, each utilizing their own strengths and experiences.

The Different Professional Cultures Shaping AO Surgeons

Because the single most important purpose of the AO was to create an organization 'by surgeons for surgeons,' it is natural to focus on them first. Although devoted to Osteosynthesis and bone trauma, the AO was not created, nor built, by a homogenous group of surgeons. Among its founders, there is a single Orthopedic surgeon (Müller) surrounded by a larger number of general surgeons, including the four others that made up the core group of G5: Schneider, Willenegger, Allgöwer, and Bandi. There are ample anecdotes referring to the different viewpoints of Orthopedic surgeons versus general surgeons, and in Müller's biography he refers to the general surgeons as "not really understanding bones," whereas the general surgeons certainly brought a special care for, and perspective of, soft tissue treatment of trauma. These general surgeons, heading regional hospitals, dealt with trauma cases as one type of caseload and did not handle trauma cases exclusively. Orthopedic surgeons joined in only later and in smaller numbers than general surgeons.

© Springer Nature Switzerland AG 2019
J.-P. Jeannet, *Leading a Surgical Revolution*,
https://doi.org/10.1007/978-3-030-01980-8_30

Looking beyond the founders in Switzerland, there were also different schools of thoughts, or experience sets, in Germany and Austria regarding the AO enterprise. In the latter countries, there were networks of accident hospitals with the specialty of *Unfallchirurgie* (trauma surgery) not present in Switzerland. In these hospitals, the main caseload was trauma of both soft tissue and bones, but not Orthopedic surgery.

As the AO expanded internationally, the general surgeons were joined by an increasing number of Orthopedic surgeons, so that over time the different types of surgeons collaborated in the general development of the AO *Instrumentarium*. Additional surgical specialties joined the AO as its *Instrumentarium* was adapted to other types of trauma. As a group of maxillofacial, or CMF, surgeons joined the organization, they created their own subgroup and became active members. Later, spine surgeons developed an AO approved *Instrumentarium*, expanding the range of surgeons active in the association. In the case of CMF, that included a number of different but related surgical and medical specialties, ranging from dental surgery to cosmetic surgery. The AO began to include an ever larger and diverse group of surgeons who, despite their various disciplines, supported its philosophy and actively participated in its further development. And, not to be forgotten, are the veterinary surgeons that found great value early on in the AO approach to Osteosynthesis, collaborating closely with the AO organization, contributing to the development of different implants and benefiting from the AO's expansion. As was the case in the US, it was actually veterinary surgeons in Europe who helped considerably in the development of, and engagement with, the AO and its philosophy in the early years.

The AO was an organization for 'many types of surgeons by many types of surgeons,' each contributing based on their own professional cultures. As has been pointed out several times by long-serving members of the AO, when attending surgical conferences surgeons would otherwise be far more segmented and not necessarily surrounded by such a full set of surgical skills and specialties. This wide range of experience and coming together in the creation of the early AO, was certainly a positive contributor to the organization's growth. These surgeons did not work in close proximity to one another but instead had to attend meetings on a regular basis, creating a network in order to bridge their separate places of work, sometimes traveling internationally to do so.

The Scientists

Early on in the building of the AO organization, there was a range of individuals who contributed in their role as scientists, although mostly from the medical or bioscience fields. They collaborated with AO surgeons in building the scientific arguments for the AO approach and became early members of the organization in the form of corresponding, or scientific, members. Some joined the Davos research operation early on and represented different areas of science. Professor and Dr. med. Herbert

André Fleisch,[1] head of the AO research group in Davos early on, was a patho-physiologist, Professor Robert Schenk was a bone pathologist and worked at the University of Basel.[2] Stephan Perren,[3] a long-time director of the AO Research Institute (ARI) at Davos, was an experimental surgeon and specialist on Biomechanics. Although the connection with the Davos research group was close, not all of these scientists were in residence in Davos. The scientific skills needed to move the AO forward did not originate from a single scientific or medical discipline. They all collaborated effectively across different institutional units and separate geographic locations.

The Metallurgists

Dealing with the early metallurgical problems stemming from AO implants, a team of metallurgical specialists at the Straumann Institute became important contributors to the AO; a number of them utilized their experience with the Swiss watch industry. This group, composed of experts in various disciplines, included metallurgists like Ortrun Pohler[4] and Samuel Steinemann,[5] a physicist, who dealt primarily with issues of corrosion. Once the corrosion issues had been identified, these team members also joined the various AOTK meetings and continued to advise the AO on metallurgical issues. The ARI in Davos did not include this expertise.

The Mechanical Designers

A unique group of contributors, already featured in our earlier chapters on the creation of the AO *Instrumentarium*, were mechanical geniuses that, through their very special skills, deserve an honored place in AO's history. Robert Mathys, Sr., who teamed up with Maurice Müller in the initial phase of the AO to come up with both implants and surgical instruments in the creation of an *Instrumentarium*, also taught the first courses in Davos. As a mechanical designer, Mathys, Sr., not only executed the requested designs but also, as a result of attending surgeries, provided his own input into the design features. As a producer, he then translated these designs into manufacturing processes so that the producers could increase production.

Two members of the Straumann Institute team were also gifted mechanical designers. Fridolin Séquin[6] was responsible for maintaining the library of drawings that formed the basis of the collaboration between the Mathys and Straumann

---

[1]Fleisch, Herbert André, Professor and Dr. Med., 1933–2007, University of Berne, 1967–1997.
[2]Schenk, Robert, Professor University of Basel, (1923–2011).
[3]Perren, Stephan, Head of the AO Research Institute, (1967–1995).
[4]Pohler, Ortrun, interview conducted on May 24, 2018, in Lörrach, Germany.
[5]Steinemann, Samuel (1923–2016), Dr. sc. ETH Zurich, Professor Lausanne (1978–1988).
[6]Séquin, Fridolin (1921–1989).

companies. He also worked with the ISO and the standardization of the AO implants and screws. Paul Gisin,[7] another Straumann staff member, was remembered for his technological contributions to the developments of AO medullary nails and drilling machines.

The AO *Instrumentarium* was not only about surgical approaches and philosophy. The creation and manufacturing of its elements benefited from a range of different mechanical skills that were essential to the assembly of the full range of instruments, and the surgeons' need for ergonomics in design was always respected.

The Entrepreneurs

AO surgeons did not act as full-fledged entrepreneurs. They provided the ideas, guidance, built surgical approaches and systems, and, of course, had the vision that their philosophy could triumph over the older, conservative, method of bone fracture treatment. The AO surgeons, however, did not assume financial risk, one essential element of becoming an entrepreneur. The AO relied, successfully, on the contributions of the producers as entrepreneurs and used their financial capital to build an entire industry. Early on in the creation of the AO, the organization helped Mathys, a small business owner, get over a financial squeeze by issuing letters of comfort, as they would be called today. But in the end, it was Mathys who had to risk his own net worth to move ahead without the comfort of legal purchase orders, or other financial help. Robert Mathys, Sr., was in that sense an 'entrepreneur' although he, on his own, would not have thought of the *Instrumentarium* without Müller and his colleagues.

The Straumann family, first father Reinhard (1892–1967), then son Fritz (1921–1988), had already been successful in a family business, operating companies which supplied components to the watch industry. For the Straumanns, access to capital was easier than for Mathys and they used this leverage to build their enterprise. The Straumanns, like Mathys, were fully engaged financially and had to absorb the risk that comes from building up fixed assets. Again, without the association with the AO they would not have grown to the size they did, but the Straumann operation as a business, or a group of businesses, was successful prior to joining up with the AO.

Hansjörg Wyss became the third entrepreneur to be involved with the AO. Originally a professional manager working for international companies, Wyss assumed the role of the risk-taking entrepreneur when he assumed responsibility for the Synthes USA business, asking for, and obtaining, a share of the capital. At that moment, he turned from an entrepreneurial manager into a full-fledged entrepreneur, driving the expansion of the US business to the point where it became larger than the Mathys and Straumann businesses combined. With his international experience, professional training in both engineering and business administration (he earned

---

[7]Gisin, Paul (1925–1995).

his MBA at Harvard), he turned into a noticeable force within the AO, which will be explored in more detail later in the book. By all accounts, he was the most business-savvy of the three producer-entrepreneurs.

All three of them, Robert Mathys, Sr., Fritz Straumann, and Hansjörg Wyss, joined important groups within the AO, such as the TK, the organization's primary decision-making body. However, when it came to voting on issues, surgeons were always kept in the majority—the three entrepreneurs were involved in the discussions of all major changes with respect to the *Instrumentarium*, commercial policy, as well as staffing. With their combined views and backed by an ever-growing clout as their enterprises grew, the producers played an increasingly influential role as the AO evolved.

The Legal, Tax, and Financial Talent

Last but not least, there was the necessary legal and financial talent that contributed to the mix of personalities joining the AO discussions. With the founding surgeons having lacked formal business or legal background, the AO relied heavily on the talents and know-how of Peter von Rechenberg (1920–1992). It was von Rechenberg who created the AO's legal and contractual framework and the financial arrangements between producers and Synthes AG Chur, the recipient of the revenue stream based on producer contributions.

There were also considerable tax implications to be recognized, all of which the AO surgeons had little idea about. Because von Rechenberg had no financial stake in the AO operations, or with the producers, he was able to play a moderating role when the main players ran into heated arguments. His accounting firm, Curia, also served as the auditor of the AO accounts. And for many years, he chaired the organizational meetings of the TK, taking a central role in the AO.

The Mix of Talents and Professional Cultures

One of the AO's achievements was the organization's ability to leverage the diversity of talents based on different professional cultures, as was just described, and to do so without a single central organization that employed all of them under one roof. If one adds to this the different national and language cultures represented within the AO, this achievement is even more astounding.

Most of the players were independent people, working in different locations, belonging to different organizations, and yet managing to act in the form of a single virtual team. In today's business world, it is not unusual to have these virtual teams, even across country boundaries. However, modern communications technologies allow for much more flexible organizations. Over the first 25 years of the AO, there were no mobile phones, no fax machines, no email, no internet, never mind internet search engines. A large amount of mailed paper correspondence is accumulated in the AO archives, and Müller commented to one biographer that in the first 20 years of the AO he was in almost daily contact with some of his key colleagues, such as Allgöwer. It is remarkable that the AO managed to achieve its goals under these circumstances.

The Private and Personal Passions of the AO Founders

The AO was not only made up of talented people with varying professional experience, educational skills and backgrounds, but the organization also attracted talent that had an enormous amount of energy and persistence, all of which must have added to the complexity of dealing with all of these personalities. Some of those passions, and how they influenced the AO, have to be mentioned—subjects that are likely to come up whenever talking about the organization to long-standing members.

Officers and Gentlemen

Whenever one peruses historical volumes from the AO, and the stories of how their founding surgeons connected with one another, the role played by the Swiss military quickly emerges. Many of the founding surgeons were officers of the Swiss military, primarily in the medical corps. Men in Switzerland are subject to military conscription and the mandated military service involved a considerable amount of time. Medical doctors and surgeons were typically assigned to the medical corps as officers, requiring them to spend significant amounts of time, on a regular basis, in the army, often for several weeks each year. Many of the AO founders served long periods in the military during World War II. These long stints of service were conducive to face-to-face discussions and to creating personal contacts, often leading to friendships. Although Müller and Schneider, two of the five core founders, had known each other from their hometown of Biel, it was during long periods of military service where their friendship was rekindled, also using their time to discuss medical issues. Müller, who was promoted as one of the youngest majors in the Swiss Army, leveraged some of his experience to train for surgery and organize courses for his colleagues later on (Exhibit 30.1).

Even if they did not all meet in the military service, the approaches and organizational norms common to all of them would invariably create some familiarity. Bandi, another member of the G5, rose to colonel, and Willenegger was also an officer who had initially heard about Müller through military contacts. These connections helped Müller recruit his core team leading up to the founding of the AO in 1958 but, of course, it was not his military experience that caused him to pursue Osteosynthesis for bone trauma.

Exhibit 30.1 Allgöwer in
Swiss Army uniform.
*Copyright by AO Foundation,
Switzerland*

The Sports Enthusiasts

Many of the early AO founders were avid sports enthusiasts, particularly of skiing.
They often combined skiing with medical meetings. The passion for skiing would
become a regular ritual of the AO courses in Davos, and it was not only recreational;
regular ski races were organized and some of the AO leaders were in a highly
competitive mode when heading to the slopes. It has also been reported that when the
early courses where organized in the US, the Swiss AO team would travel to the
Canadian Rockies at the end of a meeting or conference to have ski adventures there
(Exhibit 30.2).

There was a long tradition of ski jumping in the Straumann family where
company founder Reinhard Straumann had been a ski jumper, later becoming
involved with aerodynamics and the construction of ski jumps. This passion for
ski jumping continued even into a later era when the Straumann Organization was
involved in the development of special ski bindings for the Swiss Ski jumper Simon
Ammann, twice an Olympic Champion, winning gold medals in both 2002
and 2010.

Exhibit 30.2 Müller skiing.
Copyright by AO Foundation,
Switzerland

Aviators Among the AO Founders

As mentioned previously, aviation was a passion for many AO members. There was the flight of Robert Mathys, Sr., around Africa in 1966, and Stephan Perren's around-the-world flight in 2005–2006. The passion for flying involved several other individuals as well and was, in some ways, instrumental in the development of the Synthes business in the US. Talking to people with long-standing associations with AO, many of these stories resurfaced coalescing around certain individuals.

Robert Mathys, Sr., also had an intense interest in flying; ever since he was young he had hoped to join the Swiss Air Force after World War II as a professional pilot. Instead, he used his passion to incorporate flying into his work for the AO, even locally, and not just for the flight around Africa. One story related by several sources dealt with the situation of a blocked drill. Allgöwer and his medical team were performing a trauma operation in a regional hospital in the Swiss Rheintal Valley near Sargans. In the middle of the operation, the drill blocked, and in frustration Allgöwer telephoned Mathys for advice in his workshop in Bettlach, near Biel. Mathys immediately jumped into a small plane and flew to Ragaz, a small regional landing strip nearby, from which he was whisked into the operating room and deblocked the drill. This was flying in the service of the AO!

A second anecdote involved Allgöwer, who had himself become an avid aviator. During a flight, presumably from Chur to Basel, a warning came up to lower the landing gear during the landing approach. He apparently remarked to his fellow passengers that he did not need this warning, upon which he promptly forgot to lower the gear. When his plane survived the landing, without going into a somersault, he is reported to have said that he must have performed a pretty good landing for this to have been avoided.

Allgöwer's passion for flying eventually led to a friendship with Hansjörg Wyss. The two met over a plane purchase. Allgöwer acquired a plane in the US and did not want to fly it across the Atlantic. Wyss took care of it, and closer contact was struck up that eventually led to Wyss being nominated as head of the Synthes USA. The affinity Allgöwer felt for Wyss might, in part, be attributed to their common interest in flying. This may also have developed into a business trust, which eventually caused Müller to complain that he himself was increasingly losing influence among the core AO founder group. Wyss later remembered the time when he flew, together with Allgöwer, a twin-engine plane from Philadelphia to Basel, with two stops along the way, as a formative experience. Even to this day, Wyss remains an avid licensed pilot.[8]

Love for Animals

If there was one private passion that pulled many of the early AO members together, it was their shared love of animals. As a result, they soon found ways to include AO surgical principles and implants to mend broken bones of animals. Eventually, this love for animals led to the creation of AOVET, first as a separate but affiliated organization and later as a full member of the AO family of clinical divisions.

Famously, there was also Urs Guggenbühl (one of G13) with his large dogs in his convertible car. Another core member of AO organization, Fritz Straumann, was a horse lover and raised them on his farm near Waldenburg. He was a dog lover as well, which eventually led him to connect with the veterinarians who became instrumental in creating AOVET, as described in greater detail earlier.

There Was Always Magic

And, finally, whether it was a hobby, a skill, or a passion, there was often a show of card tricks displayed by Maurice Müller and remembered by many at the AO. Müller had achieved a very high European ranking as an amateur magician and often showed off his card tricks at dinners to entertain guests. There was a serious and

---

[8]Interview with Hans-Jörg Wyss was conducted on 2 December, 2017, in Davos.

professional side to this as well; Müller's manual dexterity was considered unmatched and connections were drawn between his ability to perform card tricks and his superior surgical skills.

A Potent Mix of Professional Cultures and Passions

Although everyone was governed by the same goals and shared values, the different personalities, when locked into a room to review a new implant or decide on a different business strategy for their enterprise, often collided and led to some intense discussions. In the early years, the role of main moderator in such clashes of points-of-view fell to von Rechenberg, the AO organization's legal and tax council. In later years, it was the power of their shared values that served as the glue for this highly diverse group of talented people who constituted the early days of the AO.

Summarizing Growth Phase   **31**

As the AO organization reached the mid-1980s, members could look back on a highly successful period, covering the first 25 years of its formal existence. This section has covered the major events that triggered a growth phase resulting in a formidable, committed, and well-resourced organization on the cusp of having achieved its initial goals of establishing the surgical concept of Osteosynthesis as the medical community's gold standard, at least in the world's higher-income countries.

As detailed in the Chaps. 19–22, the AO managed to create, together with its affiliated industrial producers, an entire industry which produced its *Instrumentarium* and distributed it worldwide. First with the Mathys and Straumann companies, and later with Synthes USA, the AO attracted three entrepreneurs willing to invest in its ideas and building three thriving enterprises. These three companies generated annual contributions to the AO of almost CHF 12 million annually and growing. This revenue stream was generated by the producing companies who could piggyback on the efforts of the AO surgeons, and bring the message to every corner of the world.

The growing revenue was invested partly in an extensive build-out of the *Instrumentarium*, growing from about 200 elements at the beginning to about 1200. In Chaps. 23–25, it is clear that the ever increasing and diversified *Instrumentarium* allowed the AO to move beyond the long bones initial trauma and create instruments that could be used in other parts of the human skeleton, such as for CMF and Spine, in addition to applications in veterinary medicine. This expansion was partly achieved through the clever leveraging of surgical experience between the various fields of surgery and supported by creative and highly effective research and development efforts.

Throughout its growth phase, the AO and its members engaged in an extensive campaign to have the AO philosophy heard, and understood, in every corner of the world. As covered in Chaps. 26–29, the AO leaders were tireless in their personal missionary work. Individual elements of the early AO were strengthened, so that the communications work became a major force; this included building a veritable

© Springer Nature Switzerland AG 2019   237
J.-P. Jeannet, *Leading a Surgical Revolution*,
https://doi.org/10.1007/978-3-030-01980-8_31

'Trauma University,' publishing an extensive stream of written materials, and cementing this with the internationalization of the AO organization.

The section ends with Chap. 30, which provides some background about the various and diverse talent that contributed to this effort. The nature of the professional talents, the wide range of backgrounds and expertise of those early contributors, and the open way with which they collaborated all played important roles in bringing the AO to the point it reached: a mature organization, which was able to disrupt the established treatment of broken bones and replace it with a radically different approach in the form of Osteosynthesis. Although the AO founders did not invent Osteosynthesis, without their effort and ingenuity it would not have achieved the position in medical treatment that it holds today. The AO founders carefully chose all of the most useful elements available, combined them and created a powerful surgical methodology and philosophy that overcame all the inherent weaknesses of the original concept.

Part III

Navigating Turbulence

Changing of the Guard

32

From Young Turks to Establishment

The leading surgeons making up the AO's core G5 group were in their early 40s when the organization was created in 1958. Those head surgeons at regional hospitals that were recruited into the founder's group, of what became known as the G13, were also about of the same age as the core founders. This was a group of young Turks willing to take on the medical establishment with a revolutionary idea. At that time, none of the founders had any university appointments. Some 20 to 25 years later, however, many changes had taken place and the AO founders had all taken on prestigious roles and positions. Since hospital-based surgeons in Switzerland are required to retire at age 65, they were also approaching the end of their active surgical careers.

Over the organization's first 20 years, the core team around Müller, Allgöwer, Willenegger, Schneider, and to a lesser degree Bandi, had worked closely with one another, shared all key decisions and appointments, and were in regular, almost daily, contact about organizational and medical issues. Discussions about the search for the next generation of leaders had been going on for some time. Lead counsel von Rechenberg had raised the issue as early as the late 1960s, when the AO was just ten years old. Things were running smoothly at that time: Schneider was comfortable in the role of chair of the Swiss AO; the TK functioned well with the four founding surgeons making the necessary business decisions together, in conjunction with producers Mathys and Straumann; licensing income into the Synthes AG Chur was growing, allowing the AO organization to continuously expand its support for ARI, the Research Institute, the Documentation Center, and the Davos courses. Also, as the principles of the AO became increasingly accepted, first in Europe and later in the US, the founders' reputations rose, and changes in positions and promotions became the norm. At the time, the founders must have asked, 'why rock the boat?'

© Springer Nature Switzerland AG 2019
J.-P. Jeannet, *Leading a Surgical Revolution*,
https://doi.org/10.1007/978-3-030-01980-8_32

Triggering Change

Despite the success enjoyed by the AO and its champions, change began to come in through retirements. Robert Schneider was the first to retire, in 1970, from his role as head of the regional hospital near Berne but maintaining his role of Chair of the Swiss AO until 1978 when he stepped down after 20 years of intensive duty on a part-time and voluntary basis. Schneider was also a key player in the AOTK and, thus, in Synthes AG Chur where he was one of four major shareholders, together with Müller, Allgöwer, and Willenegger. Synthes AG Chur was the legal unit where the producers licensing fees were collected. Schneider continued to remain active in AO affairs and in AO book publications.

To replace Schneider, the AO did not elect a younger member to head the Swiss AO. Instead, the organization appointed Allgöwer who had moved in 1967 from his appointment in Chur to assume a professorship in Basel, the same year Müller became a professor in Berne. Allgöwer remained in Basel until his retirement in 1983 and served as the chair of AO Switzerland until 1982. At that time, he took over AO International. Only then did the chairmanship for the Swiss AO get turned over to a next generation surgeon, Peter Matter, who had trained under Allgöwer and headed the hospital in Davos. He was the first of the second-generation surgeons to assume a prominent leadership position.

Müller, who had assumed leadership of the hospital of St. Gallen in 1960, after ending his stint as itinerant surgeon, was soon courted by the Berne University Hospital where he started in 1963, part-time at first and then becoming a full-time professor in 1967. He held his chair until 1980 when he decided to retire from his teaching position. Although this was admittedly early, he had grown tired of the administrative burden of being a professor. He also wanted to spend an increasing amount of time on the AO and his Protek business which, through the sale of his hip replacement business, began to generate increasing amounts of funding for his research at the University of Berne. He held on to the Chairmanship of TK until 1987.

Willenegger retired from his position in Liestal in 1975 and assumed a part-time position at the University of Basel, investing a lot of time in the AO International organization, which he helped found in 1973 and led until 1983. Bandi, meanwhile retired from his hospital appointment in Interlaken in 1978 and despite having had a severe accident, continued to remain active as a scientific advisor within the AO.

This concentration of decision-making power in the hands of a few senior surgeons did not go unnoticed. Young AO surgeons, particularly those who had been trained by the founders at the leading AO hospitals in St. Gallen, Chur, Basel, Liestal, and Berne, were increasingly unhappy with the structure that, through Synthes AG Chur and the AOTK, concentrated considerable power in the hands of a few.

Second Generation Members Ask for a Bigger Role

The younger surgeons who had trained under the founders had themselves become members of the Swiss AO in the 1960s and 1970s. Except for a few, such as Matter and Perren, who had each become the head of AO research, none of them had managed to penetrate the core organizational units of Synthes AG Chur or the AOTK. In addition, AO International, originally conceived as an umbrella unit to house all of the international chapters, as well as the Swiss AO, did not manage to fulfill this role and became largely a service organization devoted to running AO courses around the world. As a result, the increasing number of international AO surgeons could not find a way into the organizational leadership structure; it must have felt to them as being largely monopolized by Swiss-based surgeons, which it was.

The decision-making process within that small group of surgeons that was operated, by all accounts, by consensus, had been, effectively, dominated by Müller. While everyone involved agreed that this worked well for a close-knit group, the increasing complexity of the AO, its international growth, and the corresponding growth of its industrial base, required a more professional or managerial form of leadership more open to the participation of its base.

Producers Raise Their Voices

The three AO licensed producers, Mathys, Straumann, and Synthes USA, represented by Wyss, had their own concerns. As their business grew with the steady rise in sales of the AO *Instrumentarium* in their assigned geographies, there was the concern that all business decisions were made by surgeons who, in their view, had little business experience. The creation of the AO *Verwaltungsausschuss*, or Administrative Council (AOVA), which handled business decisions, was a way to give more voice to the three producers. They were, as everywhere, always in the minority since the council had more surgeons than producer representatives. This was another signal that the original structure had surpassed its usefulness.

The need for a change was all the more apparent when von Rechenberg, after many years of service and in the role of not only lead council but also moderator of the core group, decided to retire in 1983.

The steady retirements of the AO founders from their positions of influence in their hospitals or universities, and the lack of younger surgeons put into more senior positions by the leaders, would indicate that it was now no longer just a matter of appointing younger talent into existing roles, but that there was a need to change the entire structure that had, up until now, served the organization well. This moment arrived in the early 1980s with the creation of the AO Foundation, a substantial legal break from the past; a process described in the next chapter.

From Association to Foundation

33

The Association Format Had Outlived Its Purpose

When the basis for AO's growth was laid in the early 1960s with the creation of the Synthes AG Chur, and the institutionalizing of development through the AOTK, the levers of control were in the hands of just four surgeons—Müller, Schneider, Allgöwer, and Willenegger. They were all shareholders in Synthes AG Chur, the vessel built to collect the royalties from the three producers and to further fund and develop the AO. The allocation of funds from these collected fees remained in the hands of these four surgeons for most of the AO's early years.

Contributions generated by producers were not confined to sales in Switzerland, but also included revenues from other countries. At the time, Germany was the leading market, causing tensions between the German AO surgeons who had no effective decision-making participation in the AO budgeting process. The international surgeons, particularly the Germans, expected that through the creation of the AO International, they would be able to have more input in the various AO bodies. This, as we stated previously, never materialized.

By 1979, according to Allgöwer, the AO and its organizations had dispensed over CHF 32 million into its various activities, ranging from the Research Center in Davos to the Documentation Center in Berne. By 1982, the annual contributions from the producers passed CHF 10 million. The allocation of this amount to the various activities of the AO amounted to a major control lever in the organization.[1] Accumulated spending by the AO, since its creation, had reached CHF 88 million by 1984.

As early as 1975, a committee of AO members aired the idea of creating a foundation. The foundation structure was thought to be able to preserve the tax-free status of the AO. Since a foundation might then be in the hands of some

---

[1]Schlich (2002), pp. 227–232.

© Springer Nature Switzerland AG 2019
J.-P. Jeannet, *Leading a Surgical Revolution*,
https://doi.org/10.1007/978-3-030-01980-8_33

50–60 members, mostly surgeons, concerns were voiced that this could result in decisions that might be detrimental to AO's industrial partners. The major risk discussed concerned the possibility of granting licensing rights to other producers, which would essentially touch on the business of existing producers.

Synthes AG Chur Shareholder Changes

Within the core group of the Swiss founders, there was an interest in passing on some of the Synthes AG Chur shares to a younger generation of surgeons. Originally, shareholding was restricted to the four founders who could only pass on their shares with the agreement of the others. The beneficiaries of this strategy were three young Swiss surgeons of the next generation: Peter Matter,[2] Thomas Rüedi,[3] and Stephan Perren.[4]

While this helped position some of the next generation of surgeons who were highly respected, it did not do enough to stop the discussion about a bigger share of control. Müller, with 20 shares and 40% of the vote, had received the shares of Schneider upon his retirement. Effectively, he could, and to some extent did, control Synthes AG Chur.

It should be noted again that the Synthes AG Chur shares were not considered to be personal commercial investments, and no dividends were ever to be paid to shareholders. The main benefit for the shareholders was being able to participate in key decisions which they considered critical to their professional lives.

Creating a Foundation

Reviewing available sources does not completely clarify where the initial idea to change from being an association to forming a foundation came from. What is known is that Allgöwer actively supported the idea and some suspect that Wyss did as well, by then the head of Synthes USA.

The AO Foundation became formally established on 8 December, 1984.

- Persons present at the signing of the foundation documents:
  - Allgöwer, AO Founder, Synthes AG Chur shareholder
  - Müller, AO Founder, Synthes AG Chur shareholder
  - Mathys, Sr., Producer Mathys AG
  - Matter, AO Member, Synthes AG Chur shareholder

---

[2]Peter Matter, Chief Surgeon Davos Hospital, at that time Chair of AO Switzerland.
[3]Thomas Rüedi, AO Member, Chief Surgeon Chur Hospital.
[4]Stephan Perren, AO Member, Head of ARI.

- Perren, AO Member, Synthes AG Chur shareholder
- von Rechenberg Sr., Legal Counsel
- Rüedi, AO Member, Synthes AG Chur shareholder
- Schneider, AO Founder, Synthes AG Chur shareholder
- Straumann, Producer, Straumann Institute
- Willenegger, AO Founder, Synthes AG Chur shareholder
- Wyss, Producer Synthes USA
- Margrit Jaques, Minutes taker

For the new foundation to be legally and formally established, it required some assets, or starting capital: All Synthes AG Chur shareholders 'permanently and irrevocably' contributed their Synthes AG Chur shares to the AO Foundation, thus leaving Synthes AG Chur in place as a legal unit. The three producers, not shareholders of Synthes AG Chur, made cash contributions to the AO Foundation in the amounts of CHF 500,000 for Mathys, and CHF 100,000 each for Wyss and Straumann (Exhibit 33.1).

Exhibit 33.1 Signing of the AO Foundation Documents 1984, Hotel Schweizerhof, Davos. Persons present starting upper left head of table Dr. P. v. Rechenberg, and from there clockwise Dr. Th. Rüedi, Dr. P. Matter, F. Straumann, Dr. hc. Robert Mathys, Sr., Prof. Dr. St. Perren, H. Wyss, Prof. Dr. H. Willenegger, Prof. Dr. R. Schneider, Prof. Dr. M. Müller, Prof. Dr. M. Allgöwer, and, finally, a notary attending. Also attending, but not shown is Margrit Jaques who wrote the minutes of the meeting. *Copyright by AO Foundation, Switzerland*

Formal Bodies of the AO Foundation

Once the decision to create a foundation had been made, attention turned to the bodies that would govern this foundation. The governing 'parliament' of the AO Foundation would be the Board of Trustees, expanded to include about 80 active AO members, the vast majority of them working surgeons.

The first set of trustees assembled for the inaugural meeting held in 1985, in Davos, consisted of:

Swiss 25
German 14
American 14
Austrian 5
UK 4
Rest of the World 16

Membership to the Board of Trustees was by recommendation of a separate Business Council and voted on by the Board of Trustees themselves. The Board of Trustees was also the body that elected all key AO positions as per recommendations of the Business Council.

Reporting to the Board of Trustees was an Executive Committee with 15 members, including the presidents of the Board of Trustees, of key committees and commissions (Education, Documentation, and Research), as well as the heads of the Technical Committee.

Although Swiss surgeons represented less than half of the Foundation members, they still controlled key organizational units and positions in technical commissions. The board elected Martin Allgöwer as its first President, a position he was to occupy until 1992.

The last, but very important, body that came out of the reorganization was the Business Council, later renamed Board of Directors of the AO Foundation. This group was tasked with all the commercial activities that essentially funded the AO Foundation. Composed of up to five surgeons, the Council included one representative of each of the three licensed producers: Mathys, Straumann, and Synthes USA. Although they were in the minority, the producers had the right to reopen any issue should all three of them agree and find themselves in the minority of the decision.

The bodies of the Foundation, the Board of Trustees as the legislative parliament, as well as the Business Council (as mentioned, later renamed Board of Directors and then the Foundation Board) have remained the key structural elements of the AO Foundation to this day.

Struggle for a Different Role for the Industrial Partners

The formal inclusion of the industrial partners in the decision-making process was a change from previous AO practice, whereby producers were present and could provide input on discussions but could not vote. Now they had a formal voting right. As it turned out, this point was to create a substantial amount of discussion within the AO and was not really put to rest until some 20 years later when the AO changed the basis of its finance model. Opposed to the producers having a voting right was Maurice Müller himself, who had always fought to separate the business decisions from the medical ones, and who felt that a charter of a non-profit enterprise was mixed with that of a for-profit enterprise. But what were the basis of these concerns?

Looking at this through the lens of the industrial partners, they had begun to invest ever-larger amounts into the production base of the AO *Instrumentarium*. Combined sales for the three producers had reached about CHF 300 million world-wide and required substantial investments into plants, machinery, and distribution operations. Their interests were clearly directed to the business side, and because they felt they contributed the bulk of the AO Foundation budget, they wanted adequate representation. Many among the AO surgeons were sympathetic to the producers' concerns, including one of the founders, Allgöwer.

Looking through the lens of a medical doctor and social entrepreneur, which was how Maurice Müller conceived his professional role, he was always keen on separating the business from the medical side of the AO enterprise. Throughout the creation of the AO, he had argued to separate the two, meaning that business concerns should not drive decisions on *Instrumentarium* or surgical practice. Müller was also concerned that, in the case of the producers, who were accumulating wealth through the very profitable manufacturing of implants, they could find ways to influence individual members of the Business Council who did not command the same financial resources. In addition, Müller did not trust Wyss, the newcomer among the three producers, and as Allgöwer drew ever closer to Wyss regarding business decisions, Müller felt left out. Eventually, this rift led to Müller leaving the AO Foundation and stepping down from all of his AO functions in 1989.

The institutional turbulence created by the conversion from a Swiss association (the original by-laws of the AO) into a foundation, did not, of course, settle tensions arising from the conflict regarding the role of the AO and its royalty contributing producers. Although the AO now had institutional units to deal with any conflict, this does not mean that no new conflicts arose as the organization grew. Wenger, who took over from von Rechenberg to chair the Business Council meetings, remembered frequent in-fighting and heated discussions to the point where he once walked out of the meeting threatening not to return. Some of the clashes were centered on the producers' contracts and the geographic market allocation; for one, the division of Germany into two parts was the cause of constant discussions. Other disagreements had to do with the unallocated territories in Asia, particularly China.[5]

Margrit Jaques, who kept the minutes of these coordinating meetings for many years (from 1970 to 2004) and became an Honorary AO Foundation Member, also

[5]Interview with Dr. iur. Jean-Claude Wenger, founding partner of Wenger & Vieli AG, Zurich, was conducted on 14 March, 2017, in Zurich.

remembered intense and heated discussions; she was always surprised, however, that after these meetings, the members would enjoy a glass of wine and dinner together.[6] Although the overall purposes of the AO was never in doubt, certainly, the participants in this social enterprise were not always in full harmony on all details.

Conflicts Emerge Again

The conflicts over the purpose of the AO erupted a second time in dramatic fashion and culminated around 2002. At the time, even long-standing members were not sure that the AO would survive. This second conflict, long developing, had again to do with the relative roles played by surgeons versus producers.

It started in the 1990s over diverging views on developing the AO into related areas, such as Orthopedic joint replacements. With the AOTrauma *Instrumentarium* becoming increasingly mature, surgeons found new areas of interest in Orthopedics. In 1994, the AO Executive Committee recommended that the AO enter this emerging field and two years later additional details were discussed further in a brainstorming meeting.

The surgeons who were members of the AO Executive Board at that time argued that the field of Orthopedics was becoming increasingly important to them. Both Mathys and Straumann had begun to build up their respective Orthopedic business lines in parallel with the production of AO implants. After Sulzer bought Protek, the Orthopedic business created by Müller, the company cancelled distribution agreements for the Orthopedic lines made by both Straumann and Mathys. This raised the prospect that both companies might compete against each other in the future when it came to Orthopedic lines.

Sulzer Corporation came knocking on the doors of the AO Foundation expressing an interest in collaborating with the Foundation in the area of Orthopedics. The AO surgeons were interested in engaging in a research collaboration with Sulzer, due to many unresolved issues surrounding the implantation of prosthesis that also directly related to the AO trauma business. However, divergent interests between the producers in Europe, in addition to the fact that Synthes USA under the leadership of Wyss was not interested in entering the field of Orthopedics, meant that the proposal was shelved.

The three producers had become unhappy with the direction of the AO leadership and circulated a common position paper to propose changes in the AO Foundation structure. They wanted more control over some of the aspects handled by the AO, in particular shifting development responsibility to the producers. With educational programs being of central importance to producers—they saw this as a key aspect generating future sales—the producers also wanted to decentralize regional education.

---

[6]Interview with Margrit Jaques, AO Honorary Foundation Member, was conducted on 3 February, 2017, in Berne.

Improving the technical commission's (TK) decision-making process, in terms of speed and efficiency, was another constant point of discussion. Wyss complained that over the past 15 years no real development breakthrough had taken place. By all accounts, the AOTK had become too large, was not responsive enough, and lacked speed, due to the sheer number of participants.

It was agreed to put all new developments into a single 'pool' and then decide who should produce what. At about the same time, Robert Frigg, one of the ARI key developers and AOTK members, was transferred to Synthes USA, first for a temporary assignment and later on for good. Last but not least, the AO created special clinical divisions devoted to the surgical specialties for trauma, spine, and maxillofacial, thus eliminating control of the large AO-wide TK in those areas, and added several smaller ones dedicated to certain medical areas.

Surgeons Versus MBAs

Alone, these differing perspectives would not have triggered the major row that erupted in 2002 on the occasion of the trustees' meeting in Oslo. The fact that Synthes USA, under Wyss' leadership, had previously acquired Stratec Medical (the new name for Straumann's medical implant business) and thus, becoming AO's dominant industrial supplier, was certainly a major contributor to the internal tensions. Within the AO, trustees split in two groups—one that strove for more independence from producers and a second that wished to preserve the commercial links that had been so beneficial to the organization's growth. The AO CEO at that time, Wolfram Einars, strongly favored dropping the exclusivity for producers, meaning that the AO would be free to approach other manufacturers and offer product licenses.

Faced with the risk of losing exclusivity for the AO *Instrumentarium*, producers, under Wyss' leadership, assembled a coalition that resulted in the non-election of the AO President-elect, Ulli Holz, by mounting a challenge with a different candidate, René Marti,[7] who in the end edged out Holz by the slim margin of one vote. The group in support of Holz, who had advocated a more independent stance from the producers, narrowly lost out. The fact that the organization did not break apart over this dispute can be attributed to the willingness of all to pursue the greater good and the goals of the AO over the fight for commercial issues. Ultimately, the strength of the AO Foundation, and its membership was, as they were about to pass the leadership from the second to the third generation of surgeons, that the recognized, common purpose of the organization remained its most powerful glue.

The struggle for an arms-length relationship between producers and surgeons was an important one and went straight to the core of the AO Foundation as a social entrepreneurial enterprise, or a not-for-profit, versus the producers who were focused on running their business and their own vested financial interests.

---

[7]René Marti, AO President, 2002–2004. Marti was a Swiss surgeon working in the Netherlands.

The rebel group of AO surgeons, including some executive committee members, resented that producers had voting rights on all issues. There was a sense that the AO was becoming just a show for producers. These issues were actually the reasons why, after the creation of the AO Foundation, Müller bowed out. He, too, objected to granting voting rights to the producers on key committees.

The more conservative members of the AO were realistic in understanding that the AO needed a revenue base, because otherwise their programs could not continue. As this conflict erupted, the conservative members maintained the upper hand and the producers were intent on preventing any new leadership that might touch the foundation of their business, which depended on the exclusivity of the AO relationship.

Reflecting on the Struggle 15 Years Later

Even 15 years after the events in Oslo, that conflict was always referred to in interviews conducted with the attendees of that fateful meeting. Among those present was James Kellam, and Holz, who both ended up on the losing ticket, reflected positively about the outcomes and the changes over time. Kellam, who became AO President two turns later, thought the changes sought by the rebel group were eventually implemented, step by step, and that the AO again turned more towards science, with the entire funding structure changing in a direction, which was much more amenable to those opposed to the former financial model.[8]

Reference

Schlich, T. (2002). *Surgery, science and industry* (pp. 17–19). Basingstoke: Palgrave Macmillan.

---

[8]Telephone interview with James Kellam conducted on 4 January 2018, (AO President 2004–2006).

The Status of the Producer Base in 1985

The three AO-licensed producers—Mathys, Straumann, and Synthes USA—had all operated under the same exclusive AO supply agreement since 1963. Prior to the legal change of becoming a foundation, the producers had only advisory roles, with no voting rights concerning key business arrangements impacting on their businesses. With the creation of the AO Foundation, the producer's roles changed and they gained voting rights as part of the Business Council, although a small majority of seats were still held by surgeons. The change in voting rights, opposed by some of the AO founders at that time, gave the producers more status and a stronger voice in defending their interests.

Growth Continues

By the beginning of 1985, the producers' business had grown substantially. Mathys, privately-held and the original producer and co-developer of the *Instrumentarium*, had grown from being a small workshop to producing a sales volume of about CHF 100 million. Its employee headcount had risen to an estimated 400, including production employees and some staff in international sales companies.[1] The annual royalty and contribution paid to the AO Foundation at that time amounted to CHF 5.9 million.[2] In order to accommodate the growing volume, Mathys expanded its production base in its hometown of Bettlach. Sales took place in the assigned international markets as agreed under the 1963 Olten deal.

---

[1] Source: The Mathys Company, unpublished data, 2018.
[2] AO Foundation Financial Records.

© Springer Nature Switzerland AG 2019
J.-P. Jeannet, *Leading a Surgical Revolution*,
https://doi.org/10.1007/978-3-030-01980-8_34

For Straumann, who had moved its AO implant business into a separate organizational unit, no published data was available, as the company was also privately-held and ownership rested with the Straumann family. Since royalty and support payments paid for by Straumann at that time amounted to CHF 4.3 million, it can be assumed that Straumann had sales of about 75% of Mathys' volume, or about CHF 75 million. In order to deal with the growth in production, Straumann had built a new plant in Oberwil, a neighboring town of Waldenburg, its home base. Straumann's sales were restricted to its allocated territory as agreed to in the Olten deal.

The third producer, Synthes USA, under management of Hansjörg Wyss, was conducting its business in the North American markets, the US and Canada, which had originally been allocated to Straumann. When Straumann failed to make headway in the US with its US distributor, the AO founders took over responsibility for the market and became shareholders themselves. They soon realized that the US market was functioning differently and brought Wyss on board, first as a consultant and later as the managing director with a financial stake in the operation. At the insistence of Wyss, Synthes USA became the third producer of implants, directly sending royalties to the AO Foundation. By 1985, sales of Synthes USA had reached about CHF 30 million and royalties paid to the AO Foundation amounted to CHF 2.8 million.

The combined business volume of the three AO-licensed producers amounted to about CHF 200 million, with employment estimated at about 800. This was the situation at the time the AO Foundation was created. Over the next 20 years, the situation among the three producers was to chance completely. The size of their business expanded rapidly, growing tenfold, having a significant impact on the AO organization.

Management Buy-Out at Synthes USA

When Wyss assumed management responsibility at Synthes USA he did so under the condition that he could obtain a stake in the business. In 1977, he invested CHF 400,000 for a stake of about 20% . The other remaining shareholders were the AO Founders and other surgeons who had gained shares in Synthes AG Chur—the holder of the intellectual property rights and branding rights to the AO *Instrumentarium*. In the same year that Wyss had made his investment, Synthes USA produced sales of about USD 5 million.

Once Wyss was in charge, he adapted the marketing and sales strategy to closer reflect the needs of the US market. He pushed for a manufacturing plant to be built in Monument, Colorado, which was finished in 1979. Placing great emphasis on education and training programs that were located in the US and adding a sales force that was capable of advising surgeons even during surgery, volume grew rapidly. In the period from 1985 to 1987, sales grew to USD 64 million, twice the volume seen in 1984 when the AO Foundation was created.[3] This commercial push caused AO co-founder Müller to complain to Wyss about the over-commercializing of AO ideas and led to their eventual rift with Müller leaving the AO Foundation board altogether in January 1989.

Wyss proposed to buy out the existing shareholders, involving all the AO surgeons and investors who had invested into the US distribution business since the mid-1970s. The purchase price for the business reported was USD 54 million.[4] Structured as a leveraged buy-out, the purchase allowed Wyss to pay part of the price over time from the cash flow generated by the business. About 20% of the proceeds from the share sale obtained by the AO physicians, totaling CHF 12 million, was donated towards building a new AO center in Davos.

With the leveraged buy-out completed, Wyss had now reached the same status as the other two producers, Mathys and Straumann, who both owned their respective businesses outright. Being represented on the Business Council, and later the Board of Directors of the AO, the three producers began to coordinate their activities in order to act more in concert with one another. Now there were three true business entrepreneurs in charge of the production base of the AO *Instrumentarium*, and the surgeons had divested themselves of the last vestiges of business ownership while still being shareholders of Synthes USA.

Fritz Straumann's Unexpected Death

The sudden death of Fritz Straumann in 1988, at the age of 67, created significant change for the Straumann enterprises, including the AO implant business. Fritz Straumann had been a very influential figure within the AO organization, having become a Scientific Member of the AO in 1967. He played an active role in the development of the *Instrumentarium*, the science behind the metallurgy, and through his love for animals was an active supporter of AOVET from the outset. Within the AO he was member of the TK and a contributor to the first AO book *Technik*, published in 1963. After the death of his father Reinhard Straumann (1892–1967) he had taken charge of the Straumann family businesses and became Chairman and CEO of Straumann Holding.

Fritz Straumann had a major impact on the material science side of the AO *Instrumentarium*. It was his decision to go for titanium as a key raw material. In the beginning, trials were made with different combinations, ranging from pure titanium to alloys, which became the material of choice, although it was more expensive by a factor of five compared to stainless steel. The Straumann team eventually managed to settle on an alloy that had about the same strength as steel.

---

[3]Based upon available information, the purchase price at the time amounted to less than 1x sales, a relatively low amount given the profitability and growth prospects of the AO implant business in the US.

[4]"Die Schweiz ist mir zu kompliziert", *Weltwoche*, 8 October, 2014.

Key benefits of titanium had to do with patient comfort: titanium created no known allergies, was a lighter material, and did not cause problems for patients in cold weather which is of great importance in CMF implants. As it turned out, this was also of great value to dental implants, a business that Straumann was to develop later and one that was quite different from trauma implants—dental implants are not meant to be removed.[5] The AOTK did approve titanium implants in 1989, one year after Fritz Straumann's death. Full market introduction was to take longer.

Spinning Off the Implant Business

The death in the Straumann family triggered a considerable reorganization of its business. With combined sales of about CHF 120 million, the Straumann Group was divided into two separate parts: the first part was named Stratec Medical, which produced AO implants and was the larger of the two, about 75% of the business; the second part included the other businesses, such as dental, material science and testing, and electronics and watch components, all accounting for about 25%. Fritz's son, Thomas Straumann, took charge of the second, smaller part of the organization. Since 1986, the larger part of the Straumann Group was managed by Rudolf Maag, who acquired what would become Stratec Medical in 1989 through a management buy-out for a reported CHF 120 million.[6] The business was structured as a privately-held company, with some insiders maintaining that the financing had been arranged for by Credit Suisse, with the expectation that when, and if, Stratec went public, the deal would be managed by Credit Suisse. From there, the business continued under the name of Stratec Medical. When Stratec did indeed go public in 1996, stock market information indicated that Maag owned 54% of the company with the rest in the hands of public shareholders.

As owner-manager in charge of Stratec Medical, Rudolf Maag joined the other owners, Mathys and Wyss, on the AO Business Council as a voting member. Under his leadership, the business of Stratec, parallel to the other AO producers, experienced significant growth. A new factory was built in Oberdorf, a neighboring town to Waldenburg, in 1994. A second factory was acquired in the town of Hägendorf, near Solothurn, and a third factory was built in the Italian part of Switzerland, near the Italian border for easier access to a larger workforce pool. Sales grew by a factor of three since Maag assumed leadership, reaching some CHF 264 million, with a healthy profitability of CHF 47 million, and a total headcount of 900 people. Stratec's market share in Europe was about 35% and its competitive position was first in trauma, second in spine and CMF, and first again in surgical power tools.[7]

---

[5]Interview with Thomas Straumann, conducted on 1 March, 2018, in Basel.

[6]Interview with Thomas Straumann, Op. cit. This purchase price would amount to about 1.6x 1989 sales. This is higher than what Wyss paid for Synthes USA, but it is still a relatively modest amount for this type of business.

[7]Julius Bär, Analyst Investor Report on Stratec, 26 February, 1999.

Throughout this time, Wyss expressed an interest in acquiring either Mathys or Stratec. In return, Maag had put out feelers to acquire Mathys. Everybody was talking to everybody, but neither Maag nor Mathys were willing to sell. A preliminary agreement reached between Maag and Wyss was cancelled, due to a disagreement on price. So finally, in 1996, Maag took his company Stratec Medical public and listed it on the Swiss Stock Exchange. The company, now valued on the SIX Swiss Exchange, suddenly had a market value of about CHF 1.1 billion attached to it.[8]

In early 1999, Synthes USA, privately-held and majority owned by Wyss, made an offer to acquire Stratec. Since the buyout by Wyss, Synthes had experienced substantial growth from initially USD 64 million (1987) to USD 434 million (1998),[9] making the US business larger than Mathys and Stratec combined. Synthes' was the leader in the US market, having achieved the number one position in trauma and CMF, and number four in spine.[10]

This time, Maag accepted the offer to merge. A deal was struck that took care of a number of important elements. First, Wyss finally gained his entry into the European market, which he so coveted. Second, Synthes USA, privately-held by Wyss and not a listed company, could, through the acquisition of Stratec, acquire a Swiss stock market public listing on relatively good terms—two birds with one stone.

Financial analysts estimated the merged companies to be worth CHF 3.6 billion with one-third reflected by the Stratec shareholders. Effectively, the deal 'cost' about CHF 1 billion and Wyss ended up with a 70% share of the new Synthes-Stratec Company and Maag with about 17%.[11]

When newly formed Synthes-Stratec became operational, the combined companies had sales of CHF 1.3 billion and a head count of 3140, mostly in the US and Switzerland. The company set up its head office in Oberdorf, seat of the former Stratec Medical. With this merger, Synthes-Stratec remained a Swiss listed company.

Legal Threats to German Market Position

Clouds had been forming on the horizon for some time as a result of the Synthes-Stratec merger, which aroused the interest of the German Monopoly Commission. As described earlier, the producer space in Germany had been divided in the 1963 Olten deal between then Mathys and Straumann. Germany, expected to become the largest market in Europe, had been split in two and allocated to Mathys (North and East) and Straumann (South). As business volume in Germany grew, this decision,

---

[8]Julius Bär, Op. cit.

[9]Synthes USA sales were reported at CHF 618 million for 1998 as per Julius Bär Analyst Investment Report, Op. cit.

[10]Julius Bär, Op. cit.

[11]Julius Bär, Op. cit.

adopted to keep peace between the two producers, turned into an issue with the German anti-trust authorities. It became clear to everyone that sooner or later a resolution would have to be found and that the status quo was not viable for much longer.

Both the AO and the producers engaged lawyers, trying to make it clear to the German authorities that significant competition did exist in Germany through other suppliers and that German hospitals were free to source non-AO implants through them. Both Voka, a company started by two ex-Straumann executives, and Zimmer, a large international Orthopedics and implant supplier, were active in the German market. However, the threats of the German government initiating an anti-competitive legal action was enough to influence some of the moves to come.

Generational Change at Mathys

Robert Mathys, Sr., who had lead his company since 1946, started to withdraw from daily business operations in 1990, turning over the company to his three sons Reinhard, Robert, Jr., and Hugo. Eventually, it was Robert Jr., who assumed the major responsibility for the relationship with the AO, joining their TK for some time, and representing the family business on the Business Council. As Robert Jr., explained, everyone wanted to buy out Mathys, but his father was adamant not to sell the business to either Wyss (Synthes USA) or Maag (Stratec). Then Robert Mathys, Sr., died in 2000 unexpectedly.

The Mathys business had flourished, growing to a sales level of CHF 360 million and a headcount of 1420. After the local production operation in Bettlach came factories and operations in Grenchen, Balsthal, and Bellach. Throughout the 1990s, the Mathys operation had kept ahead of Stratec Medical in sales volume. The business was very profitable. Profit figures were not published as the company remained privately held; however, it could be assumed to be in the range of the Synthes-Stratec operation, which was public and reported net margins approaching 30% in 2002.[12] This represented tremendous growth over the past 40 years (Exhibit 34.1a and b). When feelers were put out again to see if the Mathys family might be willing to sell, approaches were rebuffed. Since a family shareholding agreement bound all members of the owning family together, a separate sale or even going public could not be accomplished without consent of all family members, which consisted of Robert Mathys, Sr., his three sons, and a daughter (Exhibit 34.2).

---

[12]Synthes-Stratec Annual Report 2002.

a
Mathys Gruppe Umsatzentwicklung 1966–2003

21.03.2018			Mio. CHF						
	1966	1970	1975	1980	1985	1990	1995	2000	2003
Umsatz kumuliert	2.0	13.0	28.5	59.8	98.7	124.6	230.0	360.0	489.8

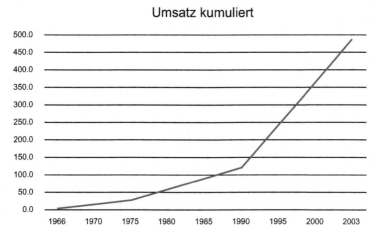

b
Mathys Personalentwicklung

21.03.2018										
	1955	1960	1965	1970	1975	1980	1985	1990	1995	2000	2003
Mitarbeiter	15	40	66	98	170	250	321	425	948	1420	1890

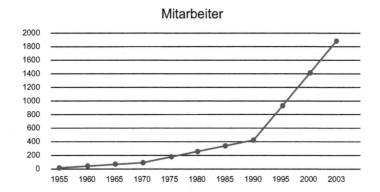

Exhibit 34.1 (a, b) Mathys Sales ("Umsatz") and Employment ("Mitarbeiter") Growth. *Source: Robert Mathys, Jr., reprinted by permission*

Exhibit 34.2 Mathys operations in Bettlach following expansion. *Source: Robert R. Mathys Jr., reprinted by permission*

Synthes-Stratec Acquires Mathys

When the decision by the Mathys family to sell its business to Synthes-Stratec was announced in 2003, it came as a surprise to many observers. Since the Mathys family had always maintained its independence, even during the Synthes USA and Stratec Medical merger, the main reasons for their change of mind caused significant speculation. One theory was that the Mathys family turned towards selling to Synthes-Stratec as a consequence of impending lawsuits in Germany by the country's anti-monopoly commission. Possible fines as high as CHF 500 million were mentioned as hanging over the various companies; selling now certainly guaranteed the Mathys family the enterprise value.

The new combined company, soon operating under the single name of Synthes, maintained all of the industrial sites of Mathys in Switzerland, as it did earlier for the Stratec Medical sites. By combining all of the original AO licensees under one single industrial roof, the new Synthes company became the largest producer of Osteosynthesis implants and surgical instruments worldwide, with a global market share of somewhere between 40 and 50%.

The two units Synthes-Stratec and Mathys continued to grow. Mathys was now a company with CHF 490 million in sales and a headcount of 1890. Synthes-Stratec achieved sales of about CHF 1.5 billion with 4100 employees. The majority of Synthes-Stratec sales were in the US. The combined company would now have almost 6000 employees worldwide and sales close to CHF 2 billion. In order to satisfy German authorities, the Mathys Germany business was divested. This concluded the threatened anti-trust lawsuits hanging over the entire Synthes and AO implant business in Germany. The total deal amounted to CHF 1.5 billion, or about 3.1 times Mathys' sales. This multiple was higher than those paid in the two previous acquisitions. Independent analysts considered this a good price for the business.

From the initial three companies, only one producer of AO-approved implants was now left. Mathys retained its Orthopedic implant business under the name of Mathys Orthopedics, with sales at that time of about CHF 45 million. The Orthopedic business is primarily active in joint replacement products and continues its operations today, having grown to about CHF 150 million with some 500 employees.[13] More recently, the company expanded into sports medicine and management is now in the hands of the third generation of the Mathys family.

With the entire AO-approved implant business in the hands of a single producing company, the relationship, as well as the licensing and operating agreements with the AO would to be impacted substantially (the focus of Chap. 49).

---

[13]Company privately held. Financial data not published and has been estimated by author.

35

Changing Business Model: From Licensing Fees to Service Agreement

Initial Business Model to Fund the AO Foundation

With the establishment of the AO Foundation in 1984, the individual AO Founda-tion shareholders donated all assets in the form of shares to Synthes AG Chur. While the creation of the AO Foundation affected the governance of the AO, it did not immediately have an impact on the revenue stream that funded the AO's activities. Over the next 20 years, however, the funding base for the organization was to change completely and a new business model was eventually adopted in 2006.

As mentioned, the agreement between the producers and the AO detailed the financial support producers were to provide annually to the AO through a transfer to Synthes AG Chur, the owner of all AO-related intellectual property and patents. These payments grew from a very small amount in the early 1960s to CHF 14.1 million annually in 1986, the first full year of operation of the AO Foundation.

Initially, producer royalty payments were not a set, fixed percentage rate. Instead, they were based on a fixed per-piece unit cost as a base amount for each element in the AO catalogue and subject to royalty payments. Once the cost basis of an element was determined, and its royalty payment set, no further adjustments were made for price increases, inflation, or currency exchanges. Effectively, this had the impact of a steadily declining royalty level as a percent of the combined producers' sales.

When measured against actual sales of the producers, the royalty payments averaged around 8%. It was a complicated system that required quite a bit of cost analysis for each of the three producers. In 1992, the agreement had been renegotiated, as it was every five years or so; it had been signed separately by the then three producers—Synthes USA, Mathys, and Stratec. The terms were left in place until 2005 when an entirely new regime was installed.

An exclusive agreement with the producers incurred risks for both sides. From the perspective of the AO, the revenue flow became dependent on the success of the producers' marketing and sales activities. Although AO surgeons were assured that the philosophy of internal fixation became the dominant treatment for bone

© Springer Nature Switzerland AG 2019
J.-P. Jeannet, *Leading a Surgical Revolution*,
https://doi.org/10.1007/978-3-030-01980-8_35

trauma—through the organization, the courses, and the development of internal fixation procedures—immediate commercial success for the association was not guaranteed. If the producers failed to build an effective supply network around the globe, other producers, marketing AO-implant copies, could step in and reap the benefit of the AO activities. In that case, the AO would not be able to obtain royalty payments at all.

From the perspective of the producers, the exclusive deal also carried risks. Although they had eliminated competition—the AO could not license to other companies—the AO producers were exposed to the risk of success related to AO surgical procedures. If the AO technique of dealing with internal fixation did not win approval around the world, the commercial prospects of producers were diminished, in addition to the fact that they had committed to not carry competitive products. Outside the trauma space, the producers were allowed to engage in other business and segments, as Straumann and Mathys did; both companies entered the general Orthopedic implant markets, which represented about 10% of sales for each of them.

Pressure and pushback against the 1992 agreement came first from the producers. Wyss, in charge of Synthes USA and later Synthes-Stratec, held the view that royalty percentages should be decreased as business volume picked up and substantial growth occurred. This did, in fact, happen and royalty payments of Synthes-Stratec for the operating year 1999 came to about 4% when measured against sales. At that point it must have been clear to the producers that they had bet on the right horse and that the AO approach to bone trauma was going to win out against competing methods globally.

Despite the steadily decreasing trend (expressed as a percent of sales), royalty transfers to Synthes AG Chur grew considerably from 1986 to 2005:

Year	Royalty CHF Mio	AO Budget CHF Mio
1986	14.1	8.7
1987	14.4	11
1988	17.2	12.5
1989	19.8	14.0
1990	22.1	16.2
1991	24.1	18.9
1992	26.8	21.3
1993	27.5	25.0
1994	29.4	25.4
1995	31.3	26.5
1996	36.1	30.5
1997	37.7	35.6
1998	44.0	38.0
1999	42.2	37.6
2000	47.9	40.1
2001	54.9	43.2
2002	57.9	48.4
2003	70.3	50.3
2004	84.1	58.6

The patterns of royalty income and budgeted expenses reveal a steady surplus accumulation on the part of the AO Foundation. During this period of almost 20 years, the AO was able to accumulate additional net reserves of about CHF 100 million, which was viewed as a necessary cushion against unforeseen circumstances. 'What if Wyss was to suddenly leave us?' was a frequently asked question and rationale for the conservative budgeting behavior.

Budget control was largely in the hands of the Business Council that was later known as the AO *Verwaltungsausschuss* (AOVA), with members that included all producers, plus a majority of surgeon voting members. This group determined budget allocations for the various expense categories, ranging from Education to Research, Documentation, and the TK process. Although producers had voting rights, they were always in the minority; they also met separately in a Producers' Coordination Committee that dealt with production allocation and pricing across the entire *Instrumentarium*.

The royalty stream grew due to a substantial and steady growth in sales transacted by the producers. Although both Stratec Medical, the ex-Straumann company, and Mathys grew steadily, the main growth came from Synthes USA. The company grew from being the smallest of the three producers to becoming the largest, even when making allowances for sales resulting from mergers. As mentioned, this growth in the US can be attributed to a very aggressive marketing strategy that saw a much greater number of sales personnel as part of their headcount than was the case for either Mathys or Stratec.

At the time of the merger between Synthes USA and Stratec Medical in 1999, the sales staff accounted for as much as 25% of total employment. The role of this sales force consisted of regular visits to operating surgeons, supporting them through their presence in the operating rooms, and providing training where needed to surgeons and surgical staff. The Synthes sales force was also highly trained in the various Osteosynthesis procedures and were, thus, becoming a group of people that surgeons in the US could rely on; they were on call 24/7. Despite concerns from Müller Synthes USA was 'over-commercializing' the AO *Instrumentarium*, Wyss contended that the company was not alone in the US market, and that other major players had also begun to market trauma implants. Only a well-supported marketing campaign had any chance of succeeding against other suppliers who sold their implants below Synthes prices in the US market. This higher level of sales support needed in the US, to some extent necessitated by the differing training schedules and intensity levels between US and European hospitals, also resulted in generally higher prices for implants in the US.

Crafting a New Agreement: CoSA—in 2006

It was during these last few years when the internal debate among AO surgeons focused on the influence of the successful producers and on the direction of the AO and its activities. Against the raising specter of a possible loss of exclusivity, and the sense of many surgeons that they should not directly benefit from the implant sales related to their surgeries, the AO and Synthes, now the remaining single producer, moved to find common ground regarding an entirely new business arrangement. They decided to sign a Cooperation Agreement (CA) that would no longer spell out payments on achieved sales, but stipulate contributions against a certain level of agreed activity, denominated in fixed, annual payments.

Monetizing the *Instrumentarium* Owned by Synthes

As a first step, it was agreed that the ownership of the Synthes brand and the rights to the accumulated *Instrumentarium* and patents, some 3500 in total, would be acquired outright by producer Synthes. This gave the merged Synthes sole possession of all the AO-related *Instrumentarium* provided, of course, that a transfer price for this could be found and the terms of a CA with future support payments could be agreed upon.

Discussions about an appropriate transfer price were lengthy and intense, as was to be expected. Initially, there was a gaping hole between asking prices versus offer prices, ranging from some CHF 500 million to multiple billions. Experts weighed in on the pricing of the total *Instrumentarium*. Since the price had to be paid for by Synthes, it had to be commensurate with the volume of business, both present and future. In the end, an amount of CHF 1 billion was agreed on, to be paid part in cash and part with Synthes shares. This payment allowed Synthes to obtain sole control over the brand name Synthes and use it for its marketing purposes. Synthes also obtained rights to all patents owned by Synthes AG Chur, renamed AO Technology. Additional details on this transaction are explained in a chapter on the battle for IP (Chap. 39).

Whether the CHF 1 billion payment was the appropriate amount for control over to the entire Synthes brand franchise and all Synthes AG Chur patents is subject to debate. It did represent a multiple of about 15 times the last royalty payments, but these payments had been steadily increasing. Given the investment climate at that time, it could be argued that the annual investment return on the amount added to the AO Foundation's endowment would yield 5–7% given the prevalent investment returns in 2006. Of course, it was hard to imagine what would happen when the financial crisis in 2008 hit, lowering the return prospects for long-term capital investments substantially below the originally planned yield of 5–7%. On the other hand, there was a second part of the deal involving a multi-year Cooperation Agreement that represented significant income to the AO Foundation and needed to be viewed in combination with the *Instrumentarium* sales proceeds.

The Cooperation Agreement of 2006 foresaw a payment of CHF 50.7 million from Synthes to AO Technology, the renamed company previously operating as

Synthes AG Chur. The services the AO Foundation was required render to the producer Synthes included:

- Courses for General Trauma (164 courses totaling 550 course days)
- Courses for CMF (56 courses totaling 140 course days)
- Courses for Spine (45 courses totaling 165 course days)
- Courses for Veterinary (12 courses totaling 40 course days)
- Courses for OR Personnel (75 courses totaling 200 course days)

All courses were to be staffed and offered, as it had been in the past, and the budget was expected to be raised. The AO surgeons were clearly left in charge of the educational experience. The courses were to use only AO-approved implants and instruments. In return, the AO Foundation would continue to provide logistical and financial support to AO educational events; for example, making skilled personnel available, in line with local and regulatory rules. In addition, the AO Foundation promised to provide a minimum of 200 standard fellowships annually.

The Cooperation Agreement also included development activities and responsibilities, with the producer Synthes taking care of development. The agreement bound Synthes to use the AOTK system for any product approvals. More basic research was to be conducted by the AO itself.

As a novelty, the agreement regulated the issue of exclusivity, something that had often been discussed within the AO. If AO surgeons were to develop new implants that Synthes declined to launch, then the AO could find alternative commercial producers. Equally, Synthes could not launch a product that covered their agreement if the AOTK declined to approve it. However, Synthes was free to enter into other cooperations outside the scope of Osteosynthesis.

How different was this new deal covered by the Cooperation Agreement? First of all, it was no longer a technology licensing, or royalty deal, based on sales volume. The new deal was compensation for a given amount of services rendered, based upon a defined formula.

In some ways, Synthes outsourced key activities to the AO Foundation that had a demonstrated track record doing this on a world-class level. If the AO did not do this for Synthes, the company would have to provide all of these services at its own costs, as Synthes competitors now had to do. Surgeons judging new implants for approval would have to be hired as consultants. Instructors for courses would have to be hired on a consulting basis as well. Since the AO Foundation was not compensating instructors and surgeons on a free market consulting level, it could be argued that replacing all of the activities rendered by the AO at market rates would be more expensive for the producer.

How good a deal was this for the AO Foundation? Many AO surgeons argued that it eliminated the impression in the market that AO surgeons were directly participating financially from the use of AO-approved implants. This image was more prevalent in the US, probably also because the US company operated under the name Synthes whereas in Europe and the rest of the world, the operating and marketing companies were Mathys and Straumann / Stratec.

Having both an enhanced endowment, which the AO Foundation decided independently how to use and allocate, and receiving an annual stipend for delivered services, which the AO Foundation was keen to render anyway (such as for education), provided AO leadership with some stability and greater certainty about the continued financing of its mission. For activities and initiatives outside of the Cooperation Agreement, the AO would be able to use its own endowment returns. Consequently, the AO Foundation gained funding certainty on some key activities, while also maintaining freedom of action on new initiatives.

The CA provided for continued renewal and renegotiation, or calibration, depending on the need for services. This renegotiation was now to be engaged in with one producing party only, where it had been three when the producers were under separate ownership. The new single producer, Synthes, also gained more commercial power as the business grew to a sales volume of USD 2.4 billion with a net profit of USD 500 million. Therefore, the agreed support payments to the AO Foundation amounted to about 2% of sales, a much smaller amount than under the previous royalty regime. It was up to the AO Foundation leadership to generate additional return for added revenue.

From Compression Plates to Anatomically Shaped Internal Fixators

36

The first period of development of the AO *Instrumentarium* was dominated by a search for better and more stable fracture compression. The move from a standard compression plate (1960) with round holes to a Dynamic Compression Plate (DCP) in 1970 represented a steady increase in clinical experience that was concentrated on making it easier for surgeons to achieve a stable compression by re-engineering and re-designing plates, holes, and screws.

Skilled surgeons who understood the surgical needs, and dictated those needs to the engineering designer, initially drove this process. Essentially, the 'Müllers of this world' dictated their requirements to the 'Mathys of this world.' Over time, as the designing process became more complex, both in terms of function and material, fixation technology became more and more driven by developers and industrial partners. This process had already started in the 1970s and was to continue over the next phases of development. With the transformation of the AO into a foundation with different governance, the ability of the developers and producers to influence the process became more pronounced. The Cooperation Agreement of 2006 made the transfer of development to the producer Synthes final.

The evolution of the AO philosophy progressed along two tracks, both connected, and at times involving the same people. One track was the development of the *Instrumentarium* and plates with two outstanding innovations and new generations of plates. The second track evolved around the refinement of the surgical technique driven by an ever more refined and deeper understanding of the bone healing process. New elements in the *Instrumentarium* affected the surgical techniques. New surgical techniques required innovations.

© Springer Nature Switzerland AG 2019
J.-P. Jeannet, *Leading a Surgical Revolution*,
https://doi.org/10.1007/978-3-030-01980-8_36

Development of Less Invasive Surgical Techniques

In the beginning, AO technique called for internal fixation of the broken bone. This conventional bone fixation with precise reduction of the bone fragments relied on an extensive surgical approach to the bone[1] and added to the injury of soft tissue, which enhanced complications. Only a high degree of surgical skill could minimize this risk. As a result, AO surgeons developed an approach named 'biological' internal fixation that avoided the need for precise reduction, especially of bone fragments. The technique aimed to align the bone fragments only and avoid exposure of the bone and the resulting surgical trauma. Adopting this technique, mechanical stabilization became less rigid. The goals of biological internal fixation were perfect alignment rather than anatomical reduction of the fractures; optimal rather than maximal internal fixation; and the inclusion of soft tissue reconstruction as part of the Orthopedic procedure. This approach became increasingly important as more and more patients arrived at hospitals with multiple injuries resulting from high-energy accidents.

A number of AO surgeons contributed to this development and published results in articles and books. Leaders among them were Reinhold Ganz, Alexander Boitzy, Jeff Mast, and Roland Jakob.[2] A second technique developed by AO surgeons was minimally invasive plate Osteosynthesis (MIPO).[3] Both developments were aimed at making the surgical procedure easier on soft tissue.

Development of New Plate Generations

To avoid the disadvantage stemming from the traditional anatomic reduction and rigid plate fixation, new plates needed to be developed. In the period between the AO Foundation's beginning (1984) and the final consolidation of the producers into a single firm (2003), five distinct generations of plate technologies and corresponding screws could be identified. Each had its own history, and development was driven by the AO 'in-house mechanics' team: Stephan Perren, surgeon, researcher, and head of the AO Research Institute; Slobodan Tepic, a mechanical engineer from Croatia; and Robert Frigg, a young local mechanic who later became an outstanding implant developer. This small group of developers were to become the principal translators between the various groups involved with the AO and bringing early ideas to prototype models that could be discussed by surgeons prior to going into testing and production. The AOTK remained the forum for these discussions.

---

[1]Perren (2002), pp. 1093–1110.
[2]Mast et al. (1988–1989).
[3]Krettek (1997), pp. S-A1–S-A2.

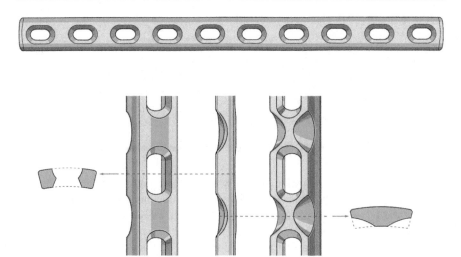

Exhibit 36.1 Limited contact dynamic compression plate (LC-DCP). *Copyright by AO Foundation, Switzerland*

The Limited Contact Dynamic Compression Plate (LC-DCP)

The first of the new generations of plates, the LC-DCP, was an extension of the previous DCP plate generation and its particular holes. The major innovation here was the feature of reduced contact with the bone to allow for better blood circulation and healing. By contouring the bottom of the plate, such that only the contours came in direct contact with the bone, the developing team at the AO took a major step away from the initial doctrine of rigid fixation through a metal plate flush on the bone, which had dominated their doctrine for so long. This design was part of the biomechanical research conducted by Perren at the AO Research Center in Davos and involved the metallurgical team from Straumann, Ortrud Pohler and Samuel Steinemann, as well as some young surgeons who had come to AO Davos through the 'Berne connection' at the Insel Hospital and interned under Reinhold Ganz.[4] This new implant also established the use of titanium as implant material (Exhibit 36.1).

The Introduction of the PC-Fix

Using standard compression plates required contact with the bone by careful adaption of the implant to the injured bone, to stabilize the fracture. Because vascular damage in the direct contact areas had been shown to account for most of the implant-related damage to the bone, the point-contact fixator (PC-Fix) was a

---

[4]Perren et al. (1990), pp. 304–310.

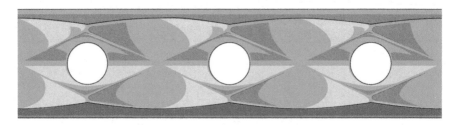

Exhibit 36.2 Internal fixator PC-Fix. *Copyright by AO Foundation, Switzerland*

general-purpose internal fixation system whereby the screw accomplished the load transfer to the bone only. This was made possible by locking the screw head into the plate of the PC-Fix. Again, contoured implants with special screws eliminated the major drawback of direct bone contact.

Developed in 1993, and first published in 1995, this ingenious technology was the product of a development effort by Perren and Tepic, a gifted engineer described by many as highly creative.[5] Locking of screws inside of plate holes became the dominant screw–plate connection used for trauma worldwide (Exhibit 36.2).

The Creation of the Less Invasive Stabilization System (LISS)

Just two years after the PC-Fix, the development team came up with a surgical aid called the less invasive stabilization system (LISS). Headed by Robert Frigg, one of the talented mechanics working for the AO at that time, a team developed a guiding system to make minimally invasive Osteosynthesis easier. The problem the team had to overcome was the fact that conventional plates did not facilitate percutaneous fixation and, thus, forced surgeons into classic open reduction techniques. With LISS, the plate was fixed to an insertion device, which acted to guide the insertion of the fixation screws (Exhibit 36.3).

The LISS system had a number of additional features of great value to the surgeon. To compensate anatomical variations, the locking screws were equipped with threaded screw heads for angular and axial fixation in the plate hole. These screws allowed the fixation of a plate without any bone contact. The self-drilling and self-tapping screws' tip made the percutaneous screw insertion easier. These were particularly advantageous for osteoporotic bones.[6] In some ways, the LISS system incorporated the advantages of the PC-Fix technology from two years earlier and made it possible to use this in a less invasive manner.

---

[5]Tepic and Perren (1995), pp. B5–B10.
[6]Frigg et al. (2001), pp. 24–31.

Exhibit 36.3 Less invasive stabilization system (LISS). *Copyright by AO Foundation, Switzerland*

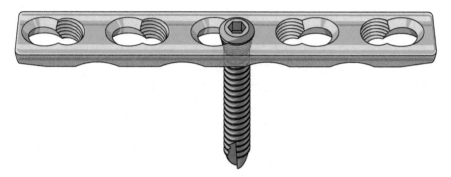

Exhibit 36.4 Locking compression plate (LCP). *Copyright by AO Foundation, Switzerland*

The Locking Compression Plate (LCP)

The locking compression plate (LCP) was the final step of this creative development period that combined previous features of compression plating (LC-DCP) and locking plating (PC-FIX/LISS) by a newly designed combination hole. The use of compression screws allowed for fracture compression; the use of locking screws provided angular stable locking of screws. The advantages of using the LCP with locking screws allowed the surgeon to use the plate with less exposure to the bone (bone bridging technique) and increased the implant anchorage in osteoporotic bones. Robert Frigg, Michael Wagner, a surgeon, and Robert Schavan, biomechanical engineer, led the development of the LCP (Exhibit 36.4).

Anatomically Shaped Plates

The anatomically shaped plates introduced in 2001 were neither a new technology nor a new system, but important with regard to enlarging the AO *Instrumentarium*. These plates, shaped for any type of bone or injury application, came as locking compression plates and applicable for the minimal invasive plate Osteosynthesis (MIPO) technique. They combined all the steps described, one by one, into single plates, causing some surgeons to comment that they are similar to fittings that could be ordered out of a building catalogue, ready for use, not requiring any or minimal adjustments, just like a carpenter would order fixtures for doors and windows. By contrast, in the early years of the AO *Instrumentarium*, surgical sets came with tools that could be used during surgery to bend plates to make them fit a given bone more precisely (Exhibit 36.5).

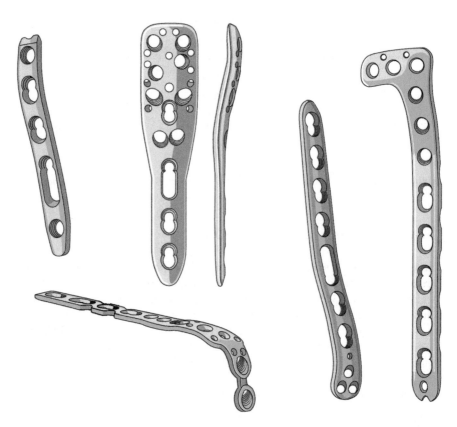

Exhibit 36.5 Anatomically shaped plates. *Copyright by AO Foundation, Switzerland*

Development Achievements of the AO System Until 2005

This is the moment to reflect on the particular pathway the AO chose to continuously improve its *Instrumentarium*. The two-track system of surgical excellence and perfection of the *Instrumentarium* certainly helped achieve ever better clinical results for patients. It also did, and this could be the major contribution, remove more and more of the risky steps from Osteosynthesis surgery, making it a simpler and more accessible procedure. Thereby, Osteosynthesis eventually became mainstream and not just the exclusive province of few, highly exceptional surgeons, such as the founders of the AO.

At the time the AO was created, the requirements to successfully use the AO *Instrumentarium* represented a high barrier for many surgeons, and often caused the rejection by established surgeons who considered this too risky a procedure. As one long-standing member of the AO, now a retired surgeon, said: "Not all surgeons are geniuses. A good percentage, maybe as many as 80%, have average surgical skills." The refinement of the *Instrumentarium* and the surgical procedures meant that many an average-skilled surgeon could achieve excellent results. Clearly, this was also the intent of the AO founders.

Taking a step back and reflecting on the evolution of the AO surgical technique, there was a profound change in the role of fixation. As the surgical doctrine moved from absolute to relative stability, the role of plate versus screws appeared to change. While at first surgeons used screws to compress the plate to the bone to achieve stability, the more recent development changed towards a plate that bridged the fracture zone seemingly 'hovering' above the bone and holding the screws in place—a reversal of surgical approach, which came about as a result of extensive research and surgical experience.

The Talent That Drove Implant Development at the AO

Although the AO was, and remains, an association led by surgeons for surgeons, this organization was masterful in incorporating non-surgical talents for the further development of the AO *Instrumentarium*. Some of those talents have been described previously but the names of Robert Mathys, Sr., and Fritz Straumann and his team bear repeating. The producers, which also applied very much to Hansjörg Wyss, became deeply involved in the development of the AO *Instrumentarium* and spent considerable amount of time in direct contact with surgeons.

Around the time that the AO was re-configured as a foundation, a working group of 'engineers of all types' brought particular skills to the task of improving the AO *Instrumentarium*. These teams were small and are described as 'just a handful of people.' However, a few names emerge due to their outstanding contributions to developing a new generation of plates. First was Stephan Perren, the head of Research and Development (ARI) who, as both a surgeon and biomechanical engineer, bridged the two sets of talents and translated the development opportunities he saw to the other surgeons. As a long-time member and chair of the AOTK, he played a pivotal role over an extended period time. The second stand-out was Slobodan Tepic, the university-trained mechanical engineer who had little to no medical training when he joined the AO and continued to innovate in various assignments in Switzerland after leaving in 1996. The third exceptional talent was Robert 'Röbi' Frigg who joined the AO in 1978 under rather unusual circumstances.[7] After the completion of his apprenticeship as a mechanic in the Grisons area of Switzerland, he was interested in becoming a photographer, and saw an ad in the newspaper that the AO in Davos was looking for someone who could do a photography job. He applied and got the job; he was just 21 years old. The resident mechanic in charge of the building and equipment left just as he had arrived and Stephan Perren turned to Frigg, as a trained mechanic, and assigned him to the vacant job.

Frigg began to work with Perren in the development of implants. He acquired knowledge and a background in measurement technologies and techniques. When he was invited into his first AOTK meeting he was only 26 and put in the same room with all these senior surgeons. As Frigg recalled his experience: "I was no competition for anyone present!"

Comparing the development processes in his early AO days to the prevailing modern processes, Frigg finds it to be like night versus day:

> The initial process was very much based on common sense. A small circle of elite surgeons with ambitions and a fighting mentality gathered around a table. They talked about problems, bad cases, and wanted to try much harder. It was in some way like performing an OP around a table.

> Early on, the clinic and surgeons indicated what they needed. Technology and development was looking for a solution. Innovation took place in a pre-phase, free from a managed process. In this setting, structure would not have worked. Everything was done on trust and oriented on clinical needs.

With the implementation of the first Cooperation Agreement between Synthes AG Chur and the AO in 2005, development responsibility formally moved to Synthes. Frigg and part of his team transferred; he eventually took on a position as Global Chief Technology Officer at Synthes, responsible for global technology and innovation. From the later perspective of working within Synthes AG Chur, he commented[8]:

---

[7]Interview with Robert Frigg conducted December 2016, in Davos.
[8]Robert Frigg left Synthes AG Chur after its acquisition by Johnson & Johnson's DePuy Division and is heading a small Medtech company, 41medical AG, in Bettlach, Solothurn, the hometown of Mathys. He has been honored by several universities, including an honorary doctorate from the University of Zurich. He serves on several advisory boards related to medical technology and material science. His name appears on more than 180 patents.

Innovation is now an industrial process. Everything turns around validation and certification. In Europe medical devices are regulated by the ISO Medical Device Directive, in the US by the FDA processes 510K and IDE. A new clinical study for a new set of implants would cost USD 5 to USD 10 million and required up to five years to prove safety and efficacy (IDE or ISO class III products). The increased regulative hurdles are the consequence of misbehavior of medical device companies like the PIP breast implant scandal. Such processes stop innovation. To change a screw takes up to five years of design, documentation, validation, verification and if a clinical trial is needed, costs of USD 300,000 are not the exception (510K or Class IIb process). Some authorities even require re-submission for approval of implants used for over 50 years in humans!"

From *Instrumentarium* Towards Instruments and Solutions

Throughout the early years of the AO, the term *Instrumentarium* had been used to signal the complete set of surgical instruments, plates, and screws developed by the AO surgeons and its industrial partners. From about 2005, and with the shift of development responsibility towards the Synthes partner, the AOTK community began a shift towards the term 'Solutions' to signal a complete set of tools for a given purpose or surgery. Projects were less about individual components but instead emphasized entire surgical solutions and instruction. At the same time, on the part of the industrial partner Synthes, the terminology had shifted towards 'Instrumentation' as a modern term instead of the older *Instrumentarium*.

References

Frigg, R., et al. (2001). The development of the distal femur less invasive stabilization system (LISS). *Injury, 32*(3), 24–31.

Krettek, C. (1997). Foreword: Concepts of minimally invasive plate osteosynthesis. *Injury, 28*(1), S-A1–S-A2.

Mast, J., Jakob, R., & Ganz, R. (1988–1989). *Planning and reduction technique in fracture surgery.* Berlin: Springer.

Perren, S. M. (2002, November). Evolution of the internal fixation of long bone fractures. *Journal of Bone Joint Surgery, 84-B*, 1093–1110.

Perren, S. M., Klaue, K., Pohler, O., Predieri, M., Steinemann, S., & Gautier, E. (1990). The limited contact dynamic compression plate (LC-DCP). *Archives of Orthopaedic Trauma Surgery, 109*, 304–310.

Tepic, S., & Perren, S. (1995). The biomechanics of the PC-fix internal fixator. *Injury, 26*(2), B5–B10.

From Eminence-Based to Evidence-Based Research

37

Retracing the Early AO Research Effort

The AO Research Institute in Davos, ARI, dates back to 1959, when the AO rented part of an underutilized facility and created the Laboratory for Experimental Surgery as a separate, not-for-profit foundation. At first, it was directed by Martin Allgöwer (an AO co-founder and head of the Chur hospital) and concentrated on research into Polytrauma (shock) and wound repair.

In 1962, Professor Herbert Fleisch, the Institute's first full-time director, began a research effort around 'bone formation.' It was not until 1967 when Stephan Perren took over the leadership of the ARI that a shift towards 'bone mechanics' took place. The Institute spearheaded research into the biology of internal fracture fixation, leading to new implants with ever decreasing contact of implants to the underlying bone. Also, during this time, a development group was formed that was responsible for the transformation of research into practical and clinical applications. Perren headed the Institute until 1995, the longest tenure of any ARI director.

From 1960 to 1985, the AO spent about CHF 125 million on its research efforts, including its Documentation Center. In the period of 1985 to 1992, some CHF 80 million was spent on the support and development of the AO philosophy. All of these activities were funded through the income stream built on implant licensing fees from the producers.

Spending covered both basic research and development work on new implants and screws. In 1992, for which there is published data, the AO operated on an annual budget of CHF 21.4 million. Out of this, research was supported with CHF 9 million, or 42%, development with CHF 2.8 million, or 13%, and documentation with about CHF 1 million, or 5%.

© Springer Nature Switzerland AG 2019
J.-P. Jeannet, *Leading a Surgical Revolution*,
https://doi.org/10.1007/978-3-030-01980-8_37

Focusing Research Activities

By the turn of the century, the ARI had fully adopted a multidisciplinary research approach to address new areas. The issue of internal fixation of osteoporotic bones, or in the areas of bone defect regeneration, became more important. ARI also began to offer its services as an independent contractor to other academic departments around the world. By 2001, ARI had moved towards three major areas of research focus that were to remain the mainstay for many years.

The first research program centered around Biomaterials for Tissue Engineering. ARI was researching biodegradable implant materials to help regenerating bone defects, as well as to gain an understanding of problems associated with repair in tissue engineering approach.[1]

ARI's second research thrust centered around a Mechanobiology program. The focus here was on tissues and how they were produced, maintained, and adapted by cells. This led to research on how to better anchor implants in osteoporotic bone, as well as an effort to understand intervertebral disc degeneration and to accelerate fracture healing.

The Institute's third research thrust dealt with the bio-performance of materials and related devices programs, such as implant surface modifications, soft issue adhesion, and implant infection resistance.

The Orthogeriatrics Project

Although the AO research effort covered a variety of undertakings, and there were many more that could be described here, there is a story from recent history that exemplifies how the AO community brings together different partners and focuses them on a single project.

Around 2006, the AO, through its global network of surgeons, "wanted to know what the next biggest thing in trauma could be."[2] Under the name of Clinical Priority Programs (CPPs), the AO began to initiate new programs. As David Helfet, one of the surgeons who participated in this process, recalled, the consensus emerged that issues around bone quality and osteoporosis would become ever more important. The AO, through its many sub-organizations, decided to put together a special team chaired by Michael Blauth,[3] a trauma surgeon based in Innsbruck, Austria. Blauth explains:

> The first program under the newly initiated CPPs was named 'Fracture Fixation in Osteoporotic Bone (FFOB).' It included the Orthogeriatric management of fragility fracture patients, not just the fixation of fractures. Jim Kellam, AO President at that time, inaugurated the

---

[1] AO Foundation Annual Report, 2003, p. 10.

[2] Interview with David Helfet conducted on 3 December, 2017, in Davos.

[3] Telephone interview with Univ. Prof. Dr. Michael Blauth, Medical University Innsbruck, conducted on 11 September, 2017.

program and established the idea. As chairman of this first CPP, I got the task to develop the program's structure under consideration of the AO Institutes and to produce tangible results within five years. There was no template whatsoever for this type of program. The core team of the program consisted of Jörg Goldhahn, Norbert Suhm, and myself.

This group's assignment was to come up with new technologies, products, and surgical guidelines. In his practice, Blauth had increasingly become interested in Traumatology for elderly patients. In his experience, some 30–50% of trauma patients in city hospitals are over the age of 80 and experience fragility fractures caused by osteopenic or osteoporotic bones, as well as the propensity to fall. For the surgeons, these bones with reduced biomechanical properties compared to those of younger adults posed unprecedented difficulties in treatment.

Standard procedure and implants may create additional bone damage or fail in providing sufficient stability for uneventful healing and immediate full weight bearing, mandatory for the older population. A typical failure mode is 'cutting through' the rarified cancellous (spongy) bone. Much more important, however, was, and is, the fact that up to 50% of elderly patients do not recover to their previous level of activity and independence, causing significant health-economic issues for society. Orthogeriatrics, the interdisciplinary and professional co-management, started to become a major priority, especially with populations living longer; a growing cohort of them living in high-income countries.[4]

This research stream eventually led to the development of the AO Philos System. The first, and nowadays more accepted, step was the development of a 'standardized implant augmentation technique' for fixation of proximal femoral fractures which are the 'classic' fragility fractures. By injecting PMMA bone cement to enhance the fixation of the implant, a form of bone augmentation was achieved. In order to make that possible, the AO team, in conjunction with Synthes, had developed a complete system that included new, perforated implants to increase contact surface. In addition, special screws were developed that allow the injection of the bone cement through the interior of the screw. The Philos System was thus a complete surgical set with implants, screws, cement, and surgical tools especially developed for this procedure[5] (Exhibit 37.1).

Blauth, who had extensive experience with the AO Philos System, admitted one could treat elderly patients with standard implants, provided one accepted the reduced health economic benefits. The incremental costs of Euro 200 to 300 per implant so augmented, however, did create a financial hurdle for some hospitals and not all payers accepted the additional cost.

According to Blauth[6]:

---

[4]Inaugurated and promoted by British and US Orthopedic Trauma Surgeons and Geriatricians like Stephen L. Kates, Daniel Mendelson, and Joseph Nicolas from Rochester, NY.

[5]Unger et al. (2012), pp. 1759–1763; Kathrein et al. (2013), pp. 273–277.

[6]Blauth, Op. cit, Telephone interview conducted on 11 September, 2017.

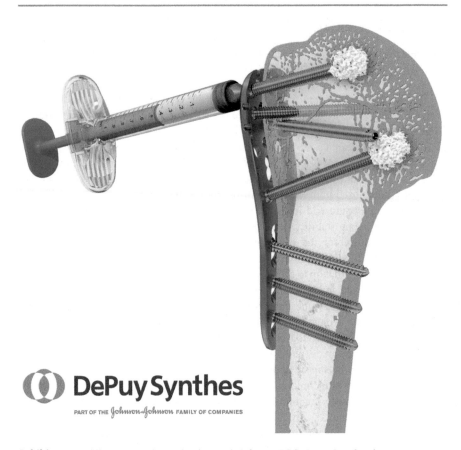

Exhibit 37.1   Philos system. *Source: Johnson & Johnson DPS. Reproduced with permission*

Implant augmentation is an excellent example for a development from bench to bedside, starting with a highly relevant and unsolved clinical problem; for example, fixation failure in osteoporotic proximal femoral fractures. As always, such inventions build on previous efforts and ideas but go much further. To make it a standard procedure, not only many technical problems with the procedures itself had to be solved but also numerous testing and experiments, including biomechanical ones, investigations in a sheep model, and finally clinical studies had to be performed. Participating were many parts of the AO, including ARI, CID, TKs, and the effort took some ten years until full introduction. To develop such an entire concept covering a full treatment, not just a single implant, you can only do with within an organization such as the AO.

To date, more than 20,000 PFNA and TFNA augmentations have been performed without any report of a failed fixation after applying this stand-alone feature in DePuy Synthes' portfolio compared to competitive implant companies.

Evidence-based Versus Eminence-based Research

The development of the Implant Augmentation System demonstrated how the AO process could bring research insights all the way into the clinic. Parallel to such developments, there was constant discussion among the AO research units on the nature and quality of its data base, or documentation, as well as the research output as presented and published in scientific papers. For this debate to be fully appreciated, it is necessary to return to the early documentation efforts undertaken by AO surgeons going back to the establishment of the AO in 1958.

The four pillars of the AO philosophy have been laid out previously (see Chap. 8) but now, the data collected included three sheets on each patient with supporting X-rays for each of these comments:

- A sheet on the type of fracture, or injury
- B sheet on the operation, type of implants used, and outcome
- C sheet on any follow-up

Müller, who started the system prior to the creation of the AO, had also seen the documentation systems of Böhler in Vienna and of Danis in Brussels, inspiring him to develop his own system. He always added a question about when the patient could go back to work, a common query in today's health economics.

The AO Documentation Center began its work formally in 1959; some 1000 cases were recorded during the first year. Based on this documentation, the AO founders were able to prove the superior clinical experience applying internal fixation. Furthermore, as the documentation grew, covering more and more cases, a team of researchers directed by Maurice Müller used the documentation base to create the 'AO Classification for Long-bone Fractures.' This system was used by surgeons all over the world and allowed for comparisons of cases under different circumstances.

Over time, the AO realized that the idea of just collecting this kind of documentation could no longer live up to modern research standards.[7] To improve on this situation, the AO created a new organizational unit named the Clinical Investigation and Documentation (CID), which was started in 1998. Under new leadership, the documentation center began to shift over time into a full-blown clinical investigation center chaired by David Helfet.[8] The new direction called for more evidence-based research.

The AO founders had practiced a form of eminence-based medicine. Müller and his colleagues experimented with internal fixation and collected the evidence that, according to their follow-up documents, worked better than standard practiced external fixation. Their approach was to practice and then tell the world, after the

---

[7]Interview with Beate Hanson, former Director of AO CID, conducted on 4 October, 2017, in Zurich.

[8]Interview with David Helfet conducted on 3 December, 2017, in Davos.

fact, how it worked. Since they were the eminent surgeons in the field of Osteosynthesis, they were listened to. Initially they toured the world and informed everyone how the Osteosynthesis technique could be made to work successfully. For example, based upon their documentation, the AO surgeons would show how they brought down an initial infection rate of 70% to 2 or 3% by the year 2000.

The Classification Exercise[9]

During the early development of the AO principles and surgical techniques, it became clear that the group lacked a coherent classification of bone fractures. Collecting documentation would only be useful if there was a common coding system to communicate among surgeons practicing at different locations. An initial approach was launched in 1966 by the St. Gallen surgeon Bernhard ('Hardy') Weber who devised a classification system of ankle fractures. Comparability of results across multiple patients required documentation of the type of affected bone, as well as the location of the fracture. Surgeons found that plain language often was not precise enough for a description of the many types of fractures. Some forms of classifications already existed but they were not generally acceptable, or sufficiently uniform, to be of help beyond a single hospital or group of surgeons.

In 1977, Müller, then the head of Orthopedics at the University of Berne, and responsible for the AO Documentation Center, also located in Berne, convinced his AO colleagues that a general classification system of the entire human skeleton was needed, not just selective parts. By that time, the Documentation Center had accumulated documents on some 150,000 surgically treated fractures. Müller tasked his residents with taking 100 fractures of each bone segment and segregating them into nine groups for the principal bones and their 29 segments, divided into three subgroups of fractures. The result was 783 fracture classifications which rose to 1500 fractures when additional qualification codes were added (Exhibit 37.2).

The Berne group led by Müller submitted the entire work to the Swiss AO in 1986 for approval, and then to the AO Foundation; both approved the classification scheme for the third edition of the AO Manual to be published in 1990.[10] The Classification System was published separately during that same year.[11]

Before 2002, the Documentation Center had published just two articles, on average, annually in relevant medical journals. Hanson, attending a meeting in Berlin, remembered one of the AO leaders pounding the table, holding the only two papers published in the previous year in his hands and challenging the organization to do better.

In order to have studies accepted in leading and relevant medical journals, it is not enough to tell old stories based on a large number of documented cases. To get into a

---

[9]Schlich (2002), pp. 114–121.
[10]Müller et al. (1990a).
[11]Müller et al. (1990b).

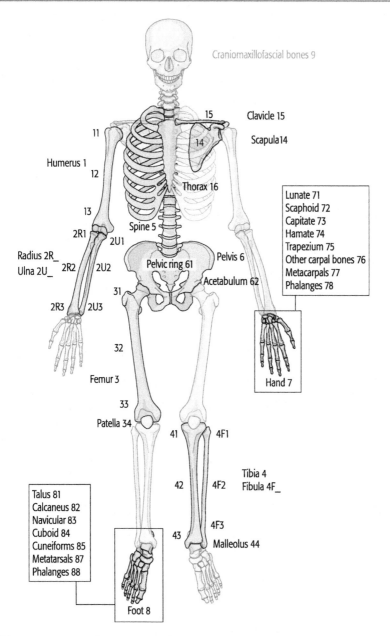

Craniomaxillofascial bones 9

Clavicle 15

Scapula 14

Humerus 1

Thorax 16

Lunate 71
Scaphoid 72
Capitate 73
Hamate 74
Trapezium 75
Other carpal bones 76
Metacarpals 77
Phalanges 78

Spine 5

Radius 2R_
Ulna 2U_   2R2

Pelvic ring 61

Pelvis 6

Acetabulum 62

Femur 3

Hand 7

Patella 34

Tibia 4
Fibula 4F_

Talus 81
Calcaneus 82
Navicular 83
Cuboid 84
Cuneiforms 85
Metatarsals 87
Phalanges 88

Malleolus 44

Foot 8

Exhibit 37.2 Structure of the A classification system. *Copyright by AO Foundation, Switzerland*

journal such as the *Journal for Bone and Joint Surgery* (JBJFA) or *Traumatology*, read by some 70,000 surgeons and with wide impact in the medical community, articles require evidence-based research results, which are written on the basis of randomized studies and control cases; something the old existing documentation center could not yield. While an eminence-based hypothesis was needed to get started, it was necessary to collect the evidence in randomized studies in order to get published.

In contrast, older studies based upon the documentation held in the AO Documentation Center were eminence-based and, thus, did not live up to the new requirements for papers. Through CID, the AO was able to support more research centers, collaborating surgeons, and hospitals, as well as create new studies that could live up to these new and demanding requirements. By 2015, the annual publication rate had risen from an average of two to a rate of 70 publications in relevant journals.

The journey of changing from an eminence-based approach to the required evidence-based approach took about 45 years. During this time, many a discussion took place among the AO founders and AO Foundation leadership about the purpose of the original documentation, enshrined as one of the four founding principles of the AO organization. It then took another ten years to change course, repurpose the effort, and support the AO philosophy with the kind of evidence that would help keep the AO surgical practice at the forefront of trauma medicine on a global scale.

References

Kathrein, S., Kralinger, F., Blauth, M., & Schmoelz, W. (2013). Bio-mechanical comparison of an angular stable plate with augmented and non-augmented screws in a newly developed shoulder test bench. *Clinical Biomechanics, 28*(3), 273–277. https://doi.org/10.1016/j.clinbiomech.2012. 12.013.

Müller, M. E., Allgöwer, M., Schneider, R., & Willenegger, H. (1990a). *Manual of internal fixation* (3rd ed.). Berlin: Springer.

Müller, M. E., Nazarian, S., Koch, P., & Schatzker, J. (1990b). *The comprehensive classification of fractures of long bones*. Berlin: Springer.

Schlich, T. (2002). *Surgery, science and industry* (pp. 17–19). Basingstoke: Palgrave Macmillan.

Unger, S., Erhart, S., Kralinger, F., Blauth, M., & Schmoelz, W. (2012, October). The effect of in situ augmentation on implant anchorage in proximal humeral head fractures. *Injury, 43*(10), 1759–1763.

From Long Bones to All Bones

38

Starting Out with Adult Long Bones

Even prior to the formal establishment of the AO organization, when surgeons assembled for practical training of their Osteosynthesis surgical techniques, the focus was essentially bone trauma in adults, mostly younger ones, still of working age. For many years, the concentration on 'long bones'—bones in the upper and lower leg, as they call it within the AO—remained the majority of bone trauma surgeries. The initial *Instrumentarium* presented for the first Davos course in 1960 reflected this emphasis.

It didn't take long until trauma in other parts of the human skeleton became a point of interest to the AO surgeons, as did patients who were children. Their first complete documentation, in the *Technik* manual published in 1963,[1] included Osteosynthesis techniques for arms, hand, shoulder, as well as a small section on fractures of the hip. As the authors mentioned in the foreword of this first complete text, the AO techniques were understood to be for the bones of the adult; they specifically reminded readers that the displayed procedures were not automatically applicable to children or young bones. Also, completely absent in that first book were references to trauma to the spine and craniomaxillofacial (CMF) areas.

Invading the Spine

In the third edition of *Technik*, published in 1991, there were new indications that were allocated considerable space. Spine trauma was added and included in the chapter.[2] Starting as early as 1977, spine indications began to be developed within

---

[1]Müller et al. (1963).
[2]Müller et al. (1991).

© Springer Nature Switzerland AG 2019
J.-P. Jeannet, *Leading a Surgical Revolution*,
https://doi.org/10.1007/978-3-030-01980-8_38

the AO, culminating in the Universal Spine System (USS), driven by surgeons Max Aebi and John Webb. Both of them were the principal authors of the large spine surgery section in the manual's third edition. To adequately deal with Spine Indications, the AO *Instrumentarium* needed to be adapted and plates, screws, and surgical tools were either adapted or re-created, many of them in titanium. Today, AOSpine is its own clinical division within the AO and spine surgery is an important part of the AO Foundation work. The journey from the first discussion in 1977 to the full deployment of the USS spanned almost 15 years and involved numerous participants across the entire AO organization and the collaborating producers.

Entering Craniomaxillofacial (CMF) Surgery

As was the case with the spine, the advance into CMF took from 1974 to 1984, until the development of specialty plates and screws for the trauma to the mandible. A first complete text on CMF trauma was published in 1986, and in 1987 the AO classification scheme was expanded to include CMF.[3] Although part of AO Trauma for many years, the creation of a separate AO clinical division for CMF, the AOCMF, had to wait until 1990. Again, the full deployment of CMF combined with courses, *Instrumentarium*, and a proper organization took 16 years, similar to the development of AOSpine (Exhibit 38.1).

Confronting Orthogeriatrics

At the outset, when AO surgeons began to develop surgical practices, they not only dealt primarily with the bone trauma of adult patients, they were also focused on younger adults. Automobile, sports, and work accidents were typical of younger people. In the previous chapter the development of surgical approaches for the growing number of fragility fractures, typical of a growing generation of older patients, was detailed. Generally, the AO recommended utilizing the existing trauma *Instrumentarium*. Experience demonstrated, however, that the weaker bones of older patients required adaptations, different implants, screws, and the practice of bone augmentation. As previously mentioned, the AO tasked a team of surgeons, under the leadership of Blauth, to tackle the development of a complete surgical kit and system, resulting in the launch of the Philos System. Again, it took about ten years for this development to come to market; most likely because this orthogeriatric indication was part of the large AO trauma effort, the timeline was shorter and the adoption process faster.

---

[3]Spiessl (1976).

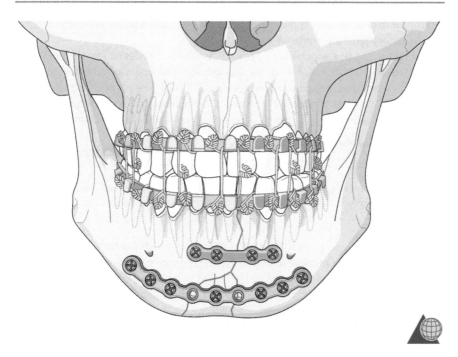

Exhibit 38.1 CMF system. *Copyright by AO Foundation, Switzerland*

Addressing Children's Bones[4]

After having 'invaded' all bones for adults and the elderly, there was still one more area that remained, namely pediatrics. The story of the development of pediatric trauma treatment, and a review of its journey to full development, is of particular interest because it shows the degree of tenacity AO surgeons needed to bring new surgical procedures into the clinic, here in the form of an Elastic Stable Intramedullary Nail (ESIN) system.

Implants developed by the AO were intended for adult patients only and children up to 13 years of age were, in case of bone trauma, treated via the conservative method, involving casts as external fixation. As experience increased, adult implants, which were quite sturdy, were simply downsized. Over time, however, the AO gravitated towards devising specific pediatric implants. The reluctance to develop dedicated implants for pediatric applications had to do with the fact that any new implant system might take some four to five years to develop. Due to the fact that solid patent protection was difficult to achieve, smaller companies could easily copy and

---

[4]This section relies heavily on two interviews held with Dr. Teddy Slongo, conducted on 13 November, 2017, at the University Hospital Berne, and on 5 December, 2017, in Davos.

develop a similar product in four to five months because they could operate below the regulatory radar umbrella.

Parallel to the developments of pediatric implants a pediatric classification system, different from the one for adults, was created. The first was published in 2006, almost 20 years after the adult version appeared.[5] Teddy Slongo, who had worked on the first two versions of the AO Pediatric Classification of Long-Bones Fractures (PCCF), believed strongly in the mission and value of the classification system:

> Classification is needed for scientific study and research. We need to be able to separate apples from oranges, Boskop from Grafensteiner, and compare Boskop to Boskop.[6] As a result, we would all speak the same language. In fact, the Davos course is now always including a lesson on pediatric classification. It was the adult classification lectures that were abandoned! Classification brings benefits to the surgeon and needs to become part of any patient's chart.[7]

Pediatrics developed slowly within the AO, although Müller had always kept two pediatric beds in his Orthopedic unit in Berne. Slongo, who had joined the trauma unit at the Insel Hospital in Berne in 1978, was one of the early pediatric surgeons within the AO. In the early 1980s, the AO was beginning to add lectures on pediatrics in its Davos courses, which later was to become a tradition. The AO trauma surgeons and the AOTK decided to create an expert group for pediatrics at that time. A curriculum task force was created to support the teaching in Davos.

When the senior AO leaders went on record that the AO needed a focus on children, movement began to gather. This led to the creation of the Pediatrics Expert Group within the AOTK in 1996, in order to develop pediatric implants and educational material. The first dedicated pediatrics course was held by the AO in Chile in 2001, and was later expanded to Davos, Germany, and other countries, including Cambodia and South Africa. Over time, Slongo, who had dedicated a considerable amount of time to teaching pediatric trauma and Orthopedics, created some 40 different sessions just for the pediatric AO community.

This effort and outreach resulted in a five-year long development of a flexible mark nail, ESIN. This nail, when first presented at a surgical conference in Germany, was met with immediate reaction and comments such as: 'You are crazy.' After 15 years, there is still resistance to the utilization of such unusual implants. For years, whenever Slongo attended conferences in Germany, a surgeon generally referred to as the 'pediatric hip pope;' would come on right after Slongo spoke to tell the audience how this procedure should really be carried out correctly. After some time, this same surgeon who had protested so loudly, suddenly wanted to speak first at conferences; he had largely copied Slongo's last paper and behaved as if he had invented the procedure himself (Exhibit 38.2).

---

[5] Slongo et al. (2006), pp. 43–49.
[6] Boskop and Grafensteiner are two popular apple varieties in Europe.
[7] Slongo, T., Interview, Op. cit.

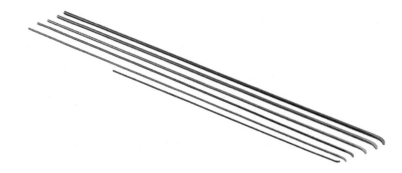

Exhibit 38.2 ESIN nail. *Copyright by AO Foundation, Switzerland*

Other experienced AO surgeons commented on the cultural differences among surgeons when faced with new approaches. A number of interviewees have volunteered that surgeons were not naturally open to new approaches, and this type of resistance has often been linked to a reluctance to enter the unsettling path of abandoning their familiar skills for new ones, leaving their comfort zone. It has been noted earlier, that at the beginning of the AO Davos courses, chief surgeons would often send their senior interns to learn the AO procedure and, although they supported AO practice in their hospitals, would not personally perform the operations. An experienced AO surgeon commented:

> In the US, it is the 'US knows best' and surgeons in a hospital were expected to follow the procedures laid down by the chief surgeons. One exception is when the head surgeon is not present. When operating alone, they can be more innovative. In Switzerland, we are less rigid, but you have to have strong arguments when you want to stray from the path of the head surgeon. Germans also tend to the view that Germans know best. In some Asian countries, there is often copying without understanding. Instructing in Latin America is best because they are open and innovative by nature.[8]

Slongo related a different experience regarding the new surgical technique that he had documented with Reinhold Ganz at the Insel Hospital in Berne. Ganz, who had followed Müller as head of the hospital's Orthopedic and Trauma Unit, had changed his mind on stability, based on his experience, and moved towards considering relative stability instead. The atmosphere at the Berne hospital was described as open, allowing for new ideas to be pursued. The idea propagated by Ganz centered on the fact that for patients under the age of 50, a total hip replacement was not ideal. Looking for ways to stabilize a hip without nailing it, he developed the technique called Slipped Capital Femoral Epiphysis (SCFE). Ganz and Slongo documented 30 cases and submitted a paper for publication. It was refused because the editors did not believe the story. Slongo wanted to use the technique also in pediatrics and, after

---

[8]An experienced AO surgeon contrasting his teaching experience in Europe, the US, Asia, and Latin America.

final acceptance of the paper for publication in 2001, he dared to move on his ideas within the AO. Presenting his ideas to a larger group in Los Angeles, he again had to hear 'You are crazy.' At the presentation to the AOTK, responsible for the approval of this procedure, he once more met with intransigence. As he recalled, everyone at the TK wanted to stabilize the hip with implants and nails and screws and was only interested in finding new screws for this particular indication. When Slongo argued for a better procedure, not the development of a new screw, he was again confronted with solid resistance which took many years to overcome.

This lengthy description of the long journey of new ideas through an organization even such as the AO, an organization generally on the side of innovation, serves to illustrate the tenacity required of innovators to push new ideas through established channels. Although the AO ended up developing implants and operating techniques for all bones, young and adult, long and short, and for veterinary surgeons, progress took time and the organization could only succeed because it combined a number of innovative surgeons with a group of producers who were skillful and added their experience to the development of an ever expanding *Instrumentarium*. Starting out in 1960 with just about 200 elements divided into five metal boxes, the *Instrumentarium* had now been expanded to over 10,000 elements for a large number of procedures.

References

Müller, M. E., Allgöwer, M., Schneider, R., & Willenegger, H. (1991). *Manual of internal fixation* (3rd ed.). Heidelberg: Springer.
Müller, M., Allgöwer, M., & Willenegger, H. (1963). *Technik der Operativen Frakturbehandlung* (pp. 3–5). Berlin: Springer.
Slongo, T., Audige, L., Schlickewei, W., Clavert, J. M., & Hunter, J. (2006). Development and validation of the AO pediatric comprehensive classification of long-bone fractures by the pediatric expert group of the AO Foundation in collaboration with AO Clinical Investigation and Documentation and the International Association for Pediatric Traumatology. *Journal of Pediatric Orthopaedics, 26*(1), 43–49.
Spiessl, B. (Ed.). (1976). *New concepts in maxillofacial bone surgery*. Berlin: Springer.

IP Issues from the Beginning of the AO

Ownership and control over the Intellectual Property Rights (IP) of the AO *Instrumentarium* has a long tradition. Given the fact that the AO created valuable products that are, or can be, sources of wealth, it should come as no surprise that over the years various interest groups have debated the question of who should control this accumulated IP.

In tracing the evolution of the AO *Instrumentarium*, it becomes clear that the AO founders where not inventors as much as they were innovators. Maurice Müller came face-to-face with the concepts and products of Osteosynthesis when visiting Danis in Brussels in 1950, eight years before the AO was established. The notion of Osteosynthesis itself is something that could not be patented, and certainly neither Danis nor his compatriot Lambotte ever tried to do so. They communicated freely to whoever wanted to know about their surgical procedures.

What Müller, and his AO co-founders, did was to take the basic concepts of the Danis *Instrumentarium*, improve upon them, further develop them, and then add a substantial amount of 'soft IP'; for example, both the explanation and skill development regarding the *Instrumentarium* elements. In doing so, the AO took this idea to the entire medical community and fought for its acceptance. They acted as the first-mover, a term that would be used in the context of today's business.

Müller in the Role of Innovator

When Müller returned from his visit to Danis and took up his appointment as senior resident at the hospital in Fribourg, he began a process of developing his own instruments. First, he ordered plates and screws from Danis' supplier in Belgium and then worked to adapt them, creating instruments that would complement his own surgical technique. He also conducted searches to find local suppliers for both

© Springer Nature Switzerland AG 2019
J.-P. Jeannet, *Leading a Surgical Revolution*,
https://doi.org/10.1007/978-3-030-01980-8_39

instruments and implants, wising to improve upon the Danis *Instrumentarium*. The instruments that Müller created were not direct copies of Danis', but even if they had been, few at the time would have cared.

When Müller later reflected on that instrument design period, he said the following[1]:

> I had been preparing for this for quite a long time. As I have mentioned, both Van Nes and Danis stressed the importance of designing and creating one's own instruments and implants. In 1952, I had already modified Charnley's compression clamps to the ones I designed with threaded connectors to be used with Schantz screws or Steinmann nails for compression as well as for distraction. After the external compression clamps came the screwdriver with a handle with a rectangular profile. Then I modified the Hohmann retractors and designed new ones with both narrow and broad tips. Then came some special bone chisels and gauges, straight and curved, and then a set of special Osteotomes. I also designed a special drill bit for bone and adapted a power drill (ARO-Motor) for more precise drilling of bone.

While working at Balgrist Clinic, Müller accumulated a number of personal instruments that he carried with him during his time as an itinerant surgeon. His special purpose, and originally designed, surgical instruments certainly contributed to his success as surgeon, always in combination with what were known to be his extraordinary surgical skills. The focus of his surgery then, particularly as he moved to Balgrist Clinic, was Orthopedic surgery, specifically relating to the hip. In very simple terms, Müller was accumulating IP related to his surgical instruments. At that time, the term IP was scarcely known; most people spoke only about patents. No definitive records have been established on Müller's own filing for patents, but it is assumed that he did. Again, Müller in his own words[2]:

> During the years I spent at the Balgrist, I worked with the existing angled blade-plates, such as those of Blount and others. These are all illustrated in my book on proximal femoral osteotomies. I had carefully noted what I considered to be their shortcomings. In the late 1950s and the early 1960s, I designed new angled blade-plates. The important features of these were the special 'U' profile of the blade portion and the different angles and different off-sets to preserve the normal anatomical biomechanical relationship of the femur, despite changes in the angle of inclination of the proximal femur after an Osteotomy.

Colleagues were impressed with Müller having his own surgical instruments; it was on that basis that the AO entrusted him with the creation of an *Instrumentarium* that would fit with both their approach and surgical technique regarding Osteosynthesis. However, when the decision to create the AO was taken in March 1958, Müller did not yet have an *Instrumentarium* dedicated to Osteosynthesis (Exhibit 39.1).

---

[1]From Schatzker (2018), p. 72.
[2]Schatzker (2018), p. 71.

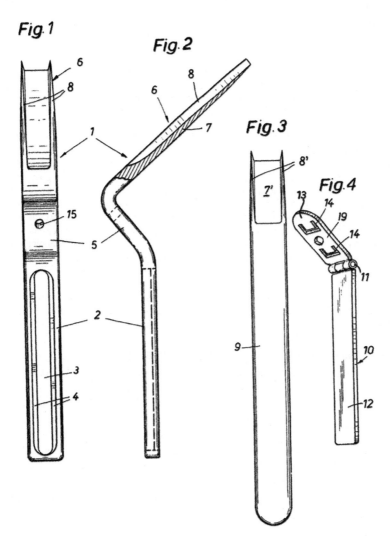

373517
1 Blatt

Exhibit 39.1 Angled blade plate Maurice Müller original patent. *Copyright by AO Foundation, Switzerland*

Müller in the Role of Chief Developer

After the Chur course in March 1958, when the other surgeons tasked Müller with a coherent set of *Instrumentarium*, he soon connected with Mathys and engaged in the development process. Müller drove development on the basis of his surgical experience during the initial development phase, while Mathys contributed the know-how of producing instruments and implants.

The emerging *Instrumentarium* was taken to the AO group, then the G13 that included the founders, who became the 'testers' for the *Instrumentarium*. Any feedback was related to Müller, who early on was the only person with direct contact to Mathys.

Müller on the details of his collaboration with Robert Mathys, Sr.,[3]:

> On 7 April, 1958, I had drawings which I made prior to my meeting with Mathys. When I met him, I was looking for someone who could make a new screw for me. Previously, I had been using material of about six different implant manufacturers. In the spring of 1958, I designed the 4.5 cortex screw with a special thread. This screw was undoubtedly an important breakthrough in the design of a bone screw. The head of the screw was rounded and had a hexagonal recess to couple with the hex profile of the screwdriver tip. The thread of the screw was designed to withstand pullout and provide optimal holding power and compression. This determined the ratio between the diameter of the shaft and the diameter of the thread, as well as the angle subtended between the thread and the shaft. The greater the surface area and the closer the angle was to 90° between the thread and the shaft, the greater the holding power of the screw. It was a non-self-cutting screw and required a tap (thread cutter) to minimize the damage to bone by the dullness of the threads of a self-tapping screw. It also made the process much more accurate. Mathys, as an expert on screw design, was very helpful.

> After the screw came the straight plates with the round holes and the external tension device or compressor, which we used in conjunction with the plates to achieve axial compression. The condylar blade-plate and the 90° and 130° blade-plates were not ready until 1960.

This commentary indicates that there was indeed substantial IP being created, and that Müller apparently considered this to be his own personal IP, formally patent protected or not, which he then brought to the AO in the context of the mandate to develop a complete *Instrumentarium*. The patents filed by Müller in his own name would not meet today's standard for patent filing.[4] The ideas behind the patents were new, but there was little 'inventiveness' to them. Most importantly, there were several ideas in one single patent, something that would not be acceptable today. In order to obtain a patent now, three main criteria have to be met: first, there should be a singular idea, feature, or solution; second, the patent should contain a new solution not found somewhere else; and third, it should include some inventiveness on the part of the filer.

---

[3]Schatzker (2018), p. 71.

[4]Interview with Urs Weber, Attorney at Wenger & Vieli, conducted on 16 March, 2017, in Zurich. Urs Weber acted as attorney for the AO Foundation for many years, covering IP and monopoly issues.

Donating the IP to Synthes AG Chur and the AO

Possibly the most important decision related to IP in the history of the AO happened right after the basic *Instrumentarium* had been completed, at the end of 1960 and right around the first Davos course. In order to settle IP and the question of how to proceed with the producer Mathys, Synthes AG Chur was created to receive payments for the rights to produce the sets. There was a need for assets to obtain legal status for Synthes AG Chur. To fulfill the legal requirements, Müller suggested that he donate his entire Osteosynthesis-related IP to this newly formed company, free-of-charge. The form of the IP was in drawings and probably some filings, covering all elements that Müller had developed up to that time (Exhibit 39.2).

This act of donating all of his IP to Synthes AG Chur, and to having Mathys pay licensing fees for use of the IP which would be used by Synthes AG Chur for the benefit of the entire AO and its mission, proved to be precedent setting for all IP treatment at AO. From then on, all developments from AO surgeons were to be handled in the same way. Synthes AG Chur would become the owner of the IP, could assign it to the producers for commercial exploitation, and earn licensing fees on it, benefiting the AO. No payments were made to AO surgeons. This policy was based on the strongly held belief that AO surgeons should not directly, or personally, make any money on the implants or surgical tools that they advocated.

A review of the list of innovations adopted by the AO reveals another important point: none of the innovations filed bear the name of any of the prime inventors. There was never a Müller this, or a Willenegger that. All innovations bear only functional and descriptive names, which serves to separate the initiator from the final product adopted by the AO community.

IP Management

Following the donation of the Muller IP at the outset, the filing of patents directly through the AO began step by step. There were sporadic filings in the 1960s, and by the 1970s there were up to four filings annually. When the AO Foundation was established, filings were entered and maintained using an Excel data sheets, which was continued until the late 1990s. When the AO Foundation, respectively Synthes AG Chur, agreed to sell its entire trauma IP to Synthes in 2006, the total number of patents involved were estimated at 3500. The number of final products that had been approved by the AOTK was estimated at exceeding 50,000 items. As the registered trademark of Synthes itself was part of the deal, the name of Synthes AG Chur had to be changed and the company owning the residual IP became the AO Technology AG.

A dedicated Synthes AG Chur patent office had been established by the AO Foundation in 2001, which offered professionalized services in IP management for all institutions of the AO Foundation, as well as consultancy for AO Members. Based upon the experience of the now named AO Technology patent office, AO surgeons could initiate and drive the innovation process as long as it concerned the

Nr. 373516   **PATENTSCHRIFT**   **Nr. 373516**

Klassierung: **30 a, 9/03**

SCHWEIZERISCHE EIDGENOSSENSCHAFT

EIDGENÖSSISCHES AMT FÜR GEISTIGES EIGENTUM

Gesuchsnummer:	77647/59
Anmeldungsdatum:	1. September 1959, 17¼ Uhr
Patent erteilt:	30. November 1963
Patentschrift veröffentlicht:	15. Januar 1964

HAUPTPATENT

Dr. med. Maurice E. Müller, St. Gallen

Einrichtung zum chirurgischen Fixieren von Knochenfragmenten in Gliedmaßen

Dr. med. Maurice E. Müller, St. Gallen, ist als Erfinder genannt worden

Es ist bereits vorgeschlagen worden, in der Knochenchirurgie und besonders beim Fixieren von Knochenfragmenten am Knochen selber verankerte Schraubverbindungen zu verwenden. Die bei solchen Versuchen verwendeten Einrichtungen haben jedoch hinsichtlich ihrer Handlichkeit und funktionellen Exaktheit nicht befriedigt.

Zweck der Erfindung ist nun, eine Einrichtung zu schaffen, welche einerseits für die Arbeit des Chirurgen hinsichtlich Exaktheit und erleichterte Durchführung die günstigsten Bedingungen schafft, anderseits selber in funktioneller Hinsicht alle nur denkbaren Anforderungen erfüllt und dabei schließlich die erwünschten Heilungserfolge ermöglicht.

Die den Erfindungsgegenstand bildende Einrichtung zum chirurgischen Fixieren von Knochenfragmenten in Gliedmaßen besitzt nun zu diesem Zwecke Knochenschrauben, und einen Werkzeugsatz zum Herstellen von mit Zentriergesenken versehenen Gewindelöchern in den Fragmenten.

Ausführungsbeispiele des Erfindungsgegenstandes sind in der Zeichnung schematisch dargestellt, und zwar zeigen:

Fig. 1a bis 1c aufeinanderfolgende Phasen beim Fixieren eines Knochenbruches mit Schrauben sowie die einzelnen Werkzeuge der Werkzeugfolge im Einsatz,

Fig. 1d eine andere Bruchstelle mit durch Schrauben fixierten Fragmenten,

Fig. 2a bis 2d aufeinanderfolgende Phasen beim Fixieren eines Knochenbruches mittels Schrauben und Platte sowie die einzelnen Werkzeuge im Einsatz.

Fig. 3 und 4 eine modifizierte Platte im Schnitt bzw. in Draufsicht,

Fig. 5 einen Schnitt nach der Linie V–V der Fig. 4,

Fig. 6 und 7 eine Hüftplatte in Draufsicht bzw. im Längsschnitt und

Fig. 8 einen Führungsteil für die Hüftplatte nach den Fig. 6 und 7.

In den Fig. 1a bis 1c ist ein Teil eines gebrochenen Knochens mit sich an der Bruchstelle überlappenden Fragmenten 1 und 2 dargestellt. Die in korrekter Relativlage aufeinander ausgerichteten Schrauben zu verbindenden Fragmente 1 und 2 werden zunächst mit einer Drahtschlinge 3 behelfsweise fixiert und sodann wird eine Zwinge 4 mit einem V-förmigen Bügel 5 auf die Bruchstelle aufgesetzt, welche die Fragmente 1 und 2 bzw. die Bruchflächen derselben aufeinanderdrückt. Dabei ist der Knochen zwischen einer Kegelspitze 6 bzw. dem kronenförmig ausgebildeten Ende einer Hülse 7 eingespannt, welche miteinander gleichachsig je am Ende eines Schenkels 5 angebracht sind. Die Hülse 7 ist dabei in ihrer Achsrichtung verstellbar in einer am Bügel 5 befestigten Führungshülse gehaltert.

Die Hülse 7 dient, wie aus der Fig. 1a ersichtlich ist, zugleich als Bohrbüchse für einen Spiralbohrer 8. Mit diesem und mit Hilfe der Zwinge 4 durchbohrt der Chirurg gemäß einer vorbestimmten Bohrlinie die am Ende der Bohrbüchse 7 anliegende Wandung des rohrförmigen Knochens bzw. im vorliegenden Fall des Fragmentes 2, wobei ein hinsichtlich der Form und Dimension korrektes Bohrloch entsteht. In dieses Loch wird nun, wie bei 9 in der Fig. 1a angedeutet, eine zweite Bohrbüchse 10 eingesetzt und bis zu der Wandung des Fragmentes 1 vorgeschoben. Das Ende der Bohrbüchse 10 ist ebenfalls kronenartig ausgebildet. Mit einem in der Bohrbüchse 10 geführten Spiralbohrer 11 wird, wie dies bei 12 in der Fig. 1b angedeutet ist, nun die Wandung des Fragmentes 1 durchgebohrt, und es versteht sich, daß auch dieses Bohrloch form- und dimensionstreu ist.

Exhibit 39.2 Patent for plates and screws (MEM). *Copyright by AO Foundation, Switzerland*

surgical procedure. Later in the development process, when a project becomes more complex, it ends up driven more by the developers, often the producer.[5]

Issues with Patent Infringement and Imitators

The AO had its first experience with imitators when two ex-Straumann executives founded Voka. As explained earlier, the decision of AO and its AOTK was, after considerable thought, not to pursue a patent infringement case and instead, to push its own quality, service, and non-profit background. Patent protection at that time (1963) was not judged to be strong enough and Voka not a major competitor.

Voka turned out to be a thorn in the side of the AO, and especially of the industrial partners, when, due to the slow and deliberate validation procedure of the AOTK approval process, the competitor could come to market with the same new product ahead of the AO. This suggested that being quick to market, but still safe, could be more important than mere patent filings and protection.

A later challenge by Zimmer, a large US implant manufacturer, came to the fore. The company copied, as did some other American companies, a large number of AOTK approved implants in considerable detail. The excuse given by Zimmer management referred to the fact that they were not copied, but that the plate and screw design were dictated by the nature of the application and therefore beyond patent protection.

Patents Are Not the Only Way to Protect IP

Although they appear to give IP protection, registered patents require considerable effort to enforce and in the medical device market, including implants, they do not always provide reliable protection. The AOIP, however, was protected by a number of other elements as well. First, there was the brand name of AO, which, once established in the market, became a sign of excellence. The AO logo, or its trademark, was another way to 'stamp' products and connote excellence and safety in origin. Brand violation, trademark or even copyright infringements are often easier to enforce and, if well utilized, can protect IP. With its distinct logo, and the trademarked and branded name of AO, the organization did implicitly move IP protection further into the commercial field, and away from the more limiting hardware and product form and function.

Because the AO Foundation and its activities were so well established, this fact resulted in a strong franchise that could form a stronger IP protection than sheer patent filings themselves. AOTK-approved products, produced by the DePuy Synthes group, are now labelled 'Approved by AO Foundation' or 'Approved by AOTK,' branding the approval process as a proof of quality.

---

[5]Interview with Christoph Nötzli, conducted on 15 March, 2017, in Zurich.

Challenging AOIP Ownership Policy

The early AO surgeons and the organization founders willingly, and without major challenges, accepted that the AO norm meant to always turn over any developed IP to Synthes AG Chur. As the AO grew, and the next generation of surgeons joined, this policy was not always accepted unchallenged and was, at times, tested. This had to do with the competitive situation where manufacturers competing with the AO paid collaborating surgeons consulting fees, allowing them to earn royalties on device developments, sometimes reaching 15% or more. In 1958, when the AO was founded, most surgeons were not aware of this. One could say, that the founders unwittingly gave up a considerable amount of money without realizing how much revenue might ever be earned on the back of their innovations.

It was not only the younger, next generation surgeons, who wanted some compensation for particular developments. Their employers, often universities, had wised up and realized that revenues from innovations and inventions, even patents, derived from scientists and surgeons on their staff could be tapped by the institutions themselves.

Some AO-affiliated surgeons, who had started to develop their own instruments or implants with non-AO manufacturers, were disciplined; there were times, however, when doctors were made to leave the AO because their actions did not respect the important AO pillar of surgeons not personally profiting from the *Instrumentarium*. In this context, even Müller let it be known that the policy he was central in creating was good for the AO at the beginning but should be modified as the organization grew beyond its infancy.

The 2006 Cooperation Agreement Triggered a Major Lawsuit

When the AO agreed to sell the entire scope of its IP to the industrial partner and producer of the AOTK-approved implants and instruments, Synthes, consisting of the majority of patents held and the trademark name 'Synthes,' as well as other product-related trademarks, a major dispute erupted with the University of Berne. Max Aebi, who was key in creating AOSpine and was the co-developer of the USS, together with Robert Mathys, Jr., became embroiled in a legal fight as to who should benefit from the IP transaction totalling CHF 1 billion.

The University of Berne claimed that it should be paid a portion for the development of the Universal Spine System (USS). Since spine elements accounted for as much as 20% of AO implant sales at Synthes, and Aebi was at that time Professor at Berne University, the educational institution sued the AO for a 'fair share' of the proceeds. The university, in the end, lost its fight on technical issues, as the court dismissed its status as a party to the suit. At the time that Aebi developed the spine system, he had signed over the IP to the development to the AO, as was customary for AO members.[6]

Even AO co-founder Müller's views on IP had evolved over time. Max Aebi remembered the following comments made to him by Müller at the time he was developing the spine system:

> If I were younger and in your position, I would leave the present AO and create a new, AO-like organization, because things have been developed in a way, which no longer reflect my original vision: in such a new organization the people who substantially contribute to the well-being of the Foundation by contributing intellectual property should be rewarded like in a University concept: one part to the University (corresponds to the AO Foundation), one part to the department of the innovator (corresponds, e.g., to AOSpine), and one part to the author.[7]

The issues of how to compensate individual efforts in the IP creation continued to be debated. The AO adopted new policies that indicated a fundamental change on the original polices and would allow for extra compensation within reason. Now that the entire trauma IP is owned by Synthes and the company that acquired it in 2011, Johnson & Johnson's DePuy Synthes (DPS) division, IP ownership on new devices and new elements, developed with involvement of the ATOK System, together with DePuy Synthes, and marketed as AOTK approved *Instrumentarium* has shifted to that company.

Whose IP Is It Anyway?

This challenge of the way the AO handles IP is raised in the form of a question: Whose IP is it anyway? Does it belong to the surgeon? Does it belong to the AO? Should it belong to the producer? While these are partly legal questions, there are also ethical issues: 'Who started this anyway?' or 'Who was the major contributor to the creation of the AO and the development of its surgical procedures?'

Clearly, these are complex questions to answer, and it would be almost impossible to find an answer that satisfies all of the parties that were at some time involved in the creation and building of the AO. Looking at the chain of events that led to the creation of the AO, and afterward, no single individual can claim having done it singlehandedly. Müller certainly triggered it, but it could have ended at any point if certain steps involving other persons had not been taken.

Starting as early as Müller's 1950 visit to Danis in Brussels, all the way to finding 12 other willing surgeons to support him, through to the *Instrumentarium* launch, and then growing the organization with education, research, and clinical

---

[6]"Die Uni Bern verliert den Patentstreit." *Der Bund*, Berne, 12 July, 2012.

[7]Source of Maurice Müller comment: Prof. Dr. Max Aebi. Müller essentially followed this strategy when he separated his hip developments from the trauma division of the AO and went on to create Protek, as described in Chap. 25.

development, the process could have been terminated at any of those points if a critical failure had occurred.

The creation of the AO and its growth over the past 60 years can be seen as a sequence of events that could have come to a halt at any step. The way the organization was created and grew, contributed to the impossible attribution of its IP to any individual. To place all IP development into a single pot, regardless of which person contributed it, may have been the stroke of genius that allowed the organization to take off. It is understandable that this original view was difficult for some to accept once the AO sold its majority of IP to Synthes for CHF 1 billion, only to see eventually the entire Synthes company to be acquired by J&J just five years later for CHF 20 billion.

Reference

Schatzker, J. (2018). *Maurice E. Müller: In his own words*. Biel: AO Foundation.

One Final Merger?

40

J&J Acquires Synthes

One More Merger Announcement in 2011

At the end of April 2011, the financial markets were surprised by the news that the largest US health care company, Johnson & Johnson (J&J), acquired the entire Synthes firm for a total amount of USD 21.6 billion (CHF 19 billion). In one single deal, the previously independent firms Mathys, Stratec Medical, and Synthes USA—all involved with the beginning of the commercialization of the AO-designed implants combined under Synthes—had become a subsidiary of a large US healthcare company. What began in a small workshop run by Robert Mathys, Sr., in the small town of Bettlach in Switzerland and bootstrapped on little capital, had just been valued at USD 21.6 billion. The date of the announcement came 53 years after the first prototypes of the AO *Instrumentarium* had been fabricated by the initial design duo of Robert Mathys, Sr., and Maurice Müller.

The company, and the original businesses, that had started out with zero sales in 1958 was, by the time of the merger, reporting global sales of USD 4 billion. About half of these sales were still manufactured in its eight plants in Switzerland; the remaining six plants were located across several other countries. At the time of its acquisition through J&J, the Synthes Group had about 12,000 employees worldwide.

The Developments That Brought Us to This Point

As recounted previously in more detail, the history of producing AO-designed and approved implants and instruments had initially begun with one company, Mathys, 53 years earlier, soon expanding to a second one, Straumann (1960), and then joined by a third one, Synthes USA (1974) started by some of the AO founders. All three companies prospered, but by the mid-1990s the US Company, Synthes USA, after several false starts, began to outpace the other two.

© Springer Nature Switzerland AG 2019
J.-P. Jeannet, *Leading a Surgical Revolution*,
https://doi.org/10.1007/978-3-030-01980-8_40

Changes in management and ownership affected the relative constellation of the three owners. First, in 1987 there was the management buy-out of the Synthes, Inc. business in the US by Hansjörg Wyss, who became the company's CEO and sole owner. The Straumann implant business also underwent a management buy-out after the death of company founder Fritz Straumann; Rudolf Maag took over, operating as Stratec Medical. Following a successful IPO[1] of Stratec Medical in 1996, that company in return was acquired in 1999 by Synthes, Inc. US and operated as Synthes-Stratec with Wyss as majority shareholder. Following the death of company founder Robert Mathys, Sr., in 2000, Synthes-Stratec acquired the AO implant business of the Mathys family in 2004, thus combining the original three companies under single ownership with majority owner Wyss at the helm. Operating under the simple name of Synthes, the company was listed on the Swiss stock market and grew rapidly to a sales level of USD 4 billion by 2011.

During a time when the AO Foundation underwent its own share of turbulence, producers of the AO implants were subject to a whole series of financial transactions that ranged from management buy-out to include IPOs, as well as several mergers and acquisitions. And yet, despite this upheaval among the ownership of the producing companies, financial support of the AO Foundation continued unabated.

The Growth of Synthes

Following the acquisition of the Mathys trauma implant business by Synthes-Stratec in 2004, combined producer sales continued to grow reflecting the continued and growing acceptance of the AO philosophy for treatment of bone fractures. This growth, partly due to the increased research and teaching programs under the AO Foundation, was used to fund the organization, based upon ever increasing royalties stemming from AO implant sales and later, unrestricted contributions from Synthes. The expansion into several additional trauma areas in the human skeleton, and the combined development of less invasive implants and surgical procedures, increased the AO *Instrumentarium* unit numbers and contributed to overall sales volume growth.

The commercial policies so successfully implemented by Synthes in the US under Wyss' leadership were another contributing factor. Wyss had enormous confidence in the value of a professional sales force driving sales in the US, a model eventually applied elsewhere in the global Synthes Company. Wyss, no longer encumbered by coordination efforts across multiple entities, was free to apply his business ideas to the development of the combined Synthes.

Some sales data stemming from the merger documentation clearly demonstrates the growth model of Synthes USA, and later Synthes-Stratec. On a pro forma basis, had the Synthes-Stratec merger taken place in 1996 and not in 1999, the sales of the

---

[1]IPO stands for Initial Public Offering, describing the first entry of a privately held company into the stock market.

two companies would have amounted to USD 593 million. In 1998, the year before the merger of the two firms, the combined sales would have amounted to USD 882 million. Much of that stemmed from the sales growth in the US. In 1999, the two companies jointly had sales of USD 695 million, only to see this grow to USD 1229 million the year before the Mathys acquisition. During this time, employment grew to 4000 for Synthes-Stratec and its operating profit (not net profit) amounted to USD 443 million. North America accounted for more than 75% of sales.

The acquisition of the Mathys business in 2004 brought in another USD 500 million in sales to the company that now operated under the name Synthes. In 2007, just three years after the merger with Mathys, the combined Synthes reported sales of USD 2759 million, growing to USD 3192 million in 2008 and USD 3687 million by 2010. Sales in the US market accounted for 58% of the total, which indicates that 'old' Synthes, Inc. had grown larger than 'old' Mathys and the 'old' Stratec Medical, combined.

The main contributor to of the impressive growth of Synthes was the success in the US. This is all the more surprising since the US market was initially very slow in adopting the AO philosophy for bone trauma. A factor that helped increase sales in the US was that the per unit price of AO implants in the country were often higher, due to the more extensive service rendered by Synthes to surgeons there in the operating environment.

Why Divest Synthes Ownership Now?

After having spent 34 years at the helm of Synthes and having reached the age of 76 without a family heir to take over, it seemed to be a logical point for Wyss to turn over the responsibility of the Synthes global enterprise to someone else. Having exerted full control over a business where he owned almost half of the share capital, it also appeared that it might be difficult for an entrepreneur like him to let someone else run the company he had built. He would still have a huge investment risk, and in some ways continue to carry the entrepreneurial responsibility in the form of ownership.

Additionally, there were major changes appearing on the horizon concerning the business of medical implants due to new technologies. Mastering these challenges would take the full time and energy of any person. Wyss had led Synthes through two major mergers with Stratec Medical and then with Mathys, eventually capping this with the acquisition of full control over the AO Foundation's patents and trademarks. The business had reached a point where its value was at its peak with all previously separate pieces coming under one roof and one single ownership. Monetizing this lifetime achievement would also allow Wyss to engage in more of his philanthropic activities (see Chap. 51).

The task then became one of finding a new owner who would respect the history of Synthes. Given that the value of Synthes had reached the dimension of about USD 20 billion, according to stock market capitalization, the potential buyer would need to be of substantial size and, most importantly, also have expertise in the Orthopedic and Trauma business. Among the companies that could be considered for such a transaction, Johnson & Johnson stood out, due to its experience in healthcare and Orthopedics; it is a global company and has a long track record of giving its individual 250 group companies a certain entrepreneurial freedom, thus preserving some of the Synthes company culture. From the perspective of J&J, this acquisition had the industrial logic of building the world largest Orthopedic implant company with a breadth of product portfolio second to none.

What Is J&J's DePuy Division?

DePuy, a wholly-owned subsidiary of J&J, itself has had a very interesting history. The company goes as far back as to 1895 when a Revra DePuy founded a company in the US state of Indiana, to make fiber splints in order to replace wooden material used at the time to set fractures. In doing so, DePuy can claim to be the very first commercial Orthopedic manufacturer in the world.

As a company, DePuy had experienced its own series of M&A activity, changing hands several times and even once connecting with the product line of AO's co-founder Maurice Müller. In 1968, DePuy was acquired by a different owner and received the exclusive marketing rights to the total hip replacement implants developed by Müller. As described earlier, Müller did not include his hip-related intellectual capital in the creation of the AO. When Müller began to market his own hip implants in the US, he was looking for a distributor and settled on DePuy, which remained the distributor of Müller implants in the US until the acquisition of Protek, Müller's hip prosthesis company, by Sulzer in 1989.

Then came a series of changes in ownership involving two pharmaceutical companies. The German firm Boehringer Mannheim acquired DePuy's parent company in 1974. Then came a time of expansion of DePuy's Orthopedic product line, followed by a move into arthroscopic surgical instruments and the launch of spinal implants. In 1997, the Basel-based pharma company Roche acquired Boehringer Mannheim, and thus became owners of DePuy. That same year, however, Roche divested DePuy to J&J in a transaction valued at USD 3.7 billion. For DePuy, this was to be the last stop, becoming a member of J&J's collection of health-related companies.

When J&J announced the acquisition of Synthes, and its intent to create the world's largest Orthopedic implant company by combining the DePuy Division with Synthes into DePuy Synthes, or DPS for short, financial analysts and observers were praising the move and suggested that only a large firm, such as J&J, could pull off a deal of this size. The Synthes division runs as a self-managed division within DPS and represents about half of DPS sales. DPS, through its various acquisitions such as Synthes, offers the most comprehensive portfolio of Orthopedic and neuro products in the world, and is itself further subdivided into several businesses, including Trauma, Power Tools, Neuro, CMF, Spine, and Joint Reconditioning (including hip, knee, and shoulder replacements).

Impact of Synthes Sale on the AO Foundation

The importance of Synthes as a licensed producer to the AO Foundation was obvious to everyone. Synthes was the sole source of funding for the AO Foundation through AO Technology, the company that used to be Synthes AG Chur. Synthes was the owner of all of AO Foundation's technology and the sole user of its trademark Synthes@. When J&J acquired Synthes, all contracts between the operating company Synthes and the AO Foundation and AO Tech remained in force.[2] This was also the case for the Cooperation and Support Agreement (CoSA) that stipulated the types of services to be rendered for Synthes through the AO Foundation, and the levels of compensation to be received for services, such as operating courses and running the AOTK system for product approval. Although Wyss left Synthes, there were still many executives at Synthes that remained from the previous regime and were familiar with the workings of the AO Foundation.

At the time of the Synthes acquisition by J&J, the collaboration and support payments received by the AO Foundation amounted to about CHF 60 million. Over the following four years (2012–2015) these payments were about CHF 64 million each year. Support payments for services rendered by the AO Foundation to J&J DPS, were regularly negotiated and adjusted, taking into consideration the needs of both the producer (DPS) and the AO Foundation.[3] Likewise, on the AO Foundation side, the same leaders remained in place, assuring a smooth handover from one ownership level to the next: namely, Synthes as a public company and J&J as the new owner, were both public companies subject to similar financial disclosure requirements but with a broader exposure to the US regulatory environment—J&J is a company that produces and sells a much broader range of health care products than Synthes does.

Following a long period of negotiation, a new Cooperation Agreement (CA) was agreed upon in 2016, the first one between the AO Foundation and DePuy Synthes. The agreement was entered into for five years with a possible extension. There were a number of important changes compared to the previous agreement (completed in 2006). The educational contributions were set at about 60% of the total budget, in order to support some 710 courses, or educational events, annually, as well as covering a targeted number of learners and about 300 fellowships. The AOTK structure would allocate about 10% of the support, and the remainder could be used for administrative support.

The new agreement stipulates that there are no obligations for AO members to purchase DPS equipment, and DPS confirmed the charitable status of the AO Foundation. Also, the CA does not create a contractual relationship between DPS and AO surgeons. There remains a certain exclusivity level limited to AO Education and the AOTK. Any IP created through the TK process continues to belong to DPS. While this high-level agreement stipulated some deliverables, authority to distribute

---

[2]Collaboration and Support Agreement between AO Technology AG and Synthes, Inc., dated 13 December, 2008.

[3]Source: AO Foundation Annual Reports from 2005 to 2015.

funding internally to the clinical divisions and regions remains entirely up to the AO Foundation Board. Similarly, the AO decides on the course contents and choice of faculty.

Major changes in the agreement concern the exclusivity of research, which is no longer part of the revised CA. First right of offer for research is reserved for DPS. AO obtained greater freedom to conduct research efforts on its own account and to link up with external bodies or universities. New initiatives can be jointly decided and added to the base funding. The new CA also includes a clause that guarantees AO funding for some time in case DPS was divested to a new owner, either in parts or in its entirety. As was the case previously, service targets were agreed upon which the AO Foundation is expected to deliver, and DPS would remit support payments. The basic support was set at a CHF 64.6 million over the first three years, and then to be renegotiated. The actual payment for 2016 was CHF 67.4 million and included contributions for some additional programs.

This new CA represents a major departure from the agreements in force around 2002 in Oslo, when the AO organization struggled with how much exclusivity to grant to producers. The new at arms-length CA in effect between the AO Foundation and DPS eliminates some of the contentious points, in part, because the IP was transferred to Synthes, now owned by DPS. The royalty issue had already been eliminated in 2006, replaced by an unrestricted grant model. As one of the central figures in the battle in Oslo mentioned, "eventually, the AO ended up where some of us wanted to be but could not, due to the strong influence of the producers. So, you could say we did get our version of Oslo implemented after all!"[4]

At this point, some might question the rationale of J&J DPS to sign any agreement at all and commit to substantial support payments on an annual basis. While the relationship has clear value for the AO Foundation, allowing it to continue its substantial and far-reaching programs, the collaboration remains of value to the producer as well. Competitors of DPS, and there are a number of them—large companies such as Zimmer and Stryker—also support their businesses with extensive training courses and collaborate with leading surgeons to extend and develop their product lines. In essence, DPS would have had to replace the AO Foundation work with its own structure. AO surgeons participate in the important training courses and in the TK development process at low daily fees, reflecting the voluntary history of the AO.

In addition, the quality of the AO teaching and its TK are generally regarded as second to none, representing the industry's benchmark. In the AO courses, only AO-approved and DPS produced implants are used, an important indirect marketing element that has proven itself over time. Tapping into the unrivaled global network of AO surgeons also represented an enormous advantage to DPS. To have all of this performed by expert surgeons, with a reputation and track record for independence,

---

[4]Telephone interview with James Kellam, Past AO President 2004–2006, conducted on 4 January, 2018.

would be of great value to any producer. Bringing all of this in-house for DPS would represent a considerable effort and expense, something that J&J and DPS leadership must certainly have been cognizant of.

Evolution of the Synthes Business Base in Switzerland

With the acquisition of Synthes through J&J's DePuy Division, the entire Synthes manufacturing base in Switzerland changed hands. These were the operations initially developed and built up by the Mathys and Straumann/Stratec businesses, representing eight locations out of a total of 14 for Synthes. With an employment of 4000 in Switzerland alone, from its total of 12,000 worldwide, there were concerns among many as to what would happen to this large industrial base.

Since the transaction took place in 2011, total employment for the DPS businesses in Switzerland has remained level. This is of great importance to the industrial basis of Switzerland and, in particular, to the industrial basis of the Solothurn region where most of the DPS employment is concentrated. Too often acquired firms are gutted and major operations transferred into a different region, leaving the original base weakened. When adding the unexpected appreciation of the Swiss Franc in 2015, adding about 10–15% to the cost base of a manufacturing organization, the red warning lights were flashing in many local supplier and government offices. That the manufacturing activity did not diminish speaks for the quality of the operation and the skill level of the staff.

A look at the manufacturing operations near Solothurn, the area where the Mathys factories once stood and remained operating under the Synthes name, now under DPS ownership, demonstrates the complexity of manufacturing operation for AO-specified implants.[5] In the two ex-Mathys plants, which still employ about 400 people each, the most modern production machinery operates in two shifts. Every year, plant leadership invested in new equipment, ratcheting up the automation level and quality of output, while keeping employments levels the same. This productivity increase, combined with a steady sales increase for implants, allowed the local factory management to remain competitive against alternative locations in different, even lower-cost countries.

The ever-growing AO-approved *Instrumentarium* had expanded from 200 in 1960 to over 10,000 individual elements. The two ex-Mathys factories in Bettlach produce annually some 11 million different elements, or parts, often in small batches of only 20. In terms of stock keeping units (SKU) it means having an inventory of over 127,000 for trauma and CMF alone, with another 45,000 for spine, not all of them originating from AO; possibly half are from DePuy itself (Exhibit 40.1).

---

[5]Interview with Sven Zybell, Head of Manufacturing, DPS, Bellach and Grenchen plants, conducted on 28 February, 2018, in Bellach, Solothurn, Switzerland.

Production at Plants Synthes Bettlach/Grenchen

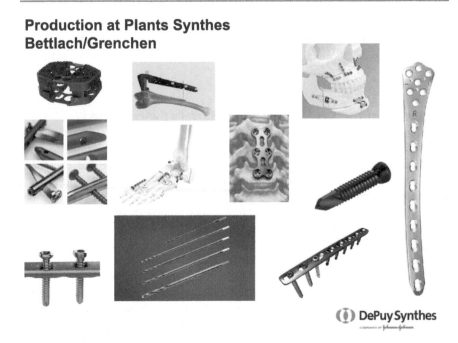

Exhibit 40.1   Typical implant parts from DPS. *Source: J&J DPS. Reprinted with permission*

The Swiss operation was kept at such a high productivity level that the plants became the model factories in the global DPS Trauma segment. Management of the operation keeps the skill level high to assure that, just in case a down-turn should ever occur, employees would find employment in other manufacturing operations in the region where watch component manufacturing remains a constant competitor for skilled staff. To stay cost competitive while producing with one of the most expensive labor forces in the world remains a challenge that can only be met if labor productivity compensates for wage levels and per-unit (element) cost beat alternative locations.

Of the eight DPS sites in Switzerland, four were former Mathys plants, another three former Stratec Medical locations, with Wyss acquiring one after the combination of Synthes-Stratec and Mathys. After taking over both Stratec Medical in 1999 and Mathys in 2004, Wyss did not eliminate any of these sites. He was a strong believer in arranging his business along several smaller operational units with dedicated production mandates and opted not to combine all operations into a single large site. In some way, the plants dotting Switzerland form a type of 'Synthes Campus,' with most plants being a one-hour drive away from each other (Exhibit 40.2).

As this manuscript went into production, news broke that J&J was negotiating with Jabil, a large US-based contract manufacturer, to transfer all of its trauma implants producing plants to Jabil. All products will continue to be marketed under DPS and J&J. This transfer affects at least 1800 employees in Switzerland

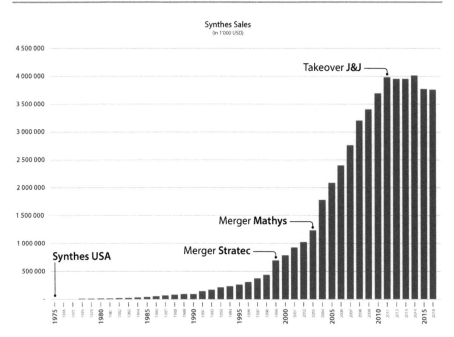

Exhibit 40.2 Development of Global Synthes Sales 1975 to 2016 including mergers and acquisition by Johnson & Johnson. *Source*: Synthes and AO Foundation. Design: IMD Institute

as well as employees from plants in Germany, US, and Mexico. Effectively, this means that the plants originally built by the Mathys organization will have operated under four different ownership structures: Mathys, Synthes, J&J DPS, and now Jabil.[6]

---

[6]"Schweizer J&J Mitarbeiter wechseln den Arbeitgeber", Neue Zürcher Zeitung, July 20, 2018.

Assessing How the AO Navigated Turbulences

41

Looking for Cruising Altitude Again

By 2011, following the acquisition of Synthes by J&J, the AO had gone through just about any kind of turbulence one could imagine. The organization had stabilized, and its activities were humming along at a record pace. The AO had grown, added resources, and overcome every one of the challenges thrown at it.

As part of its evolution, the AO had managed to replace the founding generation, step by step, and implement a new governance structure that allowed for more member participation of those at a distance from the center of gravity—Switzerland. It successfully morphed from an association to a more structured foundation, and the governance of the various bodies had provided some robustness. The price the AO paid for this growth were more processes, more commissions, more meetings, and more bureaucracy. In just a few years, AO's entire legal underpinning, set into place by its founders, had been completely reshaped.

The latest generation of AO leaders, arranged in new structures, found themselves confronted with substantial changes and challenges to the basic survival of the organization. The debates, which culminated in Oslo, were a watershed; yet, the new leadership managed to bridge the conflicting views and move on. The business arrangements underpinning the revenue and resource structure of the AO suddenly needed to be renegotiated, and with an ever-changing set of producers, which had changed from being three suppliers to just one. The research thrust also needed to be put on new foundations, and the central asset of the AO, its IP, was suddenly structured in a new setting and challenged as to how it was being managed.

While all of these challenges had to be dealt with, the *Instrumentarium* also required continued attention and expansion. The mission of the AO had to be expanded to encompass other parts of the human skeleton not envisioned when the AO was founded, including spine, CMF, and veterinary medicine.

What was the cost to the AO, while an entirely new crew led the organization and had to master all of these issues? The increased growth continued the expansion of

© Springer Nature Switzerland AG 2019
J.-P. Jeannet, *Leading a Surgical Revolution*,
https://doi.org/10.1007/978-3-030-01980-8_41

the resource base, and the ever-increasing activities led to bulking up the AO and, invariably, an increase in bureaucracy. Lack of speed in organizational matters is a typical price to be paid for this. Other than that, were there more fundamental changes at the AO—changes to its mission, to its credo, or even values?

To the outside observer, such changes were not detectable. In fact, the values and missions put into place by the AO founders were not only coming through largely unscathed, but the new leadership helped the organization overcome conflict and stress. The overriding desire to put the patient's interest first, and the attention to all of the detail that goes with the best possible processes to maximize surgical outcomes, were so paramount that they helped solve deep conflicts over business issues. Yes, compromises were made; yes, the stipends paid are now a bit higher than for what 50 years ago was done completely on a voluntary basis; and, yes, there is some compensation now for contribution to IP but, by and large, these changes did not reach the core of the AO.

When a new generation of leaders overcomes all of these challenges, while still maintaining the values of the founders, the signal is that these core values and structures are very strong. Although this does not necessarily guarantee continued success, it is likely that these values will continue to serve another generation of leaders well.

Part IV

The AO Foundation Today and Its Impact

The AO's Many Achievements

42

The achievements of the AO Foundation drive the focus of this fourth section. When J&J's acquisition of Synthes was completed in early January 2012, a major new chapter of the AO Foundation had to be navigated. The era from 1984 to 2011 was, at times, turbulent but as it came to an end it appeared to be the right moment to pause and reflect on what had already been accomplished over the course of AO's history (in this chapter).

A review of the AO organization as a whole is included, as is a discussion of the various components that constitute today's organization. Several elements and bodies of the AO are covered separately, such as the TK System, and the Institutes, which are devoted to a number of key activities (Chaps. 43–45). This will provide a sense of the governance structure that defines the AO as it celebrates its 60th anniversary.

Two chapters highlight the Foundation's continuing innovation activities—both those that are closer to the existing mission and others that are expanding into new fields and new geographies (Chaps. 48 and 49). Of particular importance in this respect are chapters dealing with the overall global impact of the AO Foundation. Interpreting the impact of the AO in a broader sense is deliberate, in an effort to go beyond what might normally be associated with the term 'foundation.' Several types of impact are identified, including health economics and AO's industrial impact. Also covered is the AO Foundation's wealth creation, including discussion of a 'wealth of all kinds', which is not limited to only economic or financial wealth (Chap. 50). Finally, there is a review of the AO's philanthropic effects and of individuals associated with the Foundation. A review of the honors showered upon the AO and its founders closes the section (Chap. 52).

© Springer Nature Switzerland AG 2019
J.-P. Jeannet, *Leading a Surgical Revolution*,
https://doi.org/10.1007/978-3-030-01980-8_42

The AO Center: The Tip of the Iceberg

To get an initial impression of the workings of the AO Foundation, a visitor is tempted to commence with the AO Center in Davos. About a mile outside of town, a wooden structure becomes visible that locals have come to refer to as the 'Toblerone,' in reference to the well-known Swiss Alps-shaped chocolate bar. The Center, inaugurated in 1992, intended to assemble under one roof different AO Foundation administrative units that had previously been located in Berne and throughout Davos (Exhibit 43.1).

Prior to making the decision to locate the Center in Davos, there was discussion about where best to locate an AO Center. Actively involved was Maurice Müller, then Professor at the University of Berne, where a number of the AO administrative offices were located. Müller had offered to donate a large tract of land outside the city of Berne but ran into difficulty obtaining approval from local authorities. Interestingly, that same piece of land owned by Müller, was later to provide the foundational resource for the *Zentrum Paul Klee* (Paul Klee Center), designed by world-renowned architect Renzo Piano and completed in 2005.

Financing came in large part from proceeds obtained when Synthes, Inc., the US-based producer of implants, was acquired by Wyss in a management buy-out. At that time, the AO surgeons who had been shareholders in Synthes USA contributed 20% of the proceeds of the share sale, and Robert Mathys, Sr., the only industrial partner not part of the US operation (because it was not his sale territory), contributed as well.[1] In 2018, a staff of about 200 worked at the AO Center in Davos, representing the bulk of AO global staff headcount of about 320.

---

[1]There have been differing stories circulating about the sale of Synthes US to Hansjörg Wyss, and the resulting payout to the original shareholders. The sale price was reported as CHF 58 million, but Wyss also owned a share of about 17%. The bulk of the shareholding was accounted for by the group of AO surgeons involved in the AOTK and Synthes AG Chur AG. The contribution of 20%

© Springer Nature Switzerland AG 2019
J.-P. Jeannet, *Leading a Surgical Revolution*,
https://doi.org/10.1007/978-3-030-01980-8_43

Exhibit 43.1   AO Center Davos, Switzerland. *Copyright by AO Foundation, Switzerland*

The biggest unit in the Davos Center is Research, or ARI, and includes about 90 professionals. Also located in the vicinity of the Center are the animal stables. If there is a negative to Davos, a physically beautiful location, it would be the travel time to Zurich, the nearest city, which requires about a two-hour drive, each way.

The AO Center in Davos, however, can be understood only as the visible tip of a large iceberg. Although some of the staff engaged in coordinating and facilitating meetings are located in Davos, the vast majority of AO Foundation activities—educational events, many professional meetings, and gatherings of the clinical divisions and their boards—takes place away from Davos all over the world. Comparing the AO Foundation to a modern business, one would describe it as a 'Distributed Organization,' with most members working off-line and coming together regularly for scheduled meetings.

A second base for the AO is located in Dübendorf, near Zurich, and serves as a kind of satellite office for some functions and staff who benefit from working and living near Switzerland's largest city. This satellite office, close to the Zurich Airport, offers meeting rooms when participants gather from several countries. The largest organizational unit in Dübendorf is AO Education, the educational unit of the AO Foundation. A total of 86 full-time employees work from the Dübendorf

---

amounted to CHF 11.6 million. The donation of Robert Mathys, Sr., brought the available funds for building to CHF 14 million. The rest of the budget was financed with a mortgage, as the AO at that time did not have substantial funds on its own.

location. Another 30 staff members are located abroad, primarily in Hong Kong, the US, and Latin America.

In a regional economic impact study conducted by the University of St. Gallen for the AO Foundation, total impact and importance of the AO for Davos, through its courses and local employment, are only exceeded by the World Economic Forum held there annually. The AO courses, mostly held in early December, and related activities generate about 11,000 overnight stays and the AO advanced to the second largest user of the Davos Conference Center.[2]

AO Foundation Organization Today

The AO Foundation has been able to achieve its massive impact and goals with only 320 paid staff members, which is largely due to the volunteer nature of the organization and its members. A vast number of dedicated boards, expert groups, task forces, and regional groupings, all staffed largely with surgeons who volunteer considerable time and effort to the Foundation, make it possible to achieve maximum impact with minimum administration.

To make this massive volunteer organization work requires both time and skill. Some members, and former members, speak freely about the difficulty of accomplishing things in a reasonable amount of time. In their opinion, the organization has grown too big and acts too slowly, but this has largely been a function of wanting to get so many surgeons involved and sharing responsibilities over thousands of participating volunteers. In terms of formal board memberships across the entire AO organization, up to 600 surgeons are involved.

The AO Foundation's structure has largely remained the same since the changes that came when transitioning into a foundation, in 1984, and the resulting adaptation of key governance bodies. What did change, however, was the sub-division into several clinical divisions with Trauma being just one of several. Also, the roles and responsibilities of the various clinical divisions changed as did many of the central functions. Research and Education, for example, became decentralized into the clinical divisions, in an effort to make them more responsive to their specialized surgeons and regional demands.

Some new responsibilities, or programs, were added and steered away from the central organization. These included new initiatives, such as incubator funding, some start-up companies, and AO Alliance, a new initiative targeting low-income countries, as well as the management of the AO Foundation endowment that had grown to CHF 1.37 billion (2017), as a result of the sale of patents and trademarks to Synthes, now owned by J&J's DePuy Synthes division. Finally, and of great importance to the financial support of the AO Foundation, was the new 2015 Cooperation Agreement (CA) with J&J's DePuy Synthes (DPS) Division, which

---

[2]"Die betriebswirtschaftliche Bedeutung der AO Foundation für Davos und den Kt. Graubünden", Strauss, Simone, et al., University of St. Gallen, 2018.

resulted in a substantial alteration in the funding and support arrangement. The AO Foundation leadership spent a considerable amount of time on these endeavors.

AO Foundation Governance[3]

The Assembly of Trustees, often referred to as the 'parliament' of the AO Foundation, consists of 131 leading surgeons (2017). It is responsible for the approval of the scientific and medical mission of the AO Foundation, important elections, and any modification of the AO Foundation charter and by-laws. Trustees transmit AO information to national institutions and other AO surgeons, as well as provide feedback regarding the specific needs of their respective regions.

The Assembly of Trustees is comprised of the following categories:

- Elected Trustees (49)
- Ex-Officio Trustees (68)
- Founding Members (4)
- Past AO Presidents (10)

Trustees serve a limited number of years, allowing for constant renewal of the body. Currently, the AO has agreed to reduce the number of trustees to 100, over time, by excluding the category of Elected Trustees and replacing them as Regional Trustees at a level number (30). The body typically meets once a year around June; the location rotates around the world. Trustees elect the AO President (a two-year term), new trustees, and members of the AO Foundation Board (Exhibit 43.2).

The AO Foundation Board (AOFB) represents the highest executive and supervisory body of the AO Foundation. The Trustees elect its members. As a group, the AOFB is responsible for the strategy of the Foundation, for allocations of funds to the various AO units, financial management, compliance and legal structure, as well as the election of key committee chair persons, and general supervision of the AO executive management. Its membership is composed of several ex-officio members such as the current President (Chair), immediate-past, and next-elect presidents of the AO, as well as the AO CEO (Vice-Chair). The other members are selected on the basis of their expertise and include one expert for each key AO clinical area, as well as experts with functional expertise, such as investment, finance, and R&D. More recently, members with clinical expertise are not expected to represent only their clinical division, as was previously the case.

The AOFB meet regularly, several times a year, in different locations. Also reporting to the AO Foundation Board is the AO Technology AG (AOTAG) group, which manages the commercial activities of the organization, including intellectual property rights (IP), and the AO Endowment. The AO's CEO, as Vice-Chair of the Endowment, heads this group (Exhibit 43.3).

---

[3] AO Foundation Annual Report 2017.

Exhibit 43.2 AO Foundation Board of Trustees (Miami 2017). *Copyright by AO Foundation, Switzerland*

Exhibit 43.3 AO Foundation Board (2017). Front row: Robert McGuire (President-Elect), Rolf Jeker (CEO and Vice-Chair AOFB), Nikolaus Renner (President and Chair AOFB), Suthorn Bavonratanavech (Past President). Middle row: Christoph Lindenmeyer (finance expertise), Florian Gebhard (trauma expertise), Ulf Claesson (investment/industry expertise), Keita Ito (R&D expertise), Jean-Pierre Cabassu (veterinary expertise). Back row: Jeffrey Wang (spine expertise), Neal Futran (craniomaxillofacial expertise). *Copyright by AO Foundation, Switzerland*

Providing guidance to the AO Foundation board are a number of advisory and executive boards covering the various AO Institutes: Education, Research, and Clinical Investigations, as well as the Executive Boards for the AOTK system and the Development Incubator. The purpose of these groups has been to ensure that the

Exhibit 43.4 AO Executive Management Board (2017). Front row: Irene Eigenmann Timmings (COO and CFO), Rolf Jeker (CEO and Vice-Chair AOFB), Eberhard Denk (AOVET. Middle row: Jayr Bass (AOSpine), Urs Rüetschi (AO Education Institute), Martin Schuler (AO Clinical Investigation and Documentation), Claas Albers (AOTK System). Back row: Tobias Hüttl (AOTrauma), Erich Röthlisberger (AOCMF), R. Geoff Richards (AO Research Institute). *Copyright by AO Foundation, Switzerland*

AOFB has the best information available for its decision-making. A similar advisory role was assigned to the four clinical divisions with respect to budget and outcome measurements.

The third major governance body is the AO Executive Management Board (AOEM), responsible for the administration and day-to-day operations of the AO Foundation. Reporting to the AO Foundation Board, and chaired by the AO CEO, its members are full-time AO employees, representing the top executive level of the organization. Members include the leaders of the key AO Institutes, such as ARI (research), AO Education, and Clinical Investigation (AOCID), managers responsible for the various clinical divisions (Trauma, Spine, CMF, VET), as well as the AOTK, and, finally, the key functional executive for finance (CFO) (Exhibit 43.4).

Despite the rather formal board structure present within the AO Foundation, there is plenty of evidence that informal decision mechanisms exist, or smaller ad hoc groups that grease the wheels of the organization, so to speak. A good example of such a grouping is the annual meeting of AO Foundation Past Presidents, typically held in Davos in December. This is what in some organizations is called a 'kitchen cabinet,' working without the formalities of statutory board meetings. There is a strong bond among these past presidents, and the connection to the AO Foundation Board is apparent. Since these past presidents were also AO Trustees, they exert noticeable influence throughout the organization.

The Emergence of the Clinical Divisions

At the AO today, key activities take place in the clinical divisions. When the AO was started, the focus of all its activity was Trauma, and at that point no one ever thought to subdivide the organization into different trauma specialties. When reviewing the AO annual reports dating back to the year that the new AO Center was inaugurated in 1992, and comparing them with more recent reports, it is clear how the AO moved, step by step, towards a structure of clinical divisions. At first, there was no recognition of any clinical division, and most of the annual reports focused on the key AO activities: Research, Development, Education, and Documentation. By the year 2000, usually at the end of the annual report, short sections were added about 'specialties,' meaning Spine, CMF, and VET, although the bulk of the annual report still focused on the key activity groups. By 2006, an important addition was the reference to 'general trauma,' plus the three above-mentioned specialties. The full reporting by clinical divisions started in 2007, and by 2008 the change towards a full 'divisionalization' along the four clinical divisions was concluded. From there on, the bulk of the annual reports was focused on developments within the clinical divisions; it was then that the functional activities took a back seat. This reflected that many of the functional activities had been absorbed into the clinical divisions.

At the AO Center, about 60 full-time employees with specific expertise work to support the clinical divisions. Each clinical division has a full-time director who is also a member of the AO Executive Board. Depending on the size of the clinical division, a number of experts are allocated to support the commissions, and in some cases the regional activities. Since many of these staff members had been working with their clinical divisions for a long time, having such resources available is important to an organization with elected chairs and commission heads subject to regular rotation. Funding for each clinical division comes almost exclusively from AO Foundation funds, either internally or externally, and is obtained through the annual contribution from its main industrial partner, J&J.

The emergence of the clinical divisions, and the decentralization of a considerable part of the AO Foundation's activities, has been an important organizational development in the years after the Foundation was fully established in 2008. This move was largely driven by the organization's spine surgeons, not the core trauma surgeons; originally it was not welcomed by everyone because some surgeons saw themselves as performing surgeries in a number of 'subfields.'[4]

Currently, there are four clinical divisions, and for the purpose of explaining the workings of the organization, some background will be given about each. The clinical divisions operate along similar lines but are not completely identical.

---

[4]Interview with Markus Rauh, AO Foundation Board CEO and Vice-Chair (2001–2011), conducted on 6 December, 2016, in Davos.

AOTrauma

Since Trauma is the AO's original clinical activity, it is by far the largest and AOTrauma was formally established in 2008. It has become, in some ways, a mini-AO within the AO Foundation, with many parallel structures. Just as within much of the AO Foundation, many activities and responsibilities are assigned to different groups and boards.

Governance of AOTrauma is in the hands of the AOTrauma International Board (AOTIB), with ten executive members who are responsible for certain commissions, such as Education, and regional chairs in charge of coordinating the AOTrauma regional boards. The commissions for Education, Research, and Community Development are global and operate on a worldwide basis. Commission members coordinate within the regions, without direct authority. The commissions' regional boards have responsibility within their five regions: Asia Pacific, Europe, Latin America, Middle East, and North America. Each regional board is fully funded and has its own budget for activities and actions, such as for education. Some regions have AOTrauma country chapters under the leadership of country councils. The total budget of AO Trauma approaches CH 27 million. Board members receive a stipend and the AO Foundation publishes these amounts annually for transparency purposes.

AOTrauma maintains a staff of about 50 (23 of which are full-time employees) in several locations. Tobias Hüttl, Medical Director for AOTrauma and in charge of the supporting staff, noted that, as was the case for all of AO, this is a "network by surgeons for surgeons." Surgeons decide on the priorities for each clinical division.[5]

Membership is managed centrally, with fees ranging from CHF 100 to 190, depending on the level of access sought. The main benefit for a surgeon is to be connected to the network and have access to the on-line services that cover a range of topics, including an on-line surgical reference. Membership is limited to trauma professionals who have attended the AOTrauma Principles course. In 2018, AOTrauma has more than 9000 paying members and about 100,000 registered users.

AOSpine

AOSpine began in steps, based on the initiative of individual spine surgeons as described earlier. These surgeons started their efforts in the late 1990s and were supported in their work by the AO organization as well as by individual industrial partners. Under the leadership of John Webb and Max Aebi, the founding surgeons, asked for, and were granted, greater operating freedom within the AO. At the insistence of the spine surgeon community within the AO, the AO Board finally gave the green light in the year 2000 to set up an AO Specialty Board for Spine Surgery—set up with the assignment to develop and grow a Spine Specialty into a

---

[5]Interview with Tobias Hüttl, Medical Director AOTrauma, conducted on 2 November, 2016, in Davos.

key competence of the AO Foundation. The AO realized that spine surgeons had different needs than regular trauma surgeons. By 2003, the AOSpine International Board was established and combined with the regional boards—and commissions for Education, Research, and professional events followed.

To some extent, the structure of AOSpine mirrors the organization of AOTrauma. The AOSpine International Board has 11 members. Three commissions deal with the coordination of global Education, Research, and Community Development. An additional five regional boards were created for Asia Pacific, Europe and Southern Africa, Latin America, Middle East and Northern Africa, and North America. Each region has its own board and is fully responsible for its budget. In many countries there are local Spine Councils as a link to local surgeons. The global budget of AOSpine amounts to about CHF 21 million.

AOSpine reports that its community comprises some 6500 paying members and about 38,000 registered users, all surgeons, researchers, and allied spine professionals. AO Spine runs a well-attended Global Spine Congress. Its staff is concentrated in the AO Dübendorf office near Zurich, a decision that at the time was interpreted as underlining the group's intent to set itself apart from AOTrauma, whose staff is mostly located in Davos. Today, the support staff consists of 30 people (including 24 full-time employees).

AOCMF

The early development of AOCMF, for craniomaxillofacial surgeries, has been described in Chap. 25. As early as 1990, CMF began to establish itself as a separate clinical division within the AO, following some early development work of key AO surgeons Bernd Spiessl and Joachim Prein. Its establishment as a separate clinical division within the AO occurred in 2008 (Exhibit 43.5).

The governance of AOCMF lies in the hands of an international board (AOCMFIB) with nine members; it consists of five regional chairs and three commission chairs for Research, Technical Development, and Community Development. There are regional chairs for Asia Pacific, North America, Latin America, Europe and Southern Africa, and Middle East and Northern Africa, following the AOSpine model. As is the case with the other clinical divisions, the responsibilities for activities rest with the regional chair and boards.

According to its own reporting, AOCMF has 3200 paying members and about 25,000 registered users globally, some 130 courses are offered, and 30 Fellowship Centers are managed. As a smaller clinical division, its annual budget amounts to about CHF 7 million. There are approximately 13 staff members (11 of them are full-time employees) who support the work of the AOCMF Clinical Division.

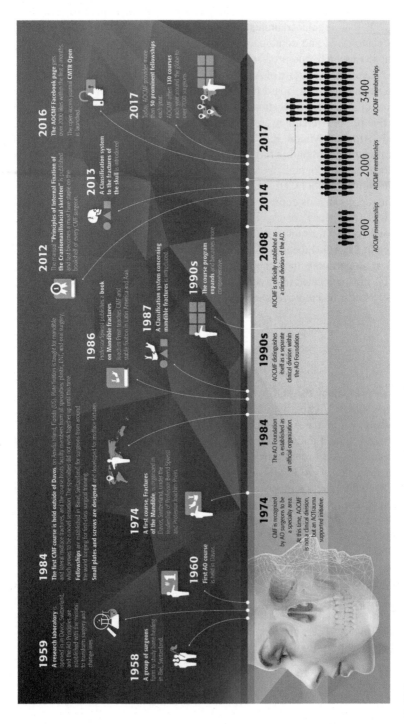

Exhibit 43.5 AOCMF timeline. *Copyright by AO Foundation, Switzerland*

AOVET

Last but not least, AOVET has been featured as a separate entity going back to 1969 (see Chap. 24). Ever since the beginning of the AO, there have always been members who were passionate about the use of Osteosynthesis implants for animals. The early AO members were supportive of the application to animals, and the producer community also backed the efforts for developing an AOVET, the Straumann family in particular.

AOVET was formally established as a clinical division in 2007. It is governed by an international board (AOVETIB), consisting of nine members, analogous to the other divisions. At the AOVETIB level, there are three commission chairs for Education, Research, and Community Development, and a chair for each of the regions: Europe, North America, Latin America, and Asia Pacific. The roles of the regional chairs, and those of the commission chairs, are similar to the other clinical divisions.

With the adoption of the new Collaboration Agreement between the AO and J&J DPS, the status of AOVET changed. While AOVET was maintaining a close relationship with J&J DPS, the division had obtained the right to work with third parties in countries where no explicit support is offered by J&J DPS. As a result, out-of-scope contributions can be generated by AOVET. The annual budget contributed by the AO Foundation to AOVET is about CHF 2 million, but the true operating budget of AOVET is actually larger. The AOVET group is supported by seven staff members (including six full-time employees).

The AOTK System Today

The AO Foundation's *Technische Kommission* (TK), or Technical Commission, was one of the organization's outstanding features that went back to the early days. The AO founders created the TK as the body they thought necessary to connect surgical practice and its instruction with the development of the AO *Instrumentarium*. Although the roles and the size of the TK evolved, it remained a central element to the AO Foundation and how its surgeon members collaborated.[1]

Where there was once a single commission in 1960, involving a few AO surgeons, the AOTK has expanded into numerous TKs dedicated to the various clinical divisions, including a large number of expert groups that sometimes serve only specific projects and are dissolved after completion. The AOTK system involves about 120 surgeons across these multiple units. At the top of the hierarchy is the AOTK Executive Board (TKEB), which functions as the main steering and supervisory board for the entire TK System. Typical for AO boards, members are independent surgeons who are dedicated to making decisions according to clinical necessities.

Membership of the TKEB consists of the chairs of each of the TK's clinical divisions (Trauma, Spine, CMF), as well as the Chair of the AOCID Advisory Committee, plus the TKEB Chairperson. As non-voting guests, the Director of the TK system, as well as the President and Vice-President of the AO Foundation, attend. Industrial partners may also attend, as needed, but have no voting rights. The main task of the TKEB is to ensure the smooth functioning of the entire group of specialty TKs, and expert groups, as well as to elect or confirm key appointments in the TK system. The TKEB and the several specialty TKs are supported by a team of about ten people (with eight full-time employees), representing the AOTK

---

[1]Interview with Claas Albers, Director AOTK System, conducted on 1 November, 2016, in Davos.

© Springer Nature Switzerland AG 2019
J.-P. Jeannet, *Leading a Surgical Revolution*,
https://doi.org/10.1007/978-3-030-01980-8_44

331

Management team. They prepare and conduct meetings, ensure documentation, and guarantee effective project management.

The AOTKs are the only bodies empowered to approve a device (sometimes called product), or a surgical method (sometimes referred to as technology), as indicated for their designated specialty. These products may be advertised and approved by the AO Foundation. All TKs operate under the procedures defined by the AOTKEB.[2] The three AOTK for Trauma, Spine, and CMF are the governing bodies for their clinical areas within the AOTK System.

Within the AOTK system, there are a number of expert groups consisting of several medical members who work together on the identification and creation of new 'Solutions' to existing clinical needs. Typically, an expert group works on one or two projects at a time. They submit clinical needs to the industrial partner, DePuy Synthes, for review. When both producer and AO agree, J&J DPS moves forward to implementation. In case of the industrial partner's refusal, the AO can then search for an external partner. As Claas Albers states:

> In a new project, the producer set-up cost might amount to USD 30 million until FDA approval, which included data, time, and about one and a half years from first submission. The TK system could help the industrial partner by showing how implants needed to look like, what the added benefit to patients, surgeon, and the health care system in terms of hospital stays, would accrue. In that sense, the TK with its approval takes away the 'market risk' for the industrial partner.[3]

Currently, there are 19 such expert groups, each comprised of five medical members; one of them is appointed chairperson. The expert groups call on other AO staff members as needed, as well as for input and collaboration from the industrial partner. The groups are built around their own medical specialties and consider inputs from both inside and outside the AO. The example cited about the development of the Philos Systems (see Chap. 37) to deal with osteoporotic bone structures was the result of such an expert group. In support of a specific project, temporary project teams or task forces can be appointed. Final approval is always given the relevant TK, not the expert group.

The AOTK system also approves a large number of surgical procedures, referred to as 'Solutions.' Solutions are accessible through the AO Foundation website and are trademarked as figurative brands, either as 'approved by AOTK' or 'Approved by AO Foundation.' Links were established to the AO Surgical Reference for further guidance to surgeons (Exhibit 44.1).

Exhibit 44.1   Approved by AOTK signs. *Copyright by AO Foundation, Switzerland*

---

[2]Source: AO website, accessed 5 May, 2018.
[3]Interview with Claas Albers, Op. cit.

The process of the TK and its expert groups has sometimes been referred to as a virtuous cycle. It starts with some clinical problem calling for a solution. If one exists, fine, it will be documented. If not, some research, either basic or clinical in laboratory, needs to be undertaken. The resulting solution, consisting of either a new procedure or device, or both, leads to innovation, which is tested and checked by the TKs who can order studies on clinical experience. Included in the cycle are descriptions about how to teach surgeons to use any new device. This is a never-ending cycle, always turning up new ideas to pursue.[4] Over the past ten years, from 2006 to 2016, the AOTK has documented about 900 active projects, which were accompanied by about 100 pre-clinical and clinical research projects. Of these, some 200 were finally 'AOTK Approved'[5] (Exhibit 44.2).

Under the current Cooperation Agreement, signed with J&J DPS in 2016, all IP resulting from activities of the AOTK system belong to J&J. In turn, J&J supports the TK system with an annual subsidy of 10% of its total contribution, allowing this worldwide approval system to be run with a budget of approximately CHF 5 million (direct costs). In return, J&J has the right to commercially exploit the AO and the AOTK trademarks with all AO-approved products.[6]

The AO Foundation obtained some flexibility for accepting the exclusive use of TK approval through J&J DPS; the new Cooperation Agreement gives the AO Foundation the right to develop IP outside the TK system, and to exploit it commercially. For that purpose, the AO Foundation has created a number of new vehicles for investment and research, addressed later in greater length (see Chap. 49).

The AOTK system is subject to some criticism, particularly from those close to it, as well as the industrial community. They found that the numerous boards got in the way of the development process, slowing down the number of innovation approvals, inevitably carrying the risk that other industrial players would undertake their own development. For the calendar year 2017, the AO reported that ten innovations had been approved by its TK system.[7]

Some of these tensions have had to do with the diverging mission of surgeons versus producers, previously described as a 'battle between MDs and MBAs.' Some of the AO surgeon leaders have often expressed the need to put patient care above sales volume. That led to extra care in the development process and longer trial periods with new procedures. Industrial partners, today essentially J&J DPS, also had their eyes on their competition who, at times, seemed to react faster in the introduction of new implants. As one of the AO leaders cautioned, "Patient driven versus market driven forces are not the same."[8]

---

[4]Interview Tobias Hüttl, Op. cit, on the virtuous cycle of the AOTrauma TK.
[5]Source: Claas Albers, AO Foundation and Director of AOTK System, 22 May, 2018.
[6]AO Foundation Annual Report 2017.
[7]AO Foundation Annual Report 2017, p. 35.
[8]Interview Chris van der Werken, AO Foundation Former President (2006–2008), conducted on 6 December, 2016, in Davos.

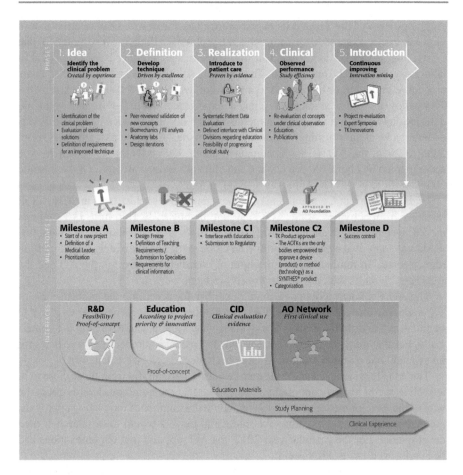

Exhibit 44.2 Expert Group AOTK. *Copyright by AO Foundation, Switzerland*

Off-Ramp Project Opportunities

2017 saw a lot of hard work within the AOTK system to devise a new strategy, enabling third party collaboration on projects categorized as unfunded, unaligned, and subsequently 'off-ramp' by J&J DPS. The AOTK has never had such a contractual flexibility regarding industry collaboration and, as a consequence, the creation of a process enabling such external collaboration has been time-consuming. It is expected that 2018 will bring significant forward movement concerning off-ramp opportunities, through identifying suitable projects and collaborators.

The AO Foundation, Home to Several Institutes

In the AO's original charter, the founders put emphasis on four pillars. Three of those pillars, namely Teaching, Documentation, and Research have remained central to the Foundation and were assigned specialized Institutes, each with their own mandates (the fourth pillar is Instrumentation).

The AO Institutes are matrixed with each of the four clinical divisions (Trauma, Spine, CMF, and VET). The Institutes, each with a special focus, perform important support roles and act as content contributors to the four AO clinical divisions. Prior to the major reorganization undertaken as part AO's Divisionalization process, the Institutes also had line and delivery responsibilities in their areas of expertise. The process is akin to what happens in many big companies which, as they increase in size, move from a strictly Functional Organization to a Divisionalized Organization, in order to manage the inherent complexity. In other words, the Institutes have moved from running programs in a line role to serving in a support role, with clinical experts providing content input to support the clinical divisions. It is the clinical divisions who set the priorities—from line to staff roles, or dotted lines, to the Institutes.

AO Research Institute (ARI) Today[1]

The majority of the assets of ARI are located in Davos, the traditional site for AO's Research Organization. Professor Geoff Richards, who has been associated with ARI since 1991, is its Director since 2009, commented that ARI had always been

---

[1]Interview with Professor Robert Geoffrey ('Geoff') Richards, Director of ARI, conducted on 2 November, 2016, in Davos.

© Springer Nature Switzerland AG 2019

335

J.-P. Jeannet, *Leading a Surgical Revolution*,

https://doi.org/10.1007/978-3-030-01980-8_45

influenced by the expertise of its directors. In the case of Richards, it was interface biology, body implant, bio compatibility, and surface topology. Previous directors have had expertise in sensing, smart implants, or different areas within bioengineering or engineering. The direction of the ARI has been heading in the direction of bioengineering for a while now.

ARI's staff has about 80 full-time employees, with roughly one-third being devoted to tissue engineering. The topics researched include bone cartilage, biodegradable polymers, different delivery vehicles, 3D printing and bio-fabrication, and degradables with living cells for AO Spine and AOCMF. Other ARI-related topics are bio-mechanical developments, pre-clinical service (such as animal research), and infections.

ARI maintains an active network with European universities and also engages in contract research; its staff are active contributors to academic journals. In fact, of the 240 contributions to the academic community in 2017, 85 were in peer-reviewed journals. The goals of ARI are naturally to contribute to the area of preclinical research and development, both explanatory and translational, with a focus on clinical solutions. ARI investigates and improves performance of surgical procedures, devices, and substances used in AO practice. In so doing, ARI supports the AO's clinical divisions.

ARI is partially funded through the AO Foundation, through the AO clinical divisions, as well as external grants and external clinical research. From the total budget of about CHF 13 million (2016), about CHF 9 million originate with the four clinical divisions. Trauma accounted for almost half of that. The AO clinical divisions contract the ARI for specific research assignments and fund them accordingly. Regarding grants for basic research from other companies, the experience of ARI management indicates that the 'US companies would rather buy an SME than support research from scratch!' Also, in the way of securing contract research there are patent issues concerning the results.

ARI management is supported by an ARI Advisory Committee (ARIAC) to provide ARI leadership with expert advice prior to funding commitments. ARI runs about 90 projects simultaneously and they are subject to regular review to assure quality output.

The AO Clinical Investigation and Documentation Institute (AOCID)

The AO's CID Institute has its roots in the previous AO Documentation Center, once housed in Berne and attached to the university there. It has been transformed from a collector of documented cases into an organization that handles evidenced-based instead eminence-based research. This evolution references the struggle to change the role of clinical research within the AO to make it compatible with scientifically accepted standards.

Since evidence-based research is being addressed, it is necessary to see if the revamped CID Institute has accomplished the goals that the new management set out to achieve in 2002, and if so, how? Because evidence-based research was the main goal at that time, the number of peer-reviewed journal articles that lived up to this standard had to grow—and they did, from two papers each year before 2002 to the new high point of 39 papers in 2015 and 2016, respectively. The steady increase went from an average in the teens until 2008, then up to the 20s until 2012 and cracking the 30s from there on. This represents a remarkable turnaround with regard to academic papers.

Such an increase in output could not be achieved without some reorganization within CID. The entire CID organization has a staff of about 28 full-time employees. The group aspires to a leading position as a Clinical Research and Health Economics Institute in the Trauma and Orthopedic surgery space. CID is comprised of three units, each with a different mandate but all contributing to the mission of the entire organization.

The first group—Clinical Operations Group (CO)—can be described as the 'engine that drives clinical research at CID.' The CO unit manages the workflow from the idea for an article, to its planning, monitoring, analysis, and eventual publication. For each of these different phases going into a planned publication, CO takes on the role of 'quarterback.'[2] It runs three separate units that specialize in each of the three main AO clinical divisions. These teams also coordinate with AO's various divisional TK units. A service pool of specialized staff supports these groups. This does not prevent any AO member from pursuing research and publications on their own, if they prefer. Access to this support group will, nevertheless, assure a higher publication rate than without, as the number of placed journal articles demonstrates.

The second group—Clinical Research Education—supports the actual ongoing research projects by working with a cadre of clinicians who are also world-class researchers. Often, surgeons need to contribute evidence for clinical research and this group offers them training to raise their skill levels, increasing the chance that the resulting study will be published in a leading journal.

The third—Health Economics—is a newer group and recognizes the need for health economics evidence to serve the trauma community over and above clinical studies. The team supports studies dealing with Health Economic issues or helps embed such evidence into larger clinical studies.

The CID at AO has evolved over the decades, away from being a storage place for thousands of patient reports and X-rays to a group that can assist the AO Foundation's deep clinical talent pool; the group enables studies, which can be published in top journals and raise the prestige of the AO within the global medical community.

Although management of CDI rests with a director, there is also a CID Advisory Committee comprised of experts from different surgical specialties. The Advisory Board provides guidance and expert advice to CID management. Both the AO

---

[2]A term used in American football for the role of the playmaker.

Foundation CEO and COO/CFO are ex-officio members of the Advisory Board, which meets twice a year to review progress.

AO Education Institute: AO's Own 'Trauma University'[3]

The AO Education Institute (AOEI) emerged from the group that used to run the AO's courses. Since the previously discussed divisionalization of the AO, the sovereignty over the courses moved to the clinical divisions, which in turn regionalized most of it by assigning execution responsibilities to the Regional Clinical Units.

This does not mean that the AOEI is not a critical player in the educational effort of the AO Foundation's operations. AOEI is the core service unit to support the clinical divisions delivering better courses. A staff of about 35 professionals, both in Davos and in Dübendorf, became specialists in the support functions to assure best practice in teaching AO courses. Each clinical division also has its own education manager.

The AOEI assumed responsibility for the educational processes that cuts through the offerings of all the divisions. This means focusing on curriculum development, faculty development, and media production. To deliver this, the Education Institute has a budget of about CHF 9 million, of which trauma used up some 80%. Just as is the case with all of the AO Institutes, an Advisory Board with three members meets regularly with the Institute director.

The curriculum development team has a small staff consisting of professionals with Master's degrees and PhDs in educational methods, measurements of results, and patient outcomes. They engage in medical education research and several of them were graduates of the University of Berne's pertinent programs. Whenever one of the clinical divisions has a new program launch, the curriculum development team assists with the design of that program; in any given year, this team might deal with up to 20 new projects.

The faculty development process is central to the AOEI and is a function that is highly regarded outside of the AO Foundation—it can be thought of as the global benchmark. With a total of 2500 faculty members engaged in the AO educational programs, all of them volunteers, training is the only way to assure consistent, high-quality courses and teaching. The AO founders realized that the quality of teaching and instruction was of the utmost importance to make sure surgeons would properly learn the various AO techniques.

Faculty training takes place on three levels. At the first level, participating surgeons learn how to be better teachers, moderators, or panelists, as well as using blended learning techniques that combine face-to-face with distance learning. At the second level, participants receive instruction on how to chair an education program,

---

[3]Interview with Urs Rüetschi, Director AO Educational Institute, conducted on 2 November, 2016, in Davos.

host an event, and adjust programs to local circumstances. The third, and top, level of instruction is reserved for educational leaders who need to know how to plan outcomes, a session, lead teams, and be the chair of a program. These courses are held and directed by AOEI staff members, several times annually, in different locations.

The acceptance in the medical community of AO courses is attested to by the number of countries who consider attending these courses important for the certification of their own surgeons. In the Netherlands, a trauma specialist is required to attend both AO courses—Principles and Advanced. In the US, the AO North America courses are required for all trauma residents. Swiss surgeons earn education points through attending AO courses.

While the teams working on curriculum development and faculty training do not enjoy much visibility outside the AO, the third unit, Media Production, more than makes up for it. Here, skilled illustrators, video creators, and App designers link the AO to the world-at-large. They assist AO surgeons in the production of well-illustrated text books, ranging from principles books to specialized books. Over time, the AO has grown into a veritable publishing company, in line with the success of the very first principles and technique books authored by the AO founders with sales volumes of more than 100,000.

Possibly the most important project in Media Production is the 'Orthopedic Surgery Reference.' This online reference for surgeons has turned out to be a real 'bestseller' with some 8000 hits per day; in 2016 alone, it was accessed by about 1.7 million devices. Access to these reference libraries has been one of the important drawing points in the recruitment of new AO members (Exhibit 45.1).

The AO as a 'Trauma University'

Coverage of the AO educational impact would not be complete without further discussion about the number of courses that are mounted all over the world. As is the case with so many aspects of the AO, only a fraction of the activity is visible to the outside observer. This also applies to educational efforts, where the AOEI is only a small part of the total educational impact (Exhibit 45.2).

First, the accumulated numbers: some 67,000 surgeons have been trained in the Davos courses, from their inception in 1960 through 2017. This pales in comparison to the numbers of courses delivered outside of Davos, which began in 1965 in Germany. Since that time, again through 2017, some 620,000 surgeons have been trained globally. Additionally, some 7800 surgeons have benefited from, and participated in, the AO fellowship programs, which started formally in 1971.[4]

In 2017, the AO and its various clinical divisions held a total of 830 courses for surgeons with a worldwide participation of 54,000. The AO faculty performed more

---

[4]Eichler, K., 'Evaluation of Health Economic Impact of AO Foundation', Winterthur Institute of Health Economics, Zurich University of Applied Sciences (ZHAW), 2018.

AO Surgery Reference

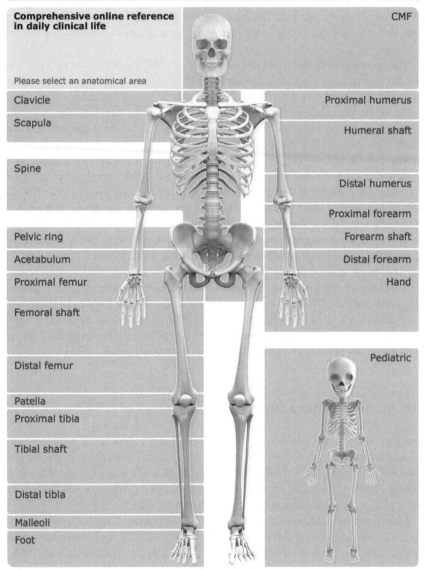

Comprehensive online reference in daily clinical life

CMF

Please select an anatomical area

Clavicle

Scapula

Spine

Pelvic ring

Acetabulum

Proximal femur

Femoral shaft

Distal femur

Patella

Proximal tibia

Tibial shaft

Distal tibia

Malleoli

Foot

Proximal humerus

Humeral shaft

Distal humerus

Proximal forearm

Forearm shaft

Distal forearm

Hand

Pediatric

Exhibit 45.1   The AO surgery reference tool. *Copyright by AO Foundation, Switzerland*

than 20,000 teaching days, delivering 113,000 participant days. The faculty are volunteers and receive only a small stipend; they are reimbursed for their travel and hotel costs. Looking at the AO Foundation's Financial Annual Report 2017, the foundation spent some CHF 47 million, or 46% of its budget, on education. How is it

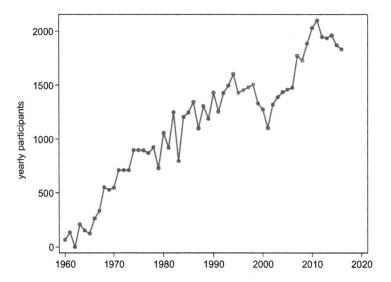

Exhibit 45.2   AO 'Davos courses' participants from 1960 to 2016. *[Source: Eichler, K.,* Evaluation of Health Economic Impact of AO Foundation, *Winterthur Institute of Health Economics, Zurich University of Applied Sciences (ZHAW), 2018].* Reprinted by permission

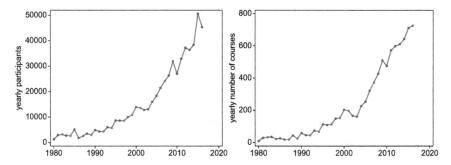

Exhibit 45.3   Yearly AO course participants (left) and number of courses (right) from 1980 to 2016 worldwide (excluding Davos courses). *[Source: Eichler, K.,* Evaluation of Health Economic Impact of AO Foundation, *Winterthur Institute of Health Economics, Zurich University of Applied Sciences (ZHAW), 2018]*

possible that on such relatively small budget, such a massive educational effort can be undertaken around the world? (Exhibit 45.3).

There are several issues to consider when looking at the AO educational budget. The indirect contributions of the industrial partners, most recently only J&J DPS, are not included in the AO's direct expenses. Additional costs borne by J&J DPS have been estimated to have reached about the same level as those published by the AO Foundation. This has to do with the fact that a large number of support personnel, either from the AO or J&J DPS, are dispatched for each course, which cannot run without this logistical help. Furthermore, surgical instruments and implants need to be made available for the practical exercises during the courses. In addition, the local or regional groups who sponsor courses also support it, and local representatives of J&J DPS, when participating, contribute as well. All told, the expenditures for the courses could be estimated as at least CHF 100 million.

Additional contributions in kind are made that do not result in cash expenditures, but would, under normal circumstances, have to be acquired from the outside. The contribution of 20,000 faculty days on low stipends would be a huge cost factor if competitive consulting rates in the open market, or salaries for full-time faculty attached to medical schools, would have to be paid. According to Chris van der Werken, "To be part of the AO faculty is prestigious. This has become the ambition of young surgeons."[5]

Also, the reported data does not have to include costs for a central campus facility.[6] The AO, operating as a virtual organization without owning any facilities to deliver courses would, if it were an independent organization, incur the costs of running a campus. And finally, there is no hospital attached to the AO, because its volunteer faculty have their own full-time assignments; they are members of a medical institution with responsibilities for patient care.

As previously noted, the AO, when expanding its courses, found it impossible to satisfy the instruction's ever-growing need for human cadaver bones. To deal with this bottleneck, the AO acquired an industrial operation named SYNBONE and had it produce artificial bone models. This operation became so successful that the product line was expanded to include some 1000 bone and torso models, accessories, and consumables, which are a staple of any AO course today. By 2018, about 210,000 such SYNBONEs were sold annually to more than 70 countries. Since 1997, SYNBONE stopped being a captive supplier for the AO and has now become a merchant supplier of its bone models. A substantial part of its operations was moved recently to Malaysia. Shares of SYNBONE AG are held by the AO Technology AG.

Tuition fees for AO courses are not centrally controlled, or available, and depend on regional support levels and local contributions from industrial partners. The 2018 Davos Principles Courses for Swiss participants were listed at approximately CHF 1700. In addition to this, a participant has to cover hotel costs and food, as well as transportation to and from Davos, making this a CHF 3000 to CHF 4000 affair. International participants incur higher costs but often can rely on scholarships from their home countries.

How does this compare to a typical medical school or university? A number of senior AO members were polled about this, and no clear answers emerged. The difficulty of this comparison is compounded by the fact that, with so many separate organizational units participating in the AO's educational effort, there is no single central cost or revenue accounting available. Experts estimated that if the AO were put together as a full-blown medical school, it would, at a minimum, equal a

---

[5]Interview with Chris van der Werken, Op. cit.
[6]'Evaluation of Health Economic Impact of AO Foundation,' Op. cit.

medium-sized institution. Large medical universities, both in the US and in Europe, have budgets of CHF 1 billion or more.

The AO 'Trauma University' operates on a decentralized model; a visitor will ask in vain for its Dean. By all accounts, it works well and has been the envy of competitors who had to field their own organizations for education and training. After all, the AO is not a business; it is a social organization. What thousands of AO staff and volunteers deliver, year in and year out, is considerable, to say the least. The AO founders, when starting their courses in Davos, believed that they would only run them a few times. Time has proven them wrong. Every year there is a new cohort of surgeons that need this training, and there is no replacement for it in sight.

Never Rest on Your Laurels

The AO Foundation had been committed to innovation since its inception. For much of its existence, innovation meant better surgical solutions in the trauma space. This took the route of improving surgical techniques, developing ever better implants, and evolving its teaching to keep up with the latest research in trauma care. Over time, some AO leaders questioned whether the organization was drawing the lines too narrowly, and if there was not a broader trauma space for innovation beyond those solutions demanded and created by the four major clinical divisions: Trauma, Spine, CMF, and VET.

AO management reflected on what the new developments critical to the trauma might be and how they should be dealt with. Three proposals were eventually put forward around 2013, involving Neuro (neurology), Recon (improving care relating to Arthroplasty), and Sports Medicine. Two were chosen—Neuro and Recon—with an initial financial commitment of three years. J&J DPS agreed to support these pilot initiatives financially on a cost basis, limited to only three years, with a possibility for extension to 2018.

AONeuro as a Testing Ground

In 2013 the AO Foundation launched an initiative around the treatment of traumatic brain injury under the umbrella of AONeuro. The initiative was supported by a number of AO CMF surgeons, among them the US surgeon Paul Manson who had supported a move towards that direction.[1]

---

[1]Telephone interview with Paul Manson, AO President 2008–2010, Member of Board of Trustees, conducted on 28 July, 2017.

© Springer Nature Switzerland AG 2019
J.-P. Jeannet, *Leading a Surgical Revolution*,
https://doi.org/10.1007/978-3-030-01980-8_46

Neurosurgeons were interested in joining AOCMF, and CMF had active collaborations with surgeons specializing in the discipline. A major change in CMF surgery came when the preponderant surgical approach changed from 'wiring' (from 1950 to 1970) to 'plates and screws' developed by the AO in the 1970s. AOCMF surgeons were using AO-developed surgical equipment in broader indications and, as a result, thought that neurosurgery as a field would benefit from the AO type of equipment. With head injuries becoming a growing problem, Manson began to champion a group called AONeuro in 2008, which would deal with cranial access as a result of brain injuries.

In response to this interest, AONeuro was started as an initiative in 2013. The group quickly developed an active educational curriculum, with 17 educational events in 14 countries, attracting some 600 participants. The courses focused on Traumatic Brain Injury (TBI).

Despite early successes, the AONeuro initiative did not connect to the core of AO Foundation's work. When the AO reviewed its scope and mission in 2017, the Foundation viewed itself as being concentrated on the muscular-skeleton system, dealing with issues of the bone or near bone, and AONeuro did not fit neatly into this definition. The AONeuro Group, under the Chairmanship of Manson, decided to separate itself from the AO and create its own, independent, foundation under the name of Global Neuro. The group aimed to reach the approximately 40,000 clinical professionals in this area worldwide. Until 2017, it had already attracted some 3000 residents and practicing surgeons via 70 successfully launched events. For the time being, the AO Foundation supported the independent AONeuro with back-office and administrative support, as well as some financial means during the group's transition.

The AO Foundation's lack of enthusiasm ran parallel to changes at the J&J DPS business, where other clinical areas were found to be more important. DPS also changed the structure of its sales force, combining sales across all clinical divisions, such as Trauma, Spine, and CMF. This move, which meant that the DPS sales force represented the full range of the AO *Instrumentation* and implants, was thought by some surgeons to be the cause for declining market share of DPS/AO in the smaller areas of Spine and CMF.

A Different Fate for AORecon

Started in 2014, the AORecon group experienced a different fate. The financial support from J&J DPS was granted under the same conditions for an initial three-year trial, with a possibility of renewal for a second three-year period. AORecon was championed by Norbert Haas, a long-serving former president of AOTK and the AO Foundation.[2] In his role as a trauma surgeon, and his involvement in

---

[2]Interview with Norbert Haas, conducted 7 December, 2016, in Davos.

Orthopedics, he had observed that Arthroplasty[3] was a surgical procedure that would become ever more important in the future, largely driven by the increase of elderly patients. In response to that, Haas started AORecon by recruiting and inviting the surgical elite and friends with an interest in that area. With regard to this surgical procedure, Haas also noticed that trauma cases declined, whereas sports medicine increased.

The mission of AORecon was to improve patient care in Arthroplasty. The procedure was often associated with hip, knee, or shoulder surgery. As a result, the curriculum development of AORecon focused on hip and knee topics. In 2016, the group's third year, there were five different courses being conducted, on four continents, all with long registration waiting lists for future courses. The network of surgeons was building slowly and AORecon is still recruiting faculty members for its courses. AORecon considered itself to be primarily an educational force in what was still an elective surgical field.

The future structure for AORecon remains undecided. AO Foundation surgeons confirmed that there was a great future for this type of surgery. Currently, by maintaining this as an initiative without formal structure, the decision whether or not to make this a fifth clinical area was put off. With its status undecided, the AO Foundation supports it with a Chair (Haas) and curriculum development through AOEI, its Education Institute. If it were not to become a separate clinical division, would it be part of Trauma? That is still being discussed within the AO.

Holding back from an all-out development could have been due to the trauma surgeons' fear of future competition. Recon often attracts a different kind of surgeon than trauma does, or at least the surgeons see themselves as part of a different specialty, one closer to Orthopedics. It is interesting to note that some time ago, when AO could have been involved with Orthopedic surgery, particularly hip replacement, two major players within AO chose to go into another direction. Müller, AO co-founder, and Weber, another AO surgeon, developed their own hip prosthesis businesses, Protek and Alopro, which were later acquired by Sulzer in the late 1990s. Wyss, in charge of Synthes USA, also said no to the prosthesis business in the early 1980s, in order to keep the focus on trauma. But today, joint prosthesis suppliers and trauma implant suppliers are combining and both product lines are offered by integrated companies under the same roof.

---

[3] Arthroplasty is a surgical procedure to replace the articular surface of a musculoskeletal joint either through replacement, remodeling, or osteotomy. Elective in nature, it is performed to relieve pain and restore function of the joint, which could have been impaired either by trauma or arthritis. Source: Wikipedia.

AO Strategy Fund: Innovating Further Afield

In 2013, the AO Foundation Board (AOFB) committed to invest CHF 15 million over three years to support strategic initiatives that were not part of the regular clinical division's innovation activities. The focus was more in the direction of unmet needs and included the following areas:

• New services or new technologies addressing unmet needs
• Projects that enhance the AO organization's visibility and reach
• Ideas to foster cooperation across the AO clinical divisions
• Initiatives to enhance AO operational effectiveness and efficiency

Selection criteria for funding was based on a proposed project's degree of innovation. The submitted projects included surgical simulation, new forms of education, or new ideas for patient care. The first call for proposals generated some 200 entries; there were 100 in response to the second. The calls were open to both external or internal applicants. The AOFB selected the 25 best proposals and provided funding for three years. The idea behind the cutoff was the expectation that the then existing AO organizations would incorporate the newly generated ideas.

AO Incubator as Next Step

Innovators can apply for funding from the AO Development Incubator (AODI) for help in bringing a new idea from concept to market; support is both financial and intellectual. This means that AODI is not just handing out funds but is actively supporting its chosen projects with regard to securing IP, proofing a concept and the valorization of ideas. AODI does not support development of surgical instruments (part of the AOTK), pure research, education, or pharmaceuticals. Of particular interest are the improvements in patient care as it applies to the main AO clinical areas.

Everyone is invited to apply, both from inside or the outside of the AO. The goal is to make an annual call for projects and have an independent board make the selection. AODI aims at supporting projects that can be brought to conclusion over a one- to five-year time frame.

AO Invest for Start-Ups

AO's most recent vehicle in the innovation space is AO Invest, a start-up capital fund. Through this investment vehicle, AO expects to partner with young companies developing new medical technologies of interest to the AO community. Bringing the connections of a purposefully-established venture fund team, combined with the experience of its 20,000 surgeon-strong network interested in the development of new technologies, AO expects to act simultaneously as an investor in, and a partner

Exhibit 46.1 Xvision
system. *Copyright
Augmedics. Yokneam, Israel.
Reprinted by permission*

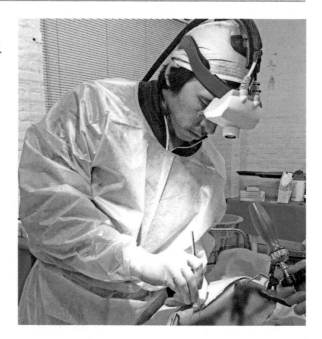

with, the developing groups. The key selection criteria: changing patient's lives for the better over the entire patient treatment journey, and not just within a given clinical field.

As of 2018, AO Invest listed two investments as part of its portfolio. The first investment is in Digital Surgery, a UK-based firm, that has developed an interactive mobile surgical simulator, which guides surgeons, step by step, through every part of an operation, helping them navigate every decision that needs to be made along the way.

The second investment was made in Augmedics, Ltd., an Israeli company, which has developed a type of helmet to be worn by surgeons in order to navigate during surgery using their Xvision technology. With this device, surgeons can continue to look at the patient without having to turn to look at a screen to their side or even behind their back (Exhibit 46.1).

To help with the management of this investment fund, the AO Foundation Board recruited a separate board of experienced investors under the AOTAG umbrella, to both make project selections and to run the contact stream with the chosen firms.

Finding Its Way Through the Innovation Space

The three types of innovations described show the different extent to which the AO is moving from its home base. The initial innovations, creating AONeuro and AORecon, were attempts to expand the Foundation's scope and move into empty spaces left unoccupied by the other, major clinical divisions. The move away from base was more of a 'leaning out,' while remaining firmly planted on its feet, within the established territory of trauma care.

The second and third move, involving the AO Strategy Fund and the AO Development Incubator, were aimed at finding new ideas that help make the organization more innovative in the area of research and development, and creating its own IP, as well as improving patient care. In terms of technology, it could be a 'step-out' but in terms of mission it still remained a 'lean-out' by the fact that it stayed close to the AO mission.

The third initiative, AO Invest, might be further afield and described as more of a 'step-out.' But, by re-inventing surgery broadly, or by impacting any form of surgery, the AO supports the modernization of its ongoing educational activities, as well as assists AO surgeons in other types of surgical practices. How these initiatives will contribute to innovative ideas that the AO may someday adopt has to be left to future experience.

AO Alliance

47

Bringing AO Philosophy to All Corners of the World

The Beginning: AO Social-Economic Committee

As AO surgeons brought their superior technique of dealing with bone trauma to the world, most of their efforts were concentrated in the high-income countries in Europe and North America, with pockets of hospitals and surgeons in Latin America and Asia. AO techniques could only be brought to patients by a cadre of trained surgeons with access to the AO *Instrumentarium*, its surgical tools and implants. The Europe-based industrial partners, Mathys and Straumann (Stratec Medical) had opened subsidiaries, or appointed distributors in many countries throughout Latin America and Asia, because surgeons from those areas joined AO courses and wanted to have access to the AO *Instrumentarium*.

This expanding footprint did not, however, reach Africa or some of the lower-income countries in Asia. As a result, some AO surgeons concerned with impacting these areas founded the AO Social-Economic Committee (AOSEC) in 1999. The AO Foundation and some of its leaders were increasingly aware that there was a huge disparity between the care they could provide to injured patients in high-income countries versus the care received by injured patients in low- and middle-income countries (LMICs).

AO's SEC played an important role for about 15 years in the areas of Sub-Saharan Africa, Asia, and in Latin America. The committee developed customized courses to be taught by local faculty, awarded fellowships, and arranged for visiting surgeons. These efforts, which have been funded and supported by the AO Foundation and selective industrial partners since the inception of the AOSEC, aimed at raising standards for fracture care in these countries (Exhibit 47.1).

A budget of about CHF 1.2 million for the activities of the AOSEC was provided by the AO Foundation. A number of AO surgeons were involved, as were the three industrial partners (Mathys, Stratec Medical, and Synthes USA) who, from early on,

© Springer Nature Switzerland AG 2019
J.-P. Jeannet, *Leading a Surgical Revolution*,
https://doi.org/10.1007/978-3-030-01980-8_47

AO Foundation

AO SEC Course on
Nonoperative Fracture Treatment

June 17–19, 2010
University Teaching Hospital, Lusaka/Zambia

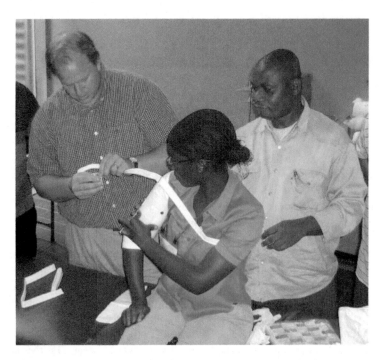

Exhibit 47.1   AO Zambia course Brochure. *Copyright by AO Foundation, Switzerland*

had voting rights on the committee and its activities. The discussions at that time centered around the development of cheaper implants, even a second brand with a different name. They also considered simpler and cheaper solutions which were surgeon-driven, or developer-driven solutions, e.g. Robert Frigg's "Tanza-Fix", a disposable external fixator developed by ADI for Tanzania and use for other African

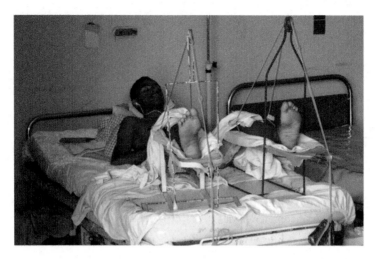

Exhibit 47.2 Conservative treatment in Africa. *Copyright by AO Foundation, Switzerland*

countries, as well as for medical interventions in natural disasters. In some courses, developed by the SEC for Africa, the proper application of the conservative treatment of broken limbs was included, to improve fracture treatment in areas without access to implants or surgical expertise[1] (Exhibit 47.2).

A story about a man from rural West Africa serves as an example of the impact of poor fracture treatment. Mohammad Kamara, age 28, lived as a subsistence farmer; he had two wives and six children on a daily income of less than USD 2.00. At the market, trying to sell his crop, he was hit by a motor bike and sustained an open fracture of his lower right leg (tibia). He was treated by a local traditional healer with bamboo splinting and herbal dressings. Five days later, his condition deteriorating, he was forced to make a two-day trip to a city looking for help. Close to death, his leg infected by gangrene, he had to undergo an amputation above the knee. Although he'd been fitted with a prosthesis six months after the injury, he would never again be able to perform his work in the fields as he had before. As a result, his eldest daughter was taken out of school to help with the farm work. Clearly, this event had significant long-term impact on Kamara and his entire family.[2]

Eventually, a plan originating in 2013 from a discussion in Lima, Peru, solidified, and it was decided to start a new organization, AO Alliance, in the form of an independent foundation, but still related to the AO organization.[3] A new board under the chairmanship of Rolf Jeker, AO CEO, who had been the initial driver behind this

---

[1] AOSEC Course offered in Zambia in 2010, Paul. J. Demmers, Chairman of AOSEC and Member of AO Board of Trustees, AO Course description.

[2] Gosselin (2009), pp. 230–232, reported in an AO Alliance Foundation internal document.

[3] Interview with Jaime Quintero, conducted on 5 December, 2016, in Davos. Jaime Quintero, AO President from 2012 to 2014, was a long-time member of the SEC and a signatory to the AO Alliance Foundation in 2014.

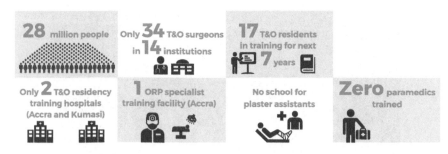

Exhibit 47.3   Situation in Ghana. *Copyright by AO Foundation, Switzerland*

new initiative, would consist of experts with practical medical and development experience in low-income countries.

The Creation of the AO Alliance

The formal signing to create the new entity, the AO Alliance Foundation, took place in December 2014 with a number of AO Past Presidents and Hansjörg Wyss as signatories. By creating a separate foundation, funding from outside the AO Foundation became possible. As a starting donation, the AO Alliance Foundation obtained commitments for CHF 75 million over ten years. One third, or CHF 25 million, was committed by the AO Foundation, and two-thirds, or CHF 50 million, would come from the HJW Medical Foundation (set-up by Wyss, the Swiss founder of Synthes USA and philanthropist), which had agreed in a memorandum of understanding to support individual project proposals up to such an amount. This would increase the annually available funding of the AO Alliance to CHF 7.5 million, a five-fold increase over the previous annual funding of the AOSEC.

The challenges faced by the AO Alliance in some LMIC are addressed by Chris Colten, former AO President and instrumental in the creation of the earlier AOSEC, commenting on his experience in Ghana[4] (Exhibit 47.3):

> Ghana has a population of 23 million and 43% of those are under 15 years. There are about 60,000 fractures annually, and they are often treated by family or a clinical nurse. There are only four teaching hospitals and about 15 regional hospitals in the country. Sometimes we have native bone healers involved with very poor outcomes for the patients. The strategy of the AO Alliance is to affect 'bone healers' to change their approach. We pay them to attend courses or for reference of patients. We get involved with recruiting village elders to pressure the bone healers. Sometimes we need to use splint types that do not cause damage. It all boils down to an educational issue exploiting the existing infrastructure.

---

[4]Interview with Chris Colton, AO President from 1996 to 1998, member of the AOSEC, and founding member of the AO Alliance, conducted on 5 December 2016, in Davos.

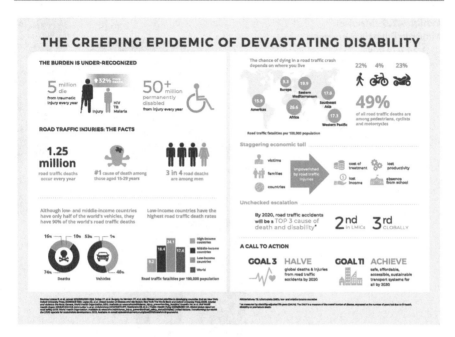

Exhibit 47.4   The bone trauma epidemic. *Copyright by AO Foundation, Switzerland*

Under the AO Alliance, in addition to other outside sources, such as the UBS Optimus Fund, funds were spent on a pediatric institute helping to improve care of children fractures, a significant percentage of all of the fractures that occur in Ghana. The AO was leveraging its experience in children fractures with the creation of the Pediatric AO Surgery Reference (AOSR) in 2014, an offshoot AOSR Trauma, with Chris Colton serving as a general editor. The creation of this guide is also supported by the AO Foundation and went 'live' in December 2017 as the first comprehensive pediatric surgery reference available online in the world.

The AO Alliance Foundation is unable to be present in all countries where its services could make a difference. Focus was required here as well, and the Foundation decided to first strengthen activities in those countries where the previous AOSEC had been active.

The AO Alliance focus on Africa was driven by a number of targets to be achieved as a result of a three-year program, aiming to provide African Trauma and Orthopedic surgeons with access to operative and non-operative fracture management courses. In the first year of operation, some 1685 participants attended the 41 courses offered in the African countries targeted by the AO Alliance. The courses were offered in 21 different countries, and involved about 400 faculty members, mostly on a regional and national basis. Courses for operating room personnel (ORP) were also delivered on the topic of sterile operative care and operative fracture management (Exhibit 47.4).

Exhibit 47.5   Maurice
Müller in Ethiopia. *Copyright
by AO Foundation,
Switzerland*

Besides Malawi and Ghana, Ethiopia was one of the AO Alliance target
countries, where the Alliance also cooperated with Australian Doctors for Africa
(ADFA)—another not-for-profit organization—to launch courses at a hospital in
Addis Ababa and to build up local capacity in the University Hospital of Hawassa,
where a new trauma unit had been established. This collaboration, while unconnected, is reminiscent of two people instrumental in the creation of the AO: Maurice
Müller had worked in Ethiopia at the beginning of his medical career in 1946–1947,
and Robert Mathys, Sr., his development and industrial partner for the first set of AO
Instrumentarium, had flown around Africa in his private plane on a humanitarian
mission, landing in Addis Ababa in 1966. Coming around full circle, in a way, the
AO Foundation's new mission in Africa certainly promises to be more permanent
than the limited visits of two of the AO's most impactful founders (Exhibit 47.5).

Reference

Gosselin, R. A. (2009). The increasing burden of injuries in developing countries: Direct and
    indirect consequences. *Techniques in Orthopaedics, 24*, 230–232.

Global Health-Economic Impact 48

The Health-Economic Contribution

As has been established, Osteosynthesis, advocated by the AO Foundation, represented a major step forward in terms of patient outcomes, certainly contributing to its rapid rise as the preferred method of treating broken limbs. The comparison to the previous 'conservative method' involving plaster and external fixation, was centered on the fact that patients were at much less risk for deformities or disabilities. What has not yet been demonstrated is that the Osteosynthesis treatment method is also more efficient from a health-economic point of view, which takes the total economic impact of better treatment on society into account.

Comparisons of traditional external fixation versus the AO-advocated internal fixation can be made at different levels. The narrowest measurement is the direct cost of the hospital treatment for either method. A unique example of such a cost comparison was recorded for a patient (born 1939) who incurred a tibia fracture on his right leg in 1959, at the age of 20, and on his left tibia in 1983, at the age of 44. The first trauma was treated using the conservative method with external fixation and leg extension, whereas the second similar trauma in the other leg was treated some 24 years later using AO implants.[1]

The comparison shows that despite the additional costs of operation and implants, the Osteosynthesis resulted in a lower overall hospitalization cost of about 15%, largely due to a shortened hospital stay by 11 days.

There are obviously other factors that could be considered in the above comparison—there is the time factor of achieving full mobility earlier, due to the absence of not having to wear a plaster cast. Furthermore, weight bearing can commence earlier by four weeks, and full healing can be completed three months earlier. These patient

---

[1]Example supplied by Professor Peter Matter and going back to the surgery experience of Professor Martin Allgöwer, AO co-founder, Chur.

© Springer Nature Switzerland AG 2019
J.-P. Jeannet, *Leading a Surgical Revolution*,
https://doi.org/10.1007/978-3-030-01980-8_48

«Hypothetical» visualization of AOF's societal impact

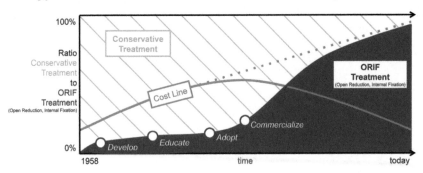

Michel Orsinger, October 2016

«Hypothetical» visualization of AOF's societal impact

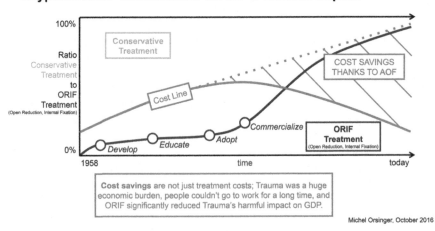

Michel Orsinger, October 2016

Exhibit 48.1   Social impact of internal fixation advocated by AO. *Copyright by AO Foundation, Switzerland*

benefits, and possibly economic benefits to insurers and employers, were not considered in this example.

The Steering Committee of the Social and Economic Committee (AOSEC), conceptualized the direct costs for Osteosynthesis versus the conservative treatment in two charts with a timeline starting with 1958, the creation of the AO organization. Results were presented to the entire AOSEC that addressed what was called 'the societal impact' of the AO approach. As internal fixation propagated by the AO began to crowd out the older, conservative plaster method, a significant savings accrued to the society-at-large over and beyond mere medical treatment costs differences (Exhibits 48.1 and 48.2).

Patient J.G.	1959	1983
Born 1939		
Accident	Right tibia	Left tibia
	Conservative Treatment	Internal Fixation
Treatment	Extension	Osteosynthesis with Plates and Screws
Hospital Stay	19 days	8 days
Plaster Applied	10 weeks	None
Full Weight Applied	After 14 weeks	After 10 weeks
Healing Completed	After 7 months	After 4 months
Hospital Charges	CHF 2,800.00 (indexed to 1983)	CHF 2,400.00

Exhibit 48.2 Hospital cost comparison between conservative treatment and internal fixation. *Source: Martin Allgöwer, AO co-founder, Chur. Copyright by AO Foundation, Switzerland*

Recent Study on Health-Economic Benefits: The Case for Switzerland

A recent study of health-economic benefits beyond mere hospital costs was conducted by a team of Zurich University of Applied Sciences (ZHAW).[2] They investigated the long-term health-economic benefits from internal fixation by putting monetary values on the time savings until return to work.[3]

---

[2]Eichler, K., Op. cit.
[3]Eichler, K., Op. cit.

anatomic localisation of fracture	YEAR	AO/OTA	treatment	exp cost direct	exp cost indirect	exp cost total
Tibia prox	2015	41-xx	OP	12868	19926	32'794
	2015		CONS	18942	122690	141'632
Tibia dia (shaft)	2015	42-xx	OP	20775	28487	49'262
	2015		CONS	18942	129117	148'059
Tibia dist	2015	43-xx	OP	26115	36154	62'269
	2015		CONS	18992	145105	164'097
Tibia total costs (CHF weighted average; per patient)	41-43		OP	17088	24934	42023
			CONS	18954	128831	147785
Difference in total costs Tibia (CHF per patient: CONS-OP)	41-43			1865	103897	105762

Exhibit 48.3 Swiss tibia fracture cost savings. *Source: Zurich University of Applied Sciences (ZHAW). Reprinted by permission*

Several assumptions had to be made, and restrictions overcome, to estimate data beyond direct hospital costs. The ZHAW team modeled the experience in Switzerland based upon data from the Swiss National Accident Insurance Fund (SUVA).[4] To arrive at indirect costs, three elements were combined which dealt with the intermediate absence from work (number of months): any permanent absence from work (number of months) resulting in disability pensions before retirement age of 65; any permanent absence from work due to death expressed in the number of years lost due to premature death prior to a regular retirement age of 65; and, improved mortality of patients under 65 resulting in productivity gains due to fewer premature deaths, and for an older population in terms of life years saved.

As the statistics per occurrence demonstrated for two of the more common bone fractures, those to the tibia and to the femur, the cost advantage in favor of the AO method remained in the 10–20% range of direct hospitalization costs. When including the indirect costs, the advantage of the AO method versus the traditional method increased substantially and reached levels of CHF 100,000 or more, per case, in favor of the internal fixation approaches (Exhibits 48.3 and 48.4).

If the savings were totaled across the bone fractures in nine major categories for all of Switzerland, annual savings as a result of the internal fixation approach over conservative treatment were considerable. The annual health-economic impact to Swiss society was estimated at about CHF 500 million, and the accumulated impact since the creation of the AO organization was estimated at CHF 15 billion. If we were to take a narrower measurement of direct health costs alone, then the savings amounted to about 2–5% of the societal impact, or in the range of CHF 20–25 million. This latter issue is of importance since the cost savings accrued to the society at large, ranging from insurance schemes to contribution to the gross national product (GNP). At the hospital level, the annual savings were much smaller, which

---

[4]SUVA (engl. SSUV) is utilized by employers, with data going back many years. SUVA data had also been used to justify the effectiveness of Osteosynthesis versus the conservative treatment during the early phase of the creation of AO.

anatomic localisation of fracture	YEAR	AO/OTA	treatment	exp cost direct	exp cost indirect	exp cost total
Femur prox	2015	31-xx	OP	21349	28527	49'877
	2015		CONS	24202	111637	135'839
Femur dia (shaft)	2015	32-xx	OP	19430	52792	72'222
	2015		CONS	24202	204558	228'760
Femur dist	2015	33-xx	OP	17638	24856	42'493
	2015		CONS	24202	196671	220'873
Femur total costs (CHF weighted average; per patient)	31-33		OP	19652	30642	50'294
			CONS	24202	157620	181'822
Difference in total costs Femur (CHF per patient: CONS-OP)	31-33			4550	126978	131528

Exhibit 48.4 Swiss femur fracture cost savings. *Source: Zurich University of Applied Sciences (ZHAW). Reprinted by permission*

could, at times, result in debates on the use of implants, because those paying for it, technically, did not profit from the entire societal benefits.[5]

Making the Case for Global Health-Economic Benefits

These are, naturally, statistics based upon the situation in Switzerland where the official, and also effective, retirement age is 65. In addition, some assumptions infer that people stayed in the labor force until retirement age, which is more typical for Switzerland but differs considerably in other countries. The medical costs accumulated for a bone fracture in Switzerland, compared with other countries, were likely to be on the high side, exceeded only by the US. All of these factors were taken into consideration by the team; adjustments were made for (1) the size of country population, (2) the level of health care costs in each country based upon international comparisons, (3) the level of income as it impacted on the loss of wages, and (4) the historical penetration level for internal fixation (Exhibit 48.5).

The global impact was a scaled-up version of the Swiss impact, adjusted for the parameters cited above. Since the Swiss share of the entire bone trauma volume accounts for only about 2%, the global societal benefit accruing annually was set at 50 times the Swiss amount, making for a very large CHF 25 billion annually. Furthermore, it should be noted, that a significant amount was saved every year by the societies of the Organization of Economic Development (OECD), countries with a high penetration of internal fixation treatment. The actual global savings are most likely lower, however, still considerable.

All of this data applied to OECD countries with developed economies but did not include the majority of the world's population. More than half of the world's

---

[5]Direct costs for implants were not available. In Switzerland, implant costs are combined with the cost for treatment under SUVA insurance and not made public. In the US, most hospitals rent the surgical sets for each procedure, again not allowing for direct comparisons on implant costs.

Intervention:

Osteosynthesis (OS) of fractures of the three index bones (femur; tibia; radius)

Comparator:

Conservative treatment (CONS) of fractures of the three index bones (femur; tibia; radius)

Outcome:

- Direct medical costs (for SSUV population <65 years; for the population aged ≥ 70 years only for proximal femur fractures)
- Indirect costs (for SSUV population <65 years)

Life years saved (calculated only for the population aged ≥70 years for proximal femur fracture)

- Direct medical costs (in Swiss Francs [CHF]) were derived using treatment costs as provided by the SSUV database or by 2015 Swiss tariffs

Indirect costs comprise:

- Intermediate absence from work (calculated as number of months off work multiplied by 2015 median Swiss monthly wages of the same age group)
- Permanent absence from work without death (number of months with 100% disability pensions before age 65 multiplied by monthly wages)
- Permanent absence from work due to death (number of years lost due to premature death before age 65 multiplied by annual wages)

Improved mortality is expressed in our analysis in two ways:

- For patients aged <65: via productivity gains due to less premature death before age 65
- For the population ≥70 years: via the number of life years saved

Observation period:

Analysis covers a time period of six decades from 1958 (founding of the AO) to 2017 (latest available data). OS and CONS were compared for each year and summed up as possible increased costs or savings of all 60 years.

Exhibit 48.5 Health-economic analysis assumptions. *[Source: Zurich University of Applied Sciences (ZHAW)]* (Eichler, K., Op. cit.)

population still does not have access to AO-inspired treatment of bone trauma, leaving a large untapped potential.

How About Monetizing Patient Benefits?

So far, benefits have been measured in health-economic terms, with only considering the economic impact for working age patients. Surely, there are other benefits, such as patient comfort. What is the value of not having to wear a cast for weeks? How can enhanced mobility both during treatment, and beyond, be valued, even if the patient is not engaged in an economic activity?

In 1959, a 39-year old teacher fell 2 m to the ground from a ladder and suffered a complicated trauma to the left lower leg near her ankle. She was operated, presumably by AO co-founder Martin Allgöwer, in the nearby hospital in Chur using an early form of Osteosynthesis. When undergoing a control in 2007, at the age of 86, 48 years later, her X-rays showed complete healing without any complications. Had she suffered this injury just a couple years earlier, she would have been treated via the conservative method involving a high risk for partial or even permanent disability[6] (Exhibits 48.6a–c).

A very important consideration in this discussion are the benefits to elderly patients, who are ever more in danger of suffering fragility fractures; a population who has been able to engage in a more active life after receiving internal fixation treatment. Because internal fixation is far superior in assuring proper bone healing than the conservative method, resulting in far fewer disability cases, also benefitting today's elderly population who wants to continue to engage in active walking, bicycling, skiing, golfing, and many other activities that, in the past, were not expected to be possible after a serious bone trauma. It is difficult to put financial figures on patient comfort and personal mobility, but the populations in the OECD countries are growing older and those benefits are most likely becoming ever more important.

---

[6]Anonymized medical records supplied by Grisons Cantonal Hospital, Chur.

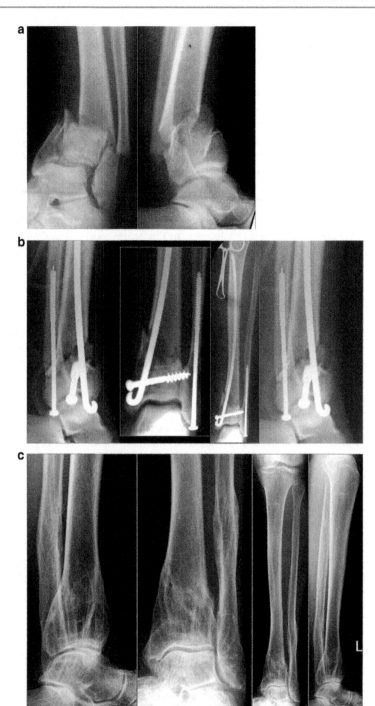

Exhibit 48.6 (a–c) Treatment of bone trauma 1959 with control in 2007. (a) Trauma fall 2 m from ladder, (b) surgery 1959, (c) control 49 years after surgery. *Source: Dr. med. Christoph Sommer, Chief Surgeon Trauma, Cantonal Hospital Grisons. Reprinted with permission*

AO Industrial and Business Impact

49

Creating a New Industry Sector

Parallel to the conquest and dominance of the internal fixation techniques propagated by the AO Foundation was the creation of an entire industry to supply the elements that made up the AO *Instrumentation*. The path of these businesses from the very beginning to the consolidation into one single supplier has been delineated already. However, an important part of the complete picture is the totality of the enterprises that make up the entire industrial sector.

How can the economic impact of an AO-inspired industrial cluster be measured? Since most of these operations were private, or if they were public wrapped up into other, large units without a detailed breakout of results, one is left to make some informed estimates. While sales figures can tell us something about the success of a company, general industrial impact is probably better described by looking at employment.

The AO-Inspired Industrial Cluster

The AO-inspired industrial cluster, at its core, comprised all the companies that were part of the original licensing agreement signed between Synthes AG Chur as the AO licensing company—the original industrial partners, at first two, Mathys and Straumann, and eventually three when Synthes USA joined the group. As Synthes USA's growth picked up and started to surpass the sales of Mathys and Straumann, a process of consolidation started, culminating in a single, combined, AO-licensed producer operating under the name Synthes, listed on the Swiss Stock Exchange. This process was led by Hansjörg Wyss, Synthes USA majority owner, and ended in 2004.

Throughout this process, the plants producing the AO *Instrumentation* elements built by the original industrial partners remained in operation, since the management

© Springer Nature Switzerland AG 2019
J.-P. Jeannet, *Leading a Surgical Revolution*,
https://doi.org/10.1007/978-3-030-01980-8_49

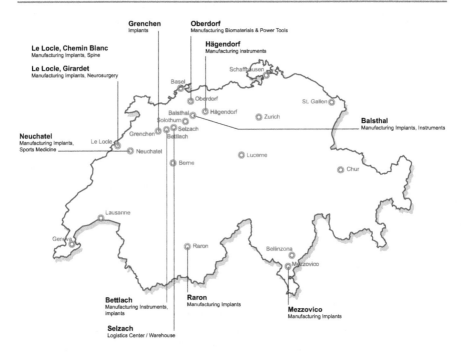

Exhibit 49.1   DPS production footprint in Switzerland. *Copyright AO Foundation, Switzerland*

philosophy of Wyss rested on the belief that several small units were a better industrial choice than a single, huge manufacturing complex. For Wyss, units of 400–500 employees achieve a greater efficiency. Therefore the acquired companies of Mathys and Straumann, each consisting of three to four separate production sites with 300–400 employees, were left intact. The factories were given specific product mandates, together covering the entire product portfolio of the AO *Instrumentation*. J&J's acquisition of Synthes made it part of the division DePuy Synthes (DPS), and maintained this operating philosophy, leaving the previous operational and manufacturing footprint intact (Exhibit 49.1).

The Global Impact of the Industrial Cluster

When Synthes was acquired by J&J in 2011, the operation employed about 12,000 people globally. This included the manufacturing operations (US, Germany, Switzerland, and the Far East) and a considerable staff involved in the distribution and selling of implants worldwide. Some experts estimated that only about half of the total number of employees were directly involved in manufacturing at Synthes, and of those two-thirds, or about 4000 people, were employed in the Synthes' manufacturing sites in Switzerland.

Looking only at Synthes omits an important fact: DPS business enjoyed a global market share of about 45%. The remaining 55% was made up of several competitors who also made trauma implants based on the AO philosophy. Whether referred to as knock-off products, imitations or copycats, it remained a fact that tight patent protection did not exist, and competitors could always find ways around the design of an implant without incurring patent infringement lawsuits.

One imitator, the former Voka Company created in 1963 by two ex-Straumann executives, Vogt and Karpf, in Selzach. At that time, many within AO organization were upset because the two founders were part of TK meetings and used insider knowledge to create their enterprise. Later renamed Osteo, the company undersold AO implants by about 20–25%. When the US company Stryker acquired Osteo in 1996, it provided Stryker its entry into the trauma market. At that time, the Selzach operation manufactured trauma implants, such as plates and screws, and had about 70 employees; under Stryker it continued to grow, reaching 480 employees in 2013, the 50th anniversary of its existence. The operation did not just produce, but also served as a development center for Stryker's trauma operation.[1]

Any industrial impact assessment of the revolution inspired by the AO needs to take into consideration all production entities, legitimized by the AO or not: without the innovation effort of the AO they would not exist. Consequently, the complete footprint of the industry inspired by the AO has to be set at about double the numbers reported for DPS alone, that is about 20,000–25,000 employees with a combined global sales volume in excess of CHF 10 billion. Given developments in Asia, and the need for low-cost implants in LMICs, as mentioned previously, the global share of the AO-branded products sold through DPS is likely to decline over time, but the global employment around implant production is likely to increase with a continuing shift towards Asia and India.

The Regional Impact of AO and Synthes in Switzerland

Regionally, in Switzerland, the impact of AO-inspired *Instrumentarium* production has been concentrated on the two neighboring Cantons of Solothurn and Basel-Landschaft (Basel-Land). Of the eight Synthes plants, now owned by J&J DPS, four are in Solothurn. In addition, the Stryker plant turning out trauma implants is located in that same area. In total, some 2600 employees could be credited to the trauma medical cluster, and about 130 apprentices were groomed in the various operations. This is the region where the watch industry had, at one time, reigned supreme with large operations in several towns in Solothurn. The medical cluster, led by the AO trauma inspired operations, having long eclipsed the watch industry in both importance and impact (Exhibit 49.2).

---

[1]"Thomas Wahl: Selzach ist ein Vorzeigewerk." *Schweiz am Sonntag*, 23 June, 2013.

Exhibit 49.2 Solothurn cluster. *Source: ConCep + GmbH in cooperation with Wirtschaftsförderung Kanton Solothurn, Vollerhebung MedTech Kanton Solothurn, Oktober 2016. Reprinted by permission*

Expanding the Circle: Indirect Industry Impact from AO

Beyond AO implants for trauma, either through Synthes or its competitors, there was a wider circle of companies spawned as a result of the industrial activity generated by the AO and its producers. These activities had to do with follow-on developments that had their roots in AO technology or applications.

There were two sources of these related investments, and both had to do with two entrepreneurial families, involved with AO since its inception, selling their AO-related operations into a consolidated Synthes and then continuing to run enterprises on related technology.

Straumann Dental

When Fritz Straumann died unexpectedly in 1988, the Straumann family split up its operation. The medical implant business became independent as Stratec Medical and taken over by its manager, Rudolf Maag, in a management buy-out. The remaining, and much smaller, part was headed by Thomas Straumann, Fritz's son, who took a small team of 20 specialists and focused them on the dental implant business. Although manufacturing AO-branded implants did not have much to do with dental implants, the technology was related and the material, particularly titanium, was of critical importance to the dental implant business. This offshoot grew rapidly, reaching sales of CHF 1.1 billion with some 5000 employees in 2017. The Straumann dental business, now about the size of Synthes in the year 2000, continues to grow rapidly. A public company since 1998, which moved from Waldenburg to Basel in 2004, Straumann Dental maintained a large manufacturing facility in Villeret, in the canton of Berne, employing about 500 people (Exhibit 49.3).

Straumann Dental would probably not have been built without the previous experience with AO implants, including the important shift to titanium and the exposure to a business model adopted by the AO industrial partners.[2]

Medartis

In 1997, Thomas Straumann founded Medartis as a way to re-enter the Osteosynthesis field the Straumanns left when the family sold Stratec Medical in a management buy-out in 1989. Medartis is focused on the development and manufacturing of metal implants used for trauma in the craniomaxillofacial (CMF) field, one AO's four clinical areas, as well as on smaller extremities (Exhibit 49.4).

Traditionally a 'titanium house,' Medartis manufactures all of its implants and screws from titanium in a new operational site in Basel where about 200 of its worldwide staff of 500 are employed. The company was started with just six employees, growing steadily to sales of about CHF 100 million in 2017. Over the first 15 years, the company did not turn a profit but it is profitable now, allowing the owners to do an IPO on the Swiss stock market and gain access to funds for future growth.

Medartis' product portfolio is focused on hand, wrist, elbow, shoulder, and foot trauma, as well as on CMF. Its signature product is the Trilock plate used in CMF and based on its patented Trilock technology, allowing for multidirectional and angular fixation. Again, Medartis was using a business model similar to AO/Synthes. Clearly, without the Straumann family's earlier involvement as a producer of AO implants, Medartis as a company would not have emerged. Technologically, the company also profited from a change in the Cooperation Agreement between AO and J&J DPS, which allowed for collaboration with other industrial partners under certain circumstances.

---

[2]Interview with Thomas Straumann, conducted on 1 March, 2018, in Basel.

Exhibit 49.3 The Straumann dental implant product line. *Source: Straumann Dental Company. With permission of Thomas Straumann*

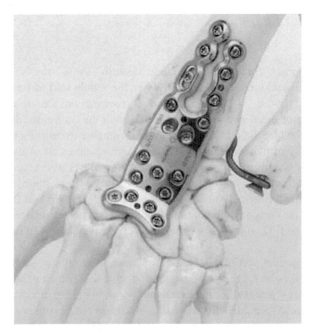

Exhibit 49.4 The Medartis wrist fusion system. *Source: Medartis Company. With permission of Thomas Straumann*

Mathys Orthopedics

Mathys, originally the largest of the three AO implant suppliers, divested its implant business in 2004 to Synthes. Divested is the right term because Mathys did not sell the entire company. It retained a smaller part, about 10% of the Mathys group, since it did not engage in AO-dependent implant and instrument business. This part was to become the nucleus of a new business, just as was the case with Straumann's dental implant business.

Robert Mathys, Sr., had long experimented with Orthopedic products, first in collaboration with Maurice Müller and his hip implants, beginning as a contract manufacturer in 1967 and distributed under the brand name of Protek. In 1996, Mathys lost the production contract to Sulzer who had acquired Protek. In 1997, for the first time, the company began marketing its products under the Mathys brand name. Throughout its history, Mathys had always been a supplier to AO or Protek for products sold under their brand names.

Since 1997, Mathys has expanded steadily its product portfolio to include prostheses for knees, hips, and shoulders, as well as bone replacement material. With this development came a change to synthetic materials, high-density polyethylene (HDPE), veering away from the original metal implants made for AO applications. Mathys' latest development is in the area of sports medicine with an implant product named Ligamys, aimed at biological self-healing for anterior crucible ligaments (Exhibit 49.5).

In 2018, Mathys, now managed by the family's third generation, runs a business with approximately 60 employees, about half of which are located outside of Switzerland, with sales of about CHF 125 million. The company maintains several sales subsidiaries in Europe and in Asia. It still operates from the same physical plant where the Mathys AO implant business had its start.

Thommen Dental

In the town of Grenchen, in the midst of Solothurn's MedTech cluster, one can find another dental implant company originating from the Synthes technology and manufacturing base. Robert Mathys, Sr., together with clinicians, had developed a dental implant system in 1975 under the brand name Ha-Ti®. This system came to market in 1986 with a breakthrough technology whose connection design has remained unchanged until today. In 1996 Robert Mathys, Sr., and Livio Marzo (member of the third generation of the Mathys family) spun the dental division out of the Mathys company into a new company named HATI Dental AG, with special focus on oral implantology and prosthetics.

In 2001, an executive from Straumann contacted Marzo regarding the Ha-Ti dental implant system and screw manufacturing. This led to the creation of Thommen Medical AG, which acquired HATI Dental AG and continued active participation in the dental implant space on the basis of the original Mathys screw

Exhibit 49.5 The Mathys knee prothesis system. *Source: Mathys Company. With permission of Robert Mathys, Jr.*

technology. The clinicians working with Thommen Medical AG continue to provide an important contribution in the further development of the system (Exhibit 49.6).

The private company remains managed and owned by the Marzo (Mathys) family, who work together with outside investors, including Novartis. As a privately-owned company, no official figures are released but employment is

Exhibit 49.6 Thommen
medical dental implant.
Source: Thommen Medical.
Reproduced with permission

estimated at about 100 people. The company has sales operations in North America, Europe, Asia, and the Middle East, and is represented by subsidiaries or exclusive distribution partners in numerous markets.[3]

Drawing a Still Wider Circle by Inspiring a Supply Base

The presence of the medical cluster centered around AO-designed implants was an opportunity for suppliers. A typical example of this is the machinery supplier Monnier + Zahner AG, established in 1964 by two entrepreneurs, specializing in machine tools for the manufacture of watch cases. The crisis in the Swiss watch industry in the early 1970s forced the company to change course. Monnier + Zahner began to specialize in machinery needed to produce bone screws and other medical and dental implants. Over time, Monnier + Zahner became a leading global supplier in the segment of milling and whirling machines used in the manufacture of high precision medical screws. Without Mathys having built this industry, which requires highly specialized equipment, it is unlikely that Monnier + Zahner would have been able to reach its present global market position. The company, privately-owned, is based in the town of Safnern and employs about 70 people[4] (Exhibit 49.7).

Appreciating the Industrial Contribution of AO Foundation and Industrial Partners for Switzerland

The success of the manufacturing base of trauma and dental implants, stemming from the development of AO *Instrumentarium* represents a major accomplishment of Swiss industry. Because this business segment was ramping up at a time when the Swiss watch industry was retrenching, the medical technology cluster in the Solothurn and Basel regions was able to balance their regional employment. Furthermore, over time, the manufacturing base was able to hold its own against foreign competition and continue to grow. That this was possible in the context of a constantly appreciating Swiss Franc, driving up the cost of operating in high-cost

---

[3]Source: Livio Marzo, CEO Thommen Medical AG, August 7, 2018.
[4]Source: Reto Jungi, Managing Director, Monnier + Zahner AG, 7 August, 2018.

Exhibit 49.7 Monnier + Zahner worm milling machine. *Source: With permission of Monnier + Zahner*

Switzerland, was largely due to the manufacturing genius of the entrepreneurs who ran the Swiss-based AO producers—namely the Mathys and Straumann families. Later, this group would include the professional managers who stepped in, such as Rudolf Maag for Stratec Medical and, in particular, Hansjörg Wyss at Synthes USA. While the AO Foundation and its surgeons were able to convince the medical world that Osteosynthesis and the AO approach were second to none, the entrepreneurs were, for their part, building, financing, and running their factories, as well as drawing upon a highly skilled and dedicated workforce. They competed against much larger firms based upon ingenuity, efficiency, and inventiveness.

50

AO as Creator of Wealth

The Different Forms of Wealth

It is only natural that one associates the term 'wealth' with financial wealth. That the AO, through its innovations and its industrial partners, created substantial financial wealth is, however, only one aspect of its wealth creation. After all, the purpose of the AO was never the creation of wealth per se; it was to improve the lives of patients suffering a bone trauma. Because wealth creation was not the AO's primary objective, it is appropriate to consider the AO Foundation as an enterprise growing out of a social entrepreneurial effort. As a result, it is important to look at the different forms of wealth generated by the AO—financial, institutional, investor, as well as social.

AO as Creator of Personal Financial Wealth

The AO Foundation and the *Instrumentarium* that it developed, directly or indirectly, resulted in creating of five billionaires. One of the five is an institutional billionaire—the AO Foundation itself—reflected by its endowment, which exceeds CHF 1 billion. Nevertheless, this enormous financial wealth creation requires some further explanation. In the course of becoming exclusive producers of the AO instrumentation, two families and two individual entrepreneurs, who actively participated in this enterprise from the beginning, were able to amass considerable fortunes. This did not happen automatically. It required entrepreneurial spirit, acceptance of risk, and enormous personal effort. On top of that, all of these fortunes had humble beginnings, and some were actually made from scratch. Of course, sacrifices were made and setbacks incurred along the way.

The key players—all involved in the AO's *Instrumentarium* business—are the Mathys and Straumann families, and Rudolf Maag and Hansjörg Wyss as individuals. The term 'family' is used in the widest sense of the term since in two

© Springer Nature Switzerland AG 2019
J.-P. Jeannet, *Leading a Surgical Revolution*,
https://doi.org/10.1007/978-3-030-01980-8_50

of these cases the founders of the enterprises, namely Robert Mathys, Sr., and Fritz Straumann, have passed away.

The Mathys Family, Continuing in Medical Technology

The small workshop owned and operated by Robert Mathys, Sr., started in 1946 in Bettlach (see Chap. 9). He was the first to collaborate with Maurice Müller on the AO *Instrumentarium*, beginning in 1958. Mathys had confidence in the famous surgeon, operated on a mere handshake, had no formal papers or purchase orders in hand, and shouldered the entire financial risk of the operation. It was a start-up in every sense of the term. The business needed constant investment and Mathys ploughed his cash flow right back into the company, not spoiling himself with large dividends.

When he passed away in 2000, his company had sales of more than CHF 400 million, about 1500 employees, was highly profitable, and still continued to grow on the back of new AO developments. Four years after the passing of Mathys, Sr., the family sold the trauma business to Synthes-Stratec in 2004, for a reported CHF 1.5 billion (see Chap. 34). The Mathys family, now in its third generation, continues to be engaged as entrepreneurs and actively participate in both the Mathys Orthopedics and the Thommen Medical companies.

The Straumann Family, Enterprising Tradition

Not unlike the Mathys family, the Straumanns were early participants in the development of the AO *Instrumentarium*, quickly becoming the second exclusive producer. They had more financial resources than the Mathys family, their other industrial ventures provided a steady cash flow, something Mathys could not rely on.

The unexpected death of Fritz Straumann in 1988, by then the head of the operation, required the Straumann group to be divided; part of it was sold, including the trauma business. In 1989 the family agreed to a management buy-out by the person in charge of the business, Rudolf Maag, who then rebranded the entity Stratec Medical. The deal totaled a reported CHF 120 million.

In line with the strong entrepreneurial and industrial tradition of the Straumann family, Fritz's son Thomas started what would become Straumann Dental, now a public company. In the eyes of analysts, the family fortune merits the term billionaire and that, essentially, had been created out of capitalizing on AO technology. Other sources have estimated Straumann family's net worth at more than CHF 2 billion.[1]

Exiting the medical business in 1989 did not make the Straumanns billionaires over night, but it did provide them resources that were used effectively to continue with entrepreneurial activities. Building two companies—Straumann Dental and

---

[1]*Fortune* Magazine website, accessed 19 May, 2018.

Medartis—represented a major industrial and entrepreneurial achievement. Both Straumann companies remain connected to the AO and have borrowed much from the AO business model in making their own companies successful.

Rudolf Maag, Stratec Medical

As mentioned above, Rudolf Maag, who ran the trauma business for the Straumann family, seized the opportunity to create his own operation in 1989 through a management buy-out, renaming the company Stratec Medical. By the time he agreed to combine his operation with the larger Synthes USA in 1999 (see Chap. 35), Stratec Medical had grown to a sales volume of about CHF 265 million, almost four times the size it had when Maag made his management buy-out ten years earlier.

Since the combination of Stratec with Synthes USA was made in the form of a share combination, folding the Synthes USA business into the Stratec Medical business to come up with Synthes-Stratec, exact terms depended on the value of the assigned shares Maag received for his smaller operation. Again, just like with the Straumanns, the Stratec Medical transaction alone did not make Maag a billionaire right away, but it did certainly serve as the foundation of his wealth. Based on some data, the value of the share package was in the range of CHF 650 million. Maag first joined Synthes-Stratec under Wyss but soon left to pursue other ventures. He invested heavily in Straumann Dental, becoming one of the largest private investors in that company, as well as in other ventures. His net worth was reported to amount to more than CHF 3 billion.[2]

Hansjörg Wyss, Building Synthes

Hansjörg Wyss is an integral part of the AO Foundation story (see Chap. 22). It began with him joining the Synthes operation in the US, and culminated in 2011 with the divestment of his Synthes company to J&J for CHF 19 billion. At that time he owned about 50% of the company.

This became the major source of his considerable fortune and, according to some sources, made him the wealthiest Swiss-born person in the world. The making of Synthes, originally a loss-making company with a handful of employees in the US, acquired at with an investment of US$ 400,000, into a company with almost 12,000 employees and global sales of about CHF 4 billion, was a major entrepreneurial achievement, requiring over 34 years of intensive effort against competition several times Synthes' size. That this wealth and success was created as the designated producer of AO approved and developed implants speaks for the genius of the surgeons, as well as of the entrepreneur. That the size of sale proceeds resulting

---

[2]"Rudolf Maag, das Imperium des unbekannten Milliardärs." *Schweizerische Handelszeitung*, 6 April, 2018.

from the J&J acquisition sometimes generated jealousy and criticism within the AO community goes with the territory.

Investor Wealth Creation

A significant part of the wealth creation benefited the investors-at-large who had allocated capital to the four entrepreneurs and their families. This was not the case with Mathys because the company had remained private. However, there were outside investors at Stratec Medical, later Synthes-Stratec, and then at Synthes USA, all of them public companies with shares listed on the stock market. Investors stepped out of the Synthes sale to J&J with half of the total, or about CHF 10 billion, and there were investor gains from the earlier combination of Stratec Medical and Synthes into Synthes-Stratec. This is also similar to the Straumann Company, Straumann Dental, that in a way emerged out of the AO.

More recently, the investor community is referring to successful start-up firms who reach at least 1 billion in market value as 'Unicorns.' Using the standards of that comparison, all three of the start-ups that arose from the AO, namely Mathys, Straumann/Stratec, and Synthes, earned Unicorn status, as did Straumann Dental.

AO Endowment as Institutional Wealth

Last but not least, it is necessary to mention the effect of wealth on the AO Foundation, whose finances depended, to a large extent, on the sales success of the producers. In 2005, when the AO Foundation was established in its present legal form, Synthes acquired all rights to the AO *Instrumentarium* outright. A transfer of CHF 1 billion was made to the endowment of the AO Foundation. This wealth contributes to the Foundation's continued activity and represents an important asset. It came from wealth created through AO *Instrumentarium* and its collaboration with the licensed producers. It also came in the form of financial wealth invested for the benefit of the AO Foundation. In fact, this is the fifth billionaire created out of the AO activities.

Social Wealth Created by the AO

In addition to the financial forms of wealth, it is important to look at the numbers regarding the health-economic contribution to society, which can be seen as indirect wealth. The contribution to health benefit (net) that Osteosynthesis of fractures in the three major bones (tibia, femur, radius) makes has been estimated at an astounding CHF 855 billion, over the 60 years of AO's existence. This would suggest that society-at-large obtained the lion's share of benefits, far in excess of the financial benefits accrued to entrepreneurs and investors.[3]

And How About the Surgeons?

In many discussions with AO Foundation members and associated surgeons, the perceived wealth discrepancy between industrial partners and surgeons has been raised throughout the years. While it might have been a minority who sometimes raised this issue, there was an underlying current questioning how the wealth created by the AO was distributed, and if it represented a fair distribution. Fairness is a rather fungible term subject to individual perception.

Referring back to the AO founders, who viewed the AO as a non-profit enterprise, is helpful. When the founders, under the leadership of Maurice Müller, separated implant sales from medical decisions, and wanted to be patient-driven rather than market-driven, they consciously gave up the spoils that came from the *Instrumentarium* production and sales. The idea was to have surgeons be surgeons, and to let the producers be entrepreneurs.

Müller, who had much to do with this orientation, was noted to say that AO surgeons should not gain from the sale and use of implants used in their own operations. However, he was quite comfortable charging for surgical skills in the operating room.

The AO, with its training, books, publications, research, easy-to-use implants and surgical tools, contributed enormously to supporting and allowing the individual surgeon to be successful at his or her essential skill. As many of surgeons have, at times, confided in interviews, it was that surgical skill that typically allowed them to earn a good income over many years. Of course, the opportunity to earn income through surgery was not equally distributed across all countries due to differing medical systems and reimbursement practices.

The discussion of wealth among the industrial partners, which apparently began in the late 1990s and was often directed against Hansjörg Wyss, contributed to the conflict that erupted at the trustees' meeting in Oslo, an incident covered in greater detail earlier (see Chap. 41). Conversations with senior AO surgeons raised several points.

The first point addressed the many benefits AO surgeons are able to gain through the association with the AO, and through the adoption of AO surgical techniques. These benefits are enhanced by academic success and access to research, both leading to prestige, and through prestige, invariably to increased income. The point here is that any active AO member probably realizes that their own income

---

[3]ZHAW report, Op. cit, p. 19, The potential net benefit of OS for fractures in the three index bones in 17 high income countries over 60 years is CHF 855 billion (base case; population age <65; 3% discount rate; in 2015 Swiss Francs).

prospects increase over the length of their professional careers through their association with the AO.

The second point concerned a common attitude existing in hospitals during the time when conservative treatment reigned supreme. At that time, a leading German surgeon referred to his younger surgeon colleagues who were routinely assigned the non-surgical task of placing patients into casts, as "Kellerkinder[4] with two left hands," a real put-down. It was precisely many of these young surgeons who grasped the opportunity that they could advance professionally through adopting the AO method of Osteosynthesis.

Some 500,000 surgeons have been trained by the AO Foundation over its 60 years of existence. Many of these surgeons, by virtue of learning the AO skills and applying internal fixation approaches, were able to earn a far better income over the course of their careers. One can look at this hypothetically: If only 15,000 surgeons of those trained were able to accumulate an additional net worth of CHF 1 million over their entire surgical career, they would have earned as much as the accumulated wealth of the producers combined. Because the wealth was distributed over many more surgeons and not just four industrial partners, the individual figures did not look as impressive.

And How About Patient Wealth?

There is yet another view, touched on briefly as the health benefits of the AO-advocated approach to bone trauma were addressed (see Chap. 48). There have been millions of patients who, as a result surgical treatment and the use of AO implants, were able to walk away from complicated fractures that before would have resulted in some degree of disability. The benefits of being able to continue leading a full life goes beyond the health-economic benefits that are largely insurance and medical cost-driven. What is the value to a patient for being able to continue a life with full mobility, to engage in the pursuit of activities without restrictions, and to return to being a full-fledged member of the community? These values are probably higher than the financial costs covered through insurance premiums or disability payments. It is almost impossible to put a financial number on such benefits, but they may well surpass any material wealth discussed in this chapter.

---

[4] 'Basement children,' or 'children stuck in the basement of a hospital.'

AO as a Philanthropic Force

51

Philanthropy or Business?

The conversation about wealth, of all kinds, might give the reader the impression that wealth generation was the end goal of many associated with the AO Foundation. Far from it. As an organization, the AO itself profited from accumulated financial wealth, but always remained dedicated to improving patient lives. Since this wealth was accrued without direct compensation to those who delivered its mission, the AO Foundation qualifies as a social entrepreneurial enterprise; social with regards to its mission and its status as a non-profit organization. Since the AO undertakes surgical development, combined with an immense educational effort that requires considerable management skills, it is also an enterprise. The AO is more than an association, not just a debating club of surgeons, but an organization that undertakes a daunting endeavor to improve fracture care globally.

Throughout its existence, the AO Foundation has triggered a vast number of philanthropic acts, including dispensing part of the wealth that has been generated. The connection between the AO Foundation and philanthropy deserves further explanation.

AO as Volunteer Organization

To repeat, the AO Founders had envisioned their organization as a form of a 'brotherhood of surgeons,' committed to the goal of making their technique of Osteosynthesis the medical community's gold standard, without compensation for their time. At first, when the AO was comprised of just a small number of committed members, everyone was expected to join in all meetings, help review texts explaining their procedures, or provide feedback on new implants or surgical tools.

As the organization grew, TK commissions were founded, and as many more tasks needed to be performed, a permanent staff was hired for administration. The

© Springer Nature Switzerland AG 2019
J.-P. Jeannet, *Leading a Surgical Revolution*,
https://doi.org/10.1007/978-3-030-01980-8_51

organization's full-time staff was compensated, but the surgeon members were not; there were, however, some exceptions in the form of stipends. It was not unusual to find that by the end of their careers, surgeons had donated enormous amounts of their time, approaching the equivalent of several years of professional activity. There was certainly some sacrifice involved, be it in terms of time away from families and frequent travel, as well as time away from their hospitals and clinics, and from their regular surgical activities.

Over time, and with the organization growing in complexity, stipends were paid for officers and for instructors in courses. These stipends have never approached what surgeons could earn using their skills in the open market. The introduction of stipends was intensively debated at that time, and some older members of the AO occasionally confided that they missed the time when no money was paid out. They accepted, however, that the current situation was different from the early AO days, but they did not like it. Still, payment for the AO Foundation's formal activity was compensated with reasonable expense coverage and a small stipend well below market rates.

It was, therefore, not too far-fetched to consider the AO, from the volunteer surgeons' point of view, a philanthropic entity. As a result, the first philanthropic act in the name of the AO was its creation as a Foundation, which continues to this day and includes the benefit of tens of thousands of service days rendered.

Founders Providing Seed Capital for the AO Organization

When the AO started, the only funds available were the amounts contributed by members. Membership fees, if they can be called that, amounted to a few hundred Francs at the time. Whenever more money was needed, the core members Müller, Allgöwer, Willenegger, and Schneider contributed a few thousand Francs each. There were few public funds available then, so its development rested largely on the shoulders of the founding surgeons. Since their contributions were for the benefit of a medical cause one can also qualify these contributions as a form of philanthropy.

Founders Donating Intellectual Capital through Synthes AG Chur

The first largest donation, not in money but as in-kind contributions of intellectual capital, came in 1963, at the time when the relationship between the producers and the AO organization needed to be clarified through creating Synthes AG Chur. It needed to be structured as a non-profit organization, and therefore had to have own assets. As a result, the founders present, under the leadership of Müller, decided to donate their intellectual capital in the form of patents, or right-of-use, to Synthes AG Chur as a gift in-kind creating an asset for Synthes and justifying its status as a non-profit organization.

At that time, there was no financial assessment of the value of these patents and, after many years, there was still considerable dispute about their commercial value.

AO records maintained by Schneider, first Chair of the Swiss AO, indicated that up to 1963, the majority of the initial developments around the AO *Instrumentarium* were due to Müller, with others beginning to contribute later. During the first ten years of the AO, there were, other than Müller, about ten other AO members mentioned multiple times, including: the core team around Schneider, Willenegger, Allgöwer, and Bandi, as well as Weber, Gisin, Stähli, Heim, Weller, Perren, and Russenberger.[1]

The statutory shareholders of Synthes AG Chur had forgone any financial benefits from their shares in the organization, such as receiving dividends. When the AO turned itself into a foundation, all shareholders of Synthes AG Chur donated their shares to the newly created AO Foundation and gave up on any benefits from their holding.

Attention should not center around the question of who did more, but on the impact on AO's development as a result of donating developments and intellectual capital, free-of-charge, to Synthes AG Chur—an organization which would in turn license their use to AO's industrial partners and receive royalties, only to be reinvested into the AO research effort. Once started, it had the effect of creating the pattern of donating any new developments to Synthes AG Chur, also free-of-charge. This pattern was maintained and accepted for many years by countless developers associated with the AO until the entire rights to the accumulated patents, brand name, etc., were sold to Synthes in 2006 for an amount of CHF 1 billion. This capital injection, passed on to the AO Foundation in the form of an endowment, represented the accumulated value of all patent rights created by the AO members over time.

Sponsoring the New AO Center Building in Davos

The new AO Center, built in Davos and inaugurated in 1992, was financed through an act of generosity on the occasion of ownership of Synthes USA. When it was decided to sell the entire US organization to Hansjörg Wyss, minority shareholder and CEO, the beneficiary owners of the company were early AO founders, who donated 20% of the proceeds of the sale of the company—estimated at about USD 60 million—to the AO for the benefit of building a new center. Additional funds came from the Mathys family, not shareholders of the US company, and the remainder of the necessary funds was financed by a mortgage. Again, this was an act of philanthropy on the part of the early AO founders, to the benefit of the AO organization.

The financial investment on the part of AO founders and shareholders in Synthes USA was possibly the only time when the previous separation of business and surgery was breached. Since the investment was made in the US, and none of the shareholding surgeons had anything to gain personally from the use of the implants

---

[1]Schneider, R., "10 Jahre AO, AO-Dokumentationszentrale," Berne 1969, p. 25.

sold in the US, this investment did not violate their own code of ethics. By helping Synthes USA to grow into a viable business, the AO stood to gain substantially from the later stream of licensing payments, reinvested into the development of the whole AO organization.

External Philanthropic Activities Related to the AO

So far, the philanthropic activity described was undertaken for the benefit of the AO in the form of donations of either time, or in-kind. Numerous other philanthropic activities were enabled by the wealth generated by the manufacturing families and were to a considerable extent devoted to humanitarian causes external to the AO.

The two families, Mathys and Straumann, as well as the entrepreneurs Wyss and Maag, engaged in their own philanthropic activities, sometimes through their companies in the form of corporate philanthropy, but also often in the form of personal philanthropy. The philanthropic activities of Maurice Müller, initiator and co-founder of the AO were a combination of personal and institutional philanthropy.

Since philanthropic activities were not always made public, the descriptions of activities in this area are confined to those in the public domain, or those mentioned in personal interviews. It is quite possible that reports of some contributions are missing, having been kept private.

Maurice Müller and His Family's Philanthropy

Maurice Müller, as a founding AO member, had participated extensively in all aspects of the AO's 'internal philanthropy.' He gave generously of his time, ranging from research, development of the *Instrumentarium*, as course instructor, and in his long role as head of the AOTK. He was also instrumental in assuring that the AO organization kept the surgical activities separate from the for-profit activities of the industrialists.

Unlike his AO colleagues, Maurice Müller had created a parallel activity developing and marketing hip replacement implants. Using the same model as the AO Foundation, Müller created a separate foundation and a company for the business operations, the Protek Foundation in 1965, and, in 1967, the Protek AG. The purpose of the Protek structure was to capture all of the profits from the production and sales of the hip prosthesis business and funnel it back into medical and scientific research. In 1974, Müller folded his Protek Foundation into the Foundation Maurice E. Müller. When Müller sold parts of Protek in 1989, and then completely in 1992, he channeled the proceeds of an estimated at CHF 300 million, into his foundation. In his view, it was not acceptable to benefit personally from the sale of implants, just as he had argued previously as an AO founder. He considered it acceptable to earn fees with his hands as a surgeon, but not through the sale of products in whose production he was not directly participating in.

Through his foundations, Maurice Müller funded a number of chairs in the disciplines of medical science and Orthopedic surgery. Donations granted to the University of Berne amounted to more than CHF 150 million over the years, where he also established the Maurice E. Müller Institute of Biomechanics (MIB) with AO member Stephan Perren as the first appointed director [a restructuring of MIB in 2003 would spawn The Institute for Surgical Technology and Biomechanics (ISTB), at the University Berne]. At the University of Basel, Müller also created the Maurice E. Müller Institute for Structural Biology in 1986, funding the Institute with CHF 50 million. Over the years, several foundations in North America, all connected to Orthopedics and the training of surgeons, received another CHF 50 million from his foundation.[2]

In 1998, Müller and his wife Martha funded the *Zentrum Paul Klee* in Berne. This center, popularly known as the Klee Museum, had a history that was in several ways connected to Müller's work with the AO Foundation. It began with an accident in 1975, when a young but already famous Italian pianist by the name of Maurizio Pollini suffered serious neck and spine injuries in an automobile accident; he was left unable to move freely his hands and legs. Looking for a surgeon who could operate on Pollini, the family came upon Maurice Müller who had the patient transferred to his hospital in Berne. Following the successful operation, Pollini was able to return to his concert tours within the year. When Müller celebrated his 80th birthday on 28 March, 1998, he invited Pollini to give a concert for his guests. Unfortunately, all the concert halls in Berne were booked on that day and the party had to be transferred to the Museum of Fine Arts Berne, to the large Hodler gallery. It so happened that shortly after that, the Paul Klee Foundation also needed that space for an important meeting, requiring that the venue be quickly vacated after the Müller event (Exhibit 51.1).

The scheduled Klee Foundation meeting was reported in the newspapers the next day; its purpose was to plan how a museum could build a museum in Berne soon enough to avoid the departure of the Klee family collection to another city or museum. The report alerted Maurice Müller to the Klee Foundation's dilemma, and within days he and his wife Martha decided to offer a significant tract of land on the outskirts of Berne, together with a cash contribution of CHF 70 million. Within two years the plans were drawn up and the museum opened in 2005, but not before another cash injection of CHF 50 million was made by the Müller Foundation.

The people of Berne might wonder what would have happened to the extensive Klee collection if a different, and better suited performance hall, would have been available to Pollini and Müller. Had the sequence of events had been different, the Müller family might never have been alerted to the issue. This same tract of land, adjacent to the Müller family home, had been offered to the AO several years earlier, as a possible location for the new AO Center, which was eventually built in Davos. The City of Berne had rejected that proposal.

---

[2]Interview with Janine Aebi-Müller and Ueli Aebi-Müller, conducted on 18 April, 2018 in Berne.

Exhibit 51.1 Zentrum Paul Klee, Berne. *With kind permission of Zentrum Paul Klee, Berne, Switzerland*

The Creation of the RMS Foundation

Robert Mathys, Sr., established the RMS Foundation in 1985 as a non-profit organization with the purpose of promoting medical and clinical research, as well as technical development and training in the respective applications. The RMS Foundation was expanded in 1992 when the research group and test laboratory of Mathys, Ltd. in Bettlach were integrated, increasing its size from 15 to 36 employees. As of 1995, the RMS Foundation was expanded to act as a service provider and contract research partner (Exhibit 51.2).

The RMS Foundation became engaged in applied research and a range of analytical, material, and technological tests for customers in the medical and material technology industries. The Foundation, initially chaired by Robert Mathys, Sr., has subsequently been chaired by Robert Mathys, Jr., for many years. The RMS Foundation has been instrumental in helping the Mathys Company build its non-trauma business and to grow its Orthopedics presence after the sale of the trauma business to Synthes in 2004. It is quite possible that the founder, Robert Mathys, Sr., used the AO Research Institute (ARI) in Davos as a role model; many of the Foundation's early activities reflected some of the ARI's mandates.

Exhibit 51.2 Robert Mathys Foundation, Bettlach. *Source: Robert Mathys, Jr., reproduced by permission*

Hansjörg Wyss and the Wyss Foundation

Wyss has a long track record of giving to charitable causes, and he had already donated several hundred million USD during the period of 2004–2008, years before he was to divest himself of Synthes, of which he owned almost half. In 1998, he founded the Wyss Foundation with the goal of supporting causes in conservation, education, economic opportunity, and social justice. In 2013, Wyss joined other wealthy donors in signing the Giving Pledge, a movement founded by Warren Buffet and Bill and Melinda Gates, promising to give more than half of his wealth to charitable causes. Covering 2015, *Forbes* magazine reported that Wyss made the 'America's 10 Most Generous Philanthropists' list with contributions of USD 330 million alone in that year, and an accumulated giving of USD 1.12 billion over his life time, accounting for almost 20% of his total net worth.[3] The assets of the Wyss charitable foundations were estimated at close to USD 2 billion.[4]

The Wyss Foundation's focus of giving included environment-related causes and, important for this readership, a number of grants to further medical research. On the environmental side, Wyss' interest in the preservation of nature was said to go back to his early student years when, in 1958, he had taken a surveyor job with the Colorado Highway Department. By 2017 Wyss, through his foundation, had

---

[3] *Forbes* Magazine, 5 October, 2016.
[4] *Forbes* Magazine, Hansjörg Wyss Profile, accessed 21 May, 2018.

Exhibit 51.3 Wyss Institute at Harvard. *Permission granted by Wyss Organization*

contributed more than USD 350 million to the conservation of national forests and other public lands in the Western United States, helping to preserve some 20 million acres (80,000 sq.-km), and another 5 million acres (20,000 sq.-km) in South America, Africa, and Europe. By comparison, this is an area twice the size of Switzerland.

Wyss has been equally active in the medical field where three large gifts stand out. In 2008 he established the Wyss Institute for Biologically Inspired Engineering with an initial gift of USD 125 million, followed in 2013 with a second donation to the same Institute for another USD 125 million. The Institute is part of Harvard University, where he earned his MBA. The Institute aims to "uncover engineering principles that govern living things, and to use this knowledge to develop technology solutions for the most pressing health care and environmental issues facing humanity"[5] (Exhibit 51.3).

---

[5] Source: Wyss Center website, accessed 21 May, 2018.

Exhibit 51.4   Campus Biotech Geneva. *Permission granted by Wyss Organization*

A second gift of CHF 100 million was made in 2013 to the Campus Biotech in Geneva, partnering with the École Polytechnique Fédérale de Lausanne (EPFL) and the University of Geneva, as well as regional hospitals, to create the Wyss Center for Bio and Neuroengineering, in the former Merck-Serono building on The Campus Biotech, part of the Swiss Innovation Park. The building had been bought back from Merck by Ernesto Bertarelli, whose family had founded Serono, and who intended to develop the site as a center for biotech development. The Wyss Center, renting space on the Campus, has been modeled along similar lines as the previously established Wyss Institute at Harvard (Exhibit 51.4).

Wyss' third major gift was establishing the Wyss Translational Center Zurich, in 2015. This new center, established by a donation of USD 120 million, to house a development center for both the Swiss Federal Institute of Technology (ETH) and the University of Zurich. Wyss himself is an ETH graduate in engineering. The center is intended to "foster translational research focused on developing treatment protocols and clinical therapies, as well as novel technologies and intelligent systems, in the emerging fields of regenerative medicine and robotic technologies."[6]

The purpose and goals of all three Wyss Institutes, whether in Boston, Geneva, or Zurich, are related to, and have their roots in, Wyss' own career as an entrepreneur in the medical field. In his role as Synthes CEO, Wyss became closely involved with the medical side of engineering. One of the AO founders described him as "the best informed person on Orthopedics, aside from top surgeons." This close connection between engineering and medical science continues in the Wyss Institutes and

---

[6]Source: Wyss Foundation website, accessed 21 May, 2018.

recalls the early history of the AO organization where surgeons, scientists, and engineers collaborated to create new medical solutions. There is a difference, though, between the two: during the first phase of the AO, scientists, surgeons, and engineers worked from separate organizations and were not located in the same space. The Wyss Institutes operate from a model of co-location of multiple science, medical, and engineering disciplines.

And, finally, Wyss supported the AO Foundation's new-born AO Alliance Foundation pledging CHF 50 million over ten years.

Significant fortunes were created in association with the AO Foundation. And yet much of that is still being returned to society in the form of further investments that have the prospect of yielding greater social dividends over long periods of time. Will these medical foundations, and their ensuing activities, uncover or create potential medical solutions that lend themselves to a revolution, such as the one instigated by the AO in Osteosynthesis? And, if they do, will they spawn similar social enterprises? Only the future will tell.

The World Honors AO Foundation and Founders

52

The Medical World Begins to Take Notice

When the AO was founded by 13 surgeons, the only notice the surgical world took of their ideas was to fight them and, sometimes, to discredit them. As the AO technique of Osteosynthesis began to take hold, the accomplishments and the ideas behind the organization led to the professional promotions of the core founders. This recognition was later also conferred to their early adherents and 'recruits,' and, to a lesser extent, the entrepreneurs who were the AO's industrial partners. In the space of a short chapter, it is not possible to render a complete account of all the honors eventually heaped upon AO and its members, but a few are mentioned as representative.

Appointments to Larger Medical Institutions

The AO founders were typically chief general surgeons in Swiss regional hospitals. With the exception of Maurice Müller, they did not see themselves as specialist surgeons, or even as Orthopedic surgeons. With their rising reputations, and the AO techniques slowly gaining traction in Switzerland, some of the AO leaders were appointed to surgical units larger hospitals. Müller first moved on to be head surgeon in the newly created Orthopedic and Trauma Department of the hospital of St. Gallen (1960–1967), and Chairman and Professor of the Department of Orthopedic Surgery at Inselspital in Berne from 1963 to 1980. Martin Allgöwer, who was head surgeon at the cantonal hospital in Chur and later took over the surgical department of the University of Basel from 1967 to 1983, remaining active in surgery. Hans Willenegger, who was chief surgeon at the cantonal hospital in Liestal from 1953 to 1975, was promoted to professor in 1968, eventually becoming a professor at the University of Basel.

© Springer Nature Switzerland AG 2019
J.-P. Jeannet, *Leading a Surgical Revolution*,
https://doi.org/10.1007/978-3-030-01980-8_52

Once the founder generation retired, many of the younger surgeons they had trained took over and stepped into their positions (this is not a complete list). This was the case for Berne (Reinhold Ganz), St. Gallen (Bernhard Weber), Balgrist (Christian Gerber), or Chur (Thomas Rüedi), as well as in some regional hospitals, such as Davos (Peter Matter), the home town of the AO organization.

Academic Honors for AO Surgeons

The second generation of surgeons all became professors early, something that had been missing in the early years of the AO when the young surgeons who lead the AO had to struggle for recognition from their peers with university credentials from leading medical schools. Then, with increased reputations both in Switzerland and abroad, the titles *honoris causa*, or Dr.h.c. (an honorary doctorate degree), began to pour in. Very often, these honors were bestowed by universities and countries where the AO founders had gone to teach and give lectures and were later followed by other AO members. There is no complete list of the honorary degrees accumulated by, and conferred upon, AO members over the 60 years of the organization's existence. A look at the accolades collected by some of the core founders of the AO will have to suffice.

Hans Willenegger, known as the 'globetrotter' among the AO founders, was accorded honorary doctorates from the Universities of Montevideo, Essen, Merida (Mexico), and Zurich. His colleague, Martin Allgöwer was honored with honorary degrees from Universities in Ulm, Uppsala, Belfast, and the TU Munich. Maurice Müller was conveyed honorary degrees from 12 universities, including Zurich, Basel, Berne, McGill (in Canada), several in Latin America, and other universities in Europe.

Many of the surgeons who followed in the footsteps of the AO founders were similarly lauded. Looking through the files and titles of AO members, the title *h.c. mult.* (Dr. h.c. mult. or Prof. Dr. h.c. mult., meaning several Honorary Doctor titles) appears frequently, providing an idea how many of them were awarded multiple honors. Without the general acceptance of the AO methodology to treat bone trauma, such widespread academic honors would not have been possible. It is a reflection not only on the exceptional talents that the AO attracted, but also of the respect for the surgical achievements and the methodology they promoted.

Honors for the Scientific Members of the AO

Beyond the surgeons, who made up the vast majority of the members of the AO, there were a number of scientists who, throughout the development of the AO, made major contributions. Honorary degree accolades were conveyed on Stephan Perren, the long-time leader of the AO Research Institute in Davos and on Robert Frigg. He was hired initially as a photographer at the ARI in Davos, but was quickly recognized for his exceptional engineering talent, and honored for his contributions to the development of many AO implants; his name appears on more than 150 patents. He has been awarded honorary degrees from the University of Zurich and two other universities. He is part of the 'Prof. Dr. h.c. mult.' club, and a prime example of the broad and deep talent that gravitated to the AO organization.

Honors and Recognitions for AO Industrial Partners and Entrepreneurs

Honors have also been bestowed on the entrepreneurs that built the industrial base for the production of AO-licensed implants and surgical instruments and export them worldwide. These honorary degrees reflect recognition for their entrepreneurial achievements in the demanding intersection between surgery and engineering. Due to their predominant presence in Switzerland, the honors came primarily from Swiss universities.

Robert Mathys, Sr., founder of the Mathys group, was recognized with an honorary degree from the University of Berne in 1974. Equally recognized were Fritz Straumann and his son Thomas Straumann, in 2009, from the University of Basel, where the founder of Stratec Medical, Rudolf Maag, was also honored in 2006. Hansjörg Wyss, the person behind the Synthes group, was honored multiple times, particularly by the University of Zurich Veterinary faculty in 2003, the University of Basel, and EPFL in Lausanne, in 2014.

As entrepreneurs, they were all cited numerous times by government bodies and industrial associations. A rather special honor was conveyed on Robert Mathys, Sr., for whom a street was named in front of the Mathys Orthopedic company offices in Bettlach.

Two Exceptional Honors for AO Founders

In concluding the list of recognitions, two awards deserve special mention as they relate to the core founder group.

The first is the Marcel-Benoist Prize, which was awarded in 1987 to three of the AO-founders, Müller, Allgöwer, and Willenegger. This prize is awarded annually to one, or several scientists, residing and established in Switzerland, who made the most useful scientific invention, innovation, or discovery, of a particularly high relevance for human life, in a given year. Established and awarded since 1920, and based upon a behest of Marcel Benoist, a wealthy French lawyer and intellectual, who bequeathed his wealth to the Swiss Government with the request, that an annual prize be established. This award is often considered the 'Swiss Nobel Prize' and is the most prestigious science recognition awarded within the country. There was a complication with the award rules stipulating that at most three recipients could thus be honored, which meant that not all of the core founders could be recognized. It was unfortunate that Robert Schneider was left out of the award (Exhibit 52.1).

Exhibit 52.1 Benoist Prize ceremony. *Copyright by AO Foundation, Switzerland*

The second important honor was Orthopedic Surgeon of the Century, conveyed on Maurice Müller in 2002 by the International Society of *Orthopaedic Surgery* and Traumatology (SICOT)'s global organization—an exceptional honor. This, in many ways, also conveyed the respect and recognition that both his professional colleagues, and the world, had for his achievements within the AO organization.

Recognition by Society at Large?

Despite the enormous health-economic and industrial achievements emanating by the AO Foundation, it remains surprising to see how little the general public is aware of the organization and the role its leading proponents have played. Over the years, millions of patients have benefited from AO designed or inspired implants to treat their bone trauma after sports or accident injuries. Even more people know of family members or friends who had been restored to full mobility without a lengthy hospital stay. That a single organization of largely voluntary surgeons were at the core of this medical and surgical breakthrough, laboring for years to improve methods and implant designs, seems to be a closely held secret that few outside the trauma surgery community appear to be fully cognizant. This remains something of a mystery. Maybe this book will bring to light an awareness for something society seems to be overlooking.

Part V

Conclusion

Did the AO Accomplish Its Mission?

As the AO Foundation and its associated organizations look back on their history, full of anticipation for the future beyond their 60th anniversary, many a current AO member and friend are likely to reflect and pose the question about the extent and value of the organization's achievement. Above all else: Have the objectives of the AO founders been met?

The AO objectives are detailed in its by-laws, which have become the credo for the organization since its creation. First and foremost is the goal of understanding issues around bone trauma, advancing experimental research on the topic, and providing a forum for exchanging experience about Osteosynthesis. This singular focus is stated in the first article of its by-laws and has spawned any number of key activities throughout the AO Foundation's history. The AO founders were clear about what they wanted to undertake; they did not, however, put forth any objectives in terms of 'developing' the bone trauma market, nor did they have any 'numerical' objectives when it came to 'growing' a business enterprise. They were surgeons and they were focused on patient care and innovating the healing process.

Over the course of this book, covering the AO's activities since its inception in 1958, it becomes clear that the AO did, in fact, center its activities as the founders intended, realizing great success on any number of measures. Some of these objectives came from early visits to originators of the practice of Osteosynthesis, particularly Danis in Brussels, and the understanding that to make Osteosynthesis widely available a massive effort by a group of surgeons was necessary. This could not be accomplished by a single practitioner but required dedicated efforts on a number of fronts: research, teaching, and the creation of an *Instrumentarium* designed specifically for Osteosynthesis. This was, most definitely, accomplished as intended.

Certainly not part of the AO mission statement was any idea that the members would create a virtual 'tsunami,' with regard to its revolutionary medical practice,

© Springer Nature Switzerland AG 2019
J.-P. Jeannet, *Leading a Surgical Revolution*,
https://doi.org/10.1007/978-3-030-01980-8_53

that Osteosynthesis would become the dominant treatment regime for bone trauma. In the high-income regions of the world, consisting largely of Organization for Economic Cooperation and Development (OECD) countries, the AO treatment philosophy and practice for bone trauma has been victorious; some 90% of trauma cases are treated via some form of internal fixation through Osteosynthesis. This accomplishment, started by a handful of surgeons from a small country and against all the odds, was not spelled out in the written by-laws, but might be the most significant achievement of all. Spreading the benefits of this methodology to the rest of the world is a task of the future.

The development of a dedicated *Instrumentarium*, with all associated elements, and the creation of an industry from scratch to supply this, was a by-product of the need for implants, as was the wrapping this into an ingenious business arrangement that provided the 'fuel' for the AO organization to undertake this journey.

The organizational structure and governance of the AO, combining a not-for-profit medical organization with an industry that could provide the funding, resulted in a unique activity of social entrepreneurship, long before the term was in vogue within the business community. This, as well as other accomplishments, was not planned but rather innovated along the way, as the need arose and with continually keeping the big long-term goal in mind.

Does this, however, mean there is nothing left to do?

Epilogue

54

Does the AO Represent a Unique Case?

The reproducibility of the AO approach to other medical indications was a frequently debated issue in interviews: Could it be done again, and today?

Examples of reproducing substantial parts of the AO philosophy certainly can be found in enterprises that originated out of the AO community. Maurice Müller with his hip business created an organization and structure around Protek that largely duplicated the setup used for the AO, and did so almost in parallel to the AO. Medical implant companies, such as Zimmer, or Straumann Dental, likewise duplicated many of the same structures and do so to this day.

Could It Be Done Again Today?

If this surgical revolution were to be introduced today, there would be a far more difficult path, with many more hurdles, taking forever until it could move into the clinic and benefit the first patients. In general, senior AO leaders often mentioned that they believe the AO approach could, in principle, be reproduced for other medical indications, but not today.

The author's sense is that a repeat would be unlikely given the present extensive, often restricting, regulatory requirements, medical and otherwise. The accomplishment of moving within five years from first pilot implants to full-scale market introduction is a feat that could hardly be duplicated today. It appears that the original positive intent of regulating medical procedures and products has often turned into its opposite of impeding beneficial innovations.

The creation of the AO fell into a time when surgeons could spend a substantial amount of time away from their home institutions to an extent not conceivable today. Furthermore, the commercialization of medicine was then far less advanced. Many AO members consider it highly unlikely that surgeons would sign away so much of

© Springer Nature Switzerland AG 2019
J.-P. Jeannet, *Leading a Surgical Revolution*,
https://doi.org/10.1007/978-3-030-01980-8_54

their intellectual property because the awareness of the potential commercial value of surgical developments is far more advanced than 60 years ago.

Is the Job of the AO "Done"?

At the end of the previous section we stated that based upon the initial goals the AO had set for itself, the organization appears to have reached its objectives. Just because of that rightful claim, does this also mean that there is nothing more left to be done?

Aside from expanding its mission and teaching into geographies not yet completely penetrated by Osteosynthesis, such as into lower-income countries, other avenues could be pursued. For example, the invention of alternatives to Osteosynthesis in trauma treatment would trigger another medical revolution. This would necessitate that the AO community cannibalize its existing treatment norms and, like its founders, turn into disrupters again. Forms of biomaterials that might do away with implants as they are used today conceivably could be such a trigger. But, as some of the interviewees pointed out during our wide-ranging talks, if there were suddenly a new technology that would eliminate much of the instrumentation developed by the AO, the organization as we know it would stand the risk of becoming obsolete and its financial base would be in jeopardy.

None of the experts were aware of any such large-scale technological threat, but digital printing and its potential impact on the family of existing implants is a concern of some AO members. However, more often the impact of digitization on surgery in general was mentioned, and the changes that digitization and distance learning were already bringing to the teaching of surgery. All of these developments would not do away with the AO and its mission, but would substantially impact on the way the organization delivered it.

What Will the Future Hold for the AO as an Organization?

Size, governance, administration, and the ever increasing amount of activities of the AO have led, in the eyes of many, to a level of bureaucracy that often gets in the way of flexibility, agility, or speed. With medical technologies related to trauma being developed and produced in many different centers around the world, the monopoly, once held by the AO during its early years, is slowly being eroded by different players, both medical and industrial.

The challenge for the AO moving into its next decades probably lies with its ability to continue to attract the very best surgeons and scientists to continue to develop its *Instrumentarium* and systems to remain world class. Even more important could be the ability to become a base for potential disrupters and medical revolutionaries in trauma care. As we have observed covering the AO's 60-year history, the organization has been able to reinvent its governance to adapt to a changing environment in the past, and to continue its mission as generations of new surgeons have taken over leadership positions.

The AO's 60-year past ability to maintain its mission and rejuvenate its governance while evolving technological and surgical systems allows for a confident outlook on the AO Foundation's future. Time will tell.

Printed by Printforce, the Netherlands